ON THE CHRISTIAN RELIGION

MARSILIO FICINO

On the Christian Religion

Translated from the Latin
with an Introduction and Notes by
Dan Attrell, Brett Bartlett, and David Porreca

UNIVERSITY OF TORONTO PRESS
Toronto Buffalo London

© University of Toronto Press 2022
Toronto Buffalo London
utorontopress.com

ISBN 978-1-4875-4354-9 (cloth)   ISBN 978-1-4875-4356-3 (EPUB)
                                 ISBN 978-1-4875-4357-0 (PDF)

Library and Archives Canada Cataloguing in Publication

Title: On the Christian Religion / Marsilio Ficino ; translated from the Latin with an introduction and notes by Dan Attrell, Brett Bartlett, and David Porreca.
Other titles: De Christiana religione. English.
Names: Ficino, Marsilio, 1433–1499, author. | Attrell, Dan, 1988–, translator, editor. | Bartlett, Brett, 1986–, translator, editor. | Porreca, David, 1974–, translator, editor.
Description: Translation of: De Christiana religione. | Includes bibliographical references and index.
Identifiers: Canadiana (print) 20220166870 | Canadiana (ebook) 2022016696X | ISBN 9781487543549 (cloth) | ISBN 9781487543570 (PDF) | ISBN 9781487543563 (EPUB)
Subjects: LCSH: Apologetics – Early works to 1800.
Classification: LCC BT1100 .F5313 2022 | DDC 239 – dc23

We wish to acknowledge the land on which the University of Toronto Press operates. This land is the traditional territory of the Wendat, the Anishnaabeg, the Haudenosaunee, the Métis, and the Mississaugas of the Credit First Nation.

University of Toronto Press acknowledges the financial support of the Government of Canada, the Canada Council for the Arts, and the Ontario Arts Council, an agency of the Government of Ontario, for its publishing activities.

A fool sees not the same tree that a wise man sees.
He whose face gives no light, shall never become a star.
Eternity is in love with the productions of time.
– William Blake, "Proverbs of Hell,"
The Marriage of Heaven and Hell, plate 7

Contents

Acknowledgments ix

Abbreviations xi

Introduction 3

On the Christian Religion 43

Internal Table of Contents 45

Appendix: Table of References to On the Christian Religion *in Ficino's Correspondence* 221

Bibliography 227

Index of Citations 235

Index 251

Acknowledgments

First and foremost, we would like to express our gratitude for the support from all our immediate friends and families, alongside our colleagues at the University of Waterloo and abroad, such as the members of the *Societas Magica*. We would like to give thanks to our many Latin teachers over the years: *inter alios/-as* Altay Coşkun, Leonard Curchin, Greti Dinkova-Bruun, Riemer Faber, Phyllis Forsyth, Sally Haag, Lucinda Neuru, Padraig O'Cleirigh, George Rigg, Andrew Sherwood, Christina Vester (and even Hans H. Ørberg!), each of whom contributed to this project in some way or another with their patience and dedication to the teaching of classical languages.

In assembling our translation and introduction we would especially like to acknowledge the work of Guido Bartolucci for his Latin critical edition of *De Christiana religione* (2019), alongside the work of many scholars like P.O. Kristeller, D.P. Walker, Francis A. Yates, Cesare Vasoli, Henri D. Saffrey, James Hankins, Michael J.B. Allen, Arthur Farndell, Valery Rees, Stephen Clucas, Carol V. Kaske, John R. Clark, Moshe Idel, Amos Edelheit, Denis Robichaud, Wouter Hanegraaff, Peter J. Forshaw, and many others, each of whom over recent decades have played some part in making a work like this possible. Thanks also to all the people at the University of Toronto Press for helping us bring this relatively obscure text of Ficino's into the light of day.

In light of the COVID-19 pandemic of 2020–2 throughout which this translation was produced, we would like to give special thanks to the invaluable archivists and digitizers of early printed books around the world. Without their dedication to keeping historical documents open access, this translation would never have come to fruition. Libraries whose digitized documents proved to be essential include the Biblioteca Apostolica Vaticana, the Biblioteca Nazionale Centrale di Firenze, and the Bayerische Staatsbibliothek. Special thanks to Ovanes Akopyan for his comments and advice on how to improve our introduction in the final stages of the editing process, and thanks also to Ben Thomson for supplying us with some references to a work which we would not otherwise have been able to access on our own in the face of pandemic closures and restrictions.

Abbreviations

Alcor.	Standard Qur'an internal reference system (sūrah.verse), followed by page references to *Alchoranus Latinus quem transtulit Marcus canonicus Toletanus*. Edited by Nàdia Petrus Pons. Madrid: Consejo superior de investigaciones científicas, 2016.
Bart. *DCR*	Ficino, Marsilio. *De Christiana religione*. Edited by Guido Bartolucci. Pisa: Edizioni della Normale, 2019.
Corp. Herm.	*Hermetica*. Edited by Brian Copenhaver, Cambridge: Cambridge University Press, 1992.
Dombart and Kalb	Dombart, Bernard, and Alphonse Kalb. *Sancti Aurelii Augustini* De civitate Dei. Turnhout: Brepols, 1955.
Eus. *Chron.*	Eusebius Caesariensis, *Chronicon*. PG 19.
Eus. *Hist.*	Eusebius Caesariensis, *Historia ecclesiastica*. PG 20.
Eus. *Prae.*	Eusebius Caesariensis, *Praeparatio evangelica*. PG 21.
Fic. *Op.*	Ficino, *Opera, et quae hactenus extitere, et quae in lucem nunc primum prodiere omnia*. 2 vols. Basel: Ex officina Henricpetrina, 1576.
Fic. *TP*	Ficino, Marsilio. *Theologia Platonica*. [Followed by book number and pp. from *Platonic Theology*. Translated by Michael J.B. Allen and edited by James Hankins. 6 vols. London: I Tatti Renaissance Library, 2001–6].

Hier. Sanctaf. *Contr.*	Hieronymus de Sanctafide (Jerome of Santa Fe), *Contra Iudeos ... libri duo*. Tiguri: Andreas Gesner and Rudolph Wissenbach, 1552.
Lact. *Inst.*	Lactantius, *Institutiones divinae*. PL 6, followed by page references to *Lactance. Institutions divines. Livre IV*. Edited by Pierre Monat. Paris: Les Éditions du Cerf, 1992.
LSE	*The Letters of Marsilio Ficino*. Translated by members of the Language Department of the London School of Economic Science. 11 vols. London: Shepheard-Walwyn, 1975–2020.
Nic. *Quaest.*	Nicolaus Lyrensis (Nicholas of Lyra), *Quaestiones disputatae contra Hebraeos*, in *Biblia: Cum postillis Nicolai de Lyra et expositionibus Guillelmi Britonis in omnes prologos S. Hieronymi et additionibus Pauli Burgensis replicisque Matthiae Doering*. 4 vols. Nürnberg: Anton Koberger, 1485. The folio numbers we cite correspond to the folios of Nicholas of Lyra's treatise, which begins on page 759 of the digitized version of volume 4 of this set, available here: https://digital.ub.uni-duesseldorf.de/ink/content/pageview/2303629, last accessed 27 October 2020.
Paul. *Scrut.*	Pablo de Santa Maria (Paulus Burgensis/Paul of Burgos), *Dialogus Pauli et Sauli contra Judaeos, sive Scrutinium Scripturarum*. Rome: Ulrich Han, 1471, which can be found digitized at the Biblioteca Apostolica Vaticana, Inc.200 at https://digi.vatlib.it/view/Inc.III.200, last accessed 27 October 2020.
PG	*Patrologia cursus completus, series graeca*. Edited by Jacques-Paul Migne. 157 vols. Paris: 1857–66.
PL	*Patrologia cursus completus, series latina*. Edited by Jacques-Paul Migne. 218 vols. Paris: 1841–55.
Ricc. *Contr.*	Riccoldus de Monte Crucis, *Contra legem Saracenorum*, cited from the critical edition established by Jean-M. Mérigoux in *Memorie domenicane*, n.s. 17 (1986), 1–144. On account

of a global pandemic we were unable to access this text in printed form, but a transcription of it is available online (with errata), accompanied by an Italian translation by Emilio Panella OP. http://www.e-theca.net/emiliopanella/riccoldo2/cls.htm, last accessed 26 October 2020. Citations of this text below will mention the internal divisions of the text by chapter and by line number, as these appear on the website.

Tert. *Apol.*	Tertullianus, *Apologeticum*. PL 1.
Thom. Aq. *C. Gent.*	Thomas Aquinas, *Summa contra gentiles*.
Thom. Aq. *S. Theol.*	Thomas Aquinas, *Summa theologica*.
Vulg.	*Biblia Sacra iuxta vulgatam versionem*. Edited by Robert Weber. Stuttgart: Deutsche Bibelgesellschaft, 1969; 5th edition edited by Roger Gryson, 2007.

ON THE CHRISTIAN RELIGION

Introduction

The Mirage of Ficino's Many Masks

Over the last sixty years Marsilio Ficino has received a considerable amount of attention in the English-speaking world, largely thanks to a proliferation of his works in translation. These various translation projects began to emerge in the wake of Paul Oskar Kristeller's *The Philosophy of Marsilio Ficino* (written in German in 1943, but published in English in 1964), D.P. Walker's study on *Spiritual and Demonic Magic: From Ficino to Campanella* (1958), and Dame Frances A. Yates's wildly popular *Giordano Bruno and the Hermetic Tradition* (1964) wherein Marsilio Ficino (alongside Giovanni Pico della Mirandola) played a prominent role in setting the standard – whether justifiably or not – for the archetypal "Renaissance magus" that she maintained Bruno embodied.[1] The image of Ficino as "magus" arose chiefly from the fact that he was the first Latin translator of the mysterious Greco-Egyptian *Corpus Hermeticum* attributed to the mythical sage Mercurius Trismegistus, and that, in his capacity as a physician, he also practised a kind of talismanic astral magic of the sort one can find in the *Picatrix* (*Ghāyat al-Ḥakīm*). Ficino consulted these and similar texts in assembling his *Three Books on Life* in the late 1480s, of which the third book *De coelitus comparanda* had its first inklings as a commentary on Plotinus.[2] The translations and publications of Ficino's eighteen-book

---

1 Paul O. Kristeller, *Philosophy of Marsilio Ficino*, trans. Virginia Conant (New York: Columbia University Press, 1964); D.P. Walker, *Spiritual and Demonic Magic: from Ficino to Campanella* (University Park: Pennsylvania State University Press, 1958/2000); Frances Yates, *Giordano Bruno and the Hermetic Tradition* (Chicago: University of Chicago Press, 1964): 20–85.
2 Marsilio Ficino, *Three Books On Life*, trans. Carol V. Kaske and John R. Clark (New York: Medieval and Renaissance Texts and Studies, 1989); Dan Attrell and David

4 On the Christian Religion

Platonic Theology (Allen and Hankins, 6 vols., 2001–6), his *Three Books On Life* and *Apologia* (Kaske and Clark, 1989, reprint 2019), his commentaries on Plato's *Phaedrus, Symposium, Timaeus, Parmenides, Laws,* and *Epinomis* (Arthur Farndell, 2008–16), and the numerous other studies produced over the decades by Michael J.B. Allen and his colleagues have each proven to be scholarly monuments in their own rights.[3] They have each served to make great strides in our knowledge about this veritable Renaissance man who became incredibly influential among the Latin West's expansive *République des Lettres* from the late fifteenth to the eighteenth century, but who had also since lapsed into relative obscurity in the English-speaking world given a rising interest in vernacular translations of Plato over Latin ones, alongside the widening incommensurability between Ficino's various roles as Platonic philosopher, Catholic priest, or magus-physician when set against the values of the paradigms laid down by the Reformation, the Scientific Revolution,

---

Porreca, *Picatrix: A Medieval Treatise on Astral Magic* (University Park: Pennsylvania State University Press, 2019); Roger Bacon, *Secretum secretorum cum glossis et notulis, tractatus brevis et utilis ad declarandum quedam obscure dicta fratris Rogeri*, ed. Robert Steele and trans. A.S. Fulton (Oxford: Clarendon, 1920); cf. Brian Copenhaver, "Scholastic Philosophy and Renaissance Magic in *De vita* of Marsilio Ficino," *Renaissance Quarterly* 37, no. 4 (1984); Wouter Hanegraaff, *Esotericism and the Academy: Rejected Knowledge in Western Culture* (Cambridge: Cambridge University Press, 2012); Wouter Hanegraaff, "How Hermetic Was Renaissance Hermetism?" *Aries* 15, no. 2 (2015): 179–209; Wouter Hanegraaff, "Beyond the Yates Paradigm: The Study of Western Esotericism between Counterculture and New Complexity," *Aries: Journal for the Study of Western Esotericism* 1, no. 1 (2001): 5–37; and Denis Robichaud, "Ficino on Force, Magic, and Prayers: Neoplatonic and Hermetic Influences in Ficino's Three Books on Life," *Renaissance Quarterly* 70, no. 1 (2017): 44–87. For a discussion of the influence of Arabic astral magic on Ficino, see also Nicolas Weill-Parot, *Les "images astrologiques" au Moyen Âge et à la Renaissance. Spéculations intellectuelles et pratiques magiques (XIIe-XVe siècle)* (Paris: Honoré Champion, 2002), 639–75; Liana Saif, *The Arabic Influences on Early Modern Occult Philosophy* (London: Palgrave Macmillan, 2015), 95–123; and Dan Attrell, "Honoring the Outermost: Saturn in *Picatrix*, Marsilio Ficino, and Renaissance Cosmology," *Preternature* 9, no. 2 (2020), 169–208.

3 Most notable here are Michael J.B. Allen, ed. and trans., *Marsilio Ficino: The Philebus Commentary* (Berkeley: University of California Press, 1975); *Icastes: Marsilio Ficino's Interpretation of Plato's Sophist: Five Studies and a Critical Edition with Translation* (Berkeley: University of California Press, 1989); *Marsilio Ficino: Commentaries on Plato: Volume I, Phaedrus and Ion* (The I Tatti Renaissance Library 34, Cambridge: Harvard University Press, 2008); *Marsilio Ficino: On Dionysius the Areopagite: Vol. 1: On Mystical Theology & the Divine Names* and *Vol. 2: On the Divine Names* (The I Tatti Renaissance Library 66 and 67, Cambridge, MA: Harvard University Press, 2015).

and the Enlightenment.[4] Although Ficino was indeed himself a fully integrated human – being far more than just the sum of his different literary personas – nevertheless, each of his works read in isolation from one another has led some to cobble together a kind of Frankenstein-like historiographical monster. That is, whenever this single actor takes to the stage of our memory, it appears he does so wearing only one mask at a time, whether that be as "Ficino the Platonic philosopher," "Ficino the astrologer-magus," "Ficino the physician," "Ficino the priest," or "Ficino the humanist." This particular translation project, admittedly, neither resolves this issue nor really makes an attempt to resolve it. Such a task is best left to biographers and prosopographers looking to trace the changes and continuities in Ficino's thought throughout his life. Instead, our project simply serves to elaborate further Ficino's current repertoire of literary personas, chiefly, with an eye set towards his aspect as "Ficino the priest."[5] It will perhaps come to the disappointment of some that this work contains no magic, no medicine, and very little astrology. What the work lacks in these matters, however, it makes up in grand flights of theosophical speculation, discussions of prophecy, miracles, and divine names, and offers a window into the history of how the angelic supercelestial theology of Christianity was in ancient times prefigured by various pre-Christian prophets and sages (*prisci theologi*) before culminating in the Incarnation of Christ and the teachings of his apostles.[6]

---

4 During the Enlightenment era Ficino was severely criticized, for example, in Johann Jakob Brucker, *Historia critica philosophiae a mundi incunabulis ad nostram usque aetatem deducta*, 5 vols. (Leipzig: Bernhard Christoph Breitkopf, 1742–4), cf. Hanegraaff, *Esotericism and the Academy*, 137–47; cf. Wouter Hanegraaff, "How Magic Survived the Disenchantment of the World," *Religion* 33, no. 4 (2003): 357–80. For a discussion of the Renaissance *République des Lettres*, see Anthony Grafton, *Worlds Made by Words* (Cambridge, MA and London: Harvard University Press, 2011). Cf. Sebastiano Gentile, ed., *Lettere, I: Epistolarum familiarum liber I* (Florence: Olschki, 1990).
5 For an article thus entitled and focused on Ficino's administrative and priestly duties (albeit with little in regard to his theological polemics), see Peter Serracino-Inglott, "Ficino the Priest," in *Marsilio Ficino: His Theology, His Philosophy, His Legacy*, in Michael J.B. Allen, Valery Rees, and Martin Davies, eds. (Leiden, Boston, Cologne: Brill, 2002), 1–14.
6 Please note that some of the research and writing for this introduction was produced in tandem with Dan Attrell's 2018–22 PhD dissertation on the prophetic sense of history and the use of the Latin polemical tradition in Marsilio Ficino and Giovanni Pico della Mirandola; as such, some material in the following pages may also appear in that work, albeit in a slightly modified form.

6   On the Christian Religion

Much like the long string of pro-Christian apologetic and/or polemical works that preceded *On the Christian Religion*, this is essentially a work dedicated to "preaching to the choir." Despite its rather bland title, the *De Christiana religione* is a veritable trove of ideas about the history of human religions as it stood in the mind of an erudite (but certainly not infallible) humanist philosopher-priest living in quattrocento Florence. Ficino was indeed a remarkable individual, and he became famous within his own lifetime not only on account of his learning, but also thanks to his ties to some of the most powerful men of his era, namely, the leading men of the Medici family: Cosimo and Lorenzo. They proverbially scratched his back, and he scratched theirs. They funded his livelihood, and in turn he helped justify Medici power and pushed to expand it in both the sacred and the secular spheres. The original version of this work was composed in Latin around the time when our humanist philosopher was ordained in the Roman Catholic Church at the age of forty, first as a deacon on 18 September 1473, then as a priest on 18 December of that year after having spent over a decade translating pagan philosophy for Cosimo. At about this same time, Ficino – a man who frequently discussed how prone he was to Saturnine bouts of melancholy and depression throughout his life – may have been in the midst of a kind of midlife crisis of conscience, not unlike St. Jerome, who relates once having a vision of Jesus chastising him for being more a follower of Cicero than a follower of Christ.[7] Ultimately, it is impossible to know for sure whether this "midlife crisis" was merely an affectation and Ficino was making use of a well-worn Christian *topos* as a rhetorical frame, or if he really was sincere in his desperation. In either case, Ficino's solution to this personal crisis had been to reconsecrate within himself the marriage of "the priest" and "the philosopher," and to restore that office to the condition it had enjoyed in Antiquity, back when priests were philosophers and philosophers were priests. In the decade leading up to this experience, Ficino had translated the complete corpus of Plato's extant works with commentaries alongside the *Corpus Hermeticum*, all while assembling arguments for his monumental eighteen-book *Platonic Theology on the Immortality of the*

---

7   Serracino-Inglott, "Ficino the Priest," 8–9; Jerome, *Epistola ad Eustochium*, 22.30, in Isidorus Hilberg, ed., *Sancti Eusebii Hieronymi Epistulae*, in *Corpus Scriptorum Ecclesiasticorum Latinorum* 54 (Vienna: F. Tempsky and Leipzig: G. Freytag, 1910), 189–90. For more on Ficino's depressive tendency and how it connects to the science of "melancholia generosa" and the modern notion of the "genius," see Raymond Klibansky, Erwin Panofsky, and Fritz Saxl, *Saturn and Melancholy* (Montreal: McGill–Queen's University Press, 1964/2019), 241ff.

Soul wherein he took aim at Averroist and Lucretian conclusions in the service of his Platonic world view.[8] *On the Christian Religion*, then, was an extension of Ficino's attempts to exalt his marriage of Platonism and Christianity – of philosophy and priestcraft. Here, however, he would accomplish this task not by attacking the philosophers of his day, but by doing battle against those who falsely interpreted Scripture. This he did not chiefly with the help of his *divinus Plato*, but by going to Scripture directly and following in the tracks first laid down by a number of ancient and medieval polemicists who were highly experienced in debating against various Jewish and "Mohammadan" modes of interpretation. Immediately after its composition in Latin, which was largely a result of the fact that much of the material he was drawing upon had originally been written in that language, the work was translated into Italian for a popular audience with Ficino's own oversight. This Italian edition was then published in 1474, prior to the Latin one, which did not see the light of day until 1476.[9] The Italian text underwent several revisions, culminating with its last printing during Ficino's lifetime in 1484 beneath the Great Conjunction of Saturn and Jupiter.[10]

---

8 Note that the *Platonic Theology* itself was not published until 1482, two years before Ficino saw the complete version of his Platonic corpus printed in Latin; see Michael J.B. Allen, trans., and James Hankins, ed., *Marsilio Ficino: Platonic Theology*, vols. 1–6 (London: I Tatti Renaissance Library, 2001–6). Gerard Passannante, "Burning Lucretius: On Ficino's Lost Commentary," *Studies in Philology* 115, no. 2 (2018): 267–85 lays out a narrative about how, in his youth, Ficino was fascinated by prevailing Lucretian currents but he ultimately rejected this fascination in a rather dramatic fashion, by burning his *commentariola*; Elena Nicoli, "Ficino, Lucretius and Atomism," *Early Science and Medicine* 23 (2018): 330–61, however, has cast doubts on this narrative, seeing his claim to have burned his *commentariola* as merely a literary *topos*. See also the recent study on Ficino's philosophy of pleasure by Raphael Egbi, *Voluptas: la filosofia del piacere nel giovane Marsilio Ficino (1457–1469)* (Pisa: Edizioni della Normale, 2019).
9 In the letters accompanying copies of *On the Christian Religion* that Ficino sent to friends and acquaintances, he repeatedly expressed his dissatisfaction with the sloppiness of the first Italian printing of his work. See Curt F. Bühler, "The First Edition of Ficino's *De Christiana religione*: A Problem in Bibliographical Description," *Studies in Bibliography* 18 (1965): 248–52. Further discussion of Ficino's references to *On the Christian Religion* in his correspondence and his later works appears below in a separate section of this introduction.
10 On Ficino's vernacular translations, see Cesare Vasoli, "Note sul volgarizzamento ficiniano della Monarchia," in *Miscellanea di studi in onore di Vittore Branca*, 5 vols. (Florence: Olschki, 1983), III, 451–74; Paul O. Kristeller, "Marsilio Ficino as a Man of Letters and the Glosses Attributed to Him in the Caetani Codex of Dante," *Renaissance Quarterly* 36 (1983): 1–47; Giuliano Tanturli, "Marsilio Ficino e il volgare," in *Marsilio Ficino. Fonti, testi, fortuna. Atti del convegno internazionale (Firenze, 1–3 ottobre*

8   On the Christian Religion

This work as a whole constitutes Ficino's attempt to reinaugurate the marriage of philosophy and religion as he perceived it to have once existed in ancient times, and to give an account of its disintegration at various junctures in history. Ficino's ideal religion constituted a set of doctrines embodied by the archetypal *Logos* (Word), the Son of God, incarnated in Jesus Christ. From the outset it should be stated that what Ficino himself meant by the word *religio* was neither popular piety nor belief but "divine law," a set of eternal and unchanging moral principles. Given that the nature of adjectives is more plastic in Latin than it is in English, the title of this work could just as correctly have been translated as *On the Religion of Christ* or *On Christ's Divine Law*, though we opted for the more immediately recognizable title. *On the Christian Religion* is a two-fold work in so far as it is part apology, part polemic.[11] In its sections exhorting men to adopt sagely piety, it addresses Ficino's immediate circle of churchmen and humanists, with Lorenzo de' Medici at their head. In its invective sections, however, it targets "Mohammadans"[12] and Jews in an all-too-familiar medieval style: that of the infamous *Contra* or *Adversus Iudaeos* polemical literary genre. On one hand, the first part of the book constitutes a history of the *prisca theologia* – the "ancient theology"[13] which sat at the centre of Ficino's

---

1999), ed. Sebastiano Gentile and Stéphane Toussaint (Rome: Edizione di Storia e Letteratura, 2006), 183–213; idem, "Osservazioni lessicali su opere volgari e bilingui di Marsilio Ficino," in *Il volgare come lingua di cultura dal Trecento al Cinquecento: atti del convegno internazionale, Mantova, 18–20 ottobre 2001*, ed. by Arturo Calzona, F.P. Fiore, A. Tenenti, and C. Vasoli (Florence: Olschki, 2003), 155–85. On the Great Conjunction of Jupiter and Saturn, see James Hankins, *Humanism and Platonism in the Italian Renaissance*, 2 vols. (Rome: Edizioni di Storia e Letteratura, 2003/4), 1.303–4.

11 For the first scholar to demonstrate that Ficino wrote *On the Christian Religion* in two parts, first a philosophical section and then later a theological section heavily derived from Paul of Burgos, see Cesare Vasoli, "Per le fonti del *De christiana religione* di Marsilio Ficino," *Rinascimento* 28 (1988): 135–233.

12 Note that it is unlikely Ficino knew any Muslims personally. None appear among his correspondents, and the few references to Turks in his letters are purely derogatory. His closest direct contact with aspects of Islamic culture involved owning a copy of a Latin translation of the Qu'ran, which he at one point lent to Giovanni Pico della Mirandola – see *Letter* VIII, 31 (dated 8 September 1486), in Marsilio Ficino, *The Letters of Marsilio Ficino. Volume 7: Being a Translation of Liber VIII*, trans. Language Department of the London School of Economic Science (London: Shepheard-Walwyn, 2003), 40–1.

13 On Ficino's *prisca theologia*, see Cesare Vasoli, "Da Giorgio Gemisto a Ficino: nascita e metamorfosi della 'Prisca theologia,'" in Giorgio Cerboni Baiardi, ed., *Miscellanea di studi in onore di Claudio Varese* (Rome: Vecchiarelli, 2001), 787–800; and Cesare Vasoli, "La tradizione cabbalistica e l'esperienza religiosa cristiana del rinascimento,"

conception of a "natural religion" as it was practised and passed down through the shared prophecies of such ancient pagan sages as Zoroaster, Hermes Trismegistus, Orpheus, Aglaophemus, Pythagoras, and Plato before ultimately being brought to fulfilment in the incarnation of Christ; on the other hand, the significantly larger second part of the work constitutes a series of attacks against various traditions of Jewish scriptural interpretation that threatened his own Trinitarian readings of the prophetic books of the Old Testament (such as those of the Talmudists or of celebrated rabbis like Moshe ben Maimon and Shlomo Yitzhaqi). In addressing their arguments, Ficino availed himself not so much of Plato and the Platonists as much as from the anti-Islamic and anti-Jewish polemics of mendicant writers like Riccoldo of Monte Croce and Nicholas of Lyra, and especially the Spanish converso Dominicans like Jerome of Santa Fe and Paul of Burgos (who themselves in turn had relied heavily upon Thomas Aquinas, Ramon Martí, and Petrus Alfonsi). In the works of such authors were often debated esoteric minutiae relating to scriptural hermeneutics and the philology of the original Hebrew and Aramaic texts, and Ficino here attempted to reiterate that approach to the best of his abilities. The Christian God, by his very Trinitarian nature, had unfurled his providence through history and in doing so allowed that direct revelations be made *not just to the ancient Hebrews* but to all of mankind as part of a grand process of cosmic reconciliation. Among the many topics he touched upon in his invective chapters, Ficino emphasized most the theme of Christological prefigurations in the words of the Old Testament prophets, and this in many ways mirrors how, in the first half of the work, he put emphasis on the theme of shared prophetic revelation among the ancient pagan sages. Here pagan and Hebrew prophecies *both* served as a *praeparatio evangelica*. The writings of the righteous among both the pagans and the Hebrews played an *equal* role in foreshadowing the fulfilment of all worldly religions in the coming of the Messiah, the Incarnate *Logos*, Jesus Christ.

Italia 9 (1994): 11–35; for more general discussions of the *prisca theologia* during the Renaissance, see Cesare Vasoli, "'Prisca theologia' e scienze occulte nell'umanesimo fiorentino," in Gian Mario Cazzaniga, ed., *Storia d'Italia. Annali 25: Esoterismo* (Turin: Einaudi, 2010), 175–205 and Cesare Vasoli, "Il mito dei 'prisci theologi' come 'ideologia' della 'renovatio,'" in Cesare Vasoli, ed., *Quasi sit deus. Studi su Marsilio Ficino* (Lecce: Conte, 1999), 11–50; see also D.P. Walker, *The Ancient Theology: Studies in Christian Platonism from the Fifteenth to the Eighteenth Century* (London: Duckworth, 1972).

The "Iron Age," *Prisca Theologia*, and Ficino's Program of Platonic Renewal

The polemical dimension of Ficino's work, written in the early 1470s, must first and foremost be understood within the wider context of aggressive Ottoman encroachment into historically Christian lands. Between 1438 and 1445, authorities from the churches of the Greek East and Latin West gathered together to form the Council of Ferrara-Florence where they hoped to find a way to bridge the great schism that had long created political and theological rifts between them.[14] If they could somehow be brought into agreement – into a "concord" or "harmony" of East and West – they believed such a union could have the strength to turn back the rising tide of Turkish invasions.[15] By the late fourteenth century, the Ottomans had rapidly spread from their holdings in Northwestern Anatolia into much of Greece and the Balkans; by the mid-fifteenth century, Mehmed II had claimed much of Anatolia and the lands to the east of the Adriatic Sea. The Ottoman conqueror made Constantinople the seat of his empire in 1453, and from there he continued to project the hegemony of the Sublime Porte into both the Black and the Mediterranean seas. Having vastly expanded its naval power in the Mediterranean, the Ottomans clashed fiercely with various Italian maritime powers like Venice and Genoa who anxiously brought home reports of an implacable Turkish advance.[16] In the meantime, at the extended council of Ferrara-Florence, Cosimo de' Medici made his acquaintance with the Greek philosopher George Gemistos Plethon, a Platonist and a pagan revivalist who dazzled Florence's humanistically inclined elites with lectures on the subtler similarities and differences between Plato and Aristotle. Though Ficino himself was not present, he gave an account of these events as such:

> At the time when the council was in progress between the Greeks and the Latins in Florence under Pope Eugenius, the great Cosimo, whom a

---

14 Joseph Gill, *The Council of Florence* (Cambridge: Cambridge University Press, 1959/2011).
15 On the theme of *"concordia"* and its conceptual counterpart *"diluvium"* see Edelheit, *Ficino, Pico, and Savonarola: The Evolution of Humanist Theology* (Leiden: Brill, 2008), 28 and 135–41.
16 See chapters I and II in Mustafa Soykut, *Image of the "Turk" in Italy: A History of the "Other" in Early Modern Europe, 1453–1683* (Berlin: Klaus Schwarz Verlag, 2001), 1–45 for a discussion of Italian perceptions of the Ottoman Empire in the fifteenth century.

decree of the Senate designated *Pater patriae*, often listened to the Greek philosopher Gemistos (with the cognomen Plethon, as it were a second Plato) while he expounded the mysteries of Platonism. And he was so immediately inspired, so moved by Gemistos's fervent tongue, that as a result he conceived in his noble mind a kind of Academy, which he was to bring to birth at the first opportune moment. Later, when the great Medici brought his great idea into being, he destined me, the son of his favourite doctor, while I was still a boy, for the great task.[17]

Over the following decades, Ficino threw himself wholeheartedly into his study of Greek literature, taking advantage of the many scholars who had recently fled the Byzantine East and settled in Florence either in expectation or in the wake of Ottoman conquest. Six years after the fall of Constantinople to Mehmet II in 1453, and thanks to the kind funding of his patron Cosimo de' Medici, a series of Greek lectures were being offered in Florence by the refugee philosopher and devotee of Aristotle, John Argyropoulos.[18] Making the most of this invaluable resource, Ficino put himself at Argyropoulos's feet.[19] Pleased with Ficino's rapid development, Cosimo offered him the opportunity of a lifetime in 1462: a villa in Careggi near Florence with access to all the resources he could possibly require, a collection of Greek manuscripts, and a request for them to be translated into Latin such that he might be able to read them for himself for the benefit of his immortal soul.[20] When modern writers

---

17 Marsilio Ficino, *Opera, et quae hactenus extitere, et quae in lucem nunc primum prodiere omnia*, 2 vols. (Basel: Henricpetrina, 1576), *In Plotini Epitomae*, Proemium, 2:1537; Ficino's claim has been criticized in Brian Copenhaver and Charles B. Schmitt, *Renaissance Philosophy* (Oxford and New York: Oxford University Press), 139 and again by Sophia Howlett, *Marsilio Ficino and His World* (London: Palgrave Macmillan, 2016), 7 and 11ff., which directs readers to Paul O. Kristeller, *Renaissance Thought and its Sources* (New York: Columbia University Press, 1975), 161. Note that Ficino was six years old at the time of the Council of Ferrara-Florence. He never met Plethon in person, but it was indeed Plethon's manuscripts of the Platonic corpus which Cosimo gave to Ficino in subsequent years.
18 Howlett, *Marsilio Ficino and His World*, 7. Before Argyropoulos, Italy had first been enchanted by the Greek teachings of Manuel Chrysoloras, who had trained Ambrogio Traversari, Guarino Veronese, and Leonardo Bruni. See Paul Botley, *Learning Greek in Western Europe, 1396–1529* (Philadelphia: American Philosophical Society, 2010), 7–12.
19 Howlett, *Marsilio Ficino and His World*, 43–4.
20 James Hankins, *Humanism and Platonism in the Italian Renaissance*, 2 vols. (Rome: Edizioni di Storia e Letteratura, 2003/4), 1.436 and 2.196; Charles Nauert, *Historical Dictionary of the Renaissance* (Lanham, MD: Scarecrow Press, 2004), 139.

refer to a "Platonic Academy of Florence," by and large they are really referring to this villa along with the informal collective of well-funded poets and philosophers rather than a formal institution.[21] For his bountiful Maecenas, Ficino diligently whittled away throughout the 1460s at his aforementioned translations and commentaries of Plato's *Opera omnia* as well as his translations of the *Corpus Hermeticum*, Alcinous, Speusippus, Xenocrates, and Pythagoras.[22]

Though Ficino began speculating on the nature of "ancient theology" around the mid-1450s, his thoughts on the matter blossomed in the wake of his translation projects from the late 1460s and throughout the 1470s.[23] Our philosopher was bent on recovering the religious philosophies of the remote past largely insofar as he felt alienated by how fractured and contentious the mainstream theological systems of his day appeared to him. Ficino felt that contemporary schoolmen and professors of theology had literally lost touch with reality and as a result had become fragmented across various subdivisions of competing *viae antiquae* and *modernae*.[24] There was a strong feeling for intellectuals working outside of the universities that the schoolmasters had divorced philosophy from true religion in their fights over Ockhamist, Scotist, Alexandrian, and Averroist positions rather than sticking to the beaten track of archetypal spirituality that had first been trod by Christ, the apostles, and the *ecclesia primitiva*. In this light there emerged a sense that there was much value to be derived from first-hand and private readings of primary documents, namely, documents from Antiquity. From an early age Ficino saw history in a somewhat cyclical mode: as a perennial struggle in which, to use Brian Copenhaver's

---

21 See especially James Hankins, "The Myth of the Platonic Academy of Florence," *Renaissance Quarterly* 44, 3 (1991): 429–75 and "Cosimo de'Medici and the 'Platonic Academy,'" *Journal of the Warburg and Courtauld Institutes* 53 (1990): 144–62, which offers a revisionist account of the mythical founding of "the Platonic Academy." Cf. Paul O. Kristeller, *Eight Philosophers of the Renaissance* (Stanford, CA: Stanford University Press, 1964), 40.

22 For a chronology of Ficino's works, see Marsilio Ficino, *The Letters of Marsilio Ficino*. Volume 8: *Being a Translation of Liber IX*, trans. Language Department of the London School of Economic Science (London: Shepheard-Walwyn, 2009), 95–6. In 1458, during the period leading up to his arrival at Careggi, Ficino had also produced translations of both Orpheus's and Proclus's *Hymns*. All of these texts would play a significant role in the construction of his *prisca theologia* narrative.

23 Hankins, *Plato in the Italian Renaissance* (Leiden, New York, Copenhagen, Cologne: Brill, 1990), 2.460.

24 Howlett, *Marsilio Ficino and His World*, 38ff.

words, "wisdom or faith, philosophy or theology, reason or eloquence might rise and fall as lights of the human spirit" rather than having been equally accessible to all people at all times.[25] He believed that prior to the Incarnation, the prophets of the Bible and the pagan sages of all nations had access to some degree of theological truth, but with the advent of the Christian era came new revelations, and particularly that mystical theology as it is found in the writings of St. Paul and those attributed to his companion Dionysius the Areopagite. It is this set of doctrines which Ficino argued had later been appropriated by the late antique Platonists of Alexandria to elucidate and understand the mysteries of their own master's philosophy.[26] With the demise of the apostolic era and the gradual disappearance of the simple life lived out in *imitatio Christi*, however, the medieval Church (and therefore the world) fell into a dark age, or in Ficino's words, an "iron age" (*saeculum ferreum*) after the iron generation set down by the poets Hesiod, Ovid, and Virgil, who cast history as a perennial cycle of decline and renewal back to man's idealized state in the Saturnine Golden Age.[27] In this model of world

---

25 Copenhaver and Schmitt, *Renaissance Philosophy*, 148.
26 Ficino's speculations on the history of philosophy might be said to have reached their final form in his introduction to Plotinus's *Enneads*, see Henri D. Saffrey, "Florence 1492: The Reappearance of Plotinus," *Renaissance Quarterly* 49, no. 3 (1996): 488–508. Cf. Michael Allen, "Marsilio Ficino on Plato, the Neoplatonists and the Christian Doctrine of the Trinity," in Michael J.B. Allen, ed., *Plato's Third Eye: Studies in Marsilio Ficino's Metaphysics and Its Sources* (Aldershot: Variorum, 1995): 555–84.
27 Hesiod, *Works and Days*, lines 109–26, trans. Hugh G. Evelyn-White, "Works and Days," in *The Homeric Hymns and Homerica with an English Translation* (Cambridge, MA: Harvard University Press 1914):

> First of all the deathless gods who dwell on Olympus made a golden race of mortal men who lived in the time of Cronos when he was reigning in heaven. And they lived like gods without sorrow of heart, remote and free from toil and grief: miserable age rested not on them; but with legs and arms never failing they made merry with feasting beyond the reach of all evils. When they died, it was as though they were overcome with sleep, and they had all good things; for the fruitful earth unforced bare them fruit abundantly and without stint. They dwelt in ease and peace upon their lands with many good things, rich in flocks and loved by the blessed gods. But after the earth had covered this generation – they are called pure spirits dwelling on the earth, and are kindly, delivering from harm, and guardians of mortal men; for they roam everywhere over the earth, clothed in mist and keep watch on judgements and cruel deeds, givers of wealth; for this royal right also they received; – then they who dwell on Olympus made a second generation which was of silver and less noble by far. It was like the golden race neither in body nor in spirit. A child was brought up at his good mother's side a hundred years, an utter simpleton, playing childishly

14 On the Christian Religion

history, as Copenhaver noted, Ficino maintained that "people *sometimes* enjoyed religious truth in periods of wisdom when the advance of piety coincided with the progress of philosophy, but sometimes the truth was veiled and philosophy parted from religion."[28] The main problem with the degenerated state of the world, in Ficino's mind, was that the aims of the philosophers had gradually drifted apart from the aims of the religious. On account of this drifting incommensurability, the philosophy of contemporary schoolmen had become corrupted by a widespread acceptance of erroneous non-Christian doctrines. True doctrine – that of Christ and his disciples, that of St. Paul, and of Dionysius the Areopagite – had become buried beneath a landslide of philosophical speculation, especially by the ideas of various pre-eminent Christian, Islamic, and Jewish Aristotelians following in the footsteps of Alexander of Aphrodisias and Averroes (e.g., the unicity of the intellectual soul, the denial of its immortality, etc.).[29] In light of all these problems, Ficino longed to spark some kind of renewal for both religion and philosophy, that they might return back to the clarity they had enjoyed among the ancients.

---

in his own home. But when they were full grown and were come to the full measure of their prime, they lived only a little time and that in sorrow because of their foolishness, for they could not keep from sinning and from wronging one another, nor would they serve the immortals, nor sacrifice on the holy altars of the blessed ones as it is right for men to do wherever they dwell. Then Zeus the son of Cronos was angry and put them away, because they would not give honor to the blessed gods who live on Olympus.

For the "golden age" in Ovid, see *Metamorphoses*, 1.89–150 and in Virgil, see his *Georgics*, 2.136–76. Cf. Dan. 2:31–35. Note that by 1492, almost two decades after completing *On the Christian Religion*, Ficino believed the transitus from Iron to Golden Age had come during his own lifetime in Florence itself through the reunion of "wisdom and eloquence, and prudence with martial prowess, as in Pallas"; see his letter to Middleberg entitled *Praises of our age as golden on account of its golden minds* (Book 11, letter 34, in Marsilio Ficino, *The Letters of Marsilio Ficino. Volume 10, being a Translation of Liber XI*, transl. Language Department of the London School of Economic Science [London: Shepheard-Walwyn, 2015], 51). This positive sentiment, however, would fade again with the invasion of Florence by Charles VIII, the deaths of Pico and Poliziano, and Savonarola's rise to power in 1494.

28 Copenhaver and Schmitt, *Renaissance Philosophy*, 148.
29 As far as Ficino's attitudes towards Peripatetic philosophy went, he made it clear by the end of his life that he believed the return to the Platonic tradition included a re-reading of Aristotle, but this was to be done along the lines of how the Neoplatonists read Aristotle, not Alexander of Aphrodisias or Averroes. Aristotle read

Between 1469 and 1474, Ficino turned his attention to the longest of all his works, the *Platonic Theology on the Immortality of the Soul*. This work was composed in the form of a polemical *summa* on the nature of the soul and structured as a progressive series of arguments in support of his anti-Averroean and anti-materialist theses.[30] In large part, Ficino assembled it to provide Christendom with a non-pagan alternative to Proclus's *Platonic Theology*.[31] The longest section of this *summa* was strictly concerned with a refutation of Averroes's ideas on what happens to the human soul at the moment of death. "The book is so extensive indeed, so packed with argument and detail, so combative in its refutation," writes its translator Michael J.B. Allen, "that it leaves us in no doubt that refuting the great Arab's arguments, and particularly what he saw as Averroes's denial of the soul being the substantial form of the body, was still an abiding concern for Ficino and presumably

---

through Averroes was thought impious while the same texts read through the lens of the Neoplatonists were not. Ficino was quite explicit about this in his introduction to Plotinus's *Enneads* (trans. from Saffrey, "The Reappearance of Plotinus," 499):

> As for us, we have tried to reveal and to explain the impact of the abovementioned theologians in the works of Plato and Plotinus, so that the poets may cease in an impious manner to introduce the events and mysteries of religion into their fables and so that the horde of Peripatetics – that is to say nearly all philosophers – may be warned that they should not mistake this religiousness for an old wives' tale. Indeed, nearly all the world is inhabited by the Peripatetics and divided into two schools, the Alexandrists and the Averroists. The first ones believe that our intellect is mortal, whereas the others think it is unique: both groups alike destroy the basis of all religion, especially because they seem to deny that there is such a thing as divine providence towards men, and in both cases they are traitors to Aristotle. Nowadays, few people, except the great Pico, our companion in Platonism, interpret the spirit of Aristotle with the same reverence as was shown in the past by Theophrastus, Themistius, Porphyry, Simplicius, Avicenna, and more recently Plethon ... Today, the will of divine providence is that this genus of religion should be confirmed by the authority and the reasoning of philosophy, whereas at an appointed time the truest species of religion will be confirmed by miracles acknowledged by all nations, as was once the case in the past.

30 Kristeller, *Eight Philosophers of the Renaissance*, 38; Bernard McGinn, *Thomas Aquinas's Summa Theologiae: A Biography* (Princeton, NJ: Princeton University Press, 2004), 140ff.; Allen and Hankins, *Platonic Theology*, 1.viii speculate that this particular work "probably played a role in the Lateran Council's promulgation of the immortality of the soul as a dogma in 1512."
31 Allen and Hankins, *Platonic Theology*, 1.xii.

16 On the Christian Religion

for his sophisticated Florentine readers."[32] In relating the truly cosmic proportions of the *Platonic Theology*, Allen and Hankins summarize most aptly that "[a]t its center is not just his spiritual search for reassurance and conviction that an afterlife awaits us and that death is not the termination of consciousness and accordingly of the self, but also his concern to redefine and thus to reconceive the constitution, the *figura*, of the human entity."[33] *On the Christian Religion* is, ultimately, a continuation of this project. Ficino was in search of a regenerative, comprehensive, and totalizing *image* of man to emulate. If man was lost, it was simply because he had lost sight of his divine exemplar and was in need of some reorientation. In opening his *Platonic Theology*, Ficino exhorted readers to "cast off the bonds of our terrestrial chains; cast them off as swiftly as possible, so that, uplifted on Platonic wings and with God as our guide, we may fly unhindered to our ethereal abode, where we will straightway look with joy on the excellence of our own human nature."[34] In spite of opening with references to the "wings" of Plato's chariot in the *Phaedrus*, the true foundations of that theological treatise were just as patristic and scholastic as they were classical, as much concerned with Augustine and Thomas Aquinas as with Plato and Proclus. Many of the arguments Ficino made therein for the immortality of the soul had not been alien to earlier medieval theologians.[35] What Ficino ultimately did that was different, however, was buttress old arguments in new terms with the support of newly available texts: that is, ancient Greek philosophical texts. If there was disillusionment in Ficino for the culture of debate in his day, it was chiefly in regard to the nature of the sources it relied upon, not necessarily the topics it debated, or even necessarily the form in which those debates took place. He was not unaware of contemporary academic discourse, he was simply disinterested on account of its complexity and its inability to rouse men to piety. It lacked both the clarity of Plato and the simplicity of the gospel, both of which had a rich history of doing just that.

---

32 Michael J.B. Allen, "Marsilio Ficino on Saturn, the Plotinian Mind, and the Monster of Averroes," in *Studies in the Platonism of Marsilio Ficino and Giovanni Pico*, ed. Michael J.B. Allen (London and New York: Routledge, 2017), 89.
33 Fic. *TP* 1.ix.
34 Allen and Hankins, *Platonic Theology* 1, 1.1.1: "solvamus quamprimum vincula compedum terrenarum, ut alis sublati platonicis ac deo duce in sedem aetheream liberius pervolemus, ubi statim nostri generis excellentiam feliciter contemplabimur." Cf. Plato, *Phaedrus*, 246a–54e and Plotinus, *Enneads*, 4.8.
35 Copenhaver and Schmitt, *Renaissance Philosophy*, 148–9.

On the Christian Religion, therefore, in keeping with the ideas in the *Platonic Theology* that preceded it, is a work that attempts to lay out, in a far less systematic fashion, how the perfect union of philosophy (wisdom) and religion (divine law) centred on the mystery of the Trinity had once upon a time been upheld by both the *prisci theologi* and in a most perfect form by the primitive Church but had since become degraded and fragmented within the course of later Church history, in what he called "the wretched divorce of Pallas and Themis."[36] Our Platonically-minded theologian wished his society to "return" or "be reformed" back in line with an ancient way of life practised during a time when the sacred and secular spheres were one. For Ficino, the concepts of "word," "form," and "reform" were inseparable, as one can see in the following passage: "By the Word of God men had previously been formed, [and] by the same Word they ought to be *reformed* – and deservingly so, for by the light of the intellectual Word, the darkness of the human intellect must be expelled; the rational animal must be corrected by the reason of God."[37] True theology was the *Logos* or Word itself descended into history. It was the very *ratio*, reason, or rational ordering principle of God dwelling among men, and as such, Ficino wished to demonstrate that Christianity was the consummation of all "natural religion" rooted in the incarnation of this *Logos*. Pagan hymns, Hermetic texts, Platonic dialogues, and Sibylline books had all foreshadowed, prefigured, and set the stage for the perfected Christian revelation. Prophecies among the pagans, just like those of the Hebrew prophets, were significant insofar as they *participated* in both Christianity's essence and its historical development. Ficino was quite clear that the Hebrews (and the Essenes), the Persians, the Indians, the Egyptians, the Ethiopians, the Greeks, the Gauls, and the Romans each played a part in the unfurling of God's plan.[38] In *On the Christian Religion*, then, we might say Ficino was not so much concerned with understanding

---

36 Proemium: "O secula tandem nimium infelicia, quando Palladis Themidisque divortium miserabile contigit!" Bart. *DCR*, 156.
37 Chapter fifteen: "Per Dei Verbum formati quondam homines fuerant, per Verbum idem reformari debebant et merito, per intellectualis enim Verbi lucem depellenda erat caligo intellectus humani, per rationem Dei rationale animal emendandum." Bart. *DCR*, 198.
38 Proemium: "Prophete igitur Hebreorum atque sapientie simul et sacerdotio incumbebant; philosophi a Persis, quia sacris preerant, Magi – hoc est sacerdotes, sunt appellati; Indi Brachmanas de rerum natura simul atque animorum expiationibus consulebant; apud Egyptios mathematici et methaphysici sacerdotio fungebantur et regno; apud Ethiopas gymnosophiste phylosophie simul magistri erant ac religionis

the Zoroaster, Hermes, or even Plato on their own terms so much as using them to confirm his ideas about God's providence. Ficino did not offer a "pro-pagan" perspective so much as a *pro-wisdom* perspective, a wisdom which he believed had dwelled among the pagan sages just as much as it had among the Hebrew prophets in the days before Christ. There were *some* exceptional figures in history who arose from pagan contexts, and on account of their elevated intellects, like the Hebrew prophets, went above and beyond the religions of their forefathers in intuiting some aspect of the divine *Logos*, but this was certainly not intuited by all pagans. Ficino is clear, as seen, for example, in chapter twenty-two, that he considered the bulk of paganism to be brutish and demonic, full of senseless violence and vain superstitions.

In this way, what anti-Islamic and anti-Jewish converso polemicists like Petrus Alfonsi, Ramon Martí, Paul of Burgos, and Jerome of Santa Fe had done in previous generations – that is, using Jewish biblical hermeneutics to refute Jews – Ficino was now attempting to do against all the enemies of his religion, but in a humanist mode, with the support of Plato and the other *prisci theologi*.[39] The union of true wisdom and divine law had clearly been upheld by sages like Zoroaster, Hermes, Orpheus, Aglaophemus, Pythagoras, and so forth, but each of these had themselves been merely preachers of logocentric reform. Their message was not "new" but tapped into a divine blueprint, the eternal *Logos*, and in doing so, they stood as analogues to the Old Testament prophets, but among the gentile nations. Since Ficino perceived Christianity – the *imitatio Christi* and the *vita apostolica* – as the prophesied fulfilment of both Jewish and gentile wisdom traditions, he searched the scriptures of pagan sages and Hebrew prophets alike, looking for points of commonality and highlighting the ways in which both groups had in their own ways foreshadowed the coming into history of a divine exemplar which fundamentally stood outside of time. While Ficino recognized Moses to be among the most significant of the prophets, he believed Christ came to fulfil the Mosaic Law just in the same way he had come

---

antistites. Eadem in Grecia consuetudo fuit sub Lino, Orpheo, Museo, Eumolpo, Melampo, Trophimo, Aglaophemo, atque Pythagora, eadem in Gallia sub Druidum gubernaculis. Quantum apud Romanos Nume Pompilio, Valerio Sorano, Marco Varroni multisque aliis sapientie simul sacrorumque studium fuerit, quis ignoret?" Bart. *DCR*, 155. For similar but ancient *prisca sapientia* narratives, cf. Clement of Alexandria, *Stromata*, 1.15.71; Diogenes Laertius, *Lives and Opinions of Eminent Philosophers*, 1.1–12.

39 Irven Resnick, *Petrus Alfonsi: Dialogue against the Jews* (Washington, DC: The Catholic University of America Press, 2006), 15.

to put an end to paganism. In Christ, the doctrines of both Plato and Moses were stripped down to their perfect form and fully embodied. It is here that we see how Ficino's reckoning of the history of religion and philosophy took a polemical turn. In *On the Christian Religion*, we get a glimpse of how the polemical tradition first devised by the Church Fathers – which began as a means of carving out a Christian identity and was kept alive throughout the Middle Ages by monastic and mendicant writers – crossed streams with humanist philosophical research projects during the Renaissance.

Christianity as "Natural Religion"

Aside from being one long and self-conscious appeal to authority, *On the Christian Religion* is also one long appeal to the natural, the necessary, and the right. For Ficino, the world of creation was like an ever-unfolding flower of vicissitudes. He leads us by the hand to envision the entire unfoldment of Christian theology as an organic process, like a rose coming into bloom, fulfilling the "rosy nature" which had been imprinted upon it from its very inception. The vocabulary of plant life – of agriculture, the vineyard, and the gardener – recurs frequently, chiefly on account of being a theme inherent to the books of the prophets themselves. When Ficino speaks of "nature," however, we must approach this term from within the scientific paradigm of the fifteenth century. Here what is "natural" is not merely about that which is "innate" or "inborn," but also that which is connected to the metaphor of birth (based on the Latin verb *nascor, nasci, natus sum*: "to be born or begotten, to proceed, to spring forth"). Simply put, what is natural is congenital. For Ficino, only Christianity was the religion of origins, or the most "radical" religion in the purely etymological sense of the term. Here he attempted to lead readers back to the very root (*radix*) of the ontological argument for the existence of God and work his way outward. Every human is linked to this primordial faith insofar as they are linked to God's process of creation and participate in the great hierarchy of being. Religion, as Ficino understood it, was the *sine qua non* of human-ness. In keeping with the teachings of not only Christian Platonism, but also those put forward in ancient Hermetic texts like the *Asclepius* and the *Pimander*, Ficino enshrined man as the nexus between the material and the divine and made "judgment in matters of religion" the essence of what distinguished man from the animals.[40] The Highest

---

40 Fic. *Op., Praedicationes*, 473–4.

Good, by virtue of being the Highest Good, is in a constant state of wishing to share itself with others. Humans, above all, have the capacity to emulate this Highest Good through self-sacrifice. Animals, who can neither practise delayed gratification nor make sacrifices, do not practise religion. Only humans do, and only some humans at that (i.e., those who participate in the perfected human form). Only humans have the intellectual capacity to grapple with the eternal Word which resides immutable and unchanging above the intellect, in the Platonic realm of forms, high up in the mind of God. Although animals can demonstrate reason in some limited capacity, none of them exhibit true religiosity; among men, however, religiosity is universal. The similarity of the rites practised by the ancient sages of the nations across the map – whether Egyptian, Indian, Persian, Greek, Ethiopian, or Latin – all cried out as a testament to the one true religion of God: the religion of sacrifice, the religion of nature, the religion that is congenital to, and in fact the determining factor of, what constituted the *genus humanum* as distinct from the other animals.

It is from this very theory of man as apex rational animal and as a demonstrator of his reason insofar as he has the capacity to be pious and selfless that Ficino established his own foundations. The central doctrine in Ficino's theology of "natural religion" is that all true philosophy and religion are true insofar as they are concerned with *caritas*, the kind of love which involves self-abnegation and, connected to this, the practice of sacrificial rites, wherein an individual willingly abscises a choice part of themselves or their property to benefit another. This was the golden chain which bound together the religion that was intrinsic to man to the religion that was intrinsic to God: "For God so loved the world as to give His only begotten Son that whosoever believeth in Him shall not perish but have life everlasting."[41] Ancient sages across the world had universally performed self-renunciation in performing sacrifices to God(s), and Ficino perceived that this was no wrong, for in those days before the Incarnation they were prefiguring God's own eternal sacrifice which had been chiseled into the hearts of men by their very natures, that is, by the fact that they were souls created in the image of God. Ficino argued that the human mind makes its own free will manifest over corporeal matters, and thereby he enshrined the freedom of virtue, truth, and religion over the life of slavery to bodily impulses.[42]

---

41 John 3:16.
42 Cf. Edelheit, *Ficino, Pico and Savonarola*, 154–5.

This liberty to do so arises purely out of the imperfection of the human intellect, which is then free either to err or to follow God. This focus on the ascetic impulse as the essence of religion made its way down to Ficino not only from Christian and Platonic sources from antiquity, but indeed directly from the works of Plato himself. Plato had made this most explicit with his chariot metaphor in the *Phaedrus*, that man alone is uniquely capable of applying his intellect to the active rejection of the senses and their passions.

In Ficino we have something like a biological reading of negative theology: God is not nature, being absolutely transcendent, but having created nature, God is in some way accessible through it, chiefly through the higher parts of a human being which extend beyond the material world. If one follows the chain of one's own genealogy all the way back to its very source, one finds oneself at the beginning of history with Adam, made in the image of God. This image, of course, is the only begotten Son of the Father, Jesus Christ, the archetypal man who is, was, and will forever be fully one and fully coeternal with God. The doctrine of procession, of God creating the world and "sending" his Son into it to make known his perfect *caritas* thus becomes a kind of Christian alternative to the Platonic doctrine of "emanation, turn, and return." Every offspring emerges from a source, every infant from a womb, every plant from a germ, and as such, every living thing endowed with reason can "turn" back to recognize the source of its origins. Human beings, unlike dogs or trees, are so fortunate as to have the capacity to return through the intellect back to the source of their origins. What was most important is that God models this very process within himself through his triune nature, particularly through the person of Christ. Just as Christ the eternal and uncreated *Logos* was made flesh, suffered pain and death as the ultimate exemplar of his perfect *caritas*, then returned to sit at the right hand of the Father, God set the model within the very structure of his own being for mankind, which is also divine, to mirror him and do the same. In this way, Ficino's universe was something like a series of internestled crystalline wombs within wombs, linked by a great umbilical cord of being. Through his only begotten Son who is simultaneously the eternal priest, the eternal temple, and the eternal sacrifice, God descends from the fullness of eternity into the imperfection of time to demonstrate to man that there can be no Platonic "turn and return" to perfect happiness (*felicitas*) without the Pauline triad *fides* (faith), *spes* (hope), and most importantly, *caritas* (love).

Ficino and the Latin Polemical Tradition

In assembling *On the Christian Religion*, Ficino applied his new Platonic philosophical perspective to try his hand at an age-old tradition: attempting to demonstrate the superiority of Christian scriptural interpretation over that of other religions – especially Judaism and Islam – largely by highlighting the various Christological clues encoded into the books of the Old Testament by the prophets. Herein he attempted to highlight God's Trinitarian composition (as transcendent Father, immanent Son/*Logos*/Word, and as unifying Spirit), the correspondence between Old and New Testaments, the coming of God as Incarnation and Messiah, and the historical nature of Jesus as a fulfiller of prophecies. Here God joined himself to the soul of a man (itself made in God's image) in order to give us the perfect religion and to bridge the fathomless gap between the finitude of man and infinitude of God. Christ, therefore, is the "priest in eternity" implicit to the very makeup of God, an ultimate unity that unfolds himself via a redemptive process by descending into his creation. To demonstrate his infinite mercy and infinite justice in perfectly equal proportion, God entered into history, bisected being and time, sacrificed himself to himself, and by this sacrifice, fulfilled the temporal laws of the ancient Hebrews with a set of eternal laws: to love God and to do unto others what you would have them do unto you.

In the chapters entitled "On the Generation of God's Son in Eternity" (chapter thirteen) and "On the Generation of God's Son in Eternity and His Manifestation in Time" (chapter fifteen), Ficino divulges the ways in which the ancient prophets foretold God's Incarnation among both the Hebrews and the pagans. Citing the Orphic tradition, Ficino maintains that the Greeks had understood the *Logos* through the guise of Pallas Athena, who emerged fully formed from the head of Zeus (using as his evidence the *Letter to Hermias* attributed to Plato, wherein the philosopher called it "the Son of God the Father"). He adds that both the Egyptian Hermes Trismegistus and the Persian Zoroaster believed the same: that God has intellectual progeny.[43] Ficino then moves on to cover

---

43 Chapter thirteen: "Hanc Palladem appelavit Orpheus solo Iovis capite natam; hunc Dei patris filium Plato in epistola ad Hermiam nominavit, in *Epinomide* nuncupavit logon, id est rationem ac verbum dicens: "Logos omnium divinissimus mundum hunc visibilem exornavit." Mercurius Trismegistus de verbo et filio Dei ac etiam de Spiritu sepe mentionem facit, Zoroaster quoque intellectualem Deo prolem attribuit. Dixerunt isti quidem quod potuerunt et id quidem adiuvante Deo; Deus autem hoc solus intelligit et cui Deus voluerit revelare." Bart. *DCR*, 194–5; cf. Plato, *Epistle* 6, 323d2–4 and *Epinomis*, 986c4–5.

the importance of the sibyls and their prophecies as contained in Virgil's *Eclogue* 4 in preparing the way for the Incarnation among the Latins (chapters twenty-four and twenty-five).[44] This rather brief narrative, however, ultimately leads into a series of *significantly* lengthier polemics directed against various ideas circulating among the Jews regarding their particular interpretations of the prophetic books (chapters twenty-six through thirty-four). It is these chapters specifically which, when taken together, make up over half the length of the book. Herein Ficino stresses his use of Jewish sources, and he does so explicitly in an effort to refute Judaism using the Jews' own weapons against them. This is telling because this approach to Hebrew literature is entirely in keeping with a polemical style set down in previous centuries by such Spanish conversos as Petrus Alfonsi, Ramon Martí, Abner and Paul of Burgos, or Jerome of Santa Fe, sources which he cites explicitly in chapter twenty-seven.[45]

---

44 See Wendell Clausen, *A Commentary on Virgil, Eclogues* (Oxford: Clarendon Press, 1994), 119–29 and Pierre Courcelle, "Les exégèses chrétiennes de la quatrième Églogue," *Revue des Études Anciennes* 59, 3–4 (1957): 294–319, the latter of which provides a detailed account of the various receptions of *Eclogue* 4 by Christian sources, some of whom saw Christ in the prophesied child, while some held these interpretations in contempt.

45 Chapter 27, Bart. *DCR*, 240:

> De Iudeis autem interim quid est dicendum? Raro et pauci electi erunt. De iis enim illud Isaie intelligitur: "Et relinquetur in eo sicut racemus et sicut excussio olive duarum aut trium olivarum in summitate rami." Postquam enim propter illorum perfidiam a naturali arbore, ut Paulus Apostolus inquit, excussi sunt et ab olive radice separati, adhuc nonnulli vel ibi relicti, vel potius interdum denuo videntur inserti, qualis fuit Evaristus Hebreus, vir illustris, qui septimus a beato Petro Pontifex Christianorum fuit, annos plures quam decem in ea dignitate dignissime vixit martyrque obiit. Preterea Gotorum tempore Iulianus Iudeus primum Hispanie sanctissime rexit episcopatum. Petrus quoque Alfonsius, eiusdem generis, dialogum conscripsit contra perfidiam Iudeorum; Alfonsus Burgensis, summus methaphysicus, in sexagesimo etatis sue anno fidem Christi suscepit pluraque adversus Iudeos egregia scripsit. Quid dicam de Nicholao Lyrensi, mari doctrine magno viroque sanctissimo? Quid de Hieronymo physico, qui tempore pontificis Benedicti contra Iudeos subtiliter disputavit? Fuerunt et alii numero quidem multi, quamvis egregii, tam longo seculo pauci, de quibus illud Hieremie dictum censeo: "Assumam vos unum de civitate et duos de cognitione [sic]" – (aliter "congregatione") – "et adducam vos in Sion," scilicet celestem. De iis diligenter Paulus Burgensis episcopus, theologus insignis, tractavit.

Cf. Bernard McGinn, "Cabalists and Christians: Reflections on Cabala in Medieval and Renaissance Thought" in *Jewish Christians and Christian Jews*, ed. R.H. Popkin and G.M. Weiner (New York: Kluwer Academic Publishers, 1994), 12–16 for a discussion of Petrus Alfonsi's relation to the development of Christian Cabala.

When it came to attacking the subtler points of doctrine that the Jews maintained about the Messiah, Ficino's own approach was mediated by two key converso figures. In arguing against those who proclaimed that the Messiah had not yet come – an idea that had been debated for centuries by rabbis like "Moses the Egyptian" (Maimonides, *Rambam*), Moses ben Nahman of Girona (Nachmanides, *Ramban*), and Shlomo Yitzhaqi of Troyes (Salomon Isaacides, *Rashi*) – Ficino chiefly relied on the polemics of the Christian converts from Judaism Paul of Burgos (a.k.a. Pablo de Santa Maria or Paulus Burgensis, formerly Solomon ha-Levi, c. 1351–1435) and Jerome/Gerónimo of Santa Fe (a.k.a. Hieronymus de Sancta Fide, formerly Joshua ha-Lorki, fl. 1400–30). Both of these men had, in their own days, become Dominican friars after their respective conversions and had dedicated their lives to preaching to Jews and proving their *bona fides*.[46] Like the Andalusian astronomer and physician Petrus Alfonsi who set the model for good converso behaviour back in the twelfth century, both Paul of Burgos and Jerome of Santa Fe had been erudite Talmudists before undergoing their own conversion experiences. Prior to undergoing Christian baptism on 21 July 1391 and changing his name, this later-to-become bishop of Cartagena had been a wealthy rabbi in his own community, renouncing every aspect of his former life to assume the vows of poverty, chastity, and obedience.[47] All this took place in the immediate wake of that terrible massacre of Jews that began on 6 June 1391, though Paul himself claimed he had been moved by his readings of Thomas Aquinas.[48] Both Paul of Burgos

---

46 For brief biographical entries, see Walter Drum, "Paul of Burgos," in *Catholic Encyclopedia* vol. 11, ed. Charles Herbermann (New York: Robert Appleton Company, 1913); Richard Gottheil and Meyer Kayserling, "Ibn Vives Al-Lorqui (Of Lorca), Joshua Ben Joseph (Hieronymus [Geronimo] de Santa Fé)" in *The Jewish Encyclopedia*, vol. 6 (New York: Funk & Wagnalls, 1906), 552. Paul of Burgos is especially notable in that he not only wrote the anti-Jewish polemic *Dialogus Pauli et Sauli contra Judæos, sive Scrutinium scripturarum* (Rome: Ulrich Han, 1471) modelled in some ways after Petrus Alfonsi's *Dialogi contra Iudaeos*, but also the *Additiones* to Nicholas of Lyra's *Postilla*, which appear in the latter's *Biblia: Cum postillis Nicolai de Lyra et expositionibus Guillelmi Britonis in omnes prologos S. Hieronymi et additionibus Pauli Burgensis replicisque Matthiae Doering*. 4 vols. Nürnberg: Anton Koberger, 1485), excerpts of which appeared in Paul of Burgos, *De nomine divino quæstiones duodecim*, ed. Johannes Drusius (Franeker, 1604; Amsterdam, 1634; London, 1660; Utrecht, 1707) which pertains to correct pronunciation of YHVH.
47 Benzion Netanyahu, *The Origins of the Inquisition in Fifteenth-Century Spain* (New York: Random House, 1995), 171.
48 Leon Poliakov, *The History of Anti-Semitism*, vol. 2 (Philadelphia: University of Pennsylvania Press, 2003), 160–1.

and Jerome of Santa Fe took to a life of attacking the traditional knowledge which they had received in the yeshivas in their youths, and this was done precisely as a means of proving the validity of their spiritual renewal to their new co-religionists, who were ever wary of relapsing "crypto-Jews."[49] Alongside their voluminous literary endeavours, both authors actively campaigned to persecute Sephardic Jews in the century leading up to the great expulsions of the 1490s, endeavouring by all manner of arguments to convince secular rulers to strip Jews of their traditional rights, ultimately forcing them to convert or flee the Iberian peninsula empty-handed. In 1413, Jerome of Santa Fe – at the time a physician for the antipope Benedict XIII – was personally responsible for initiating the infamous Disputation of Tortosa with his work on the Midrashim drawn up from Ramon Martí's *Pugio fidei*.[50] Shortly thereafter, in 1415, Jerome's fellow converso Dominican, Paul of Santa Maria, was made archbishop of Burgos in northern Spain for his learning and long service in the spiritual war against the Jews. From this elevated position of ecclesiastical authority, he doubled down on his anti-Jewish interests. Under the immediate influence of the Dominican polemics of Thomas Aquinas and the Franciscan biblical exegesis of Nicholas of Lyra, the work Paul of Burgos penned in the final year of his life – the *Dialogus Pauli et Sauli contra Judaeos, sive Scrutinium Scripturarum* (1434) – is most significant for our own purposes. In form it bears remarkable similarities to Petrus Alfonsi's *Dialogi contra Iudaeos* (1110), which consists of a kind of Socratic dialogue between "Moses Sephardi" and his Christian alter ego "Petrus." Paul of Burgos's text consists of a war of words between "Saul the Jew" and "Paul the Christian" wherein Paul acknowledges that Saul will not be convinced by arguments from New Testament scriptures, but with Old Testament scriptures alone.[51] Here

---

49 Paul of Burgos gives formerly Jewish converts to Christianity pride of place in his *Scrutinium Scripturarum*: in an early chapter replete with Christian authorities like the evangelist Luke, Paul the Apostle, and Augustine, he asserts that if the Jews take up the faith of Christ, they too can attain "Christian dignity" (*dignitas Christiana*), just as the Christians had attained "the dignity of Israel" (*dignitas Israelitica*); then in the last two chapters he returns to this subject, in the penultimate one recalling the few but important Jewish converts during the first coming of Christ and the prophesied conversion of all Jews during the second, and in the final one commemorating the illustrious converts of the *tempus medium* between these two transformative ages (Paul. *Scrut.* 1.2.1,12r–13v; 1.2.4, 18r–20v; 2.6.13, 284r–286v; 2.6.14, 286v–288r).
50 For more on Ramon Martí's *Pugio fidei*, see Robert Chazan, *Daggers of Faith: Thirteenth-Century Christian Missionizing and Jewish Response* (Berkeley: University of California Press, 1989).
51 Paul. *Scrut.* 1.1.1, 4r.

the strategy is familiar: locate a particular Christian belief which Jews do not share, find precedent for it in the Hebrew (or Aramaic/"Chaldean") original, and demonstrate how contemporary Jews have fallen off the path of the *veritas Hebraica* into the *falsitas Iudaica*. In a similar fashion, Jerome of Santa Fe composed his own anti-Jewish polemics, the *Tractatus contra perfidiam Judaeorum* and the *De Judaeis erroribus ex Talmuth*, which also borrowed its arguments from this single unbroken line of medieval anti-Jewish polemicists. By the time Ficino was writing *On the Christian Religion*, every one of these anti-Jewish polemicists were being extensively cited in that work, comprising the very DNA of his most extensive chapters.

With no real knowledge of Hebrew or Aramaic, Ficino was not nearly as well equipped to deal with Old Testament scripture in its original form as his younger friends Giovanni Pico della Mirandola or Johannes Reuchlin would become in later decades. It was chiefly for this reason that he had to rely so heavily on arguments taken directly from the pages of older authors who had spent their whole lives dissecting all manner of esoteric Talmudic minutiae in the service of Christendom. Indeed, what Steven J. McMichael says of Alfonso de Espina (a contemporary of Ficino), that "because his sources are all Christian, even when he is quoting from a Jewish text, there is no actual engagement with the living Jewish community on their interpretation of the Mosaic law," can equally be said of Ficino's understanding of the Talmud when he composed *On the Christian Religion*.[52] When arguing about the presence of Christological theophanies or prefigurations in the Old Testament, Ficino typically used St. Jerome's Latin Vulgate translation, but there are also a handful of instances where he expressly tried to leverage his crude knowledge of transliterated Hebrew into arguments about the nature of God, the Holy Spirit, and the Messiah. While on the one hand we cannot entirely call Ficino's approach "Kabbalistic," given that he made no direct recourse to Kabbalistic texts like the *Zohar*, no reference to the sephiroth, and no use of Abulafian combinatorial arts (or any type of gematria, notarikon, or temurah); on the other hand, we can certainly see Hebrew grammatical arguments similar to those used against Talmudists in the twelfth to fifteenth centuries by polemicists in the line of Petrus Alfonsi and Ramon Martí. Such arguments would be the

---

52 Steven J. McMichael, "Alfondo de Espina on the Mosaic Law," in *Friars and Jews in the Middle Ages and Renaissance*, ed. Steven J. McMichael and Susan E. Myers (Leiden: Brill, 2004), 222.

closest Ficino came to touching upon what Moshe Idel called "Kabbalistic thinking" in the 1470s, and it is similar kinds of speculative arguments that also went on to play a prominent role in Giovanni Pico della Mirandola's 900 *Conclusiones* and *Heptaplus*, written during the mid- to late-1480s and deeply influenced by the translation work of the converso Flavius Mithridates.[53] Ficino's awareness of Kabbalistic sources at the time he composed *On the Christian Religion* was much less extensive than during his later career, though it must be admitted that the discussion in chapter thirty about the Tetragrammaton being derived from three different tenses of the verb "to be" has its origin in Kabbalistic texts. Bartolucci posits that Ficino's awareness of this argument was likely the result of conversations with Jewish scholars who may have suggested it to him in person at an early enough date to influence the composition of *On the Christian Religion*.[54] Ultimately, both Ficino and Pico were bound together by a shared belief that arguments dealing with the grammar of the Bible's original languages were the most valuable weapons in the Church's arsenal. This was not only because such a mode of attack had a long precedent in the stratagems of mendicant and converso polemicists – tapping into a much longer medieval philological tradition as it had been practised by Talmudic scholars and their converso adversaries – but also because they provided another outlet with which to explore newer and more fashionable humanist proclivities to return *ad fontes* and to cut off various theological problems at the source.

For Ficino, contemporary Jewish approaches to Holy Scripture were an affront to the perfect *Logos* embodied by the religion of Christ.

---

53 For more on an early encounter between Ficino and the themes of Kabbalah, see Guido Bartolucci, "Per una fonte cabalistica del *De Christiana religione*: Marsilio Ficino e il nome di Dio," *Revue de la Société Marsile Ficin* 6 (2004): 35–46 and Guido Bartolucci, "Marsilio Ficino e le origini della Cabala Cristiana," in *Pico e la Cabalà*, ed. F. Lelli (Florence: Olschki, 2014): 47–67. For Ficino's influence on Jewish thinkers like Yohanan Alemanno, see Moshe Idel, *Kabbalah in Italy 1280–1510* (New Haven, CT and London: Yale University Press, 2011). For the influence of Kabbalistic texts on Pico, see Chaim Wirszubski, *Pico della Mirandola's Encounter with Jewish Mysticism* (Cambridge, MA: Harvard University Press, 1989). There is one instance of Kabbalistic literature explicitly cited in chapter twenty-seven of *De Christiana religione*, namely, the *Sefer HaBahir* (Latin: *Lucidus*) by "the ancient and illustrious theologian Rabbi Nehunya," but this appearance is not of much significance overall given that Ficino's only acquaintance with the text was through Paul of Burgos's *Scrutinium Scripturarum*; see Guido Bartolucci, *Vera religio. Marsilio Ficino e la tradizione ebraica* (Turin: Paideia, 2017), 45–64.
54 Bartolucci, "Per une fonte," 42–6.

Throughout *On the Christian Religion* Ficino shines light on his vision of a marriage of Christianity and Platonism not so much in order to settle contemporary academic debates over philosophical minutiae directly, but more so to discursively build up a grand cosmic narrative which he could subsequently employ to illustrate why Christianity and no other religion – especially not contemporary Judaism and Islam – was heir to his supercelestial theology. As touched on above, Ficino maintained that it was austerity, asceticism, renunciation, and above all, love (*caritas*) to the point of martyrdom as exhibited by the primitive Church – in other words, the transvaluation of worldly values – that provided the clearest proof that Christ's first followers did not have ulterior motives.[55] The apostles had lived out their lives in imitation of the Old Testament prophets, then suffered and died in order to participate in the death and suffering of Christ, not that they might achieve some paradise of earthly delights, or be reunited with their ancestors, but that their immortal, divine, and individuated souls might rise up, *become like God*, and come to rest in eternal, transcendent, and perfect happiness (*felicitas*) with God. Beyond invoking the fulfilment of various prophecies in confirming the truth of Christianity, Ficino enshrined the *imitatio Christi* and the *vita apostolica* as his religion's surest signs of being true. Though Ficino himself did not employ such a term, today we might say that it was the "transvaluation" of pagan values – a moral inversion he saw present neither in Judaism nor in Islam – which he perceived as the essence of the Christian message. By condensing a handful of Christ's most celebrated aphorisms, Ficino tried to summarize the very essence of Christianity, in the following words:

> "Give all your possessions to the poor; reject who you hold dearest; if someone strikes you turn your cheeks; do good to your enemies; regard this life and all its pleasures as worthless; deny even yourselves; take up this cross of ours – the terrible cross; please follow us immediately. For if you follow us, without doubt you will undergo everything that mortals judge evil throughout the rest of your life." ... What persuasion, full in all respects of every sort of dissuasion! Do we believe that Demosthenes or Cicero could have persuaded anyone of anything using this method? Nevertheless, that speech, nay the speaker persuaded many great men against all expectation.[56]

---

55 Cf. 2 Cor. 13:13.
56 Chapter eight: "'Date vestra omnia pauperibus; carissimos vestros respuite; porrigite genas percutienti; benefacite inimicis; vitam hanc omniaque eius oblectamenta pro

A life modelled in imitation of the *Logos*, Ficino maintained, spoke louder than empty rhetoric ever could. For as much as he was concerned with transcendent Platonic, incorporeal, and supercelestial matters, he first had to broach the subject by an appeal to the experiences of exemplary men who lived in a bygone age. What is truly transcendent on this plane of existence is found only through total abasement: the highest things are brought down to the lowest, and the lowest things are brought up to the highest. With the backing of the very Hebrew prophets' actions themselves, Ficino believed radical acts of renunciation to be unique to Christianity, making it a completely different entity altogether than the "carnal" faith of the Jews, the "lewd" and "unjust" faith of the pagans, or the "lascivious" faith of the Mohammadans.[57] To be a Christian was to renounce this world in love, and to renounce this world was to practise the one true "natural religion" long ago foreshadowed by the sacrificial rites of the *prisci theologi*, for nature itself had been set in place for rational souls to climb up and out of, to return back towards the one true super-natural God. For the Hellenistic world, it was Plato who preached most articulately this renunciation of the flesh for the life of the mind, but for Ficino, this ideology was perfected most completely centuries later in the men of the New Testament, namely, in those who established the perfect marriage between the *vita activa* and the *vita contemplativa*.

For as much as poverty, suffering, martyrdom, and death played a role in historically legitimating the Christian faith, the concept of revelation

---

nihilo habetote; abnegate vos metipsos; crucem hanc nostram, crucem terribilem, substinete; sequamini nos quamprimum precamur. Si enim nos sequemini, procul dubio quecunque a mortalibus mala existimantur per omnem vitam subibitis.' ... O suasionem dissuasionis omnis undique plenam! An putamus Demostenem, Ciceronemque hac ratione quicquam persuadere cuiquam potuisse? Persuasit tamen contio illa, immo contionator, subito multis magnisque viris." Bart. *DCR*, 173; Matt. 19:21; Luke 12:33, 18:22, 14:25–7; Matt. 4:44, 6:19–20, 16:24–6.

57 Chapter 8: "Si religionis maxime propria est puritas, hec certe divinissima est, que neque viles posteriorum Iudeorum superstitiones et spurcissima *Talmut* deliramenta, neque obscenas et iniquas Gentilium fabulas, neque abominabilem Mahumethensium licentiam et *Alcorani* ineptias admittit, que neque terrena premia, ut leges alie, sed celestia pollicetur, neque adversarios fidei legisque sue interfici iubet, quemadmodum iussit *Talmut* et *Alcoranum*, sed vel ratione doceri, vel oratione converti, vel patientia tolerari." Bart. *DCR*, 178. Cf. *The Letters of Marsilio Ficino*. Volume 11: *Being a Translation of Liber XII*, trans. Language Department of the London School of Economic Science (London: Shepheard-Walwyn, 2020), 107–9 for Sebastiano Salvini's letter commending *On the Christian Religion*, which concludes in sum that in it "you will find ... the obstinacy, errors, and false statements of the Jews, and the Mohammedans' arrogance, ineptitude, temerity, and delight in the physical."

and prophecy – a concept "naturally" held in common by pagans, Muslims, Jews, and Christians – played no small role in Ficino's theology either. This is, of course, because the *vita apostolica* was entirely patterned upon the lives of the prophets from its inception. It was through the lens of the historic lives of the prophets and their words that the moral transvaluations of Christ and his apostles acquired their force. Historically speaking, inasmuch as Christ and his apostles lived lives of religious renunciation, they had done so in imitation of the Old Testament prophets who preceded them. They emulated men who walked about the streets dressed in sackcloth, who mortified their flesh or ate dung, who reproached hostile priests and kings at great peril, all in service of something that transcended mundane earthly concerns: their ideals about *justice* on the one hand, and *mercy* on the other.[58] It was the prophets who had first "prepared the way for the Lord" with their thunderous admonitions for a return to a just society, and it was through their emulation that Christianity legitimized its own ostensibly transgressive character. In Ficino's Platonist scheme, however, the apostles were not so much emulating the prophets as much as the prophets and the apostles were both *participating* in the eternal pattern embodied by and manifested in Christ. One only needed the "spiritual understanding" to see it. If the lives of most Christians did not reflect the lives of the prophets, of the primitive Church, or ultimately, the life of Christ, it was because the light of truth was being ignored. Fortunately, truth had been preserved within the very letters which constituted Scripture – that very Scripture which Ficino perceived in his own age was being shoved aside at the expense of non- or even anti-Christian innovation.

Throughout the gospels, Christ himself is depicted as a kind of prophet above all prophets, namely, one who fulfils the prophecies of others as much as he gives and fulfils his own. Among all the prophecies issued by Christ, however, Ficino upheld the destruction of Judaism to be among the most important. Throughout chapter eight, in giving his list of reasons as to why Christianity is supreme above all other religions, Ficino asks the rhetorical question: "What of the fact that Christ, the teacher of life, not only predicted His own death, the future persecution against His disciples everywhere, the propagation and immutability of His religion, the wretched ruin of the Jews soon to come, the conversion of the pagans, the obstinacy of some Jews to endure all the way to the end of the world, but also inspired His

---

58 Cf. Mic. 6:8.

disciples to say the same?"[59] Here the ultimate prophet, who through his own life fulfilled the very religion of the prophets, is praised in his foretelling of Judaism's inevitable two-fold demise: first with the destruction of the Second Temple, then with their mass conversion upon his final return at the end of history. In this we can see how the very legitimacy of Christ as Prophet-Messiah was held in a kind of inverse proportion to the legitimacy of contemporary Judaism: Christ is Christ insofar as he fulfilled and ended the faith of the Old Testament with a new one; to suggest anything else would be to throw God's gift back in his face. It is here within this very incommensurability between Christianity and Judaism that Ficino carved out his theological home. This niche, of course, had long been carved out by other polemicists before Ficino had come to inhabit it. It is indeed a regrettable aspect of our Florentine philosopher-priest that constructing his own identity was part and parcel with tearing down that of his neighbours, but it was certainly not a practice unique to him. The fact that he was trying to garner favour from the Church and further his own career by composing a work focused on slandering Jews as *pertinaces, homunculi*, and *miseri* is rather telling of the virulently anti-Semitic climate of the Church during the latter half of the quattrocento.[60]

It is not surprising that this polemic ultimately made few, if any, waves in actual Jewish circles.[61] Not only were Ficino's hermeneutics quite unoriginal, being cobbled together from the works of a discrete handful of widely respected medieval mendicant and converso polemicists, but to a learned rabbi they would not have been terribly convincing either. Among scholastic authors, Ficino also received little attention, largely because most of the ideas he put forward were already present

---

59 See page 65 below.
60 For context, one should keep in mind that the infamous blood libel controversy revolving around Simon of Trent occurred in 1475, a scandal which climbed its way up into the very highest levels of Church authority; see Paul O. Kristeller, "The Alleged Ritual Murder of Simon of Trent (1475) and its Literary Repercussions: A Bibliographical Study," *Proceedings of the American Academy for Jewish Research* 59 (1993): 103–35.
61 For a discussion concerning Ficino and the ongoing debates between the converso Kabbalist Flavius Mithridates and the peripatetic Elia del Medigo at various houses in Florence in 1485, see Harvey J. Hames, "Elia Del Medigo: An Archetype of the Halachic Man?" *Traditio* 56 (2001): 217–18. Throughout the 1480s, Del Medigo resisted the rising trend of Ficino's Christian Platonism in Florence with his emphasis on Jewish *halakha* and Aristotelian philosophy as interpreted by Averroes, a position he attempted to impress upon one of his disciples, Giovanni Pico della Mirandola.

32 On the Christian Religion

in authors that most fifteenth-century *doctores* already knew quite well (from Eusebius and Augustine to Thomas Aquinas and Nicholas of Lyra). Relying on transliterations and second-hand information, Ficino himself was simply not very well equipped with the linguistic tools to "beat the Jews at their own game," as it were, in the manner of men like Petrus Alfonsi, Ramon Martí, Paul of Burgos, and Jerome of Santa Fe. In any case, despite being rhetorically addressed to the Jews in its polemical sections, the actual intended audience for this work was Ficino's inner circle of churchmen, poets, princes, humanists, and patrons. As mentioned from the outset, Ficino chiefly preached to the proverbial choir. He was far more interested in sparking a *"rinnovazione"* in Christendom – of inaugurating his up-and-coming translations of the *prisci theologi* and demonstrating how they might be useful to Christians – than he was in actually trying to convert Jews directly.

On the Christian Religion through Ficino's Own Eyes

As far as we are able to gather, Ficino made reference to *On the Christian Religion* in a small selection of other later printed works, such as the *Platonic Theology*, and in his summaries of Plato's *Cratylus* and *Phaedo*. Throughout his career, he made thirty-five more-or-less explicit references to it in subsequent writings. Many mentions to the work arose in the process of sharing and distributing copies among his friends, acquaintances, and colleagues, since Ficino appended his printed editions with introductory epistles addressed to individual recipients.[62] Most of the letters that refer to *On the Christian Religion* are undated, and of those that have dates (twelve of the thirty-two), eight cluster between the dates of 13 February 1477[63] and 10 November 1479, with three outliers from the 1480s. Since the Latin version of Ficino's text first saw print on 10 December 1476, most of the dated letters fall within three years of that date of publication. Bartolucci's critical edition includes three appendices containing many of the letters that mention *On the*

---

62 Details on the appearances of *On the Christian Religion* in Ficino's letters, and the identity of the recipients and dedicatees of this book can be found in Paul O. Kristeller's *Supplementum Ficinianum*, 2 vols. (Florence: Olschki, 1937), 1.LXXVII-LXXVIII and Mario Emilio Cosenza, *Biographical and Bibliographical Dictionary of the Italian Humanists and of the World of Classical Scholarship in Italy, 1300–1800*, 6 vols. (Boston: G.K. Hall & Co., 1962).
63 The letter in question, 3.57 to Ficino's friend Naldo Naldi, is dated 13 February 1476, but the Florentine date for cycling to a new year was 25 March at the time, such that the letter would be labelled as being from 1477 by modern time reckoning standards.

Christian Religion. Entire paragraphs contained in each of these letters can also be found verbatim elsewhere within the published collections of Ficino's correspondence, but the addressees and dates differ.[64] In the letters, only three times does he refer to the book by its full title *"De Christiana religione."* Elsewhere, he calls it his "Religion," his "book on true piety," and his "book on the holy (or, true) faith." He states that the book is an expression of his "faith and devotion," "wholly composed of Christian piety." He describes it as his "pledge of religious love," "a handmaiden of Truth" in which his "mind [is] reasoning with all its power on divine faith and hope," since "as a follower of the ancients, [Ficino] always joins the religious to the philosophical to the best of his ability, not only in this one book *On Religion* … but in all his writings." In writing the book, Ficino alleged himself to be aiming "not to instruct, but to fulfill his duty to Piety itself," while revealing "the true nature" of his religion. In one instance, he sent *On the Christian Religion* at the same time as his treatise *On Love* to the same correspondent, Filippo Controni, and in so doing, he claimed to demonstrate that his "love is religious, and his religion full of love." He proclaimed that the book should serve as a "proof and pledge of how constant" his future affection towards its recipient, Gian Stefano Castiglioni, will be. Most significantly, he sent the book to a papal commissary, Pietro Placentino, so that it could be used as "arms" to fight "against the enemies of divine wisdom" – arms with which Ficino himself claimed in his letter to be striving "unceasingly with all [his] strength against the enemies of truth."

Ficino's dismay at the poor quality of the first Italian edition that was printed two years before the Latin edition is a topic that came up several times in his letters. He urged his readers, if they happened upon mistakes, to "bear in mind [that] we have no printers here [in Florence], only misprinters."[65] Ficino wrote to his book's recipients such things as "it may not seem beautiful, but I hope that at least it is not ill-informed," or "if it should seem very poor, remember that the Christian religion was founded in poverty." Ficino evidently became quite self-conscious about the quality of his final product. Another instance of Ficino drawing

---

64 Clearly, Ficino was treating his own epistolary compositions as form letters, where he would copy and paste a paragraph from here and there to create new letters for new correspondents.

65 References to all the letters cited or alluded to in the previous two paragraphs appear in the appendix below, which offers a summative table of all references to *On the Christian Religion* in Ficino's correspondence.

attention to the humble nature of his work can be gleaned from a subtle change in wording between two letters he addressed to the same person, Girolamo Rossi, one being a first draft, the other being the one that actually accompanied the book. Where the original version read: "Read well our book on the holy faith ... do not measure the stature of what is divine from the base level of *humanity*," the version he actually sent was changed to "do not measure the stature of what is divine from the base level of *my feeble intellect*" (emphasis added).

The social status and occupation of Ficino's correspondents reveals with what sorts of people our philosopher-priest deemed it fit to share his work. Among the twenty-five individuals who became recipients of *On the Christian Religion* as gifts, all but one were Italian. Some were high-ranking churchmen: Rainaldo Orsini, the archbishop of Florence who took office in early 1474 shortly after his predecessor – a Franciscan named Pietro Riario who had been responsible for Ficino's ordination – died;[66] Raffaele Riario, cardinal, bishop of Viterbo, and grand chancellor of the University of Rome; and Filippo Controni, archbishop of Urbino. Others were high-ranking diplomats, such as Bernardo Bembo from Venice and Filippo Sacromoro and Gian Stefano Castiglioni from Milan. Still others were high-ranking noblemen, including – unsurprisingly, since he was Ficino's patron – Lorenzo de' Medici, and Federico da Montefeltro, the Duke of Urbino. Others were prominent scholars in the humanist tradition and personal friends of Ficino, such as Angelo Poliziano. Most of the recipients, however, were local churchmen (Francesco Marescalchi, Giorgio Antonio Vespucci) or men who had taken monastic vows (Antonio of Forli, Daniel Placentino, Girolamo Rossi, and Donato Ugolino). Still others were holders of lesser political office in various northern Italian towns (Francesco Guarini from Florence; Antonio Ivani from Volterra; Antonio Lanfredini from Florence; Alberto Parisi from Bologna). Clearly, Ficino was eager to share his work with a wide but strategically targeted audience.

The first of Bartolucci's appendices offers an edition of a hitherto unpublished letter by Sebastiano Salvini, Ficino's cousin, fellow priest, doctor of theology, and a close collaborator in the preparation of the Latin text of *On the Christian Religion*.[67] This letter offers the most elaborate of the descriptions of the book that appear in any associated

---

66 Serracino-Inglott, "Ficino the Priest," 8.
67 See Bart. *DCR*, 311–12. A translation of this letter appears in Ficino, *Letters*, vol. 11, 107–9.

epistolary. Its final paragraph summarizes both the book's contents and the opinion of it held by one who worked closely on it with Ficino:

> Wherefore, most pious and devout man, we are sending you the book *On the Christian Religion*, produced as attractively as the material permits and in great detail, by our Marsilio, who, as I think, is no less a Christian than a Platonist, and he is no less zealous for you than for himself. In this book you will find the true humanity on which the fine religion of the Christians is founded, its modesty, moderation, justice, sanctity, hope, love, faith, and at the end, the obstinacy, errors, and false statements of the Jews, and the Mohammedans' arrogance, ineptitude, temerity, and delight in the physical.[68]

Clearly Ficino's intentions were not lost on his earliest readers: he had demonstrated that he was no less a Christian than a Platonist, all while exposing the enemies of Christendom. This letter accompanied a copy of the book that Salvini sent to Guido, the prior of the Santa Maria degli Angeli monastery in Florence, on 1 January 1487, placing it outside the window of time when Ficino was sending most of the dated letters that accompanied copies of *On the Christian Religion*. Bartolucci's Appendix III provides an edition of a letter that also appears in the published collections of Ficino's correspondence. It was addressed to his friends (*Ad familiares*), and amounts to a brief and abstract summary of *On the Christian Religion*. Several other letters refer to this summary and allow it to be dated to sometime before 15 September 1477. Ficino eventually re-used the text of this letter as part of one of his Italian sermons.

Turning now to the explicit references to *On the Christian Religion* in Ficino's non-epistolary works, his *Platonic Theology* refers readers back to the more extensive discussion on the numbers of the principal angelic orders "following the position of Dionysius" in chapter fourteen of *On the Christian Religion*.[69] Elsewhere in his *Platonic Theology*, however, there are extensive passages, sometimes pages long, that are word-for-word identical with what appears in *On the Christian Religion*. Although this was not an uncommon practice in scholarly writing at the time, it goes some way in helping to explain Ficino's prolificity.

---

68 Ficino, *Letters*, vol.11, 109.
69 Fic. *TP* 16.1.9 (Allen and Hankins 4.302–3 and note at 362); cf. chapter fourteen and Bart. *DCR* 196–7.

The long parallel passages combined with the explicit mutual cross-referencing between the two works confirms that they were indeed composed around the same time, though the *Platonic Theology* was first begun in 1469.[70] In his summary of Plato's *Cratylus*, which he subtitled "Concerning the True Principle of Names," he discusses the importance of divine names and refers back to his book *On Religion* for a fuller discussion of how, foreshadowing Reuchlin's 1494 *De verbo mirifico*, Jesus proved his divinity through his "true understanding and pronunciation of [the] tetragrammaton name."[71] In the very first sentence of Ficino's summary of Plato's *Phaedo*, he states: "Our book on religion confirms something that is sufficiently well-known of itself: that the life of Christ is the ideal pattern of all virtue."[72] The relative paucity of references to *On the Christian Religion* in Ficino's later works suggests that, in his view, the book spoke for itself and served its intended purpose. Even in his more emphatically Christian works, such as his translations and commentaries of pseudo-Dionysius's *Mystical Theology* and *Divine Names* composed much later in his career (1490–2), he rarely circled back to it. This fact to some extent confirms our belief that *On the Christian Religion* was composed primarily to cement Ficino's ordination as Catholic priest and to establish the *bona fides* of his up-and-coming Platonic revival in the eyes of contemporary Church authorities.

Translators' Notes

In producing our English translation of *On the Christian Religion*, we diligently availed ourselves of Guido Bartolucci's timely and commendable 2019 critical edition of *De Christiana religione* (Pisa: Edizioni della Normale). We made a few minor modifications whenever we disagreed with his editorial choices vis-à-vis the earliest printed copies (whether in Latin or Italian). When these instances arose, if they were significant (i.e., not just typographical errors), they were footnoted. We have kept Bartolucci's paragraph divisions, with a few exceptions where numbered lists were involved. His edition is accompanied by a lengthy Italian introduction with special attention to Ficino's sources and the

---

70 For a discussion of some of the numerous overlaps between *On the Christian Religion* and the *Platonic Theology*, see Bart. *DCR* 29–30 and 52–9.
71 Arthur Farndell, *Gardens of Philosophy: Ficino on Plato* (London: Shepheard-Walwyn, 2006), 95. This passage is also discussed in Bartolucci, "Per una fonte," 42.
72 Farndell, *Gardens of Philosophy*, 130.

transmission of *On the Christian Religion*. While we did not attempt to reproduce the whole body of his ample research here, we did avail ourselves of a good deal of his footnotes in assembling our own apparatus, checking each one for accuracy along the way, reformatting, and adding in our own notes and corrections wherever necessary. It is important to note also that in our references we did not in every instance refer to the same printed and critical editions of texts as Bartolucci did, and as such our notes may diverge in many places. We worked to use the same editions for the most part, but on account of pandemic restrictions, we had to avail ourselves of what texts were at hand.

Although our version is primarily a translation of the Latin, we often made recourse to the earliest printed editions in Italian (1474 and 1484) to provide more context and further clarify obscure passages. Ficino's Latin in *On the Christian Religion* was not always clear, and having contemporaneous vulgar versions on hand – prepared by Ficino himself – to compare was most useful. The Italian editions, beyond their benefit in clarifying grammatically ambiguous passages, also shed light on confusions that are particular to Latin, such as the tendency to render both *item* ("likewise") and *idem* ("the same") as simply *item*. In interpreting the Italian whenever the need arose, we availed ourselves of a 1611 Italian-to-English dictionary whose editor listed Ficino as one of the authors he intended to illuminate for an English audience.[73]

In selecting the right words, we employed Charlton T. Lewis and Charles Short's *A Latin Dictionary*, *The Oxford Latin Dictionary*, with additional help from Deferrari and Barry's *A Lexicon of St. Thomas Aquinas*, Ashdowne et al.'s *The Dictionary of Medieval Latin from British Sources*, and Du Cange et al., *Glossarium mediae et infimae latinitatis*. For Greek, we used Liddell and Scott's *Greek-English Lexicon* and for what little Hebrew Ficino discusses, Strong's *Exhaustive Concordance of the Bible*. To provide the most harmonious rendering possible, we also occasionally found ourselves looking up terms in Allen and Hankins's *Platonic Theology* or Kaske and Clark's *Three Books on Life* to see how other Ficino translators had dealt with them.

In the matter of biblical quotations, which are numerous, we clung as much as possible to the sixteenth-century Douay-Rheims English translation as our point of stylistic reference. Whenever a verse appears, it is cited in the notes, and where necessary, we made adjustments to

---

73 John Florio, *Queen Anna's New World of Words, or Dictionarie of the Italian and English Tongues* (London: Melchisidec Bradwood, 1611).

harmonize that Vulgate-based English translation with what was actually present in Ficino's Latin. In some instances, however, we attempted to rid our translation of certain archaisms too incommensurate with modern English definitions (e.g., we rendered the Latin *caritas* as "love" rather than its closest cognate "charity," which has a different sense now than it did in sixteenth-century English). Thematic words and certain wordplay, like puns, that could not be fully conveyed in translation are provided in brackets embedded into the English text (e.g., *voluntas, caritas, ratio, seculum, leonem/lenonem, philosophus/philopompus*, etc.). In the matter of special vocabulary: for the word *gentiles*, which we encountered in numerous different contexts, we oscillated between "pagans" and "gentiles" depending on what felt better in that particular location. The word "gentile" results from the shadow cast by the Hebrew prophets just as the word "pagan" is the shadow cast by Christianity. As such, when dealing with the word in the context of the Hebrew prophets, we opted for "gentile," while we used "pagan" more broadly when translating *gentiles* in a more Christian context.

An additional challenge in translating words of ethnicity, civic or religious identity, and race stems from the sheer variety of Ficino's sources and the often incompatible paradigms underlying each of them despite their shared vocabularies. Given that Ficino's work is cobbled together from such a mix of disparate sources, we strived to cohere in terminology with modern treatments of his sources. As noted above, we translate one of these words, *gentilis*, as "pagan" or "gentile" as the context demands, but have broken somewhat with the conventional translation of *gentes*, the plural of *gens*, which translators often render as "gentiles." This translation of *gentes*, however, is inadequate, as Aaron P. Johnson points out in his discussion of the term's Greek counterpart, *ta ethnē*: "[I]n the current English usage, the meaning of 'gentile' is not always clear. As an oppositional term to the Jews, 'gentiles' may be taken in a racial or cultural or religious sense, depending on the speaker's conception of Jewish identity as particularly racial, cultural, or religious ... However, both in the Septuagint and early Christian authors, *ta ethnē* carried connotations of racial and political elements along with the religious."[74] For this reason, where the Douay-Rheims English translation has "gentiles" for *gentes*, we have opted to translate it as "nations," with its concomitant broader connotations of racial and cultural distinctions. Similarly, in our translation of *genus* – itself a translation of Greek *genos* into

---

74 Aaron P. Johnson, *Ethnicity and Argument in Eusebius' Praeparatio Evangelica* (Oxford and New York: Oxford University Press, 2006), 42.

Latin – we have opted to use the term "race." This distinction in terms between *gens* (or *ethnos*) and *genus* (or *genos*) should not be taken as a clear conceptual separation of nation and race: *gens* is itself a category or kind of *genus*, one that carries specifically genetic and ethnic connotations, whereas *genus* is far broader in meaning, allowing for distinctions in class, caste, gender, or species.[75] Thus, in our translation of 2 Cor. 11:26, we have modified the Douay-Rheims English translation to read, "in perils from my own race (*genus*), in perils from the nations (*gentes*)," where *genus* seems almost to function as a singular form of *gentes*.[76] Nevertheless, despite these subtle distinctions, the notions these words convey often overlap to such a degree that one can translate each as "race" to little detriment.[77] Moreover, in rendering Ficino's Latin terms "homo" and "homines," we have opted to retain his fifteenth-century practice of assuming that the terms "man" and "men" (in reference to "mankind") also embrace women, and indeed, all of humanity.

As work designed to bridge the gap between Platonic philosophy and Christian theology, to provide a history of the Christian religion and the primitive church – all while doubling as an anti-Jewish polemic – *On the Christian Religion* was such an ambitious undertaking that many of the skills required to accomplish such a feat flawlessly occasionally went beyond Ficino's capacities. Throughout the work, Ficino made a good deal of errors, some of which were inevitable. Of these errors, many involve lists of names. Such errors were most likely to appear whenever Ficino was working closely with the various Spanish polemicists and copying the names of significant figures from Jewish history. For example, Sa'adiah Gaon, whom Paul of Burgos renders repeatedly as *Cahadias*,[78] is named thrice in chapter twenty-seven, each time in a different form: *Chadias*, *Chahadias*, and *Chalchadias*. Though some errors certainly originate with Ficino, we frequently noted occasions where

---

75 Johnson, *Ethnicity and Argument*, 35–51; cf. the Loeb translation of *genos* of Eus. Hist. 1.6.9–10 (*PG* 20.87–90) in *The Ecclesiastical History* vol. 1, edited by E. Capps, T.E. Page, and W.H.D. Rouse and translated by Kirsopp Lake (London: William Heinemann, 1926), 53 and our translation of Ficino's use of that material on page 124 below.
76 See below, page 61; cf. Johnson, *Ethnicity and Argument*, 49–50, who points out the subtle distinction in these two uses: *genos* tends to be reserved for the singular to mark out a particular people with a degree of specificity, whereas *ethnē* gets applied to an undifferentiated plurality of peoples.
77 Cf. Sabrina Inowlocki, *Eusebius and the Jewish Authors* (Leiden and Boston: Brill, 2006), 107, 113, 127, 267–8 who often translates both *ethnos* and *genos* as "race."
78 Cf. Paul. *Scrut*. 1.3.2, 23v; 1.3.4, 33r; 1.9.13, 144v.

he preserved corruptions from his sources or even compounded these corruptions with further corruptions of his own. Eusebius, particularly his *Praeparatio Evangelica*, served as a common source for many of these names that had long ago been corrupted in transmission, though Ficino for the most part faithfully preserved them as he received them. Again in chapter twenty-seven, Ficino introduced new errors when he provided the names *Ventozara* and *Ravanais*, which he took from a copy of Paul of Burgos's *Scrutinium Scripturarum* containing the names *Ventozra* and *Ravanay*, themselves corruptions of the Latinized forms Ben Cos(i)ba and Rab(bi) Huna.[79] As a general rule, whenever we encountered names, we tried to render them into their modern recognizable forms but left the original Latinized names in footnotes. We made an exception and maintained the erroneous forms of names when the error itself proved integral to Ficino's argument, such as when he recounts the Bar Kokhba revolt twice as two different events, once with Rabbi Akiba (naming Ventozara as the messiah) and again in the next paragraph with one Achilayl (naming Bar-Kozeba as the messiah). In this we can see how a minor divergence in the transmission of names could snowball into many more misattributions down the line. Here Ficino wound up predicating one of his key arguments against the Jews – that they have such various and sundry false messiahs – on these two mistakes. In addition to frequently garbling Jewish names, it is notable that Ficino often mistook names belonging to the third declension in Greek as second-declension Greek or Latin nouns.[80]

Perhaps somewhat ironically given Ficino's emphasis on the importance of following Scripture to the letter, his citations were frequently sloppy, in many instances consisting more of paraphrases than word-for-word reproductions. Whether citing the prophets, Christ and his apostles, the Church Fathers, or his favourite Dominican polemicists, he often added a jot here or removed a tittle there, condensing and expanding with alternatives whenever he saw fit.[81] As such, whenever trying to figure out what was actually going on in some of Ficino's more

---

[79] Cf. Paul. *Scrut.* 1.2.1, 13v; 1.3.4, 32v.
[80] E.g., "Manethus" for "Manetho," "Heros" for "Hero," "Melitus" for "Melito," and "Zophirus" for "Zopyrion."
[81] E.g., in applying his knowledge of biblical Greek, Ficino departed from the Vulgate to render a new Latin translation from the original Greek text: once to apply a peculiar grammatical rule of Greek to the Latin, one that makes no significant impact on the meaning of the text (note 654 below on *abscondita*), and once to change the content of a prophecy to add an implication of logical necessity to the upheavals to

opaque arguments, especially when those arguments were being lifted *ex situ* from other authors, we always made recourse to those authors' works. Sometimes our curiosity led us to chase down the origins of specific arguments even further into the past, such as those we find stretching all the way back to Petrus Alfonsi's twelfth-century *Dialogi contra Iudaeos* and "Rabbi" Ramon Martí's late thirteenth-century *Pugio fidei*, upon which the conversos Paul of Burgos and Jerome of Santa Fe had both relied. It was these two anti-Jewish polemical authors, Paul and Jerome, who most clearly shaped Ficino's style, which itself vacillates markedly throughout the work according to whichever author he was copying at any given moment. There is a tendency towards shorter, less grammatically complex sentences in sections that are largely derived from anti-Jewish polemical sources, with the relatively fewer long sentences being held together by conjunctions or parataxis. When, however, he draws on Church Fathers in his chapters dedicated to accounting for Church history, there is a marked tendency towards longer, periodical sentences, often with several levels of hypotaxis. This, ultimately, is but one of the many ways Ficino's work is marked by an inconsistent Latin style, cycling as he did between various sources and the generic conventions they provided him.

---

come (note 656 below on *necessitas*). Additionally, Ficino frequently tries his hand at philology, often citing alternative readings, especially between the Vetus Latina and Vulgate versions of the Bible, interrupting quotations with the word *aliter* followed by the alternative to convey these discrepancies in Scripture, which we have bracketed off and translated with "or" (see also Bart. *DCR*, 122–4).

ON THE CHRISTIAN RELIGION

Marsilio Ficino

Here are the chapters contained in this book.

Chapter 1	Religion, Above All, Is Particular to Man and Truthful	49
Chapter 2	On the Divinity of the Soul through Religion	51
Chapter 3	Youths Should Beware Lest They Offer an Opinion on Religion Lightly	52
Chapter 4	Every Religion Has Some Good, so Long as It Is Directed towards God Himself, the Creator of All Things; Christianity Is Faultless	53
Chapter 5	Christ's Disciples Never Deceived Anyone	54
Chapter 6	In What State of Mind Christ's Disciples Would Toil	56
Chapter 7	No One Deceived Christ's Disciples	62
Chapter 8	The Christian Religion Is Founded on the Power of God Alone	65
Chapter 9	Christ's Authority Is Not from the Stars but from God	72
Chapter 10	Christ's Authority Was Not at All without Miracles	74
Chapter 11	Christ's Authority among the Pagans	81
Chapter 12	Christ's Authority among the Mohammadans	85
Chapter 13	On the Generation of God's Son in Eternity	86
Chapter 14	The Order of the Heavens, Angels, and Souls around the Trinity Is like the Order of the Spheres around the Centre	88
Chapter 15	The Generation of the Son in Eternity and His Manifestation in Time	90
Chapter 16	It Is Fitting for God to Have Joined Himself to Man	92
Chapter 17	Of What Kind Is the Union of God and Man	94
Chapter 18	How Becoming Is the Union of God and Man	95
Chapter 19	Christ's Coming Gives Blessedness with Faith, Hope, Love	97
Chapter 20	Christ's Coming Served to Lift the Burden of Sin	98
Chapter 21	Christ Fulfilled the Perfect Kind of Instruction	99
Chapter 22	Christ Expelled Error, Revealed the Truth	100
Chapter 23	Christ Is the Idea and Exemplar of Virtues	104
Chapter 24	The Authority of the Sibyls	106
Chapter 25	The Sibyls' Testimonies about Christ	109
Chapter 26	On the Prophets' Authority, the Old Testament's Nobility, and the New Testament's Superiority	112

Chapter 27	The Prophets' Testimonies about Christ	116
Chapter 28	Resolving Doubts around the Prophecies	156
Chapter 29	Against the Jews: That They Are Wretched in Christ's Vengeance	166
Chapter 30	Confirmation of Our Material from Jewish Sources against the Jews regarding the Holy Books	175
Chapter 31	Confirmation of God's Trinity and of Christ's Divinity from the Jews	179
Chapter 32	Confirmation of the Messiah's Suffering against the Jews from Jewish Sources	185
Chapter 33	Confirmation against the Jews of Original Sin, and Thereby of the Messiah's Suffering, from Jewish Sources	190
Chapter 34	Proof against the Jews, from Jewish Sources, that the Ceremonies of the Old Testament Have Been Completed and Fulfilled by the Arrival of the New Testament	196
Chapter 35	On the Authority of Christian Doctrine	206
Chapter 36	That the Holy Scripture of the Christians Is Not Corrupted	214
Chapter 37	The Cause of the Error of the Jews, Mohammadans, and Pagans	219

PREAMBLE

In everything that I wish to assert, whether it is treated here or elsewhere, I only wish to assert as much as the Church approves.

Book by Marsilio Ficino the Florentine, *On the Christian Religion*, to Lorenzo de Medici, guardian of the fatherland, a preamble.

That the Greatest Kinship Exists between Wisdom and Religion

The eternal wisdom of God determined that the divine mysteries, at least at the very beginnings of religion, are only to be handled by those who are the true lovers of the true wisdom. Therefore, it happened that among ancient men, the same men investigated the causes of things and diligently conducted sacrifices to the highest cause of things itself, and the same were themselves also philosophers and priests among all the nations. And this by no means was wrong. For, since the soul – as our Plato agrees – is able to fly back to the heavenly father and fatherland only on two wings, namely, the intellect and the will, and the philosopher relies most on the intellect, while the priest relies on the will, and the intellect illuminates the will, while the will sets the intellect alight, it follows that they, who through intelligence first discovered the divine (whether by finding it by themselves or by arriving at it through divine inspiration), through will first worshipped the divine correctly, spread correct worship of it, and the reason for their worship to others.[1] Therefore, the prophets of the Hebrews and Essenes were inclined to wisdom and priesthood simultaneously.[2] The philosophers among the Persians, because they were in charge of sacred rites, were called Magi (i.e., priests). The Indians consulted the Brahmins on both the nature of things and the purification of souls. Among the Egyptians, mathematicians and metaphysicians took up the priesthood and the kingship.[3] Among the Ethiopians, the gymnosophists were at once teachers of philosophy and prelates of religion. The same tradition prevailed in Greece under Linus, Orpheus, Musaeus, Eumolpus, Melampus, Trophimus, Aglaophemus, and Pythagoras.[4] The same applies in Gaul

---

1 Plato, *Phaedrus*, 246a–d.
2 Eus. *Prae.*, 8.11.3 (*PG* 21.642–3).
3 Fic. *TP* 14.10 (Allen and Hankins 4.300).
4 Cf. Eus. *Prae.*, 10.8.2; 10.11.27–30 (*PG* 21.798–9, 826); Tert., *Apol.*, 21.29 (*PL* 1.462).

under the governance of the druids.⁵ Who can ignore how much zeal for both wisdom and sacred rites Numa Pompilius, Valerius Soranus, Marcus Varro, and many others among the Romans had? Lastly, who does not know how great and how true a doctrine there was among the ancient Christian bishops and priests? O happy times that kept this entire divine marriage of wisdom and religion intact especially among the Hebrews and the Christians! O utterly woeful times, at last, when the wretched divorce of Pallas and Themis happened! What an abomination! Thus, the sacred was given to dogs to mangle! For the doctrine was in large part handed over to the profane, and so – as most often happens – it became an instrument of iniquity and wantonness and is better called "cunning" than "knowledge." The most precious pearls of religion, however, are often handled by the ignorant and trod upon as if by swine. For it often seems that this inept administration at the hands of the ignorant and cowardly must be called "superstition" rather than "religion."⁶ In this way, they do not faithfully understand the truth which, being divine, shines alone on the eyes of the pious.⁷ However much they may try, those men either worship God incorrectly or misconduct the sacred rites since they are entirely ignorant of matters human and divine.

How long shall we endure this harsh and wretched lot of an iron age, gentlemen, citizens of the heavenly fatherland, and inhabitants of the earth? Please – any time now – let us, if we can, deliver philosophy, the sacred gift of God, from impiety. What is more, we can, if we but will. Let us redeem the holy faith with all our strength from execrable ignorance. Therefore, I urge everyone, and beseech the philosophers for their part, to take religion to heart, or arrive at it; but I beseech the priests to incline themselves diligently towards the pursuit of lawful wisdom.⁸ I myself do not know how much I have accomplished or will accomplish in this matter. Still, I have tried, and I shall not cease from trying, not relying on my own limited skill but on the clemency and powers of God.

Benevolent Lorenzo, your grandfather, the great Cosimo, then your pious father Piero, sustained me with their wealth from the tender age when I could first practise philosophy. Recently, as is your custom in a good many other matters, by your own will you have joined in me – to the best of your ability – the zeal for philosophizing with the duty of

---

5 Cf. Diogenes Laertius 1.1.
6 Cf. Plutarch, *De superstitione*, 1.1.
7 Cf. Matt. 7:6.
8 Cf. Lact. *Inst.* 4.3.4–9 (*PL* 6.453–6; Monat, 44–7); 4.4.1–6 (*PL* 6.456–8; Monat, 52–5).

piety. You have, with distinction, honoured your Marsilio Ficino with a priesthood. Would that I had never or will never let myself down since the favour and aid of God Himself and of the Medici has never let me down! When I was initiated into the sacred rites of the priesthood, I composed the work *On the Christian Religion* to better procure divine grace for myself and gratify you and to not let myself down. I saw fit to dedicate this treatise to you, the supporter of my profession, not only as the chief guardian of wisdom but also as the chief cultivator of piety.

CHAPTER 1 – RELIGION, ABOVE ALL, IS PARTICULAR TO MAN AND TRUTHFUL

We see that every endowment of the human race appears at some point in certain animals, at least in terms of there being some kind of similarity, with the exception of religion.[9] Brutes do not display the mark of religion, such that it is the characteristic of us alone to raise our mind towards God, the king of heaven. So too, it is particular to us to raise our body towards heaven, and thus divine worship is altogether natural for man, in the same way that neighing is for horses or barking is for dogs. If someone were to affirm rather pedantically that some beasts now and then venerate heavenly things – which I find hardly believable – the Platonists will respond that these sorts of beasts are doing something else at that moment when they seem to be honouring heavenly things; or if perhaps they are honouring them, they still do not know what they are doing; or if they do know, they too are participants in intelligence and immortality. But in truth, to return to our purpose, man, the most perfect animal, not only excels in his perfection, but also differs from his inferiors in that particular characteristic by which he is joined with the most perfect, that is, the divine. Similarly, if man is the most perfect among mortal animals, inasmuch as he is a man, he is the most perfect of all in particular on account of the endowment that, among the animals, he has as his own and that is not shared with the other animals. This is religion. Through religion, therefore, he is most perfect. In turn, if religion were empty, man would be the least perfect of all creatures since by it he would be completely mindless and most

---

9 Cf. Sallust, *Bellum Iugurthinum*, 1.

miserable; accordingly, many men abandon all advantages of a temporal life, and certainly all men abandon many and undergo hardships, out of either love or fear of God. No other animal, however, abstains from immediate benefits due to the worship of God and an expectation for what is to come. Add to this that the goad of conscience relentlessly prods us alone; divine vengeance and the fear of hell most bitterly distress us alone.

Therefore, if religion – as we have said – is groundless, there is no animal more mindless and unhappy than man. Therefore, on account of religion, man would be the least perfect of all, yet just a moment ago, he appeared more perfect than all through it. But no one can endure things so contrary through the same part of himself that according to it, not only is he perfect to the highest degree, but also utterly imperfect.[10] Therefore, religion is true, especially since, just as nothing can be made bitter cold by bringing it close to fire, so too one, for this reason, cannot become the most foolish and wretched man because he cleaves to the wisest and most blessed God alone. Likewise, God, who is the utmost truth and good, cannot deceive the human race, His children. This natural and shared belief about God was put in us by God, our shared origin and the author of our natures. We ought also to remember that the divination performed by an entire species of animals, since it is performed out of an instinct of a universal and of a particular nature, is true: at sunrise, many reptiles creep out from Earth's bosom, portending a fog in the air; in the evening, a thickly crowded murder of crows flies across the sky from a specific expanse of air, presaging winds, and innumerable other examples of this kind. Religion, therefore, is true because of man's shared divination, for everyone has always worshipped God everywhere for the sake of the life to come. Therefore, it is true that God provides for us and that there will be another life, if only this most perfect animal species has the truest judgment, which is for it the most natural thing of all. So great appears the case for religion, not only from the fact that it belongs to each and every man, but also from the fact that all the beliefs, feelings, customs, and laws of men change, except for shared religion.[11] Therefore, should anyone be found entirely devoid of religion, since this is outside the nature of the human species, he has

---

10 Fic. *TP* 14.9 (Allen and Hankins 4.292–4); Kristeller, *The Philosophy of Marsilio Ficino*, 171–99.
11 Fic. *TP* 14.9 (Allen and Hankins 4.294).

either been an abomination from the start or has been polluted by contact with another abomination.[12]

CHAPTER 2 – ON THE DIVINITY OF THE SOUL THROUGH RELIGION

Our Plato in the *Protagoras* has it that the greatest proof of our divinity is that on earth we alone as participants in a divine lot through a certain affinity, recognize and desire God, invoke Him as Creator, love Him as Father, venerate Him as King, and fear Him as Lord.[13] For just as the Sun cannot be seen without the Sun, and just as the air cannot be heard without air, but the eye filled with light sees light, and the ear full of air hears air resounding, so God cannot be known without God.[14] The soul, however, being filled with God, lifts itself towards God to the extent that it both recognizes God when illuminated with divine light and thirsts for Him when set aflame by divine heat. For the soul is not raised towards that which is above and infinite, unless it is raised up by a higher, infinite power. Hence, the soul is made a temple of God, as Xistus the Pythagorean reckoned.[15] In fact, he judged that the temple of the eternal God would never be destroyed. The human mind meditates on God every day, the heart burns for God, the breast heaves for God, the tongue sings of Him, the head, the hands, and the knees adore Him, the arts of man refer to Him. If God does not hear this, perhaps He will seem unaware; He will perhaps appear thankless, if He does not heed it, and cruel in a way, if He compels us whom He does not heed to cry aloud every day.[16] But God, who is infinite wisdom, goodness, and love, cannot be ignorant, thankless, or unmerciful. In sum, since a superior mind comprehends an inferior one rather than the other way around, if

---

12 See Edelheit, *Ficino, Pico, and Savonarola*, 225 for commentary on this passage.
13 Plato, *Protagoras*, 322a.
14 Cf. Matt. 6:22.
15 Cf. 1 Cor. 6:19; Edelheit, *Ficino, Pico, and Savonarola*, 227; in Fic. *TP* 4.361, n. 48 states that Jerome referred to this author as "Sextus Pythagoreus" (the author of the so-called *Sentences of Sextus*), who is not to be confused with Pope Sixtus II (r. 257–8). The quote also appears in Augustine, *De natura et gratia*, 64.77 (*PL* 44.285), which Allen and Hankins suggest was likely Ficino's source, despite also appearing in Porphyry's *De abstinentia* and in Rufinus, who translated the work and is the root of the misattribution of this mysterious "Pythagoreus" to Pope Sixtus II.
16 Fic. *TP* 14.8 (Allen and Hankins 4.280).

the human mind gets an inkling of the divine mind, the human mind is necessarily comprehended and governed by the divine mind.

CHAPTER 3 – YOUTHS SHOULD BEWARE LEST THEY OFFER AN OPINION ON RELIGION LIGHTLY

Even if a man is naturally religious at any age, with the exception of a very few men – and they are certainly misshapen – there are two stages of life that are more religious, as Plato says, namely, childhood and old age. For children are born religious, and they are raised in religion, and in adolescence they persist most firmly until reason is aroused. Reason by its nature demands causes and reasons for each and every thing. If, in this stage of life, they either eagerly pursue the studies that diligently examine the causes of things or chance upon the conversations that do likewise, they begin to posit, as it were, that no assertion can be made unless they themselves have discerned its reason. They then first largely turn their backs on religion, unless perchance they commit themselves to the laws and counsel of their elders. Because the most hidden reasons for divine things are only observed with difficulty after a long while, with a mind that has been purified, with the most exact diligence, youths do not yet get an inkling of these kinds of reasons and, because they assert nearly nothing whose reason they do not see, they disregard religion in some way – if they rely only on their own judgment. Many who settled on this opinion on account of pride and intemperance give themselves over to the pleasures of Aristippus, eventually thinking of religion as nothing more than old wives' tales. Others, however, on account of meekness and modesty, cleanse their mind of the senses in the Pythagorean manner through moral, natural, mathematical, and metaphysical disciplines, lest they – just as those mentioned above – be blinded by suddenly raising hitherto bleary eyes to the divine sun, but instead, by approaching it step by step, first, to see the divine light in the moral as if it were the light of the Sun on Earth; second, to see it in the natural as the light of the Sun in water; third, to see it in mathematics as the light of the Sun in the Moon; fourth, to perceive clearly and soundly the divine light in metaphysics as the light of the Sun in the Sun itself, the supercelestial as much as the celestial.[17] These Orpheus

---

17 Cf. Plato, *Respublica*, 515c–d. It is unclear as to who "those mentioned above" are; the parallel passage from Fic. *TP* (Allen and Hankins 4.305) is alternatively rendered as "lest they are forced, like the Aristippeans, to blind their eyes ..."

calls the lawful priests of the muses, who finally at an older age form much better thoughts on religion, just as we read in Plato's *Epistle to King Dionysius, Phaedrus*, in the first book of *The Republic*, and in the tenth of *The Laws*.[18] The divine Plato warns youths not to rashly offer an opinion on divine matters, but to trust the laws until age itself teaches them, whether through the steps of the disciplines that we have mentioned or through experience or through some separation of the soul from the body, which moderate old age brings about, such that the soul at that age distinguishes things that are separate from bodies more clearly than it had previously been accustomed since it is seeing them up close in a way.[19] Indeed it is always fitting to remember that neither is it possible by nature for there to be wisdom in youths, nor is anything more dangerous, whether in judgment or in action, than bold ignorance and ignorant boldness. Wisdom without daring is indeed advantageous, albeit not advantageous enough, but it never does any harm; daring without wisdom, however, is some sort of untamed beast, completely out of control. Since we have very broadly discussed the truth of our shared religion, the providence of God, the divinity of souls in our book of *Theology*, may these brief assertions about them suffice for the present, for we are making haste towards the mystery of the Christian religion.

CHAPTER 4 – EVERY RELIGION HAS SOME GOOD, SO LONG AS IT IS DIRECTED TOWARDS GOD HIMSELF, THE CREATOR OF ALL THINGS; CHRISTIANITY IS FAULTLESS

Nothing displeases God more than being despised; nothing pleases Him more than being worshipped. He punishes more mildly those who transgress His divine laws in part but strikes with thunder those who rebel against His authority out of ingratitude, malice, and arrogance. Therefore, divine providence does not at any time permit any region of the world to be utterly devoid of every religion, though He does permit different rites of worship to be observed in different times and places. Indeed, perhaps this kind of variety, ordained by God, begets a certain

---

18 Plato, *Phaedrus*, 241a–b; *Respublica*, 328d–9d; *Leges*, 888a–d.
19 Fic. *TP* 14.10 (Allen and Hankins 4.302–4).

kind of marvellous elegance in the universe. It is of more concern for the greatest King to be honoured in earnest than for Him to be honoured by this or that token gesture. As many nations as King Alexander ruled over, so many were the ways in which he was honoured when he would set out for the nations in person or send envoys. He approved, to some degree, of everything that was being done for his glory but still regarded one approach as more acceptable than another. More or less the same is to be judged regarding the king of the world. He prefers to be worshipped in whatever way, even incompetently, provided it is in keeping with human nature, than not to be worshipped at all out of pride. Indeed, for men who are intemperate but submissive to Him to a degree, He either corrects them like a father or at least punishes them less. As for the impious, the utterly ungrateful, and those rebelling out of their own free will, however, He casts them out and torments them as enemies. Although God indeed utterly disapproves when no human worship is taken up for His sake as if it were a wilful impiety, what worship does He still approve of most of all, nay, solely? In and of Himself, God is the highest good, the truth of things, the light and fervour of minds. Therefore, they who venerate God diligently through the goodness of their actions, with truthfulness, with what clarity of mind they can, and with what love is due, they above all others – indeed alone – worship Him unerringly. But such men are, as we shall demonstrate, whoever worship God in the same manner as Christ the teacher of life and His disciples instructed.

CHAPTER 5 – CHRIST'S DISCIPLES NEVER DECEIVED ANYONE

Had the disciples of Christ thought to introduce a fiction for the sake of deceiving the human race, they certainly would have had some reason: to persuade all the more easily. Nevertheless, they did the opposite, for they set themselves on a thing that was not only the most difficult to believe but also to observe. Also add in under how many very difficult circumstances, if you consider the times, places, and people, namely, in the most cultivated times, in the largest cities, filled with all sorts of teachings, against the powerful, and emperors, both learned and numerous, when the disciples themselves were the weakest, the most lacking in everything, uncultured from the beginning, and very few in number: for Christ left behind eleven apostles; in fact, the apostles were guiding the seventy-two disciples of Christ. Let us hear Paul speaking thus to the Corinthians: "Observe your vocation, brothers, because there are few who are wise, few who are powerful, few who are noble according to the flesh, but God chooses those things of the world that are foolish so as to confound the wise, and God chooses the weak to confound the strong, and He chooses the ignoble and contemptible things of the world, and those things which do not exist, so that He may destroy those things which do exist."[20] Therefore, one must not believe the disciples made anything up, especially since they bravely persevered to the end under the most difficult of circumstances owing to the utmost harmony of good practices and beliefs among themselves. They would have otherwise obtained nothing: they neither received nor expected any payment for such toil in this life, nor did they promise any to the nations. And this is what Paul said: "If in this life only we have hope in Christ, we are of all men most miserable."[21] They often declared that they would die for their faith, and afterward that everyone who followed their teaching would suffer bitter and unspeakable hardships. Not to mention that they used to cast aside whatever is regarded as good by mortals, and they ordered these things be cast aside, nor did they whisper it in secret, but boldly broadcast their teaching out in the open before the crowd. Accordingly, Paul, even while bound by his neck in chains, preached publicly what he writes to the Philippians: "The things which have happened to me have fallen out rather to the furtherance of the gospel: so that my bonds are made manifest in Christ, in all the court and in all other places."[22] And elsewhere he says that "the gospel has now been preached to every creature that is under heaven."[23] Likewise, none of these things was conducted in secret.[24] Therefore, they believed they were preaching the truth to men, and it is all the more certain that they understood what they preached. Hence this verse of Peter: "Always be prepared to provide a reason to anyone asking regarding those things that are inside of you: hope and faith."[25] Hence these verses of Paul to the Corinthians: "So I run and fight, not as at an uncertainty, I so fight, not one beating the air, but I chastise my body, and bring it into subjection, lest perhaps, when I have preached to

---

20 1 Cor. 1:26–8.
21 1 Cor. 15:19.
22 Phil. 1:12–13.
23 Col. 1:23.
24 Cf. Acts 26:26.
25 1 Pet. 3:15.

others, I myself should become a castaway."[26] Hence Paul and Apollo, when discussing the mysteries of Christ with learned men wherever they went, would cite the books of the prophets. Often Paul orders his disciples, especially the priests, to apply themselves diligently to a profound understanding of the prophets. Therefore, as I have said, they believed and understood what they were preaching. Otherwise, they would never have subjected themselves so fearlessly and so freely to continuous labours, dangers, beatings, and certain death for the affirmation of our teaching. For the glory of Christ, Paul laboured continuously for thirty-seven years, beyond all belief, unto his last breath, under every kind of punishment. Peter also laboured the same amount of time; John the Evangelist laboured for sixty-eight years, and similarly all the others for their entire lives. For this reason, it seems exceedingly clear that they had never pondered any concern of men whereby they might more easily win these men over since they relied on the force of truth alone. This is based on the fact that we have to accept neither the original ceremonies from the Jews nor additional gods from the pagans. For had the disciples of Christ wished to allow both Jewish ceremonies to be preserved along with their Christian counterparts, and the gods of the pagans to be worshipped together with Christ, everyone would have immediately and without doubt received the worship of Christ into their hearts.

CHAPTER 6 – IN WHAT STATE OF MIND CHRIST'S DISCIPLES WOULD TOIL

Paul explains in what state of mind the disciples of Christ toiled in the *Letter to the Romans*: "Who," he says, "shall separate us from the love of Christ? Shall tribulation? Or distress? Or persecution? Or famine? Or nakedness? Or danger? Or the sword?[27] As it is written: 'For thy sake, we are put to death all the day long. We are accounted as sheep for the slaughter.'"[28] "For I am sure that neither death, nor life, nor Angels, nor Principalities, nor Powers, nor Virtues, nor things present, nor things to come, nor might, nor height, nor depth, nor any other creature, shall

---

26 1 Cor. 9:24–7.
27 Rom. 8:35.
28 Rom. 8:36; Ps. 44:22 (Vulg. Ps. 43:22).

separate us from the love of God, which is in Jesus Christ our Lord."[29] Afterward, Paul listed to the Corinthians the many kinds of labours and torments he had both endured and was enduring, and he added that in these he rejoices, boasts, is strengthened.[30] He writes to the Philippians while imprisoned in Rome: "In nothing shall I be confounded, but with all confidence, as always, so now also, shall Christ be magnified in my body, whether it be by life or by death. For to me, to live is Christ: and to die is gain. And if to live in the flesh: this is to me the fruit of labour, what I shall choose I know not. But I am straitened between two: I want to be dissolved and to be with Christ, a thing by far the better for me; but to abide still in the flesh is necessary because of you."[31] He adds below, divining in this way: "And having this confidence I know that I shall abide and I continue with you all, for your furtherance and joy of faith, that your rejoicing may abound in Christ Jesus for me, by my coming to you again."[32] And a little after: "Unto you it is given for Christ, not only to believe in Him, but also to suffer for, having the same conflict as that which you have seen in me and now have heard of me."[33] He was freed from his chains, as he predicted, and he returned to the Philippians. Paul writes to the Colossians: "Continue in the faith, grounded and settled, and immovable from the hope of the gospel which you have heard, which is preached in all the creation that is under heaven, whereof I Paul am made a minister, who now rejoice in my sufferings for you and fill up those things that are wanting of the sufferings of Christ, in my flesh, for His body, which is the Church."[34] Paul writes to the Thessalonians: "That no man should be moved in these tribulations. For you yourselves know that we are appointed thereunto; for even when we were with you, we foretold you that we should suffer tribulations: as also it has come to pass, and you know."[35] Paul writes to Timothy: "God had not given us the spirit of fear: but of power and of love and of sobriety. Be not thou therefore ashamed of the testimony of our Lord, nor of me His prisoner, but labour with the gospel, according to the power of God."[36] And a little after: "For the gospel I suffer these

---

29 Rom. 8:38–9.
30 1 Cor. 4:9–21.
31 Phil.10:20–4.
32 Phil. 1:25–6.
33 Phil. 1:29–30.
34 Col. 1:23–4.
35 1 Thess. 3:3–4.
36 2 Tim. 1:7–8.

things, but I am not ashamed; for I know whom I have believed and I am certain that He is able to keep that which I have committed unto Him, against that day."[37] Likewise, he writes a bit later: "In preaching the gospel I labour even unto bands, as an evildoer but the word of God is not bound. Therefore I endure all things for the sake of the elect, that they themselves may also obtain the salvation which is in Christ Jesus, with heavenly glory. A faithful saying: for if we be dead with Him, we shall live also with Him; if we suffer, we shall also reign with Him; if we deny Him, He will also deny us; if we believe not, He continueth faithful, He cannot deny Himself."[38] Likewise, he writes: "You know what persecutions and afflictions I suffered at Antioch, at Iconium, and at Lystra; and out of them all the Lord delivered me. And all that will live godly in Christ Jesus shall suffer persecution."[39] He similarly writes to the Corinthians: "Always bearing about in our body the mortification of Jesus, that the life also of Jesus may be made manifest in our bodies. For we who live are always delivered unto death for Jesus's sake: that the life also of Jesus may be made manifest in our mortal flesh."[40] Hence he writes to the Galatians: "I bear the marks of the Lord Jesus in my body."[41] Likewise he writes to the Corinthians: "For I think that God hath set forth us apostles, the last, as it were men appointed to death, since we are made a spectacle to this world and to angels and to men."[42] And a bit later he writes: "Even unto this hour we both hunger and thirst and are naked and are buffeted and have no fixed abode, and we labour with our own working hands,"[43] that is, for the sake of providing sustenance, for he never wished to live off another's labour; and he continues: "We are reviled and we bless, we are persecuted and we suffer it, we are blasphemed, and we entreat; we are made as the refuse of this world, the offscouring of all,"[44] that is, rubbish and filth. Paul writes to the Romans: "We glory in tribulation, knowing that tribulation worketh patience, patience trial, and trial hope. And hope confoundeth not: because the love of God is poured forth in our hearts, by the Holy Spirit who is given to us."[45] Similarly to the Galatians: "God forbid that I

---

37 2 Tim. 1:12.
38 2 Tim. 2:9–13.
39 2 Tim. 3:11–12.
40 2 Cor. 4:10–11.
41 Gal. 6:17.
42 1 Cor. 4:9.
43 1 Cor. 4:11–12.
44 1 Cor. 4:12–13.
45 Rom. 5:3–5.

should glory in anything save the cross of our Lord Jesus Christ, through whom the world is crucified to me, and I to the world."[46] Likewise, he writes: "As I am crucified with Christ, therefore I no longer live, but Christ lives in me."[47] But listen to what he says to the Romans: "For you have not received the spirit of bondage again in fear, but you have received the spirit of adoption of sons, whereby we cry: 'Abba Father!' For the Spirit Himself giveth testimony to our spirit that we are the sons of God. And if sons, heirs also; heirs indeed of God and joint heirs with Christ: yet so, if we suffer with Him, that we may also be glorified. For I reckon that the sufferings of this time are not worthy to be compared with the glory to come that shall be revealed in us. For the expectation of the creature waiteth for the revelation of the sons of God."[48] Paul writes to the Corinthians: "For if the dead do not rise again, why also are we in danger every hour? I die, brethren, daily by your glory which I have in Christ Jesus our Lord. If according to a man I fought with beasts at Ephesus, what doth it profit me if the dead rise not again?"[49] In turn he writes: "We are in tribulation, brethren, for your exhortation and salvation, which worketh in you the enduring of the same sufferings, which we also suffer, that our hope for you may be steadfast, knowing that you are partakers of the sufferings, so shall you be also of the consolation. For we would not have you ignorant, brethren, of our tribulation which came to us in Asia, since we were pressed beyond measure."[50] Likewise he writes: "I exceedingly abound with joy in all our tribulation. For also, when we were come into Macedonia, our flesh had no rest, but we suffered all tribulation."[51] Hence he says to the Ephesians: "I Paul, the prisoner of Jesus Christ, for you Gentiles, I pray you not to faint at my tribulations for you, which is your glory."[52] Finally he says that he is fulfilling an embassy in chains on behalf of Christ; he says to the Philippians that he considers everything, even the greatest matters, of no import, and regards it as shit that he may gain Christ and share in His suffering, and being made conformable to His death to earn His resurrection.[53] Likewise, he writes: "Our conversation is in heaven,

---

46 Gal. 6:14.
47 Gal. 2:19–20.
48 Rom. 8:15–19.
49 1 Cor. 15:29–32.
50 2 Cor. 1: 6–8.
51 2 Cor. 7:4–5.
52 Eph. 3:1; 3:13.
53 Phil. 3:8; 3:10.

from whence also we look for the saviour our Lord Jesus Christ, who will reform the body of our lowness, made like to the body of His glory, according to the operation whereby also He is able to subdue all things unto Himself. Therefore, my most beloved and desired brethren, my joy and my crown, so stand fast in the Lord, dearly beloved."[54] He writes to the Thessalonians: "And you became followers of us and of the Lord, receiving the word in much tribulation, with the joy of the Holy Spirit.[55] You know, brethren, our entrance in unto you that was not in vain, but having suffered many things before and indignities, as you know at Philippi, we had confidence in our God to preach unto you the gospel of God in much carefulness.[56] You are become followers of the assembly of God which are in Judea, in Christ Jesus; for you also have suffered the same things from your own countrymen, even as they have from the Jews;[57] we were comforted in you, brethren, in all our necessity and tribulation, by your faith, because now we live, if you stand in the Lord."[58] In addition, he thus admonishes the Hebrews: "Call to mind the former days, wherein, being illuminated, you endured a great fight of afflictions, and on the one hand indeed, by reproaches and tribulations, were made a spectacle, and on the other, became companions of them that were used in such sort; for you both had compassion on them that were in bands and took with joy the being stripped of your own goods, knowing that you have a better and a lasting substance in heaven. Do not, therefore, lose your confidence which hath a great reward."[59] Likewise, he writes: "Having therefore a great high priest that hath passed into the heavens, Jesus the Son of God, let us hold fast our confession."[60] Likewise, he writes: "And therefore we also having so great a cloud of witnesses over our heads, laying aside every weight and sin which surrounds us, let us run by patience to the fight proposed to us, looking on Jesus, the author of faith, who, having joy set before Him, endured the cross, despising the shame, and now sitteth on the right hand of the throne of God."[61] By some unknown impulse, however, I am compelled to return to what he writes to the Corinthians: "I am more, in many more labours, in prisons more frequently, in stripes

---

54 Phil. 3:20; 4:1.
55 1 Thess. 1:6.
56 1 Thess. 2:1–2.
57 1 Thess. 2:14.
58 1 Thess. 3:7–8.
59 Heb. 10:32–5.
60 Heb. 4:14.
61 Heb. 12:1–2.

above measure, in deaths often; of the Jews five times did I receive forty stripes save one; thrice was I beaten with rods, once I was stoned, thrice I suffered shipwreck, a night and a day I was in the depth of the sea; in journeying often, in perils of waters, in perils of robbers, in perils from my own race, in perils from the nations, in perils of the city, in perils in the wilderness, in perils in the sea, in perils from false brethren, in labour and painfulness, in much watching, in hunger and thirst, in fasting often, in cold and nakedness; besides those things which are without, my daily instance, the solicitude for all churches. Who is weak, and I am not weak? Who is scandalized, and I am not on fire? If I must glory, I will glory of the things that concern my infirmity. The God and Father of our Lord Jesus Christ, who is blessed forever, knoweth that I lie not; at Damascus, the governor of the nation under Aretas the king, guarded the city of the Damascenes, to apprehend me, and through a window in a basket was I let down a wall, and so escaped his hands."[62] Truly he also praises the Corinthians because they suffer if a man bring them into bondage, if a man devour them, if a man take from them, if a man be lifted up, if a man strike them on the face.[63] For Paul was not seeking his own but Christ's glory alone, as he discloses here. "Among you one says: 'I indeed am of Paul,' another: 'I am of Apollo,' are you not men? For what is Apollo? What indeed is Paul? The ministers of Him whom you have believed: and to every one as the Lord hath given. I have planted, Apollo watered, but God gave the increase. Therefore, neither he that planteth is anything, nor he that watereth, but God that giveth the increase. But he that planteth and he that watereth, are one."[64] "Let no man therefore glory in men. For all things are yours, whether it be Paul or Apollo or Cephas or the world or life or death or things present or things to come. For all are yours. And you are Christ's and Christ is God's."[65] But listen even to these verses: "Love seeketh not her own,"[66] "love beareth all things, believeth all things, hopeth all things, endureth all things, she never falleth away."[67] Similar to that is this verse of John: "Fear is not in love, but perfect love casteth out fear."[68] Let us now conclude the words of Paul with his letter to Timothy: "In this we labour

---

62 2 Cor. 11:23–33.
63 2 Cor. 11:20.
64 1 Cor. 3:4–8.
65 1 Cor. 3:21–3.
66 1 Cor. 13:4–5.
67 1 Cor. 13:7–8.
68 1 John 4:18.

and are reviled, because we hope in the living God."[69] "A faithful saying, and worthy of all acceptation, that Christ Jesus came into the world to save sinners of whom I am the chief, but for this cause have I obtained mercy, that in me first Christ Jesus might shew forth all patience for the information of them shall believe in Him unto life everlasting. Now to the king of ages, immortal, invisible, the only God, be honour and glory for ever and ever."[70] So writes Paul the Apostle.

John the Apostle also, in Revelation, calls himself a witness and a participant in the afflictions of Christ and urges certain people to endure.[71] Similarly, he strongly commends many for their endurance in his letters; just as even other apostles and evangelists do. Luke the Evangelist, finally, writes that the apostles, after being struck by the Jews, proceeded rejoicing because whoever suffered injustices in the name of Christ were regarded as worthy;[72] furthermore, he writes that they decided everything among them and their own was to be held in common and they wished that the management of goods was to be alien to the apostles. He adds that when a certain Cornelius had wished to worship Peter, Peter rebuked and forbade him.[73] Furthermore, when the Lycaonians wanted to offer sacrifices to Paul and Barnabas as gods for working miracles, Paul and Barnabas did not allow them.[74] John, also, in Revelation did not permit himself to be worshipped.[75] From this it is clear that the apostles did not seek their own advantage or honour, but only the glory of Christ. Therefore, if anyone suspects the apostles made anything up, either he never read these passages and the like or he is mad.

CHAPTER 7 – NO ONE DECEIVED CHRIST'S DISCIPLES

Christ's disciples and their followers have seen far clearer and greater miracles than we have. For although we have been born and raised in this religion, we would still never toil to the same degree for something familiar to us as they toiled for something new and, if I dare say,

---

69 1 Tim. 4:10.
70 1 Tim. 1:15–17.
71 Cf. Rev. 20:4–5.
72 Cf. Acts 5:40–1.
73 Cf. Acts 10:24–7.
74 Cf. Acts 14:11–14.
75 Rev. 19:10; 22:8–9.

almost preternatural. Furthermore, the more preternatural it appears, the clearer signs and portents it lacked from the beginning to lend it credence. For who would easily believe that some unlettered youth, the son of a carpenter, as it was believed, a beggar who had been subjected to a shameful public execution, is the very divine mind which is forever in God, through which all things are forever made and governed? This was never believed about anyone else, for which reason, as Luke the evangelist writes,[76] when Paul the Apostle was debating on this matter before King Agrippa and Porcius Festus, the governor[77] of Judea, Festus exclaimed, "Paul, thou art beside thyself, much learning doth make thee mad."[78] This passage of Tertullian to the Roman judges also addresses the subject: "We too mocked these things at one time. We come from you: men are made, not born, Christian."[79] Therefore it must be thought that those who made these declarations, and those who offered faith to the former who were making these declarations, had seen miracles clearly worthy of God. Hence Paul to the Corinthians: "The Jews require signs, the Greeks seek after wisdom, but we preach Christ crucified, unto the Jews indeed a scandal, and unto the Gentiles' foolishness; but unto them who have converted, Jews or Greeks, Christ, the power of God and the Wisdom of God, for the foolishness of God is wiser than men, and the weakness of God is stronger than men."[80] By miracles alone, and those the most manifest miracles at that, Paul, the noble, powerful, wisest, and bravest man, could suddenly become the defender of Christians, from their bitterest enemy, and to subject himself of his own volition to so many troubles that no one is able to count, out of the love of Christ alone. Truly God foretold according to Luke: "This man is to me a vessel of election, to carry my name before the Gentiles and kings and the children of Israel. For I will shew him how much he must suffer for my name's sake."[81] Therefore, one must by no means believe the heralds of Christ had been deceived by anyone's tricks. In fact, the writings and deeds of Christ's disciples as much as of those who suddenly received this sort of teaching at that time and

---

76 Cf. Acts 25:23–4.
77 The Latin word Ficino uses ("*praeses*") implies "governor" while historically speaking, Porcius Festus was *procurator* (imperial title implying non-military authority in a province) of Judea.
78 Acts 26:24.
79 Tert. *Apol.*, 18.4 (PL 1.378).
80 1 Cor. 1:22–5.
81 Acts 9:15–16.

at the greatest peril attest that the first fruits of Christians were in the hands of such men of sound mind that they neither wished to deceive nor could be in any way deceived. What reason was there that as many Jews as Gentiles – most learned in any teaching whatsoever and many wealthy men – would rather give up their pleasures and estates, and die cruelly with those simple, beggarly disciples of Christ, than live with worldly delights? Let us hear that divine man from Carthage, Tertullian, in the *Apology* crying out thus to the Roman judges: "And now, good judges, go on, crucify, torture, condemn, grind us down. Your iniquity is proof of our innocence. It is to that end that God suffers us to suffer these things. For by the most recent condemnation of a Christian woman to a pimp (*lenonem*) rather than to a lion (*leonem*), you concede that a stain on one's chastity is considered more atrocious among us than any torment or death. And nevertheless your rather exquisite barbarity accomplishes nothing: it is more a lure of our order. The more we are mowed down by you, the more we rise up; the blood of Christians is a seed.[82] We cover everything. And were it not more agreeable to be killed than to kill according to such a teaching, against you we could have fought unarmed and not rebellious, merely at variance, by the hate of division alone. For if such a host of men had retired to one of the most remote places in the world, away from you, the loss of so many citizens would have at any rate enfeebled your dominion; indeed, what is more, even the desertion itself would have been punishment enough; without doubt you would have grown frightened at your desolation, at the silence of things, due to a certain astonishment as if that of a dead city, you would have sought for who you could command, for nearly all the citizens you have are Christian."[83] Origen likewise, in book four of his *On the First Principles*, says: "Countless men, in every region of the world have suddenly abandoned the laws of their fathers and taken up the Christian law, and have freely suffered and freely suffer daily all kinds of tortures and death for His glory."[84]

But now, if I wished to count the thousands of men in any teaching whatsoever, especially in philosophy, who were disciples of Christ or the successors of the disciples of Christ and who, in a long line all the way back to the time of Emperor Julian, amid arms and fire, defended Christ through their holiness, speech, letters, prolonged labour, peril,

---

82 Tert. *Apol.*, 50.12–14 (*PL* 1.534–5).
83 Tert. *Apol.*, 37.4–7 (*PL* 1.462–3).
84 Origen, *De principiis*, 4.1 (*PG* 11.343).

and death, I would be compelled to compose a work that is by no means brief – not to mention the myriad of preachers and philosophers who among the Greeks, barbarians, and Latins, after Julian, spent their whole lives most devoutly in Christian work.

CHAPTER 8 – THE CHRISTIAN RELIGION IS FOUNDED ON THE POWER OF GOD ALONE

If the Christian religion was in no way founded on human power or wisdom or delight, but rather if, not only without the support but also everywhere under the active resistance of many powerful or learned men and human pleasures, it so unexpectedly sprung up, it so suddenly spread over the entire earth – for which reason Paul writes to the Romans that their faith is being proclaimed over the whole world[85] and writes to the Colossians that the gospel is present all over the world;[86] John also writes, "whatsoever is born of God overcometh the world. And this is the victory which overcameth the world: our faith"[87] – it necessarily follows that this very religion was founded on divine power, wisdom, and hope. What of the fact that many centuries ago an exceeding number of prophets and Sibyls in long succession predicted each and every one of these things, which we shall show in the following section? What of the fact that Christ, the teacher of life, not only predicted His own death, the future persecution against His disciples everywhere, the propagation and immutability of His religion, the wretched ruin of the Jews soon to come, the conversion of the pagans, the obstinacy of some Jews to endure all the way to the end of the world, but also inspired His disciples to say the same? Additionally, what is marvellous, Christ described beforehand no differently than Josephus would after the catastrophe, the future siege in a sabbatical year, the destruction and unprecedented slaughter to be carried out by the pagans through famine and iron, and moreover the captivity of the Jews among all the nations.[88] Additionally, it is worth hearing what speech Jesus and each of His disciples employed

---

85 Rom. 1:8.
86 Col. 1:5–6.
87 1 John 5:4.
88 Cf. Eus. *Hist.*, 3.7 (*PG* 20.234) and Josephus, *De bello Iudaico*, 4.420.

to persuade listeners: "Give all your possessions to the poor;[89] reject who you hold dearest;[90] if someone strikes you turn your cheeks; do good to your enemies;[91] regard this life and all its pleasures as worthless;[92] deny even yourselves; take up this cross of ours – the terrible cross;[93] please follow us immediately.[94] For if you follow us, without doubt you will undergo everything that mortals judge evil throughout the rest of your life."[95] They said this. What persuasion, full in all respects of every sort of dissuasion! Do we believe that Demosthenes or Cicero could have persuaded anyone of anything using this method? Nevertheless, that speech, nay the speaker persuaded many great men against all expectation. But how? By God was that miracle done, more amazing than any other miracle, since Jesus, as those who heard Him attest, spoke not as scribes and Pharisees, but as one with power.[96] What is more, they were so persuaded that, as followers of Christ, they always loved Him more than is possible for human nature alone. Certainly whoever has contemplated their works and writings with a clear mind will in no way deny this; indeed, it is all divine. If there is anyone who would doubt it, let him carefully read and reread the books of the prophets, the evangelists, and the apostles, and let him read the commentaries of those who followed them at that time: the truth of this matter will immediately show itself. For in these men there is a new force, also an unparalleled simplicity and temperance, and passion, dignity, profundity, and majesty. This in fact shows that the divine force and flame was not wanting in them, nor does the truth require the adornment of words, nor divine force human stratagems. In addition, in so many volumes of the Old and New Testament, nothing is found anywhere that is not harmonious, which has not been conceded concerning everything else and is the greatest proof of divine truth. Those writers have a certain air of piety and venerability about them and, what is pitiable, this air is shared among them but is completely foreign to everyone else. This indicates that God favoured all of them above the rest. What should we say to the fact that although all the other writers waver and

---

89 Matt. 19:21; Luke 12:33 and 18:22.
90 Luke 14:25–7; cf. Matt. 10:33–5.
91 Matt. 5:44.
92 Matt. 6:19–20.
93 Matt. 16:24–6.
94 Matt. 4:19.
95 Cf. Matt. 10:5–42.
96 Matt. 7:29.

hesitate, nevertheless, they nowhere doubt anything, but spoke with as much – by God Almighty – as much certainty as the bravery they had in enduring the greatest hardships. Listen to that fisherman John the Evangelist: "That which was from the beginning, which we have heard, which we have seen with our eyes, which we have looked upon and our hands have handled, of the word of life; for the life itself became known, and we have seen and do bear witness and declare unto you the life eternal, which was with the Father and hath appeared to us; that which we have seen and have heard, we declare unto you, that you also have fellowship with us and our fellowship may be with the Father and with His Son Jesus Christ. And these things we write to you, that you may rejoice and your joy may be full. And this is the declaration which we have heard from Him and declare unto you: that God is light and in Him there is no darkness."[97] Likewise, consider in the following with how forcefully he affirms: "God is testified in His Son and this is the testimony, that God hath given us eternal life, and this life is in His Son. He who hath the Son hath life, he who does not have the Son of God, does not have life. These things I write to you that you may know that you have eternal life who believe in the name of the Son of God. And this is the confidence which we have toward God, that, whatsoever we shall ask according to His will, He heareth us. And we know that He heareth us whatsoever we ask, we know that we have the petitions which we request of Him."[98] We know that whoever is born of God sinneth not but the generation of God preserveth him and the wicked one toucheth him not. We know that we are of God and the whole world is seated in wickedness. And we know that the Son of God is come and He hath given us understanding, that we may know the true God and may be in His true Son. This is the true God and life eternal."[99] Similarly: "There are three who give testimony in heaven: Father, Word, and Spirit. And these three are one. And there are three that give testimony on earth: spirit, water, and blood. If we receive the testimony of men, the testimony of God is greater."[100] "Wonder not, brethren, if the world hates you. We know that we have passed from death to life."[101] Thereafter: "In this we know that we abide in God, and He in us, since He hath given us of His Spirit, and

---

97 1 John 1:1–5.
98 1 John 5:10–15.
99 1 John 5:18–20.
100 1 John 5:7–9.
101 1 John 3:13–14.

we have seen and do testify that the Father hath sent His Son to be the saviour of the world, and we have known and have believed the truth, which God has in us."[102] Likewise, elsewhere: "He that saw hath given testimony, and his testimony is true, and he knoweth that he speaketh true."[103] Likewise: "This is that disciple who giveth testimony to these things: and hath written these things and we know that his testimony is true."[104] But look, moreover, how vehemently he declares: "In the beginning was the Word, and the Word was with God, and the Word was God. The same was in the beginning with God. All things were made by Him, and without Him was made nothing that was made; since in Him was life, and the life was the light of men, the light shineth in the darkness, and the darkness did not comprehend it."[105] Similarly, elsewhere he says: "Now is the Son of man glorified, and God is glorified in Him. If God be glorified in Him, God will also glorify Him in Himself, and glorify Him continuously."[106] I do not know who could at the same time declare something more straightforwardly and affirm it more effectively. Let us conclude the words of John with these indisputable words of his: "I love you in truth, and not I only, but also all they who have known the truth for the sake of truth, which dwelleth in us, and shall be with us forever."[107]

James says this to the twelve scattered tribes: "My brethren, count it all joy when you shall fall into diverse temptations, knowing that the trying of your faith begetteth patience; and patience hath a perfect work: that you may be perfect and entire, failing in nothing. But if any of you lack wisdom, let him ask of God who giveth to all men abundantly and upbraideth it not, and it shall be given to him. But let him ask in faith, nothing wavering."[108] And a bit later: "Every best gift and every perfect gift is from above, coming down from the Father of lights, with whom there is no change nor shadow of alteration. For of His own will hath He begotten us by the word of truth, that we might be some beginning of His creature."[109] And let us hear of Peter's faith: "You are a chosen race, a kingly priesthood, a holy nation, a purchased people, that you may declare His virtues, who hath called you out of darkness

---

102 1 John 4:13–14 and 16.
103 John 19:35.
104 John 21:24.
105 John 1:1–5.
106 John 13:31–2.
107 2 John 1:1–2.
108 James 1:2–6.
109 James 1:17–18.

into His marvelous light."[110] "Do not fear, but if you partake of the sufferings of Christ, rejoice that when His glory shall be revealed, you may be glad with exceeding joy. If you be reproached for the name of Christ, you shall be blessed: for that which is of the honour, glory, and power of God, and that which is His Spirit, resteth upon you."[111] "The ancients therefore that are among you, I beseech who am myself also an ancient and a witness of the sufferings of Christ, as also a partaker of that glory which is to be revealed in time to come: feed the flock of God which is among you, taking care of it, not by constraint but willingly, according to God."[112] "But the God of all grace, who hath called us unto His eternal glory in Christ Jesus, after you have suffered a little, will Himself perfect you, and confirm you, and establish you, to Him be the glory and the power forever and ever, Amen."[113] Peter, elsewhere: "For we do not by following ignorant fables make known to you the power and foreknowledge of our God Jesus Christ, but we are made eyewitnesses of His greatness."[114]

Moreover, we ought to consider Paul's hope, glory, and steadfastness; having such hope we enjoy much confidence: "The Lord is indeed a Spirit; and where the Spirit of the Lord is, there is liberty. But we all, beholding the glory of the Lord with open face, are transformed into the same image from glory to glory as by the Spirit of the Spirit of the Lord."[115] "Therefore, having this ministration, according to what mercy we have obtained, we faint not, but renounce the hidden things of dishonesty, not walking in craftiness nor adulterating the word of God, but in manifestation of the truth commending ourselves to every man's conscience in the presence of God. And if our gospel be also hid, it is hid to them who are lost, in whom the god of this world hath blinded the minds of unbelievers, that the light of the gospel of the glory of Christ, who is the image of God, should not shine unto them. For we preach not ourselves, but Jesus Christ our Lord; and ourselves your servants through Jesus. For God, who commanded the light to shine out of darkness, hath shined in our hearts, to give the light of the knowledge of the glory of God, in the face of Christ Jesus. But we

---

110 1 Pet. 2:9.
111 1 Pet. 4:12–14.
112 1 Pet. 5:1–2.
113 1 Pet. 5:10–11.
114 2 Pet. 1:16.
115 2 Cor. 3:17–18.

have this treasure in earthen vessels, that the excellency may be of the power of God and not of us. In all things we suffer tribulation, but are not distressed; we are straitened, but are not destitute; we suffer persecution, but are not forsaken; we are cast down, but we perish not."[116] And a bit later he adds: "For we know that He who raised up Jesus will raise us up also with Jesus. For which cause we faint not, but though our outward man is corrupted, yet the inward man is renewed day by day. For that which is at present momentary and light of our tribulation worketh in us above measure, exceedingly an eternal weight of glory, while we look not at the things which are seen, but at the things which are unseen, for the things that are seen are temporal, but the things which are not seen are eternal.[117] For we know, if our earthly house of this habitation be dissolved, that we have a building of God, a house not made with hands, but eternal in heaven."[118] So Paul writes to the Corinthians. He, however, warned Timothy in this way: "Be thou vigilant, labour in all things, do the work of an evangelist, fulfill thy mystery,[119] be sober. For I am even now ready to be sacrificed, and the time of my dissolution is at hand. I have fought the good fight, I have finished my course, I have kept the faith; for the hereafter, there is laid up for me a crown of justice, which the Lord the just judge shall render to me on that day, and not only to me but to all who love His coming."[120] In these words he prophesied that his own impending martyrdom was at hand, which soon followed. I am unable to contain myself from adding to this how confidently in his assertion and how majestically he sang in the epistle to the Hebrews about the eternal generation and power of the Son of God: "God, who, at sundry times and in diverse manners, spoke in times past to the fathers by the prophets, last of all, in these days, hath spoken to us by His Son, whom He hath appointed heir of all things, by whom also He made the world; who, being the splendour of His glory and the figure of His substance and upholding all things by the word of His power, making purgation of sins, sitteth on the right hand of the majesty on high, being made so much better than the angels as He hath inherited a more excellent name than they,"[121] and so on. In the

---

116 2 Cor. 4:1–9.
117 2 Cor. 4:16–18.
118 2 Cor. 5:1.
119 In 2 Tim. 4:5 the Vulgate has *"ministerium"* ("ministry") rather than *"mysterium"* ("mystery"). This change is Ficino's, whether deliberate or accidental. It may also be a kind of error that could arise from dictating to an amanuensis.
120 2 Tim. 4:5–8.
121 Heb. 1:1–4.

following he says of the same Son of God: "For the word of God is living and effectual and more piercing than any two edged sword, and reaching unto the division of the soul and the spirit, of the joints also and the marrow, and is a discerner of the thoughts and intents of the heart; neither is there any creature invisible in His sight, [but] all things are naked and open to His eyes, to whom our speech is."[122] To the Colossians: "The Son is the image of the invisible God, the firstborn of every creature, for in Him were all things created in heaven and on earth, visible and invisible, whether Thrones, or Dominions, or Principalities, or Powers. All things were created through Him and in Him, and He is before all, and by Him all things all things consist. And He is the head of the body, the Church; who is the beginning, the firstborn from the dead, that in all things He may hold the primacy, because in Him, it hath well pleased the Father that all fullness of divinity should dwell and through Him to reconcile all things unto Himself, making peace through the blood of His cross, both as to the things that are in heaven and the things that are on earth."[123]

However, lest I be compelled to go on too long through what wonders the truest oracle, as it were, pours forth about the Son of God in the letters to the Ephesians, to the Colossians, to the Philippians, and about the Holy Spirit to the Corinthians and about the remaining mysteries of theology elsewhere, I shall wrap it up concisely.[124] If anyone carefully reads the holy letters, he will be compelled to admit that Christian law is in accord with divine virtue, since our steadfast heroes adhere to its unmoving foundation, clear of mind, burning in their will, simple and sure in their words, unwearied in their action, unconquered in argument; others too anxiously seek out petty rationalizations through ambiguities and, as David said, being wicked they wander about in circles, neither sufficing as leaders for themselves or for others.[125] Finally, if purity is the chief quality of religion, this one is certainly the most divine because it allows neither the base superstitions of the later Jews and the foulest absurdities of the Talmud, nor the lewd and unjust fables of the pagans, nor the abominable wantonness of the Mohammadans and the silliness of the Qur'an. Indeed the Christian law neither promises earthly rewards, as other laws do, but rather

---

122 Heb. 4:12–13.
123 Col. 1:15–20.
124 Cf. Eph. 1; Col. 1:15–20; Phil. 3:7–14; 1 Cor. 12.
125 Cf. Ps. 12:9 (Vulg. Ps. 11:9) and Th. Aq., *C. Gent.*, 1.6.3.

it promises heavenly rewards, nor does it command opponents of its faith and law to be killed, in the way the Talmud and Qur'an have commanded, but rather it commands they be taught by reason, converted through speech, or tolerated with patience. This law – that makes the case for virtues through toil before talk, as became self-evident during the first fruits of the Christians – does not merely cut away at vices but uproots them entirely. For such was their condition and lot that they could not make the case in any other way than the through exercise of both virtues and miracles. Furthermore, this law eagerly exercises virtues not for the sake of ambition or pleasure or human tranquillity, but for the sake of God alone, and does away with this whole world and regards it as worthless in pursuit of the world to come.

CHAPTER 9 – CHRIST'S AUTHORITY IS NOT FROM THE STARS BUT FROM GOD

In our *Theologia* [*Platonica*], we have proved that the common religion is from neither the stars, nor men, nor illness, but from God and the common nature of the human species. But for the time being, we shall briefly show here that the Christian law is not from, nor is it maintained by, some fate from the stars.[126] The coming of Christ was foretold as divine from the beginning of the world by prophets and Sibyls, who were not trained in astrology but inspired by the divine. Additionally, the celestial spheres, being remote universal causes, tend to guide – and not without some favourable intermediaries – particular effects on earth to their purpose; however, not only did they not manage all human matters favourably for Christians, but it is recorded that for three hundred straight years, matters had been adverse to the Christians. Hence, according to Luke, when Paul, during a disputation with the Jews at Rome, had said, "For the hope of Israel, I am bound with this chain," the Jews added: "We have discovered concerning this sect that it is everywhere contradicted."[127] On this very account, Tertullian thus exclaimed: "Truth has been hated since her inception. Just as she has appeared, she is thought an enemy. For her enemies are as many as there are outsiders: the Jews by their rivalry; soldiers by their extortion; even our very

---

126 Cf. Fic. *TP* 14.10 (Allen and Hankins 4.301–29).
127 Acts 28:20, 22.

own family members by their nature. Day by day we are besieged, day by day we are betrayed, in our very gatherings and congregations we are oft-suppressed."[128] Likewise, he says: "Truth does not plead her own case, because she does not even have any regard for her own condition. She knows that she is making a journey as a stranger on this earth, that she easily finds hostile outsiders, that otherwise she has in the heavens her race, her home, her hope, her grace, her dignity; meanwhile she desires only that she not be condemned to be unknown.[129] For what is more unjust than that men hate what they do not know, even if it warrants hatred?[130] We thus refute them in each of the following ways: so long as they hate, they are ignorant; and so long as they are ignorant, they wrongly hate."[131] So he says. In addition, material causes produce laws that are concerned with pleasure or ambition or surely concerned with no more than civic matters. Christian law condemns all these or rises above them. Likewise, the celestial spheres cannot pour in a loftier desire than a desire for the heavens; Christian piety rejects and transcends the celestial spheres and worships God alone above heaven, seeing that it is not born of heaven or of heavenly spirits but of the supercelestial God alone. Countless men among all the nations have offered themselves freely in the name of Christ to harm and certain death for the sake of divine blessedness alone. When else has such heavenly motion effected such struggles? What sage by his piety alone could ever have spread his teaching over the entire earth, and what God could ever on account of His virtue alone have been everywhere believed in the face of opposition from ancient tradition and power? If these things came from the stars, certainly someone would also have had the same or a similar destiny from the stars as another at birth.[132] What fate, pray tell, has confirmed that it is the very creator of the universe who has taught and teaches that the fates have no power? How, therefore, does fate contradict itself and preach that it does not exist? Eusebius proved it thus: "How have those who for the sake of preaching the gospel, either have fought now for many years, or are fighting even now been compelled toward a single will and faith, and toward the same virtue of the soul, and toward a way of life at different times, and so many within living memory? Who with a sound mind could ever have believed that

---

128 Tert. *Apol.* 7.3–4 (*PL* 1.307–8).
129 Tert. *Apol.* 1.2 (*PL* 1.259–60).
130 Tert. *Apol.* 1.4 (*PL* 1.261).
131 Tert. *Apol.* 1.5 (*PL* 1.262).
132 Cf. Augustine, *Confessiones*, 7.6.8–10.

both the young and the old, men and women, slaves and free men, learned and unlearned, neither born in a single clime of the earth nor in the same hours, but all over the world and in different times, forced by the stars, had chosen one and the same new, unheard of doctrine – and indeed at risk of death – over the rites of their forefathers, and preferred the doctrines of true philosophy and the harsh life rather than pleasures?"[133] So says Eusebius. Therefore we ought not to listen to certain impious and fatuous advocates of fate, who at the very beginning of the Christian religion proclaimed it would fail as soon as it had completed its 365th year, and they even corroborated this claim with an oracle.[134] Nor would any astrologer ever dare to proclaim that it will fail, which depends not on some temporal motion of the heavens but on the eternal immovability of God, which has from the beginning of the world up to the times of emperor Octavian consisted in the declarations of the prophets, in the hope of the people, in the likeness of things; it has thereafter endured until our time for now 1,474 years in spite of the heavens and earth. For this reason God banished the first persecutors of this religion, namely the Jews, as we shall show elsewhere; He defended it from the long and fierce persecution of pagans and heretics. This religion, therefore, which has God as its champion and defender, can never be destroyed, even if it should be poorly practised by its own and cruelly assailed by its foes. For under the kingship of God stands the religion which is treated no worse by its own adherents than by others. Finally, if human matters turn out favourably for Christians, the ceremonies will not go unobserved; if many misfortunes befall Christians, at long last this religion will grow and be perfected; for since it previously arose and matured in some extreme and long-lasting adversity, it will necessarily be sustained and fulfilled by the same adversity.

CHAPTER 10 – CHRIST'S AUTHORITY WAS NOT AT ALL WITHOUT MIRACLES

It seems to me, magnanimous Lorenzo, that those who demand new miracles every day as relentlessly as they do shamelessly to confirm their faith in Christ need to be vehemently refuted. For if the miracles

---

133 Eus. *Prae.* 6.6.70–1 (*PG* 21.431).
134 Augustine, *De civitate Dei*, 18.53–4 (*PL* 41.616–20; Dombart and Kalb, 653–6).

are few and far between, they are portents; if they were done in great numbers, they would appear contrived or natural. Let it suffice for us to know that the world had once, not without ostensible miracles, taken up and carried out so miraculously such miraculous practices and works. Origen says against Celsus: "We know for certain that those who came earlier would not have believed that Christ was the Son of God, since He had been slain so disgracefully, unless the whole thing had been predicted by the prophets; additionally, unless He had performed miracles as much as His followers had. Moreover, the steadfastness of the Christians' works and the diligence of their speech will be favoured by those who judge them; they establish that the Christians did not make up their miracles."[135] What of the fact that the pagans, the Jews, and the Mohammadans have conceded to us that Christ performed miracles? The disciples of Christ preached and wrote openly and daily, as much in Judea as elsewhere, about the miracles of the star from the East, the eclipse of the Sun, the earthquake and rending of the temple, and many others revealed to many thousands of men. Indeed this was at the time when there still remained countless numbers of those who could have most easily refuted the disciples as lacking any substance, unless the latter had been speaking the truth, since the former were alive and already adults at Christ's death. How ever did Herod commit such an abominable and hazardous crime, in particular when he murdered so many infants and his own son, if he had not been terrified by some awe-inspiring new portent?[136] News of this crime was in fact sent to Octavian as soon as Herod committed it. Listen to Macrobius: "When Augustus had heard that among the boys under the age of two, whom Herod, king of the Jews, ordered to be killed, Herod's own son was also slain, he said: 'It is better to be Herod's pig than his son.'"[137] Moreover, Origen, in the books against Celsus, writes that he had himself read in a book *On Comets* by Chaeremon the Stoic that now and then comets signified good fortune and health, and such was the comet that shone in Octavian's time. Origen asserts that the history concerning this comet was disclosed by Chaeremon and adds that the Chaldeans, since they had examined the comet and kept noticing that their own demons had been weakened of late, went to Judea to worship someone greater than their demons. Nor, indeed, should it be surprising that Chaldeans

---

135 This is more of a paraphrase than a direct quotation; cf. Origen, *Contra Celsum*, 2.47–8 (*PG* 11.870–1).
136 Matt. 2:1–16.
137 Macrobius, *Saturnalia*, 2.4.11, ed. J. Willis (Stuttgart and Leipzig: Teubner, 1994), 144.

noticed it; for in that same Eastern region, as Origen attests and as others corroborate, long before in the same city as the Magi, the prophet of Baal distinguished himself and predicted that the Messiah would rise up like a sceptre out of Israel, when the new star of Jacob rises, specifically in these words: "A star shall rise out of Jacob and a sceptre shall spring up from Israel."[138] One Calcidius the Platonist confirms the sacred history and writes that the descent of God was signified by the rising of a certain star preceding it and it was confirmed by the Chaldeans who venerated the newborn God.[139] It is worthwhile to listen to Pliny on the earthquake, for he says: "The greatest earthquake in living memory occurred during the principate of Tiberius Caesar, leaving twelve cities of Asia in ruins."[140] Perhaps that was the earthquake that happened during Christ's passion, not only because he says that it was so great that there never had been one like it before, but also because it was in Asia during the rule of Tiberius – that is, where and when Christ suffered.[141] Eusebius writes that he had read in the commentaries of the heathens that in the eighteenth year of Tiberius's reign, there was a solar eclipse, Bithynia was shaken by an earthquake, and most of the temples were cast down in the city of Nicea: all this coincides with what happened during the passion of the saviour. Indeed even Phlegon,[142] who is the eminent reckoner of the Olympiads, writes about this in the thirty-third book, saying this: "On the fourth year of the two hundred and second Olympiad, great and outstanding among all that preceded it, a solar eclipse occurred: on the sixth hour, the day turned into such a dark night that the stars in the sky were seen, and an earthquake overturned many temples in the city of Nicaea in Bithynia." So says Phlegon.

The Gospel of John offers an argument for the fact that the saviour suffered in this year. There the following is written: "After the fifteenth year of Tiberius Caesar, the Lord preached for three years."[143] Josephus, also, a native writer of the Jews, attests that the priests around these times on the day of Pentecost had first sensed disturbances in the area and some loud noises, then from the inner sanctum of the temple suddenly

---

138 Origen, *Contra Celsum*, 1.59–60 (*PG* 11.767–71); cf. Num. 24:17.
139 Calcidius, *Commentarius*, 126, ed. J. Magee (Cambridge, MA: Harvard University Press, 2016), 328–31.
140 Pliny, *Naturalis historia*, 2.200.3–5.
141 Concerning the great earthquake of 17 AD, see Suetonius, *Tiberius*, 48.2; Strabo, *Geographica*, 13.4.8; Tacitus, *Annales*, 2.47; 4.13.1–5; Velleius Paterculus, *Historia Romana*, 2.126.4.
142 Latin: Phlegro, here and below.
143 Luke 3:1.

there burst forth the unexpected sound of many saying: "Let us depart from this abode."[144] This much Eusebius says. Luke the Evangelist, who says that Christ was baptized in the fifteenth year of Tiberius when he was nearing the age of thirty, also states that Christ suffered in the eighteenth year of Tiberius. Eusebius, however, calculates that Christ was born in the forty-second year of Augustus's reign but that he had begun preaching the gospel in the fifteenth year of Tiberius's reign.[145] Dionysius the Areopagite, foremost of the Athenian philosophers, and Apollophanes, an eminent sophist and expert in the natural sciences, were together near Heliopolis on the day Jesus was killed. These men then saw the Moon's globe wondrously setting in the East and wondrously standing before the width of the Sun from the ninth hour until the evening – outside the time of conjunction. They observed that such a setting of the Moon reached the edge of the body of the Sun and then in the end its course turned back in the diametrically opposite direction. Since they understood that this had clearly happened against the entire natural order, Dionysius was immediately dumbstruck and Apollophanes, turning to Dionysius, cried: "Splendid Dionysius, these are certainly the reversals of divine things." Dionysius the Areopagite wrote this to the wise Polycarp and asked him to meet Apollophanes, himself still alive and not yet Christian, since neither would he deny that those things happened against the natural order nor, beyond that, would he reject Christian truth, but rather take it up with humility.[146] Lactantius corroborates that Christ was crucified on the twentieth day of March.[147] What is more, one Cecco d'Ascoli the astrologer, although not very religious, nevertheless asserts that by astrological calculation it is certain that on the day that Christ was crucified, the Sun was in the first degree of Aries, the Moon in the first degree of Libra, and an eclipse could not possibly have happened naturally, not only because it was a full Moon – it is necessary for an eclipse to happen during a new Moon – but also because that eclipse began in the East, although a natural eclipse usually begins in the West.[148] Others are of the opinion that the Sun was in Pisces, the Moon in Virgo; nevertheless, they also

---

144 Eus. *Chron.* 2 (Schoene 2.149; *PG* 19.535–6); cf. Eus. *Hist.* 3.8.6 (*PG* 20.238); cf. Josephus, *De bello Iudaico*, 6.288–304.
145 Cf. Eus. *Hist.* 1.5.2 (*PG* 20.82).
146 Ps.-Dionysius, *Epistula*, 7.2 (*PG* 3.1077–81).
147 Lact. *Inst.* 4.10.18 (*PL* 6.474; Monat, 90–1).
148 Cecco d'Ascoli, *Sphera cum commentis*, 23r (Venetiis, 1518).

78 On the Christian Religion

come to the same conclusion as Cecco d'Ascoli about the eclipse. The Jews show the same, since as their law demanded they always observed Passover on the fourteenth Moon and they sacrificed Jesus on Passover. There was indeed an eclipse, for it was impossible to lie at the time about such a manifest thing, for miracles of this sort were also preached and written about in the same age and among the same men as they are reported to have occurred. But for the sake of Christ alone that miracle was produced in the sky.[149] For what, either then or at any other time, has been produced more miraculous than Christ, whether under the sky or above it? Paul, His herald, says of this matter: "God exalteth Him, and hath given Him a name which is above all names, that in the name of Jesus every knee should bow, of those that are in heaven, on earth, and under the earth, and that every tongue should confess that the Lord Jesus Christ is in the glory of God the Father."[150] And, what adds to the astonishment, the tongues of men confessed this after He had emptied Himself, taking the form of a servant, becoming humble and obedient unto death, even unto the death of the cross.[151] If the world admits, without seeing any miracles, that a man of such a lot and appearance constituted the highest God, then this fact alone surpasses the astonishment of all other miracles. I cannot be led to believe that John the Evangelist, the most simple and sober writer of all, had dared to cry out with such a wondrous voice, if he had not seen many miracles: "There are also many other things which Jesus did which, if every thing were written, the world itself I think would not be able to contain the books that should be written."[152] I omit the fact that the evangelists often say that Jesus miraculously healed thousands of sick at once. The great Paul teaches us how great was the apostles' preaching, by which many people were converted. For to the Corinthians he says: "I, brethren, when I came to you, came not in loftiness of speech or of wisdom, declaring unto you the testimony of Christ. For I judged not myself to know anything among you except Jesus Christ and Him crucified. And I was with you in weakness, and in fear, and in much trembling, and my speech and my preaching was not in the persuasive words of human wisdom, but in shewing of the Spirit and power, that your faith might not stand on the wisdom of men, but on the power of God. We speak wisdom, however, among the perfect."[153] In another

---

149 Cf. Eus. *Hist.* 5.23 (*PG* 20.491–4).
150 Phil. 2:9–11.
151 Phil: 2:7–8.
152 John 21:25.
153 1 Cor. 2:1–6.

letter to the Corinthians he says: "The signs of my apostleship have been wrought on you, in all patience, in signs, and wonders, and mighty deeds."[154] But let us listen to what he writes in his letter to the Thessalonians: "You know, for our gospel hath not been unto you in word only, but in power also, and in the Holy Ghost, and in much fullness."[155] Had the ever prudent Paul forgotten himself to such an extent, or did he think the people to whom he was writing so forgetful that he would recall the miracles he performed before them, had he not performed them? The refutation and the disrepute would have come quickly, had it happened that he had lied.[156] He also writes to the Romans about the miracles he performed, and from this letter and others like it we conclude that in those times there was no shortage of miracles, and by their power the house of God was actually then built as a light and exemplar for our own home. Of this house of God, as Paul says: "It is the church of the living God, the pillar and ground of the truth, and evidently great is the sacrament of piety, which is manifest in the flesh, is justified in the spirit, appeared unto angels, hath been preached unto the Gentiles, is believed in the world, is taken up in glory."[157] So he says to Timothy.

Why therefore do we prattle on in disbelief? Why do we insolently demand more? Can it be that our great God has a daily quarrel with us before a judge?[158] Can it be that at a moment's notice God is compelled to redeem His authority with miracles, not only from each and every one of us, but from future generations, who will make similar demands, and He is forced, as some illusionist for hire, to appear on stage for everyone's approval? It is, however, not even natural and fitting to force a man, an animal free by nature, using some forceful displays, but rather to win him over with inspiration and teaching. For virtue and blessedness is promised to the willing, not to the unwilling: not by inquiring but by believing, the authority of the one who commands is confirmed. What do we make of the fact that there are few who are worthy to see miracles and far fewer who are worthy to receive them? Miracles among men are, as most often is the case, harmoniously performed by God through the souls of men thoroughly detached from their bodies and attached to God, as if through instruments. So plunge yourselves into the mire of the

---

154 2 Cor. 12:12.
155 1 Thess. 1:4–5.
156 Rom. 15:17–19.
157 1 Tim. 3:15–16.
158 Cf. Horace, *De arte poetica*, 1.78 for the expression "sub iudice lis est."

body, wretched souls! Shall you thereby see heavenly miracles? Oh! How foolishly you long to see the sublime with your head downcast towards the earth! How foolishly you wish to be swept aloft by portents, not to climb the steps of virtue! What on earth is more miraculous, what more divine than a soul completely the master of its own body? Let us put this command to the test, if we can; and indeed we can if we but have the will: then not only shall we perceive miracles, but we shall perform them ourselves. With certainty, I reckon that in different places God often makes wondrous signs for us, even though we are not worthy, but they are not all clear to everyone. Also, many things are not written, or are written but not believed, and the ambiguities of this fact seem to give an opportunity for some exceedingly detestable men who, in imitation of true miracles, introduce false ones. Imitation and forgery necessarily follow a true thing, with the result that someone tries to imitate and copy it; counterfeit money would not have been introduced, unless legitimate money had been introduced at some point. Fake miracles would not have been devised if by the very existence of true miracles, men had not been enticed to the imitation of and trust in them. The miracles Aurelius Augustinus and Gregory say they had seen were such that they ought not to be distrusted.

For my part, I have heard that in our age, and even in our city of Florence, some wondrous and also believable things have occurred, though some are more hidden. For sure, from many trustworthy men we learned about the miracle that occurred in plain sight before many thousands of men, who both saw it and are still alive; it happened at Ancona in 1470 AD. A girl, on account of one of the worst muscle contractions, from earliest infancy walked using her buttocks instead of her legs; moreover, Bindello, a Florentine, was not able to speak for many years due to trauma to his throat and chest; when both had suppliantly commended themselves to the Virgin Mary in the same place, they were immediately healed. To all people they had been known to be infirm for many years, and afterward, four years on now, are known as healthy to all people.

Do not be surprised, Lorenzo, that Marsilio Ficino, a student of philosophy, brings up miracles; for what we write is true, and it is the duty of the philosopher to confirm each and every thing with its proper reason. There are, however, proper reasons for natural matters, which are in accordance with nature, but for divine matters, which are of the sort that is beyond nature, there are not only metaphysical proofs but also – perhaps especially – miracles. For God not so much by words as by miraculous works proves His mysteries and confirms His commandments, whence this verse: "Though you will not believe the words, believe the works."[159]

CHAPTER 11 – CHRIST'S AUTHORITY AMONG THE PAGANS

No one has ever denied Christian miracles, although some men ascribed the miracles to the power of demons, unaware that demons tend to either inspire worship of themselves, or of vices and, finally, destructive discord; the heroes of Christ, however, were most hostile towards these things. But how in the world can the religion that condemned and overthrew the worship of demons, and both put those demons to flight and still has them in flight, have itself sprung from demons? Nearly the whole world suddenly took up the worship of Christ and continues to worship with the exception of a few vagrant money-lenders, who have been wholly enthralled to greed and are unable to make correct judgments on divine matters. In fact, all the pagans agreed that Jesus was either God or at least divine. When the Milesian Apollo was consulted, he thus commended Christ: "He was mortal in body, wise, a producer of signs, but under the leadership of the Chaldeans, He was arrested by arms and suffered a bitter death by nails and rods."[160] Porphyry in his book *On Responses* says the gods pronounced that Christ was the most pious and they asserted that He became immortal, so favourably giving witness about Him; Porphyry adds that the goddess Hecate, when she was asked about the soul of Christ, answered: "That soul belongs to a man of most outstanding piety; they worship it, a stranger to severity," and after much else, Hecate added: "The Christ Himself, being pious, has ascended into heaven, as the pious do." Therefore do not disparage Him; Porphyry himself concedes that Christ was both wise and pious, although, not only clearly struggling against the truth but also against himself, he calls Christians part uneducated, part Magi.[161] Tertullian in *Apologeticus* wrote that, when Pilate reported to emperor Tiberius concerning the doctrine of the Christians, Tiberius referred the matter to the Senate that the sacred rites of the Christians should be accepted among the other sacred rites. However, when by decree of the senators it had been decided that the Christians were to be expelled from the city, due

---

159 John 10:37–8.
160 Lact. *Inst.* 4.13.11 (*PL* 6.484; Monat, 116–17).
161 Augustine, *De civitate Dei*, 19.23.2 (*PL* 41.651–2; Dombart and Kalb, 691).

to the fact that a judgment of this thing had not been brought before the Senate earlier (for there was an old decree that no god should be consecrated without the authority of the Senate),[162] Tiberius, through an edict, threatened death against the accusers of Christians; many senators and Roman aristocrats were killed. Eusebius affirms the same.[163] Vespasian and Titus, when they heard of the works of Christ, feared His power. Hadrian, just as Julius Capitolinus tells, determined to make temples to Christ and accept Him among the gods, and for that reason he ordered temples to be made without images in all cities, which today, because they do not have divine presence (*numina*), are said to be Hadrian's. He was said to have planned these temples for this purpose but was stopped by those who, while consulting the oracles, had discovered everyone would become Christian, if it had happened as he wanted, and the remaining temples would be abandoned. Alexander Severus determined to build temples to Christ, but he did not follow through; in the morning he would pray in his shrine before a statue of Christ. So Capitolinus says.[164] But hear what Eusebius reports about Hadrian: "The philosophers Quadratus, a disciple of the apostles, and Aristides the Athenian gave books composed in defense of the Christian religion to Hadrian, and the legate Granius Serenus, a nobleman of the highest order, sent a letter to the emperor, saying it was unjust to give in to the cries of the mob for the blood of innocent men, and, without even an accusation against their name, for them to be made guilty of sectarianism; Hadrian, moved by this letter, wrote to Minucius Fundanus the proconsul that Christians were not to be condemned without submitting an accusation, and a copy of this letter has endured up to our age." So Eusebius says.[165]

Antoninus Pius, when he had heard that Christians frequently use the proverb "Do not do to others what you do not wish done to you," studied the life of Christ carefully and dedicated a statue to Him as a god. For my part, I reckon Antoninus was especially persuaded to do this by the philosopher Justin, who dedicated to him a book composed in defence of our religion. Eusebius relates that Philip was the first of the emperors to be Christian; for the emperors above worshipped Jesus not alone, but with the other gods, but all seemed to have feared their people more than God.[166] In the end Constantine, since he had

---

162 Tert. *Apol.* 5.1 (*PL* 1.290–2).
163 Eus. *Hist.* 2.2.1–6 (*PG* 20.139–42).
164 Eus. *Hist.* 4.3.1–3 (*PG* 20.307).
165 Eus. *Chron.* 2 (Schoene, 2.166; *PG* 19.557–8); cf. Eus. *Hist.* 4.3 (*PG* 20.307) and 4.8.6 (*PG* 20.326).
166 Eus. *Hist.* 4.18 (*PG* 20.374).

experienced Christ's miracles more clearly in his own affairs, came to fear God more than the people, and he worshipped Christ alone and openly, overturned the temples of the idols, and built temples to Christ at great expense far and wide. Eusebius, who wrote during Constantine's time, writes this about Him.[167] It is agreed that the emperors, however, who raged violently against Christians, had been led to do so by their cruel nature and rash anxiety rather than by the consideration of justice, if anyone should consider those insane Neros and Domitians, which Rome had in abundance in those days. To those who condemn us, Tertullian says we ought to glory in our religion because they condemn nothing but what is some great good; indeed such persecutors of ours have always been unjust, impious, shameful, and condemned by all people, while the emperors more moderate towards the Christians have behaved more honourably; but whatever emperors raged most monstrously above all others, such as Nero and Domitian, paid a wretched price.[168] Not to mention that Judas, the betrayer of Christ, suddenly hanged himself with a noose, and in those days the disciples of Christ publicly spoke and wrote of it; furthermore, that Pontius Pilate, the man who condemned Christ, at last, after enduring many misfortunes, killed himself by his own hand, and Eusebius asserts that he read this among the historians of the Greeks and the Romans.[169] Herod I faced a similar end by killing himself; there was a similar end to Herod II as well: this Herod immediately after the murder of James and the imprisonment of Peter, stricken by an angel, as Luke attests, died and, as Josephus says, he saw an angel standing over his head as an attendant to his death, and at last, suffering harsh torture, forcefully broke the thread of life.[170] Emperor Aurelian too, when he had initially set in motion the persecution of Christians, was first deterred by a thunderbolt then soon after slain.[171] Julian the Apostate also, while setting out against the Persians, vowed Christian blood to the gods after his victory, but still on the march lost his army to famine and thirst and was also himself ignominiously killed. Diocletian killed himself, Maximianus was slain dishonourably.[172] I do not think I should let pass in silence that Celsus the Epicurean, Porphyry as well, and Julian, and

---

167 Eus. *Hist.* 10.9 (*PG* 20.902–3).
168 Tert. *Apol.* 5.3–4 (*PL* 1.292–5).
169 Eus. *Hist.*, 2.7.1 (*PG* 20.455).
170 Acts 12:3–17; Eus. *Hist.* 2.9.4 (*PG* 20.458); cf. Josephus, *Antiquitates Iudaicae*, 19.8.2.
171 Eus. *Hist.* 8.13, 15 (*PG* 20.779).
172 Cf. Byron J. Nakamura, "When Did Diocletian Die? New Evidence for an Old Problem." *Classical Philology* 98, 3 (2003): 283–9; Anon. *Epit. de Caes.* 39.7.

Proclus, the Platonists, and several other men noted for their teachings, who partly on account of some outrageous arrogance, partly to indulge their own people and the powerful among them, impiously brandished their tongues and pens against Christian piety, while the arms of the powerful raged against it on all sides. Doubtless they really proved that neither the fathers of our religion were by any means to be held in contempt, since distinguished philosophers saw fit to meet them in battle and were bested by them, nor that the religion itself had arisen by the might of men, since it so astonishingly overcame human wisdom and power. As God predicted in Isaiah: "I will destroy the wisdom of the wise men, and condemn the understanding of prudent men,"[173] and Paul the Apostle confirmed it, saying: "The wisdom of this world is foolishness with God";[174] "for the foolishness of God is wiser than men, and the weakness of God is stronger than men."[175] Elsewhere this vigorous soldier of Christ cried out in this way: "Our weapons are not carnal, but mighty to God, to destroy the fortifications and counsels, and every height that exalteth itself against the knowledge of God, then to bring into captivity every understanding unto the obedience of Christ and to revenge more readily all disobedience."[176] Justly, therefore, Gamaliel, the great teacher of the Hebrews, feared these weapons when he counseled not to persecute the teaching of Jesus: for if it were from God, it could not be stopped; if it were not from God, just like other fictions that had occurred in those times, it would last only briefly. The divine Plotinus, foremost of the interpreters of Plato, also feared them, as did Numenius, Iamblichus, and Amelius, who endeavoured not to disprove Christian theology, but rather to imitate it. During roughly the same times, Arnobius the African, a most famous rhetorician, feared them even more; when he, still an idolater, was compelled by dreams to believe in Christ but could not gain the trust of a bishop whom he had always attacked, he burned the midnight oil writing against his first religion – as Jerome says – the most brilliant books and, as if through an exchange of some hostages of piety, gained at last the trust of the bishop.[177]

---

[173] Cf. Isa. 29:14.
[174] 1 Cor. 3:19.
[175] 1 Cor. 1:25.
[176] 2 Cor. 10:4–6.
[177] Jerome, *De viris illustribus*, 79 (PL 23.723).

CHAPTER 12 – CHRIST'S AUTHORITY AMONG THE MOHAMMADANS

The Mohammadans resemble Christians in some way, although as followers of the Arians and the Manichaeans, they are heretics. Their king, Mohammad, certainly acknowledges that Jesus Christ is the power, wisdom, mind, soul, spirit, and word of God, born by some sort of divine inspiration from Mary, the eternal virgin; that He raised the dead and, above all others, He performed a great many other miracles with divine power; that He was more eminent than all the prophets of the Hebrews; and that they would have no prophet after Jesus. Mohammad held Jesus above all men and Mary above all women. He added that the uncorrupted body of Jesus had risen to heaven; he placed Christians above Jews by a long measure and absolutely hated the Jews.[178] All this is in his book, the Qur'an. Thus, his followers do not initiate the Jews into their sacred rites until the Jews admit that the Christians' ancient sacraments are good and true.[179] Those who visit the tomb of Mohammad are deemed insufficiently purified until they have visited Mary's tomb. They punish with severity whosoever makes insulting use of Christ's or Mary's name. They are a race of religious men, some dedicated to Elijah, others to John the Baptist, others (and these especially) to Jesus Christ.[180] They celebrate the prophets and the gospels. They learned from Mohammad in the Qur'an that the Qur'an is the confirmation and manifestation of the Hebrew prophets and the gospel. One reads in it that none will be perfect unless he obeys the Old and the New Testaments, and also the Qur'an, since it is the union and manifestation of both.[181] However many times he mentions the gospel, which he does often, each time he calls the book by the proper name, "light."[182] Finally, he also adds that the gospel is the light of the [Old] Testament, the instruction and the straight path for the God-fearing. Besides, he introduces God in the Qur'an, speaking thus: "Since we ranked some prophets above others and spoke to them, we have bestowed our spirit appropriately on Christ, son of Mary, and to him have given a strength and power beyond all others."[183]

It seems, however, that there are two principal errors of Mohammad: the one is that although he places some divinity in Christ, far greater than in all men, whether present, past, or future, he nevertheless seems

---

178 Ricc. *Contr.* 1.41–60.
179 Cf. *Alcor.* 5.82–5 (Petrus Pons, 80); 22.17 (Petrus Pons, 200); 61.14 (Petrus Pons, 335).
180 The Italian text specifies that there are three orders ("*regole*") of religious men.
181 Cf. *Alcor.* 5.46 (Petrus Pons, 82).
182 Latin: *lucidus*.
183 *Alcor.* 2.253 (Petrus Pons, 36).

in some places to assert that divinity to be distinct from and lesser to the substance of the Highest God, something he in fact learned from the Arians; but in this matter he is struggling with himself: for the epithets which he attributes to Christ signify that His divinity is the same as the Highest God's.[184] Mohammad's other and indeed more obvious error is that, when the attendants of the priests who tried to lay their hands on Christ fell down, God – as Mohammad reckons – immediately and secretly swept Jesus up to heaven. When they stood back up, seizing hold of someone else resembling Jesus, they flogged and crucified him; this it seems he learned from the Manichaeans. There is no need to refute errors of this kind: for whosoever has refuted the Arian and Manichaean heresies, surely seems also to have refuted Mohammad.[185]

We may conclude that all sects of pagans, Jews, and Mohammadans agree that the Christian law is truly the most excellent of all. For although each of them prefers his own heresy on account of some affinity of nature and custom, or some affinity to fiction, he nevertheless places the Christian religion before all others, with the exception of his own. Therefore, when it is being judged objectively, it is indisputably preferred to all the rest.

CHAPTER 13 – ON THE GENERATION OF GOD'S SON IN ETERNITY

All life generates its offspring internally before doing so externally, and the more superior a life is, the more deeply within itself is the offspring it generates.[186] Thus vegetative life, so in trees as in animals, generates its seed – in one way a tree, in another an animal – within its own body before either casting it out or generating an external tree or animal therefrom. Thus sensitive life, which is superior to vegetative life, through its imagination furnishes in itself an image and an intention for things before moving its limbs and shaping things in external matter; but the first offspring of the imagination, because it is in the soul itself, is for that reason closer to the soul than the offspring of vegetative life, which is not made in the soul, but in the body. Thus rational life, which is above sensitive life, carries within itself the reason not only of things but also of its

---

184 Ricc. *Contr.* 1.12–25.
185 Ricc. *Contr.* 1.35–40; 1.50–1.
186 Cf. Fic. *TP* 11.4 (Allen and Hankins 3.262).

very self before it brings its progeny – as it were – into the light, whether by speaking or acting; the first progeny of reason is closer to the soul than the progeny of the imagination; for the power of reason is reflected back onto its progeny and – through it – back onto itself. This the power of reason achieves by seeking, understanding, and loving itself and its action, something that the imagination does not achieve. Thus angelic life is above rational life; it produces within itself notions of itself and of things by some impulse from God, before bringing them down into the matter of the world; this offspring is even deeper within an angel than reason's offspring is within it because it is neither moved nor changed by individual external objects. For this reason, divine life, because it is the highest and most fruitful of all, generates offspring much more like itself than the rest and generates it within itself before birthing it outside itself. It generates offspring, I repeat, by understanding just as God – by perfectly understanding Himself and everything in Himself – conceives the perfect idea of His entire self and of everything in Himself, which is in fact the complete mirror image of God and the complete exemplar of the world above.[187] This Orpheus called Pallas, who was born from the head of Jupiter alone;[188] this Plato named the son of God the father in his *Letter to Hermias*, in the *Epinomis* he dubbed it *Logos*, namely, "reason" and "word," saying: "The *Logos*, most divine of all, has ordained this visible world."[189] Mercurius Trismegistus often makes mention of the Word and the Son of God and also of the Spirit; Zoroaster also attributes intellectual offspring to God.[190] Indeed, they said what they could, and even that was with the help of God. Only God, however, understands this, and whoever He wishes to reveal it to. The fertility of God, which is infinite good in actuality, extends itself infinitely from eternity in actuality by the nature of a boundless and eternal good; whatever is outside of God is finite. Therefore, God extends Himself in Himself; here certainly the infinite Son is of an infinite Father. It then follows that an offspring of this kind is innermost to God by a much greater degree, I would say, than the notion of an angel is to the angelic mind. In an angel, since "being" is certainly something other than "understanding," the notion that is generated in the process of understanding is something other than the essence of the angel itself; in God, however, because "being" and "understanding" are the same thing, the notion that God begets by understanding Himself

---

187 Cf. Thom. Aq. *C. Gent.* 4.11.1–7 and 1.3.5.
188 Plato, *Epistolae*, 323d.
189 Plato, *Epinomis*, 986c; Fic. *TP* 11.4 (Allen and Hankins 3.250): "ἔταξεν λόγος ὁ πάντων θειότατος ὁρατόν."
190 Corp. Herm. 1.9 (Fic. *Op.*, 1837); Lact. *Inst.* 4.27.20 (*PL* VI.535; Monat, 230–1).

is an image of His very self that is ever the most faithful. The Son is the same in essence as the very one who generates, although by the generation of some wondrous relation He is distinguished from the one who generates. Finally, God, the infinite good, understanding Himself from eternity through an eternal notion of this kind, breathes infinite love from eternity through the same notion in Himself towards Himself.[191] Therefore, theologians call the Father and the Son and the loving Spirit three persons, and they, by their divine nature, are a unity between themselves, such that God is one and simple, but they do differ by some inconceivable relation. Thus we have two extremes in the order of things and two middles: in any given angel – as some posit – one person is angelic in the one nature of its species, and likewise for the opposite. In any given pregnant woman, however, there are more persons in more natures and vice versa. In any given animal there are more natures in one person, but in God there are more persons in one nature. I have said enough of this for now, but never really enough. Attaining sufficiency in this contemplation is not to be sought from philosophers but from those heroic leaders of the Christians and from God.[192] For Isaiah rightly says: "What the eye hath not seen, what the ear hath not heard, what hath not entered into the heart of man, God hath revealed to them that love Him."[193]

CHAPTER 14 – THE ORDER OF THE HEAVENS, ANGELS, AND SOULS AROUND THE TRINITY IS LIKE THE ORDER OF THE SPHERES AROUND THE CENTRE

Above the four elements, which are subject to change according to substance and quality, there are the seven heavens of the planets. It is not their substance, but somehow a certain quality or disposition of theirs that is changed. Since their motion is almost erratic, the eighth heaven, whose motion is more orderly, is placed above them. But that heaven has two kinds of motion, that is, from the East to the West and back again, and also at least two qualities, namely, radiance and splendour; therefore, one is raised up from that heaven to the crystalline one, whose motion is simple from the East and whose quality is also simple: radiance. Since, however, its status is superior in motion, and its light is

---

191 Fic. *TP* 11.4 (Allen and Hankins 3.262–4).
192 Cf. Lact. *Inst.* 4.25.3–5 (*PL* 6.524–5; Monat, 204–7).
193 Isa. 64:4; cf. 1 Cor. 2:9.

superior in radiance, thus from this heaven, one is raised to the Empyrean, which is entirely immutable and utterly brilliant. The Empyrean heaven is well suited to the immutability and light of the Trinity; the remaining nine heavens are suited to the nine orders of angels. There are three hierarchies of divine spirits, just as Dionysius the Areopagite sees it, each of which itself contains three orders: each order, as some theologians calculate, contains many legions. They reckon that a legion consists of 6,666 units and that there are as many legions in each order as the legion itself has units; but I agree more with Dionysius when he says that there is such a multitude of those spirits that it exceeds the human capacity to calculate. The one and only essence of God is extended into a threefold number of persons. The number of the three hierarchies and that of the nine angelic orders, just like the number of spiritual spheres, encompasses this number of three persons. The first hierarchy is attributed to the Father, the second to the Son, the third to the Spirit. In the first the Seraphim contemplate the Father in and of Himself, the Cherubim contemplate the Father in as much as He begets the Son, the Thrones contemplate the Father who begets the Spirit with the Son. In the second hierarchy, the Dominions contemplate the Son in and of Himself, the Virtues contemplate the Son who emanates[194] from the Father, and the Powers contemplate the Son who begets the Spirit with the Father. In the third hierarchy, the Principalities contemplate the Spirit in and of itself, the Archangels contemplate the Spirit that comes from the Father and the Son, and the Angels contemplate the Spirit that proceeds from the Son and the Father. Although each, as we have said, observes some things in one manner and others in another, especially God; each, nevertheless, beholds the whole Trinity and everything in it. As Dionysius says, they have yet another difference because the first hierarchy draws its clarity (*liquor*) solely from the Trinity, the second by way of the first, and the third by way of the second and the first. Likewise, the Seraphim examine the order of divine providence in the goodness of God as an end. The Cherubim observe it in the essence of God as a form, and lastly the Thrones observe it in and of itself. The remaining orders now descend to perform works, but the Dominions, like architects, command what the rest carry out. The Virtues are concerned with and move the heavens and, like instruments of God, they cooperate to perform miracles; the Powers ward off the things that seem able to upset the order of divine governance. The rest of the orders descend even further to human

---

194 Here the Latin diverges in a Christologically significant way from the Italian, which has "*nascente*" here instead of "*manentem*."

affairs: the Principalities take care of public affairs, nations, leaders, and magistrates; Archangels direct the divine worship of each and every one and take part in sacred rites; Angels order minor things, and each one attends to an individual as a guardian.[195]

In the same way that there are nine orders of angels, thus the souls of the blessed are separated into nine orders: for, as Plato says in *Timaeus*, each soul ascends to the order and the spirit, just as to its own star, to which it rendered itself similar in its lifetime.[196] Although our souls, while they are in our bodies, produce the fourth hierarchy under the Moon, nevertheless, because of the free movement of their rational nature, they can ascend through all the benign spirits and descend through all the malign ones, especially since they occupy the middle of all things, and therefore contain certain qualities of all things in themselves. Therefore, it happens that the progression of souls is most expansive. The Moon is the boundary of the Elysian confines of life and death, as the Pythagoreans hold; whatever is under the Moon is allotted to death and the dead where there are as many degrees of punishment according to the throngs of malign spirits as there are rewards in the heavens according to the orders of benign spirits. For the Styx flows between the wretched nine times and surrounds them, just as the Elysian Fields nine times embrace the blessed.[197]

CHAPTER 15 – THE GENERATION OF THE SON IN ETERNITY AND HIS MANIFESTATION IN TIME[198]

Since before the beginning of the temporal world, there has been the eternal world, which in fact is the exemplar of this world, the reason and intelligible Word of the architect of the world, the splendour of its glory, and the image (*figura*) of its substance. The Word of this kind is always with God and is God Himself; thereby, divine power was

---

195 Cf. ps.-Dionysius, *Caelestis hierarchia*, 6–7 (*PG* 3.199–212); 8.1 (*PG* 3.237–41); 9.1–2 (*PG* 3.257–60).
196 Plato, *Timaeus*, 41d–42b.
197 Cf. Virgil, *Georgica*, 1.242; 4.480; *Aeneid* 6.439; cf. Fic. *TP* 18.8 (Allen and Hankins 6.135–7) and 16.1 (Allen and Hankins 5.235).
198 Note that this title is a truncated version of the one in Ficino's table of contents, "On the Generation of God's Son in Eternity, and His Manifestation in Time."

speaking with itself from outside of time, and in speaking it impressed not only itself but also everything else onto the world from within; thereby, at some point, the ages were expressed from without as much as everything within the ages. After the mysteries of the prophets, the heavenly spirits – John the Evangelist and Paul the Apostle – poured these divine oracles from heaven onto man. At some point, however, the human race rebelled against God and, without God, was never able to rise again towards God because it had fallen to the lowest depth; but at some point it behooved human minds to rise again, lest God had created in vain that which He had created to follow Him. By the Word of God men had previously been formed, by the same Word they ought to be reformed – and deservingly so, for by the light of the intellectual Word, the darkness of the human intellect must be expelled; the rational animal must be corrected by the reason of God. Therefore, when the times were set by the divine will, God created by the rational Word a man's soul which, in the same moment, He joined to the tender fetus in the womb of a virgin conceiving through the Divine Spirit. Also in the same moment, the Word itself assumed a human nature, and from an immortal soul and a mortal body was made entirely like a man. Thus, from that man and the Word of God, Christ became one, God and man.[199] Thus, infinite goodness, which wants to share itself with everything, then shared itself with all things in a most fitting way when it joined to itself a man, and in him, in the middle rank of things as it were, everything is contained. Then neither did the divine majesty change its abode, since it exists everywhere and always, nor did the divine sublimity lower itself to the human as if through a deficiency, but rather it elevated the human to itself; nor could the infinite light of the divine Sun be corrupted in any way by being joined to a man, but by this joining, man has always been able to be illuminated and perfected; and, just as in the case of man, to grow and to diminish thus concern the body in such a way that they never penetrate to the soul, so too, in the case of Christ, to suffer what is human particularly concerned the man and did not penetrate to the divinity. Christ therefore suffered what is human as a man and wrought what is divine as God.

---

199 Cf. Origen, *De principiis*, 2.6.3 (*PG* 11.211).

CHAPTER 16 – IT IS FITTING FOR GOD TO HAVE JOINED HIMSELF TO MAN

Why was God made man long ago? For man to be made God somehow, at some point. For whosoever desires and strives to be divine by natural instinct can become God in some way; he, however, cannot rise towards God unless at some point God so draws him towards Himself so that he would wish to rise to the extent that He had previously drawn him towards Himself. Let us go over this matter again from a fresh start.

The greatest craftsman ought to produce work that is clearly the greatest; indeed, it is so great that no better thing can be made. So great a thing, therefore, is manifestly what the highest God ought to make. This work is either solely uncreated or created or a composite of both: that first work is in fact not manifest, but its maker is, for it is God alone who is not derived from another. The second kind of work, since it is entirely finite, is an immeasurable distance away from the infinite God. In this distance, surely as much on account of the interval itself as on account of God being infinite, another work can still be made, and likewise another more outstanding work can always be made. Therefore, no simple creation can be that greatest work which we seek, but in this way we are confident to find a work of this kind eventually, provided we can find a single thing that is made both from creator and creation; because of the creation, it is called a work; because of the creator, however, it is called immeasurable. God is able, knows how, and wishes to make a work of this kind. For God is immeasurable Power, Wisdom, and Goodness, therefore at some time or another, a creation ought to have been joined to the Creator. Only the eternal is above the rational soul; only the temporal is below it, but the soul itself is part eternal and also part temporal; it mirrors God in His unity, angels in their intellect, its own species in its reason, beasts in their senses, plants in their nutritive power, and non-living things in their essence.[200] The soul of man, therefore, is everything in a way – as we have argued at greater length in our *Theology* – especially since it is in a body put together from the powers of everything and the most moderate image of heaven.[201] It is appropriate, however, for the whole of creation to be somehow joined to God, the shared leader of all things, and not just joined haphazardly – since God is the highest unity – but indeed from the top down. Therefore, it is fitting that God be united with human nature, in which everything

---

200 Cf. Thom. Aq. *C. Gent.* 4.27.1.
201 Cf. Fic. *TP* 1.2 (Allen and Hankins 1.18–27).

exists. For were He joined to those extremes of created things that are above human nature, a union of this kind would pertain neither to the middle of things nor to the other extremes, and likewise were He joined to those things that are below us. Surely the infinite unity united His works with Him to the highest degree, both to one another, and to itself, since from the beginning He enclosed everything in man, and then He bound man to Himself.

Perhaps on account of those things which we have stated above, the prophet Habakkuk said: "Thy work, O Lord, in the midst of the ages bring it to life; in the midst of the ages thou shalt make it known; when thou art angry, thou wilt remember mercy"[202] because clearly that work is completed in the species at the centre of things, which is made up of both ages, namely, eternity and time. Some also add that the work is completed in the middle of the world's course. For they hold that it is not the world that is completed in ten thousand years, but precisely the world's course, since it was set up for the sake of a still motion, and in this middle of the world's course, God revealed Himself to men so that His coming would be equidistant from the extremes of both ages, lest either the expectation of the future coming be drawn out too long or the memory of the past coming utterly fade away. But God, who governs the times, has beheld the times.

If the property of goodness is to diffuse and to communicate itself, since God is infinite good, He ought to fulfil every means of communication. There seem to be four of these: presence, power, unity of essence, and unity of person. The first is fulfilled in everything, for God is present everywhere. The second is spread through all forms, even the smallest, for every form has some effective power from God, but matter itself does not. The third happens only within God, for the essence of God cannot become the essence of another, otherwise either what is infinite would become finite or what is finite would become infinite. The fourth means of communication cannot happen in things without reason, for a divine union according to personhood is not suited to things that, by nature, entirely lack the awareness and love of God. Also, it does not follow that one person is made from an angel and God. Obviously there is no sufficient remedy for the wretched angels since they are impenitent; for the remaining angels, that ancient possession of divine light suffices for their own blessedness. And this light among the Seraphim somehow becomes a Seraph, also among the Cherubim a Cherub, and likewise among the others, in the same manner as the light of the Sun

---

202 Hab. 3:2.

when it passes through glass of different colours transforms into various colours. But in man, God justly renders a man divine, for just as in natural things, the most excellent of the natural is made from ultimate matter and supreme form, as a rational animal is, so likewise in divine things the divine thing received, most excellent of all, is produced from a supreme and ultimate Spirit, namely, from God, and from the soul of a man. A divine ray poured into man's mind was not enough for him to be awoken (for he deviates from the mind on account of the senses); it is therefore fitting in a specific man, namely, Jesus, for the soul to have been joined to the divine alone in such a way that an abundance of rays overflowed both in His body and into the senses of men.[203]

CHAPTER 17 – OF WHAT KIND IS THE UNION OF GOD AND MAN

Since the union of God and man happened according to the divine person rather than the divine nature, it is not fitting for that reason that the Father and the Spirit be similarly united when the Word is united to man.[204] Although they are suitable by nature, they nevertheless differ in the properties of their persons. Therefore, just as with the Trinity three persons exist in the same nature, so with Christ one person exists in three natures: God, soul, and body, and there man is comparable to God just as the hand is comparable to the soul, or indeed the tongue to the intellect.[205] For God, strictly speaking, does not become the form of a natural man, but man becomes the specific and harmonious instrument of God for carrying out God's specific works most excellently. There are not, however, two persons in Christ, but one: namely, the person of the Word conjoined not to the person of a man, but to His nature. For just as the rational soul exists in its own being, and by its being the body also exists, so too the Son of God exists all the more in the being of His person, and exalts human nature towards it.[206] Accordingly, just as our words are imperceptible when conceived by the mind and only once they are uttered aloud by the voice become perceptible, thus the Word of the divine mind remains invisible from eternity in God but has

---

203 Cf. Thom. Aq. *C. Gent.* 4.54.
204 Thom. Aq. *C. Gent.* 4.39.2–3.
205 Thom. Aq. *C. Gent.* 4.40.13.
206 Thom. Aq. *C. Gent.* 4.41.8.

been made visible through the assumption of a man. Therefore, Christ is the Word, and from eternity the divine mind speaks this Word with and within itself by understanding itself and everything. The divine Spirit had already uttered this Word when it assumed a human body as a voice and conveyed the will of God to whosoever listened. He conveyed the will of God to everyone insofar as they were able to grasp it; He bestows eternal blessedness upon everyone insofar as one were to exert oneself in this short life. Indeed, He handed down many highly celebrated commandments but brought them all together in so few words when He ordered: "Love God with your whole self. Love your fellow man as you love yourself. Do not do to others what you do not wish them to do to you."[207]

CHAPTER 18 – HOW BECOMING IS THE UNION OF GOD AND MAN

For the most part reforming the deformed is no less than simply forming something from scratch; accordingly, being good is no less than simply being. Therefore, it was becoming of God, the maker of all things, to perfect those things that had been imperfect, and, just as He had created all things by the imperceptible Word – for what else are creatures than the result of God's thoughts, like some utterances pronounced aloud? – so it was becoming of God to reform the perceptible through the Word now somehow made perceptible. Since, however, God created everything in a powerful, wise, and benevolent manner, it was thus becoming of Him to restore everything to display His power, wisdom, and benevolence. What is more powerful than to reduce the extremes to one person and to render the lowest as the highest? What is wiser than coupling the first and final reason to wondrously adorn the universe? What is more benevolent than for God, Lord of the universe, to assume the form of a servant for the salvation of His wayward servant? So therefore, when He joined the worldly to the king of the heavens and made the worldly in some way equal to the heavenly, He both demonstrated and made it so that there was nothing deformed in the world, nothing utterly despicable. Moreover, since man had fallen from God the most powerful, the most wise, the most benevolent, he had therefore sunk into imbecility, ignorance, and evil. Because of this fall and because

---

207 Cf. Luke 10:27; Matt. 7:12; Luke 6:31; Gal. 5:14; James 2:8.

man became profane from pious, he was now thoroughly unsuited to imitate divine virtue, to recognize the light, and finally to love goodness. For man, therefore, to ascend again from this ruin towards the sublime, it was most fitting for the sublime God to extend His hand from on high to him, clearly for this reason: to make Himself visible, lovable, and imitable for man. There was no method more suited to this goal than for God to be made man, so that man, who would look to the physical world (*corporalia*) since he was already made with a body (*corporalis*), might now know God more clearly as both physical (*corporalis*) and human, love God more ardently, imitate God more easily and also more diligently, and thus become blessed. Finally, man could not be healed entirely unless he were to recover his innocence of mind, the friendship of God, and his own excellence, which from the beginning had been subject to God alone by nature, nor could man obtain excellence unless his healer were God, to whom alone man is by nature subordinate. Nor could man obtain God's friendship except through some appropriate mediator who could extend a hand to both and somehow be a friend and relative to the extremes of each. There is no such mediator at all, unless it is at the same time God and man, nor could man recover his innocence unless his guilt were forgiven, which justice does not permit to be forgiven without satisfaction. Only God could make satisfaction on behalf of the entire human race. Still neither was it becoming for anyone but man, who had sinned, to suffer, nor was it possible for God. Therefore, it was proper that the human race be rectified through God who had been made man. Hence, excellence could not be secured except through the most excellent healer, nor could friendship be reconciled except through the most friendly mediator, nor could innocence be recovered except through the most sufficient satisfier. But the most excellent healer is God alone, the most friendly mediator is man, and the most sufficient satisfier seems to be Christ in particular, because He is equally God and man. Therefore, what John said was extremely conducive to the healing of man, that the divine Word took on human flesh so that, just as the human race had been created through the eternal Word but had fallen into guilt by abandoning the inspired Word, so through the visible Word it would be redeemed from guilt.[208]

---

208 John 1:1–5.

CHAPTER 19 – CHRIST'S COMING GIVES BLESSEDNESS WITH FAITH, HOPE, LOVE

No one can obtain the blessedness which resides in divine contemplation unless he loves God ardently; we cannot love God ardently unless we hope to be able to attain Him at some point; we cannot hope unless we have a prior belief not only that God exists, but also that at some point we are able to enjoy God. Therefore, God, the Father and healer of men, once assumed humanity in wondrous ways and offered Himself to our senses so that through those senses – which we use all the time and trust very highly – we might be more confident that God exists by seeing His body and His miracles. From this arose faith, the foundation of knowledge. Whoever believes that God had descended into the mass of a body for the sake of healing the human race will hope that he will soon obtain all things, no matter how great, from God. Whoever sees even a fraction of such favours, whoever hopes for even a fraction of them, unless he is utterly insane and ungrateful, cannot not love God. Likewise, once you understand that God had been joined to a soul by some union of person, you ought to hope that the soul can be joined at some point to God by some union of activity, in which the highest blessedness resides. You ought also to desire to cleave closely to God above all else, for God completely poured Himself into the soul and body of man alone. Therefore, because God joined Himself to man without an intermediary, it is proper to remember that our happiness (*felicitas*) dwells in Him, so that we may cleave to God without an intermediary. Also, because friendship exists between equals, as long as you consider God to have made Himself equal to man in some way, you should not deny the friendship God has with you, nor should you forsake your friendship with God. So let men cease, I repeat, let them cease despairing of their divinity at once! It is due to this despair that men overwhelm themselves with mortal concerns. Let them revere themselves as divine, and let them hope that they can ascend to God, since the divine majesty deemed worthy in some way to descend to them. Let them love God with all their hearts, that they may be transformed into Him who miraculously transformed Himself into a man out of His immense love.[209]

---

209 Cf. Matt. 22:37.

CHAPTER 20 – CHRIST'S COMING SERVED TO LIFT THE BURDEN OF SIN

The life of the body is the soul, the life of the soul is God.[210] The order of nature demands that the body be obedient to the soul, and the soul be obedient to God. The order of justice requires that, if the soul becomes discordant with God, by pain of retribution, the body would become discordant with the soul, and the senses with reason. The soul of the first parent rebelled from God, and the body and senses rebelled from Him. The first rebellion was a sin, the second rebellion was the penalty for the sin, and it was sin itself since the penalty detracted him from reason and God. The rebellious complexion and inclination flowed forth from the first parent like some feeling into all those who emanated therefrom like streams from a source. This is the original sin, the origin of all other evils of the body and soul. This is confirmed in the scrolls of the Hebrews, and the divinity of these scrolls is confirmed by their greatest antiquity beyond everything else, by their agreement on nearly all things, by their propagation throughout the world, by their unfailing longevity, concord, majesty, prudence, and miracles. Hence the well-known opinion of the Magi descended from Zoroaster that all the evils of the body derive from the evils of the soul, and a healed soul wards off all other evils. Plato merely hints at this in the *Timaeus*, but states it openly in the *Charmides*.[211]

To get back on topic, a rebellion of this kind, since it detracts from the majesty of the infinite God, made mortals most unfit for infinite blessedness and unable to be guided except by an infinite God. Nevertheless, they had to be given guidance eventually, lest from the start God just ordained them for blessedness in vain. It is through pleasure that sin was committed, and through the opposite of pleasure that pain is to be purged. In some way every human nature once sinned in the man who played the part of everyone; all who are in far more accord with God than the one who was discordant, in some way must once suffer similarly in whoever also plays the part of everyone. But after Adam, the only one who could play the part of everyone was He who had been deeply joined to God, the founder of all things. Therefore, He was at the same time God and man: He was God that He might embrace everyone and could wash away the infinite guilt; He was man, that He

---

210 Fic. *TP* 13.1.4 (Allen and Hankins 3.114–16); 16.7.12 (Allen and Hankins 5.302); *In Charmidem* (Fic. *Op.* 1306).
211 Plato, *Timaeus*, 42a, 43e; *Charmides*, 157b–e.

could suffer for their guilt, and that a man might suffer just as a man had sinned. Thus, the punishment and merit of that man had some sort of infinite power, inasmuch as he had truly been joined to an infinite God, but there had been need for some kind of infinite suffering and merit to utterly wash away the infinite guilt.

CHAPTER 21 – CHRIST FULFILLED THE PERFECT KIND OF INSTRUCTION

Divine providence did not wish to omit any kind of instruction for its sons. The instruction is twofold: through teaching, obviously, and through example.[212] The teaching is perfect, and one cannot rightly doubt this since there is a consensus that such a teaching is rooted in God alone. God the Father, therefore, sent man such an instructor that both was God, lest one would see fit to doubt His teaching, and also man, so that He might properly carry out all of man's duties and complete all of man's labours on behalf of our virtuous God, and by this example to instruct men perfectly towards virtue. Indeed, in matters of education – especially of the moral variety whose proper end lies in action – works are far more inspiring than words. His miracles proved Him to be God so that His teaching might be trusted among those willing to be taught, but His human sufferings proved Him to be a man. Therefore, there appears to be no room left for excuse, unless we want to be excessively obstinate; if we insolently persist in rejecting His teaching as less true, His divinity and miracles cry out in protest; if we insolently persist in rejecting His teaching as harsh beyond measure, that teacher and leader's humanity and labours show that what He bore as a man is possible for man. Finally, because the culmination of sins resides in the fact that we cling excessively to material things (*corporalia*), or we depart from spiritual things, Christ, the teacher of life, by His life and teaching, sent into the world something like a sword and fire, that is, the cleansing power of a purified soul, in order to cut to the quick and burn up all the deadwood of corporeal (*corporalis*) vices.[213] He also freely and willingly bore every single thing that others flee from as if it were evil: vagrancy, hunger, thirst, lack of clothing, disgrace, abuse, floggings, a short life, and a most ignominious, bitter death. Moreover,

---

212 Cf. Lact. *Inst.* 4.12.20 (*PL* 6.482; Monat, 108–11); 4.23.10 (*PL* 6.520; Monat, 194–5).
213 Cf. Lact. *Inst.* 4.24 (*PL* 6.520–3; Monat, 194–205).

100   On the Christian Religion

He fled every single thing that others pursue as if it were good, that He might show us by this reckoning that what we call evil is not truly evil, nor are the things we call good truly good, and that no material things should be thought to be of any value, but rather that whatever is outside of God should be treated like the dream of a meagre shadow.[214] But since He was free from all the things mortals choose as good, surely He alone merited (*meruit*) the only miracles on earth until today, and He deserved (*meruit*) immediately to be thought the highest God.

The Hebrews call their holy men prophets; when the pagans call their great men gods, they understand them to have been already made divine and servants of God; the Mohammadans believe that their king Mohammad, son of Abdalla son of Abdal Muttalib king of Arabia, was certainly merely a man but still a messenger of God, which is also what he calls himself in the Qur'an.[215] He adds that he had been sent by God in force of arms and that Christ had been sent by God with the power of miracles and that God had made Jesus and Mary as a miracle for man.[216] Deservedly (*merito*), by His astounding works, Christ alone merited (*meruit*) what neither many emperors could achieve by contending for it with both threats and rewards, nor could Zoroaster, Pythagoras, Empedocles, Apollonius of Tyana, or many other philosophers achieve through marvellous wisdom and a long life (although Iamblichus the Chalcidian celebrated Pythagoras in a long disputation and indeed Philostratus eloquently celebrated Apollonius, as did Porphyry with his wit, and so did many emperors with whatever favour they could offer).[217]

CHAPTER 22 – CHRIST EXPELLED ERROR, REVEALED THE TRUTH

Before the coming of Christ, many gods were worshipped nearly throughout the entire world. These gods were in fact demons and priests, and were certainly evil, as Oenomaus the philosopher admits: "Who does not see that those who cared nothing for the purification

---

214 Cf. Pindar, *Pythian Odes*, 8.95.
215 Herman of Carinthia, *De generatione Machumet*, in *Machumetis Saracenorum principis Alcoran*, ed. Theodor Bibliander ([Basel]: Iohannes Oporin, 1543), 204–7.
216 Herman of Carinthia, *Doctrina Machumet*, in *Machumetis Saracenorum principis Alcoran*, ed. Bibliander, 194.
217 Iamblichus, *De vita Pythagorica*, 28.145–7.

of souls, those who only focused on worldly things and always demanded worldly things from their worshippers, were evil? They used to order the most obscene and cruel sacrifices be made, and they sowed as much discord as possible by their responses; living tyrants were worshipped everywhere instead of gods, that is, the blessed dead; the souls of men – some intemperate, some unjust – were worshipped. The human race was once oppressed by these most terrible monsters; it was not the armed Hercules, but the unarmed Christ who then snuffed them out when He checked the evil demons' power."[218] Plutarch reports the opinion of barbarians that it was possible for demons of the air to suffer distress and death; he also cites the testimonies of many that during the reign of Tiberius it had been ascertained by definite signs that the great demon Pan and many other demons had clearly cried out then died. Proclus the Platonist even showed that it was possible.[219] We ourselves, however, know that at that very time Christ had entered Limbo and risen from the dead. Plutarch also writes that by his time, oracles, with one or two exceptions, had already gone out across the whole world.[220] Listen to how Porphyry lamented this: "After people started worshipping Jesus," he says, "we could gain nothing worthwhile from the gods." If they are gods, Porphyry, why do they not suppress the power of Jesus with their own strength?[221] But let us hear the great Tertullian speaking thus in front of Roman judges: "Judges, let anyone who we can agree is possessed by a demon be summoned to appear before your court. When he is ordered to speak by any Christian at all, that spirit will truthfully confess itself a demon as much as it will falsely profess itself a god elsewhere. Likewise, let anyone be brought forth from among those who are thought to be enthused by a god: if all the spirits of this kind do not confess themselves to be demons, since they dare not lie to a Christian, spill the blood of that most insolent Christian on the spot! What could be clearer than the fact of this miracle? What is more reliable than this proof? The simplicity of the truth is plain for all to see, its own power stands in its defence.[222] It will leave no room at all for suspicion that it happened by means of magic or some deception of the sort. Yet, all this mastery and power of ours in that matter works solely by the naming of Christ. Thus by both our touch and

---

218 Cfr. Eus. *Prae.* 5.26.4 (*PG* 21.378–9); 5.29 (*PG* 21.386–7); 5.32 (*PG* 21.390).
219 Eus. *Prae.* 5.17.6–9 (*PG* 21.355).
220 Plutarch, *De defectu oraculorum*.
221 Eus. *Prae.* 5.1.9–11 (*PG* 21.311).
222 Tert. *Apol.* 23.4–7 (*PL* 1.413–14).

our breath they also withdraw from bodies at our command, unwilling, lamenting, and visibly ashamed before those present among you. Believe them when they speak the truth about themselves, you who believe them when they lie. No one lies to bring dishonour, but rather to gain honour for themselves.[223] They openly deny that they are gods when Christians compel them to tell the truth, nor do they respond that there is another God but one, whom we ourselves serve."[224] These have hitherto been the words of Tertullian. Lactantius writes that during his time, this lesson was publicly learned every day: whenever the pagans sacrificed to their demons, if someone was present bearing the sign of the cross on their forehead, the soothsayer being consulted could not render a response, nor could the demons depict the future in the entrails of beasts.[225] He says that this was the main reason for the persecution of Christians by wicked kings. For they did not notice that it was the sign of the cross, being more powerful, that was putting the demons to flight, weak as they were.[226] Socrates, Plato, and Varro rightly ridiculed the superstitions of the pagans, but only privately, on account of the mob. At long last, Jesus destroyed the superstitions lest man be destroyed. Shortly before the light of Christ, Greeks and Romans had more and more by the day begun to be corrupted by the infectious impiety of Aristippus and Epicurus. When countless martyrs from everywhere among the nations – some unlearned, some most learned – set aside all fear for their present lives for the sake of the one God and a future life, they provided man the most effective antidote against the venom of Aristippus and Epicurus.[227]

In addition to all this, among the many nations there used to exist the most unjust laws: Persians would come to know their own mothers through the most unspeakable nuptials; Scythians would gorge themselves on human flesh; Carthaginians, and in fact many other men besides would even slit their sons' throats and sacrifice them to demons; the Massageteans and the Decerbices would make sacrifices of their relatives and neighbours and feast upon their flesh once they had grown old; the Bactrians would cast their elderly to dogs raised

---

223 Tert. *Apol.* 23.15–17 (*PL* 1.415).
224 Tert. *Apol.* 23.19; 24.1 (*PL* 1.415–16).
225 Cf. Virgil, *Georgica*, 3.491.
226 Lact. *Inst.* 4.27.1–3 (*PL* 6.531–3; Monat, 222–5).
227 By referring to an "antidote" for a "venom," Ficino is here making a mocking inversion of the Epicurean concept of the "Tetrapharmakos" or four-fold remedy: "i) God is not to be feared, ii) Death is of no concern, iii) And the good is easily gotten, iv) The terrible easily endured."

for this purpose; the Scythians would bury alive the loved ones of the recently deceased; the Tibarenians were accustomed to throw their living elders headlong from great heights, while the Hircanians and Caspians would throw them to carrion birds and dogs (the former cast away the still living while the latter, the dead). Formerly, they would do these and a great many things of the same sort with the utmost religious care; this most savage pestilence was then from everywhere banished solely by the preaching of Christ and His disciples. This also had the result that fewer people are now possessed by demons or commit suicide.[228]

Before the coming of Christ, the Jews would commonly touch upon only the surface of the law of Moses and their prophets, but Christ and His disciples taught in the most perfect way possible how to penetrate to the profound meanings of the divine mind with the eyes of a Lynceus – nay, with divine eyes – as even Philo the Jew attests when he praises the acumen and the holiness of the Christians in his discussion on contemplation. The ancient theology (*prisca theologia*) of the pagans, in which Zoroaster, Mercurius, Orpheus, Aglaophemus, and Pythagoras are in agreement, is entirely contained in the volumes of our Plato.[229] In his *Epistles*, Plato prophesies that mysteries of this sort could at long last be made manifest to man after many centuries, as indeed so happened; for in the era of Philo and Numenius, the mind of the ancient theologians first began to be understood in the pages of the Platonists (that is, immediately after the speeches and writings of the apostles and the disciples of the apostles).[230] The Platonists used the divine light of the Christians for interpreting the divine Plato; hence the fact that, as Basil the Great and Augustine show, the Platonists appropriated for themselves the mysteries of John the Evangelist.[231] I have certainly discovered for myself that the principal mysteries of Numenius, Philo, Plotinus, Iamblichus, and Proclus had been taken from John, Paul, Hierotheus, and Dionysius the Areopagite. For whatever grand thing the former had to say about the divine mind, the angels, and everything else regarding theology, they obviously appropriated from the latter.

---

228 Eus. *Prae.* 1.4.7 (*PG* 21.39); 4.16.8 (*PG* 21.271).
229 Fic. *In Phil.* (Fic. *Op.* 1233).
230 Plato, *Epistolae*, 314a.
231 Basil of Caesarea, *Homilia* 16 (*PG* 31.472); Augustine, *Confessiones*, 7.9.13.

CHAPTER 23 – CHRIST IS THE IDEA AND EXEMPLAR OF VIRTUES

What else was Christ except a kind of book of morality, indeed a living book of divine philosophy sent down from heaven and the divine idea of virtues itself made manifest to the eyes of man? To Him, therefore, to Him, I repeat, let us all turn our eyes and minds: He who once suddenly turned ignorant little men into sages will teach us true wisdom; He who possessed nothing of His own, and granted what is His to God and man, will teach us true justice, for to God He granted reverence for the father and reverence for more than the father; to man, however, He granted the goodwill and care for brothers; He who desired nothing for its greatness on earth, who feared nothing for its difficulty will teach us greatness of spirit and the most outstanding bravery; He in whom scarcely the first motions of the soul appeared, and those in fact were relaxed and becoming, will teach us an unrivalled moderation; He will teach us the incredible meekness with which we may utterly banish pride, the plague of human society. For who is meeker than He who made Himself equal to the lowliest beings despite being the highest of all? He who lived not only for Himself but also for the entire human race, and who died willingly in order to redeem the rest of us from death, will teach the most ardent love for all men. He who often applied Himself to remedying the errors and ills of man, and most often to contemplating the divine will teach us the most perfect rule of both contemplation and action. We have from the beginning as witnesses of His life many writers and the most authoritative ones of all at that, as well as the greatest number of imitators, and finally the whole world. Christ showed Himself openly to men for a brief time (for it was not fitting for Him to go beyond that), and that was enough for us. He performed so many miracles that John says that if they were written out one by one, not even the world itself could contain the books. We learn from our tradition that over fourteen men had written about His life as being the most celebrated and admired by everyone. However, only those writers who wrote not with a human, but a divine hand – such as Matthew, Mark, Luke, and John did – are used or ever were. Matthew wrote in Hebrew, and Jerome says that, in his time, Matthew's Hebrew text was extant in Pamphilus's library. Jerome also says that the Nazarenes, who were using this scroll in Bersabe and throughout Syria, provided him the opportunity of transcribing it.[232] Even Panthenus the Stoic, a martyr of Christ, when he had penetrated all the way into the heart of India preaching the words of Christ,

---

232 Jerome, *De viris illustribus*, 3.2 (*PL* 23.643–5).

discovered there not only the seeds of the Apostle Bartholomew, but also brought with himself the Hebrew gospel of Matthew. So says Eusebius.[233] The remaining three, who are called evangelists, wrote in Greek. The Christians of antiquity also read the gospel of a fifth evangelist, which was called *According to the Hebrews*. Ignatius and Origen submitted this gospel to sufficient tests, and Jerome translated it from Hebrew into Greek and Latin. So says Jerome.[234] The truth of Christianity especially shines forth in the fact that from the very beginning the assembly of Christians did not admit just any writer rashly, but the holy, simple, sober, and most select writers, who were truly from among the top in value, some of whom had heard Christ firsthand, others His disciples. These writers, even if they wrote in different languages, in different times, and in different places, and even if they did not see each other's writings – except perhaps John – all nevertheless corroborated each other's work throughout, with the truth as their guide. Sometimes, something like a dissonant dissimilarity appears between them concerning minor details, but indeed never a contradiction. From such dissimilarity, one can simply see that each had composed his history removed from one another, but none of them had done so removed from the truth; in fact, they preached so many and such great miracles so openly for so many years in Judea and Jerusalem, where they are said to have been performed, that everyone agrees they preached the highest truth. How in the world could they have continued in such a difficult task among the most learned of men by asserting falsehoods? How could they have come to be admired if they had conveyed conflicting accounts? Indeed, the kingdom of Christ would have suddenly dissolved had those leaders actually disagreed with one another. The evangelists and the apostles said many things in common regarding the life and teaching of Christ, and each one brought something unique to the table: if, on the one hand, any of them had provided the entire story, the rest would seem superfluous; if, on the other hand, each had only provided something novel, the continuity and the authority of the story would be lost. To be sure, what is amazing is that the writings of Matthew, Mark, Luke, John, Peter, Paul, James, and Jude are such that there are numerous witnesses present at the start of it all, and, if we should listen to all these witnesses, we would – I reckon – hear nothing unnecessarily or inappropriately repeated.

---

233 Eus. *Hist.* 5.10.3 (*PG* 20.455).
234 Jerome, *De viris illustribus*, 2.11 (*PL* 23.642).

CHAPTER 24 – THE AUTHORITY OF THE SIBYLS

The philosopher Varro, in his books *Of Divine Things*, diligently records the names, times, and homelands of the ten Sibyls, and to this end he cites many writers as witnesses. He affirms, moreover, that the Sibylline books had been laid away by the Romans in a shrine, where they were guarded by fifteen men (*quindecim viri*) and specific priests designated for this purpose. Livy adds that during Tarquin's reign, the Romans had restored from the verses of the other Sibyls the six books of the Cumaean Sibyl that some old hag had burned.[235] These six books they had collected with the greatest care by sending delegates out into the world.[236] Therefore, three books from among them then were from the Cumaean Sibyl, the rest from the others. But these books were distinguished by having no title or name of their own, except that of the Erythraean Sibyl, who inserted her own name into a poem. The Romans would consult these poems on matters of greatest import, nor was it permitted for just anybody to look at them. I nevertheless reckon that Maro had been granted permission to read those books under Augustus, and Lactantius under Constantine, because of their close personal relationships.[237] At times, the emperor and the books' caretakers would yield and so granted this permission to some other great learned men. Therefore, it was possible for Lactantius, a close friend of Constantine, to understand the Sibyls' testimonies that he cites about Christ from their books, since at the time the books were still extant since Rome had not yet been sacked by anyone. He wrote about those things to Constantine; it is therefore unthinkable that he was lying either to that learned emperor or to other erudite men, then as numerous in Italy as they were in Greece – and a good many were still seriously misrepresenting Christian writers, even in the smallest matters.[238] Does Virgil not read in the same books of the Sibyls what the prophets and the evangelists say of Christ? And, most importantly, did Virgil not understand that the predictions in the Cumaean Sibyl's text, as I imagine, would come true in the Sibyl's own times, when Jesus was born, although Virgil, to fawn over Pollio, twists the Sibyl's oracles to be about his newborn son named Saloninus, none of which at all could have corresponded with Saloninus, who died as a boy and accomplished

---

235 Ficino is mistaken about his source here since this story is not contained in Livy; rather, it comes from Lactantius quoting Varro: Lact. *Inst.* 1.6 (*PL* 6.144–7); cf. Aulus Gellius, *Noctes Atticae*, 1.19.
236 Augustine, *De civitate Dei*, 18.23.1 (*PL* 41.579; Dombart and Kalb, 613).
237 Maro = P. Vergilius Maro.
238 Cf. Augustine, *De civitate Dei*, 18.23.2 (*PL* 41.579–80; Dombart and Kalb, 614).

On the Christian Religion   107

nothing? Whatever one reads in it does, however, correspond with Jesus, who was born in those times. But what does Virgil see in it? In such a time as that one clearly was, it would happen that in the final age of waiting some great order of the ages would be born anew, extending down from eternity (meaning hereafter from the eternal Father the eternal Son would also be born at the time when a virgin would blossom) the Golden Age would return (meaning the Son would come forth from the virgin and the age of true and blessed teaching would flourish) and "a new child (*progenies*) would be sent down from high heaven."[239] These words explain the previous ones: we know that the Sibyl had foretold that the boy would be born of a virgin, since she added that it was a new generation (*progenies*), meaning born in a new way, and setting out not from earth but from heaven – that is, from God, in whom he existed from eternity. Virgil's poem itself goes like this:

> *The last age of the Cumaean song has already come*
> *The great order of ages is being born anew.*
> *The Virgin now returns, the reign of Saturn returns,*
> *Now a new child* (progenies) *is being sent down from high heaven.*[240]

For my part, I reckon that Virgil stitched together poems of this sort from the Sibyl's words, such as I recounted a little earlier. Virgil adds to what I imagine he had read in the Sibyl, that is, that the Iron Age would revert to a Golden Age with the birth of the child, and that there would then be the glory of the age. All of this seems to pertain to the purification of souls and the teaching of Christ. And the traces of that ancient deceit (*prisca fraus*) would be wiped clean. He had then read in the Sibyl's writings, I believe, that the original guilt we received in the beginning by the Devil's deceit ought to be expunged. Although he himself did not understand these kinds of mysteries at all, he nevertheless combined the words of the Sibyl in his poem in such a way that they seemed to put forward a different sense. Maro appended what sort of child (*progenies*) this would be:

> *He will receive the life of the gods, and he will see heroes*
> *mixed with gods, and he too will be seen by them.*
> *He will rule a world made peaceful by his father's virtues.*[241]

---

239   Virgil, *Eclogae,* 4.7.
240   Virgil, *Eclogae,* 4.4–7; cf. Augustine, *De civitate Dei,* 10.27 (*PL* 41.304–6; Dombart and Kalb, 301–3).
241   Virgil, *Eclogae,* 4.15–17.

It seems that Virgil had read there that that child would be God born of God, soon to govern and judge the entire world by the virtue of His father, God, and nothing divine would be hidden from Him, and He would have all the angels as His attendants. The poet adds that at the same time, the serpent would die along with the treacherous toxic plant, and later he adds: "Few traces of the earliest deceit would still survive."[242] What Virgil meant when he wrote this I do not know; for our purposes, it is enough that he had it on the authority of the Sibyl, whom he did not at all understand, that the serpent – that is, an evil demon – would be undone by the work of the child, and that the toxic and treacherous plant would be tamed – that is, the power of demons which beguiled men since before Christ with a false religion presented as true and which had deceived them from the beginning in the appearance of the serpent and with the inducement of a certain plant. The demon has still been tempting souls after Christ, although he has not been achieving as much as before, and for this reason it has been said that few traces of the deceit would survive. Porphyry also acknowledges that mortals had been in the habit of being induced to crimes and false religions by malign demons, and this he argued carefully in his book *On Abstinence*. In addition, Virgil thus addresses the child (*progenies*):

Take up your great honours, for the time is nigh
dear offspring of the gods, great germ of Jove.[243]

I believe the poet had it on the authority of the Cumaean Sibyl that this most awaited man would be the offspring of God, not of a man, and – on which nothing more can be said – that it would be the great germ of God, that is, the eternal offspring of God and the extension of God all the way to temporal matters and perception by which the kingdom of God – that is, the number of the blessed – would grow. I know that Maro was so prudent and moderate that I cannot think that he would have used so great a hyperbole for the infant son of the private citizen Pollio, unless he had drawn some such extraordinarily remarkable things from the Sibylline songs; the Sibyl also would not at all have made such marvellous pronouncements about

---

242 Virgil, *Eclogae*, 4.31.
243 Virgil, *Eclogae*, 4.48–9.
244 Virgil, *Eclogae*, 4.50–2.

a simple man who was not a god. But hear how over the top a hyperbole Virgil adds:

See the world tottering under the weight of its vault:
the lands, the sea's expanse, and the boundless heaven;
See how all things rejoice at the age to come.[244]

Perhaps the Sibyl had written that the offspring of God would be honoured by the elements and the heavens; the sky honoured Jesus with an eclipse, the air and fire honoured Him with a shining comet, the water obeyed His commands and supported His feet, and the earth honoured Him with a quake when He was crucified during the reign of Tiberius.

Finally, the poet, though not knowing what he demands, cries out: "O may the final chapter of my life last so long."[245] Perhaps the Sibyl hoped for what the prophets also hoped for: to live just long enough to see the day of Christ before dying, as Simeon cried out after he had long held out hope and had reached a ripe old age: "Now thou dost dismiss thy servant, O Lord, according to thy word in peace because my eyes have seen thy salvation," and so on.[246]

CHAPTER 25 – THE SIBYLS' TESTIMONIES ABOUT CHRIST

As we have said above, the Roman Senate kept the Sibylline books. Lactantius, a close friend of the emperor Constantine, read certain things obviously pertaining to Christ the son of God in those books: firstly, the utterance of the Erythraean Sibyl, when she proclaimed that God is the nourisher and creator of all, who distributed His sweet Spirit to everything and made it the foremost of all the gods; similarly, she says: "God gave it to faithful men to be honoured"; and another Sibyl commanded that this Spirit ought to be known when she said: "Know that your God is the one who is the Son of God."[247] In the *Psalms* of David, one reads the following: "The Lord said to my Lord: Sit thou at my right hand."[248] Likewise: "From the womb before the day star I begot thee."[249] Likewise: "The

---

245 Virgil, *Eclogae*, 4.53.
246 Luke 2:29–30.
247 Cf. Lact. *Inst.* 4.6.5 (*PL* 6.462; Monat, 64–5).
248 Ps. 110:1 (Vulg. Ps. 109:1).
249 Ps. 110:3 (Vulg. Ps. 109:3).

Lord hath said to me: Thou art my son, this day have I begotten thee";[250] and in the Proverbs of Solomon: "The Lord made me in the beginning of His ways by His works, before the ages; He laid my foundation in the beginning, before making the earth."[251] And a little later: "When He prepared the heavens, I was with Him," and so on.[252] In addition, Lactantius compiled the following on the works and death of Christ from the Sibylline books: "There will be a resurrection of the dead, a swift sprint of the lame, the deaf will hear, the blind will see, the unspeaking will speak";[253] which Isaiah also sang: "Strengthen ye the feeble hands, and confirm the weak knees. You who are fainthearted do not fear, do not dread, our Lord will render judgment; He Himself will come and save us. Then shall the eyes of the blind be opened, and the ears of the deaf shall hear, then the lame man shall leap like a stag and the tongue of the dumb will be free, for water is broken out in the desert and a river in the land for the thirsty," which signifies the time of baptism.[254]

Still let us follow what Lactantius compiled from the Sibyls: "He will simultaneously satisfy the hunger of five thousand men in the wilderness with five loaves and two fish, and while picking up the leftovers, He will fill twelve baskets for the hope of many";[255] He will restrain the winds with a word; He will lay flat the raging sea by treading on it with the feet of peace and with faith";[256] "He will walk upon the waves, He will banish the illnesses of man. He will bring the dead to life, He will shield many from pain, doing everything with a word, curing every illness";[257] "wretched, disgraced, hideous to bring hope to the wretched";[258] "He will come into the iniquitous hands of unbelievers, and they will strike God with polluted hands, and they will spew forth venomous spit from an impure mouth. He will simply give His holy back to the blows";[259] "and He will remain silent while receiving blows, lest anyone discover what the word was or how He came to speak with the dead. And He will be crowned with a crown of thorns";[260] "but they gave

---

250 Ps. 2:7.
251 Prov. 8:22; cf. Lact. *Inst.* 4.6.6 (*PL* 6.462; Monat, 66–7).
252 Prov. 8:27.
253 Lact. *Inst.* 4.15.15 (*PL* 6. 492–3; Monat, 136–7).
254 Isa. 35:3–6.
255 Lact. *Inst.* 4.15.18 (*PL* 6.493; Monat, 138–9).
256 Lact. *Inst.* 4.15.24 (*PL* 6.494; Monat, 140–1).
257 Lact. *Inst.* 4.15.25 (*PL* 6.494; Monat, 140–1).
258 Lact. *Inst.* 4.16.17 (*PL* 6.498; Monat, 150–3).
259 Lact. *Inst.* 4.18.15 (*PL* 6.506; Monat, 166–7).

Him gall for food and vinegar for drink. They will show this table of inhospitality";[261] "for you, foolish nation, did not understand your God when He was toying with mortals' minds, but you crowned your God with thorns and mixed a drink of horrid gall";[262] "the veil of the temple will be split and there will be night at midday, excessively dark for three hours";[263] "and the fate of death will end. After undergoing a slumber of three days and then returning from the dead, He will come back into the light, after first showing the beginning of the resurrection to those who are called";[264] "when what I have said is accomplished, every law will be fulfilled in Him."[265] Likewise, the Sibyl says elsewhere: "There will be a blessed race of heavenly Jews,"[266] that is to say, through the excellence of Christ, for whose sake many Jews, cleaving closely to Him, became divine above the others. The Erythraean Sibyl added: "They will say the Sibyl to be mad and mendacious, but once everything has happened, then they will remember me, and no longer will anyone say me to be the mendacious prophetess of the great God."[267] Aurelius Augustine cites many songs of the Erythraean Sibyl translated into the Latin language, which he saw in Greek in the writings of the proconsul Flaccianus, a man most distinguished by his teaching. In their chapter headings, the order of the letters was such that these words were read in them: "Jesus Christ, Son of God, saviour."[268] In these songs, the resurrection of bodies, the change of ages, the coming of God in judgment, the eternal rewards and punishments for men are described.[269] One also reads such things in the writings of Mercurius Trismegistus. Plato too, when asked how long one ought to remain in his precepts, is reported to have answered: "Until someone more sacred should appear on earth, to open the source of truth to all, and at last for all to follow."[270]

---

260 Augustine, *De civitate Dei*, 18.23 (*PL* 41.580–1; Dombart and Kalb, 615); cf. Lact. *Inst.* 4.18.18 (*PL* 6.507; Monat, 168–9).
261 Cf. Lact. *Inst.* 4.18.17 (*PL* 6.506; Monat, 168–9).
262 Lact. *Inst.* 4.18.20 (*PL* 6.507; Monat, 168–9).
263 Lact. *Inst.* 4.19.5 (*PL* 6.511; Monat, 176–7).
264 Lact. *Inst.* 4.19.10 (*PL* 6.513; Monat, 178–9).
265 Lact. *Inst.* 4.17.4 (*PL* 6.499; Monat, 152–5).
266 Lact. *Inst.* 4.20.11 (*PL* 6.516; Monat, 182–5).
267 Lact. *Inst.* 4.15.29 (*PL* 6.495; Monat, 142–3).
268 I.e., ΙΗΣΟΥΣ ΧΡΙΣΤΟΣ ΘΕΟΥ ΥΙΟΣ ΣΩΤΗΡ.
269 Augustine, *De civitate Dei*, 18.23.1 (*PL* 41.579–80; Dombart and Kalb, 613–14).
270 Fic. *Op.*, *Epist.* 4.19, 769–70 (*LSE* 3.45–6); *Epist.* 8.7, 867 (*LSE* 7.11).

CHAPTER 26 – ON THE PROPHETS' AUTHORITY, THE OLD TESTAMENT'S NOBILITY, AND THE NEW TESTAMENT'S SUPERIORITY

Dionysius the Areopagite writes to the learned Polycarp that the Persians, the Babylonians, and the Egyptians wrote down in their annals that they worshipped miracles in their rites, as if they too were divine, and they worshipped the portents that are done by God, as the Hebrews recounted regarding the position and regression of the heavenly bodies in their own annals.[271] Plato did not remain silent about the regression of the Sun, the flooding of water, or the devastation of fire. Many pagans are cited as witnesses to these things by Josephus, Aristobulus, Tertullian, and Eusebius: in particular, Berossus the Chaldean, Manetho[272] the Egyptian, Hiram the Phoenician, king of Tyre,[273] Ptolemy the Mendesian, Menander of Ephesus, Demetrius of Phalerum, King Juba, Thallus, Apion, Nicolaus Molus of Damascus,[274] Hesiod, Hecataeus, Hellanicus, Acusilaus, Ephorus, Theophilus, Mnaseas,[275] Aristophanes, Hermogenes, Euhemerus, Comon, Zopyrion,[276] Abydenus, Hestiaeus, Sibyl, Eupolemon, Alexander, Artapanus, Molon, Theodorus, Philo the Pagan, Aristaeus, Ezekiel, Timocharis, Polyhistor, Numenius, Choerilus, Sachoniato, Africanus, Alphaeus, Megasthenes.[277] Each one of them confirmed nearly each and every detail, and everyone certainly confirmed all that pertains to an antiquity that precedes everything else: the wondrous deeds, the greatest teaching of the Hebrews, and the miracles of the Bible. From all this, it is evident that Clement of Alexandria, Atticus the Platonist, Eusebius, and Aristobulus prove that the pagans, if they had any eminent teachings or mysteries at all, they obviously appropriated them from the Jews, but what is contained in their writings in the form of simple history they had merely translated into poetic tales.[278] The ruin of Phaethon and the story of Deucalion make this clear, and so too does the multitude of other such tales. Plato imitated the Jews to such an extent that Numenius the Pythagorean

---

271 Ps.-Dionysius, *Epistulae*, 7 (PG 3.1081).
272 Latin: Manetus (see page 40 and note 80 above).
273 Latin: Hieronymus Phenicis, Tirii rex.
274 Latin: Nicolaus Molus Damascenus; Ficino conflates two people from Eusebius: Nicolaus of Damascus and the poorly attested Molus.
275 Latin: Manasses.
276 Latin: Zophirus (see page 40 and note 80 above).
277 Tert. *Apol.* 19.6 (PL 1.445); Eus. *Prae.* 9.11, 13 (PG 21.697, 701).
278 Cf. Eus. *Prae.* 10.1–2 (PG 21.767–72).

said that Plato was nothing other than a Moses speaking in the Attic tongue.[279] He adds in his book *On the Good* that Pythagoras too had followed Jewish teachings. Plato in the *Epinomis* says that the sciences were introduced by a barbarian who first discovered these teachings; afterward, Plato adds, everything flowed from the Egyptians and the Syrians.[280] In fact, writers always held that Judea was partly in Syria, which part Pliny called "Galilee," and the earliest writers also called another part of it "Phoenicia," as Eusebius shows.[281] Proclus the Platonist also venerates the Syrian and Phoenician theology above others. Pliny says that the Phoenicians had been the inventors of the alphabet and astrology.[282] Those who praise the Chaldeans strike me as also extolling the Jews, since they too have been named Chaldeans, as Lactantius shows. As I see it, it is for this reason that Orpheus said that God had been known only to a certain Chaldean, signifying Enoch or Abraham or Moses. The Platonists posit that Zoroaster is signified by Orpheus.[283] This man, moreover, as Didymus posits in his commentaries on *Genesis*, was the son of Ham, son of Noah, and was called Chanaham by the Hebrews.[284] As Eusebius demonstrates, he was still alive at the time of Abraham. We ought to remember that the endowments and merits of the Jews could easily have passed over to the Egyptians, for they were neighbours and had always commingled. Alexander and Eupolemon write that Abraham had been the most distinguished man of all in his holiness and wisdom, that he first taught astrology to the Chaldeans, then to the Phoenicians, then finally to the Egyptian priests; it is customary for them to say that they received astrology from the successors of Enoch, who invented it and was named Atlas.[285] Julius Firmicus the astronomer calls Abraham divine because of his wondrous wisdom;[286] whatever things are said of Mercurius Trismegistus, Artapanus shows they had been present in Moses and done by Moses, and that he himself was Mercurius, and that he was also called Musaeus.[287] But since the teaching of the pagans was strengthened by Moses, no one will be discouraged who hears Porphyry saying, on the basis of the evidence of

---

279 Eus. *Prae.* 9.6.6–9 (*PG* 21.694).
280 Eus. *Prae.* 10.4.20–1 (*PG* 21.786); cf. Plato, *Epinomis*, 986a–7a.
281 Eus. *Prae.* 10.5 (*PG* 21.787).
282 Pliny, *Naturalis historia*, 7.192.
283 Eus. *Prae.* 13.12.5 (*PG* 21.1098–102); *Orph. frg.* 246–7 Kern.
284 Cf. ps.-Clement, *Recognitiones*, 4.27.1–4 42–4 (*PG* 1.1326).
285 Cf. Eus. *Prae.* 9.10.3 (*PG* 21.695–8).
286 Iulius Firmicus Maternus, *Mathesis*, 4.17.2.
287 Eus. *Prae.* 9.27.3 (*PG* 21.727–30).

the elder Sachoniato, that Moses had lived fifteen hundred years before the first Greek philosophers. In the same Porphyry's book *On Responses*, he cites an oracle of Apollo where it is stated that the Hebrew people – illustrious and exceedingly holy beyond all others – knew, received, and transmitted true wisdom, the best worship of God, and the blessed life.[288] Moreover, in his book *On Abstinence*, he lavishes some certain devotees and philosophers of the Jews, whom they call Essenes, with such words of praise that he held them up above all others as prophets, saints, and divine.[289] To the same end, he employs the testimony of the peripatetic Theophrastus, who says the Jews assiduously observe fasting and prayer and that the Jews of old were philosophers by nature. This claim was not without merit, for the Sibylline books called the race of the Jews celestial and blessed.[290] The peripatetic Clearchus writes that Aristotle was a Jew, and in India the Calami philosophers were also Jewish;[291] in addition, Megasthenes claimed that the Brahmin philosophers of India had descended from Jews;[292] Ambrose, if I recall correctly, showed that Pythagoras was born of a Jewish father.[293]

I am failing to mention that Strabo, Justin, Pliny, Pompeius Trogus, and Cornelius Tacitus could not remain silent about the antiquity and wisdom of the Jews.[294] Drawing on the opinion of Pompeius Trogus, Justin asserts – especially among the many things he says about the excellence of the Jews – that Abraham and Israel and Moses and Aaron, the son of Moses, reigned in Syria, and amazingly their wealth, once coupled with justice and their religion, increased greatly. Justin recounts the history of Joseph, son of Israel almost as the Bible does: his brothers sold him; he became most dear to a king of the Egyptians, inasmuch as he held the most wisdom in matters of portents and was the foremost interpreter of dreams, and there was nothing he did not know about human and divine law, and he openly provided so many responses to testing that his responses seemed to be given by God, not by a man. He says that Moses was the son of Joseph, similar to his father in virtue and wisdom, but fairer in appearance, and that he had miraculously led his people out of Egypt to their homeland.[295]

---

288 Eus. *Prae.* 9.10.1–2 (*PG* 21.695–8).
289 Eus. *Prae.* 9.3 (*PG* 21.682).
290 Eus. *Prae.* 9.2 (*PG* 21.682).
291 Eus. *Prae.* 9.5.6 (*PG* 21.691).
292 Eus. *Prae.* 9.6.5 (*PG* 21.694).
293 Ambrose, *Epistulae*, 6 [28].6 (*PL* 16.902).
294 Strabo, *Geographica*, 16.2.34–8; Tacitus, *Historiae*, 5.110.
295 Justin, *Epitome*, 36.2.

The antiquity of the Jews, then, whose writings were not held in contempt by the pagans, but had actually been appropriated by them, is not to be regarded as some small matter. From what Aristobulus provides, we gather that the books of Moses had been translated into Greek before Alexander and before the Persian Empire, and the entire Bible was translated during the reign of Ptolemy Philadelphus; as Aristaeus attests (he was present at the time), the peripatetic Demetrius of Phalerum persuaded the king to make this translation.[296] In a letter to the king, he says that he had read some of the Jews' scrolls that had been translated long ago, scrolls of surely such a wondrous character that it seemed as if only the laws sanctioned by the Jews were perfect and divine. Hecataeus of Abdera affirms the same regarding this law.[297]

Why did Ptolemy pay for the translation with nigh countless expenditures? Why did he heap such honour upon the translators and the high priest after they had done the translation? Whoever doubts this need not read any further than Aristaeus and Josephus. Tell me, please, what sort of city do you think Jerusalem was, where the high priest chose the seventy-two most outstanding men, skilled above all in Hebrew and Greek from among a number of other men?[298] Pliny rightly calls Jerusalem the most outstanding of all the cities in the East.[299] The philosophers Aristaeus and Hecataeus recount in abundant detail that the city was the largest and best fortified. Josephus and Eusebius, in fact, show that it had been so large that, when it was besieged by the Romans, over 1,100,000 Jews perished in the city, in addition to the over 90,000 who were sold into slavery.[300]

It was, however, not our purpose to discuss the worldly aspects of that city, but rather its heavenly endowments. If indeed anyone wants to know this, not only should he think on what we have discussed above, but more importantly he should also read and reread their writings; only then will he discover how weighty is the authority of the prophets, whose laws and oracles the Jews, Christians, Mohammadans, and – if I can cut to the chase – all the nations which the earth sustains have believed and obeyed for so many ages. Christ's teaching transcends Moses's as much as the power of purgatory transcends that of the state. In the gospels, Christ runs through every thicket of vice, and those which Moses had pruned in that more uncultivated age (for it was appropriate that such an arrangement be

---

296 Eus. *Prae.* 8.3.3 (*PG* 21.589–91).
297 Cf. Eus. *Prae.* 8.1.6 (*PG* 21.585–7); 8.2–3 (*PG* 21.587–900).
298 Cf. Eus. *Prae.* 8.2 (*PG* 21.587–90); 9.4 (*PG* 12.687–92).
299 Pliny, *Naturalis historia*, 5.15.70.
300 Eus. *Hist.* 3.7.2 (*PG* 20.233–4); cf. Josephus, *De bello Iudaico*, 6.420.

followed) He uproots entirely; for instance, where one considers adultery and murder, one now denounces the adulterer and the murderer, and no longer does one permit that a tooth be pulled for a tooth for the sake of vengeance, but orders that the other cheek be gently offered to the one striking it, and that one is to pay back evil with good. "If thy right eye or hand scandalize thee," He says, "pluck it out and cut it off," that is, put out entirely the first incitement to lust or vengeance.[301] There are also many other examples of the same sort from which it appears that the New Testament is the absolute end of the Old Testament and better than it, insofar as an end goes beyond what is for that end.

CHAPTER 27 – THE PROPHETS' TESTIMONIES ABOUT CHRIST

"Search the scriptures (*scrutamini scripturas*), in which you think to have life everlasting; they are the same that give testimony of me."[302] This is how, in the writings of John against the Jews, our Jesus proclaims these words with utmost confidence, since it is He who knows all the very abundant evidence of His own divinity, which will not fail anyone who asks for it, but He warns them to not so much engage with the rind of the divine oracles as to try to penetrate to their pith.[303] For in the prophet's writings God had predicted: "I will open my mouth in parables. I will utter things hidden from the foundation of the world."[304] Since ancient times, the Jews have had two sets of sacred writings: the one is in Hebrew, written in Hebrew characters; the other is in Chaldean, but written in Hebrew characters. As Rabbi Salomon and Rabbi Moses the Egyptian report, no one has ever dared to contradict the Chaldean text.[305] Among the Jews, therefore, the authority of both is equal, with the same meaning in each, but what is concise or obscure in the one is often more elaborate and clearer in the other. The same principle applies to the holy scriptures among us, which we now have translated

---

301 Matt. 5:21–39.
302 In John 5:39, Jesus uses these words as a rebuttal to his Jewish persecutors. See Paul. *Scrut.* 1.1.1, 1r for the use of this verse to begin his anti-Jewish polemic *Scrutinium Scripturarum*.
303 Cf. Paul. *Scrut.* 2.6.14, 287v for Paul's use of this same metaphor to a different end in the closing words of his *Scrutinium Scripturarum*.
304 Ps. 78:2 (Vulg. Ps. 77:2); Matt. 13:35.
305 Nic. *Quaest.* 3ra–b.

into Greek by the seventy-two Jews and then again by Jerome from Hebrew and Greek into Latin.[306]

But let us now listen to the testimony of the prophets. Jeremiah: "Behold the days come, saith the Lord, and I will raise up to David a just branch, and a king shall reign, and shall be wise, and shall execute judgment and justice in the earth,"[307] and a little later: "And this is the name by which they shall call Him: the Lord our just one."[308] Where in Hebrew it says "David," in Chaldean there is "Messiah"; when it says "Behold the days come," it shows that the Messiah would come not long after Jeremiah because it would certainly be a false statement if He were still to come. Besides, he reveals that the Messiah would be God, for where our translation says "Lord," the Hebrews have the name, the *Tetragrammaton*, that is, the name of four letters which among them is to be venerated more than all other divine names to a degree that is suitable for no creature; Moses the Egyptian discussed this at length in his book *On Guidance*.[309] Hence in the book *Tren*, when asked what the name of the Messiah is, Abba the Jew responds: "His name is Adonay," substituting that for the wondrous Tetragrammaton and adding this statement from Jeremiah: "This is the name by which our just Lord shall call him." But it is not "he shall call (*vocabit*)" but rather "they shall call (*vocabunt*)": this is what the Chaldean translation and the Septuagint's translators taught.[310]

ISAIAH: "A child is born to us, and a son is given to us, and the government is upon his shoulder, and His name will be called: Wonderful, Counsellor, God the Mighty, Father of the World to Come, the Prince of Peace."[311] So says the Hebrew; their Chaldean text has: "An infant is given to us and will receive upon Himself the law in order to search through it, and His name from before will be called: Wonderful, Counsellor, Mighty, God, Everlasting unto the Ages of Ages, Messiah in whose days peace will be multiplied." It showed that the Messiah would be God, His kingdom – a spiritual one and of another world[312] – to come during the reign of Octavian, under whom there was a universal and long-lasting peace. It was the most far-reaching and the happiest monarchy of the world, an ordering of the whole world. What is clear, however, is that these things cannot be used

---

306 Jerome, *Prologus Regum*, in Vulg., 364–5.
307 Jer. 23:5.
308 Jer. 23:6.
309 I.e., *The Guide for the Perplexed*.
310 Paul. *Scrut.* 1.10.6, 163v–164r.
311 Isa. 9:6.
312 Cf. John 18:36.

for king Hezekiah, because Isaiah adds: "His empire shall be multiplied, and there shall be no end of His peace."[313] Likewise: "Upon the throne of David, and upon His kingdom He shall sit, to establish it and strengthen it forever."[314] These things can only pertain to the divine peace of souls and to a spiritual empire; hence Moses the Egyptian in his letter to the Africans regarding the Messiah puts forth six names for the boy who was born, namely, "Wonderful," "Counsellor," "Mighty," "God," "Father of the world to come," "Prince of Peace." But why does the Septuagint translation put only "Angel of great counsel" in place of the six words? Because, when they interpreted the divine pronouncements for the pagan Ptolemy, they often skipped over or modified the things which pertain to the divinity of Christ, lest perhaps Ptolemy think that the Jews consider the Messiah to be a god inasmuch as he is a man, and a god distinct from the highest God, and that there are two gods. But the Hebrew and Chaldean texts, and the translation from Hebrew make clear the divinity of Christ. There are, however, some Jews who are worthy of ridicule: those who in the words of Isaiah above posit that "will call" (*vocabit*) is said rather than "will be called" (*vocabitur*). For the Septuagint translators rendered it as "will be called" and the Chaldean translation shows that "will be called" is how it should be said.[315]

MICAH: "And thou Bethlehem Eufrata, art by no means the least among the thousands of Judah, for out of thee shall He come forth who is to be the ruler in Israel: and His going forth is like from the beginning of the days of eternity."[316] After "shall He come forth," the Chaldean text adds "Messiah": it shows that the Messiah had existed as God from eternity, and as a man who would come forth from Bethlehem. Therefore, whoever offers this explanation concerning king Hezekiah, merely a temporal man, is obviously mad. Rabbi Salomon nevertheless adapts this prophecy to be about a Messiah king.[317]

ZECHARIAH: "Rejoice greatly, O daughter of Zion, shout for joy, O daughter of Jerusalem: behold thy holy" – or "just" – "king comes to thee, saviour: he is poor, riding upon an ass, and its colt. And I will scatter the chariot out of Effraim, and the horse out of Jerusalem, and the bow of war shall be broken, and he shall speak peace to the

---

313 Isa. 9:7.
314 Isa. 9:7; cf. Luke 1:32 and Hier. Sanctaf. *Contr.* 1.2, 27–8.
315 Paul. *Scrut.* 1.10.5, 159v–162r.
316 Mic. 5:2.
317 Paul. *Scrut.* 1.10.7, 166v–167r.

nations, and his power shall be from sea to sea, and from the rivers even to the end of the earth."[318] Rabbi Salomon the Jew, explaining this passage, says that these words cannot be understood except as referring to a Messiah king, and the rest of the Jews agree on this.[319] From this, it is clear that the Messiah would come to Jerusalem as a poor man, riding upon an ass, and his kingdom would not be of this earth, and from Him the salvation of souls rather than of bodies would be through only His holiness and His death: for Zechariah adds: "thou, furthermore, by the blood of thy testament hast sent forth thy prisoners out of the lake," that is ancient men from limbo. But such things are read about Jesus alone, whom Zechariah hinted would be a man and a God when he said that he would be poor, riding upon an ass, unwarlike, making use of no weapons but only the doctrine of peace, and still he calls Him "saviour" and "king reigning everywhere": this is the office of God.[320]

JACOB IN *GENESIS*: "The sceptre shall not be taken away from Judah, nor a ruler from his thigh, till he come that is to be sent, and he shall be the expectation of nations."[321] Where the Hebrew text has "ruler," the Chaldean has "a scribe from the sons of his sons"; where the Hebrew has "till he ...," the Chaldean has "till the Messiah ..."; where it says "and he shall be ..." and so forth, the actual Hebrew has "around him nations will be brought together." It is, however, agreed upon that Jacob is speaking about the coming of the Messiah: for the Chaldean book thus makes it clear and those following this fact, the Jews Moses Gerondi,[322] Sa'adiah,[323] and Kimhi[324] admit that the words are made about the Messiah. It is agreed that Jesus was indeed the Messiah, since He called and saved the pagans just as He did the Jews, and the pagans worshipped Him more, and what is more, since around His time, the Jews' sceptre was taken, and although 1,474 years have now elapsed from then until our own day, the power of the Jews is still not restored, nor is it appropriate for little old grannies to imagine that

---

318 Zech. 9:9–10.
319 Hier. Sanctaf. *Contr.* 1.7, 81.
320 Paul. *Scrut.* 1.3.1, 21r–22r; 1.5.2, 45v; 1.5.10, 62v; cf. Hier. Sanctaf. *Contr.* 1.2, 25–6.
321 Gen. 49:10.
322 I.e., Rabbi Moses ben Nachman (1194–1270), also known as Nachmanides or the *Ramban*, a man who became infamous in Christian circles for his 1263 disputation against the converso Dominican polemicist Pablo Christiani in Barcelona before King James I of Aragon.
323 Latin: Chalcadias; i.e., Rabbi Sa'adiah ben Yosef Gaon (882–942), also known as the *Rasag*.
324 Latin: Chanihis; i.e., Rabbi David Kimhi (1160–1235), also known as the *Radak*.

a Jewish kingdom still survives in Babylon or beyond the Caspian mountains, for all of history cries out in contradiction. Indeed, Moses the Egyptian and all the other teachers of the Hebrews state that it had never been allowed – nor could it ever be allowed – for any Jew to make any judgment in criminal trials outside of the Promised Land. Whoever, therefore, attributes a kingdom to the Jews in exile outside of Judea is obviously mad. Let us hear the prophecy of Hosea: "The children of Israel shall sit many days without king, and without prince, and without sacrifice, and without altar."[325] We see that such is the present condition of the Jews, and all the interpreters of the prophets – Jews as much as Christians – confirm that the prophet had spoken about these times. It is clear that the Jews today lack a legitimate sacrifice because their law only allows Jewish sacrifices that are performed in the Promised Land. No few Jews counter that the sceptre had been taken from Judah a hundred years before Jesus, namely, when power over affairs was transferred to the Maccabean priests, who were not from the tribe of Judah, but of Levi, as Josephus also reports. But Jesus was born in the time of Herod, who is said to have succeeded the Maccabees.[326] To this there is a threefold response: the first is that since the Maccabees were at least of the tribe of Judah by their mother's line, the power of Judah was not entirely overthrown during their reign; the second is that the prophet Jacob did not understand it to be about this tribe or that, but about the entire Jewish people; the third is that, to the extent that all the Jewish teachers agree, there was always among them a certain council of seventy learned men to whose judgment decisions on more serious matters were referred. They called this council "the Sanhedrin," and it was like a sort of senate, both adhering to the living ruler and managing the succession when the ruler died. Moses himself had in fact established it, and during the Babylonian captivity it would assist the Jewish leaders of the Jews in Babylon, and after the return, it would assist the leaders in their homeland. The authority of this council lasted until King Herod, who, according to Josephus, had been born from an Idumean father and an Arab mother and received the kingship over the Jews from the Romans; it was under his rule that Jesus was born. Herod killed all the men from the college, and he destroyed the council, which even the Jews confirm both in the book *The Jerusalem Sanhedrin* and in the *Avodah Zarah*. Therefore, not only was the sceptre then taken away from Judah, but so too was the scribe

---

325 Hosea 3:4.
326 Eus. *Hist*. 1.6.2 (*PG* 20.85–8).

taken from Judah's sons, as the Chaldean text had predicted. For that reason, when Herod, who was a foreigner, assumed the kingship and on top of that killed everyone he could find from the royal line of David, only then was the kingdom of the Jews completely destroyed. In the end, when he destroyed the council, it is thought to be at this moment that the scribe was taken from the sons of Judah.[327] Eusebius writes that the emperors Vespasian and Domitian had ordered all who were from the line of David to be killed in order that there might not be a single remnant of the kingdom of the Jews, for they feared the coming of Christ just as Herod did from the start. Eusebius received this from Hegesippus.[328]

HAGGAI: "The Lord of Hosts saith: 'Yet one little while, and I will move the heaven and the earth, and the sea, and the dry land. And the desired of all nations shall come, great shall be the glory of this last house more than of the first.'"[329] To us today, "one little while" means that the Messiah had already come some time ago; "I will move the heaven," namely, through the eclipse of the passion and also through the star seen by the Magi;[330] "the earth," namely, through the earthquake during the Passion and beforehand through the earthquake that Josephus writes about, which had come to pass during Herod's reign in Judea. It was so terrible that neighbouring nations thought that every town in Judea had collapsed. Were there not then earthquakes happening everywhere, when Jesus was being born, when the whole world was being enrolled in the census by the edict of Caesar Augustus? Everyone had to return to their homeland from wherever they were so that each one could be duly enrolled in the census. Josephus also claims that because of the faction of Judas of Galilee against the Romans, Judea at the time was shaken by numerous massacres.[331] "The sea," namely, when Christ commanded the sea and the winds. When he adds that the Second Temple would be more fortunate than the First, he understands that it would receive the Messiah; for it was more abject and wretched in every other way. Each of these things, however, corresponds with Jesus the Nazarene alone, especially since He came welcomed by the pagans, for He saved more of them than He did of the Jews because the former held Him in higher honour. Let not the Jews await the construction of the third temple under a new Messiah! Haggai called the Second Temple "the last," but

---

327 Paul. *Scrut.* 1.3.2, 22r–27r.
328 Eus. *Hist.* 3.17 (*PG* 20.249–52); 3.20.1–7 (*PG* 20.251–4).
329 Hag. 2:7–8,10; cf. Nic. *Quaest.* 4rb.
330 Eus. *Hist.* 1.8.1 (*PG* 20.99).
331 Eus. *Hist.* 1.5 (*PG* 20.79–86); Luke 2:1–5.

that it would never be restored is attested in what Ammianus Marcellinus the pagan historian writes in his life of the emperor Julian. For, he says, since Julian was eager to amplify the memory of his rule by the greatness of his works, he considered restoring at exorbitant expense in Jerusalem the formerly ostentatious temple that had been stormed in many a murderous battle when Vespasian and Titus laid bitter siege, and he assigned the task to be completed to Alypius of Antioch. And so, while Alypius was boldly pursuing this project, and the governor of the province was helping, fearsome balls of flames continuously burst forth in many onslaughts near the foundations and rendered the place [inaccessible], as they consumed the workers on several occasions. Since the element was quite determinedly driving them back in this way, Alypius left the work unfinished.[332]

MALACHAI: "Behold I send my angel, who will prepare the way before my face, and presently the Lord, whom you seek, and the angel of the testament, whom you desire, shall come to His holy temple. Behold, He cometh, saith the Lord of Hosts, and who supporteth the day of His arrival?"[333] "Behold I send" and again "Behold, He cometh" declares not so much a delay as the Jews think, but a swift coming of the Messiah: He is not, therefore, still yet to come. "Angel, who will prepare the way" means John the Baptist, the herald of Christ; "before my face" shows John the Baptist would preach prior to Christ that Christ Himself is God, for God Himself, who is speaking, calls the face of Christ "His own face." "The angel of the testament" designates the messenger of the New Testament, the Messiah; "and who shall support" designates the uncertainty and the obstinacy of many in the recognition of the Messiah; add to this the ruin of the Jews and the fall of idolatry.[334]

ISAIAH: "The voice of one crying in the desert: Prepare ye the way of the Lord, make straight His paths, every valley shall be filled and every mountain and hill shall be made low, and the crooked shall become straight, and the rough ways plain. And all flesh shall see the salvation of our God." These things are quite similar to the above, and obvious.[335]

---

332 Ficino's text provides a difficult reading for this section: we have translated "onslaughts" using *adsultibus* from Ficino's source (see Ammianus Marcellinus, *Res gestae*, 23.1.2–3), whereas Ficino himself has "and expenses" (*ac sumptibus*); we have also supplied "inaccessible" (*inaccessum*), which Ficino omits, from the same source; cf. Bart. *DCR*, 131–2.
333 Mal. 3:1–2.
334 Hier. Sanctaf. *Contr.* 1.12, 110–11; cf. Paul. *Scrut.* 1.8.16, 119r-v.
335 Isa. 40:35; Ps. 98:2 (Vulg. Ps. 97:2); Hier. Sanctaf. *Contr.* 1.12, 110–11.

DANIEL: "Seventy weeks are shortened" – or "cut down" – "upon thy people, and upon thy holy city, that transgression may be finished, and sin may have an end, and iniquity may be abolished; and everlasting justice may be brought; and vision and prophecy may be fulfilled; and the saint of saints may be anointed."[336] The Jews Moses Gerondi, Jose, David, Saʿadiah,[337] and Abraham explained Daniel in such a way that 490 years would pass from the destruction of the First Temple until the destruction of the Second Temple, and around the end of that period the Messiah would be born.[338] Also, Nicholas of Lyra counted the weeks in such a way that Christ suffered during them; he also demonstrated that this was Daniel's intention.[339] The Jew Barachiah, in his book *On the Order of the World*,[340] explains this verse of Isaiah: "My salvation is near to come, and my justice is to be revealed,"[341] where he states that the part "my justice" means the Messiah about whom Daniel said: "So that everlasting justice may be brought."[342] Similarly, Moses Gerondi, while explaining Daniel's words uttered by the angel that were mentioned above, says this: "Everlasting justice and Holy of Holies, or saint of saints, is none other than the Messiah sanctified from the sons of David." So he says. And rightly did David thus sing: "In His days shall justice spring up,"[343] and Jeremiah: "This is the name that they shall call Him: 'the Lord our just one.'"[344] Certainly Jesus wiped away the calamity of the original transgression and granted the gospel's grace and justice.[345]

But lest anyone be allowed to imagine Daniel's weeks to be sevenfold numbers of months, or centuries, or millennia, or ages, it is important to remember in that book of the Jews, *On the Order of the World*, all their

---

336 Dan. 9:24; Paul. *Scrut.* 1.3.3, 27v.
337 Latin: *Chadias*.
338 Hier. Sanctaf. *Contr.* 1.2, 43–4. It is noteworthy that Ficino uses different names (*Chalchadias* above, *Chadias* here, and *Chahadias* later in this chapter) for the same historical person, Saʿadiah Gaon. Moses of Girondi (Nachmanides) is also usually presented as *Moses Gerundensis*, yet here he appears as *Moses Tyronensis*. These misspellings likely reflect errors arising from Ficino dictating to a scribe, neither of whom had established conventions for the transcription of Hebrew phonemes. Jerome of Santa Fe has "*Sahedias*" for Ficino's "*Chadias*," and "*Zirona*" for Ficino's "*Tyronensis*"; examples such as these suggest that Ficino may not have recognized the identity of all names he was citing.
339 Nic. *Quaest.* 4va.
340 I.e., *Seder Olam*.
341 Isa. 56:1.
342 Paul. *Scrut.* 1.3.3, 28r; Hier. Sanctaf. *Contr.* 1.2, 43–4.
343 Ps. 72:7 (Vulg. Ps. 71:7).
344 Jer. 23:6.
345 Paul. *Scrut.* 1.3.3, 29r.

writers appear to agree on this: that those weeks are only numbers of years. Salomon and Moses Gerondi attest the same, acknowledging in their commentaries on Daniel that Jewish sacrifice had been put to an end in the last of those weeks during the destruction of Jerusalem by the Romans.[346] And Salomon himself asserted that the weeks of Daniel were finished in the destruction of the Second Temple.[347] It was certainly foretold by Daniel either that it would happen in the end of those weeks, or at least after sixty-two weeks. For it was foretold by Daniel thus: "And after seven and sixty-two weeks Christ" – or "chrism," i.e., the anointing of priests – "shall be ruined and judgment will not be in Him. The people shall corrupt the temple and the inner sanctum, with their leader that shall come, and the end of this shall be waste."[348] Certainly, as Josephus attests, after Herod the priests were never appointed following the succession of the race of priests[349] nor for lifetime appointments in accordance with the law of Moses, but rather each and every year, anyone, even the most ignoble, would buy the priesthood from the ruler or from the Romans.[350] Certain men, although they cannot otherwise avoid the true interpretations of the Christians in this passage, say that Daniel is in error here, but he said everything else well throughout; nit-picking pedants of this kind, however, are to be ignored as those who wrestle with themselves and are always in error, here and elsewhere. For there are those among them who dare to overhaul the times of Jesus that everyone knew very well. Josephus disputes such people, where he writes about Jesus's times and where he says that in the twelfth year of Tiberius Caesar, Pontius Pilate had undertaken the procuration of Judea and had remained there for ten consecutive years.[351] The pagan Cornelius Tacitus says Christ was killed by Pontius Pilate, the procurator of Judea during the reign of Tiberius.[352]

Furthermore, to put everything in order, there were many opinions among the Talmudists (i.e., the canonical interpreters of the Jews) regarding the coming of the Messiah. The first is of Jose, who in the book *Seder Olam*[353] (i.e., *On the Order of the World*), explained the end of

---

346 Hier. Sanctaf. *Contr.* 1.2, 43–4.
347 Paul. *Scrut.* 1.3.3, 29v.
348 Dan. 9:26.
349 On the term "race of priests" see Johnson, *Ethnicity and Argument*, 35–6 and page 39 above.
350 Eus. *Hist.* 1.6.9–10 (*PG* 20.87–90); cf. Josephus, *Antiquitates Iudaicae*, 20.1.3; 20.10.1.
351 Eus. *Hist.* 1.9.1–2 (*PG* 20.105–8).
352 Tacitus, *Annales*, 15.44.3.
353 Latin: *Ceder Lophan*.

the seventy weeks in the way we have mentioned above. The second is of Akiba, who, following the calculation of Daniel on the destruction of the Second Temple, reckoned that the Messiah would come, and for that reason believed that a certain foolish and warlike man by the name of Ventozara who claimed himself to be the Messiah and whom a gigantic crowd of Jews followed forty-eight years after the destruction of Jerusalem, as they themselves say.[354] Therefore, almost all those who had assembled in the town of Betar rebelled against the Romans, inasmuch as they had a great deal of trust in the luck and weapons of that famous leader. But the emperor Hadrian, after laying siege to the town, killed Ben-Kozeba along with all of his followers.[355] The Jews relate all these things in the book called *Demai*. Third, the Jews accept the view from the book *Of Ordinary Judges*, which is of no small authority among them.[356] There, it is stated that the world is six thousand years old, two thousand of them for emptiness and void, the same number for the law, and the same again for the Messiah. Furthermore, they say that this had been said by some disciple of Elijah, son of Sarepta, whom Elijah had raised from the dead.[357] But according to the Hebrews' calculation, two thousand years passed from Adam to Abraham, which were the years of emptiness. From this to Jesus the Nazarene, there were also two thousand, which were the years of the law. Therefore, based on the Jewish calculation, the years that come after Jesus seem to have begun with the Messiah, especially since in that book the claim is made that there are four thousand years between the beginning of the world and the Messiah. But according to the

---

354 Ficino's source for this name is Paul. *Scrut.* 1.3.4, 32v which provides "Ventozra"; this form of the name appears to be a corruption in transmission of "Ben Cos(i)ba," a Latinization of Ben-Kozeba, the name given by posterity to Simon ben Kosiba, better known as Simon bar Kokhba. Bar Kokhba is referenced again in the next paragraph as a different person by the name of Bar-Kozeba (Latin: Barcosiba). As Paul of Burgos's own source Ramon Martí notes, the names Ben-Kozeba and Bar-Kozeba, both meaning "son of lies," are applied to Simon ben Kosiba in the Talmud. For his name in the Latin polemical tradition, see Ramon Martí, *Pugio fidei*, 2.4.23 and 3.21.9 (Leipzig: Friedrich Lanckisus, 1687): 325–6 and 907 and Mor Menahem, *The Second Jewish Revolt: the Bar Kokhba War*, 132–136 (Leiden and Boston: Brill, 2016): 403–4 for his name in ancient sources.
355 Paul. *Scrut.* 1.3.4, 32v.
356 *Avodah Zarah* 9a; cf. Pico della Mirandola, *Heptaplus*, 7.4; Douglas Carmichael, "Heptaplus" in *Pico Della Mirandola: On the Dignity of Man*, trans. Charles G. Wallis, Paul J. W. Miller, and Douglas Carmichael (Indianapolis and Cambridge: Hackett Publishing Company, 1965/1998), 160.
357 Nic. *Quaest.* 5rb; cf. 1 Kings 17 (Vulg. 3 Rg. 17) where Elijah raises from the dead the son of a widow in Sarepta.

computation of all the Hebrews, the world today is passing through its 5,234th year. Therefore, the Messiah has already come.[358] The fourth opinion was that of a certain great man they called Rab, who says in a book called *Sanhedrin* that all the temporal boundaries assigned to the coming of the Messiah have already passed and that redemption consists of penitence alone. Although perhaps he was not speaking about Christian penitence, he somehow nevertheless could not keep silent about the truth. At the same time, somebody – relying on the authority of this man and so believing that all temporal boundaries had been passed – shouted: "Woe to the souls of those calculating the temporal boundaries of the Messiah!" The fifth was Saʿadiah,[359] who in the book called *On What to Believe*[360] concluded by means of diligent calculation that there was a certain temporal boundary of the Messiah that had already passed 340 years ago. The sixth opinion was that of Moses the Egyptian, a man of the utmost authority among the Jews, who, although he prohibited inquiry into the times of the Messiah in *Deuteronomy*,[361] nevertheless wrote in a letter to the African Jews that he has on the authority of the most trustworthy tradition of the ancients that the Messiah would be born during the 4,474th year after the beginning of the world. But this time based on their calculation came 760 years before us. The seventh opinion is that of Moses Gerondi, who in his commentaries on the *Pentateuch* affirms that the Messiah would arise in the 5,118th year after the creation of the world. Levi Ben Gershom agrees with him in his commentary on Daniel, but this temporal boundary precedes us by more than a century.[362] Therefore, the Jews await a future Messiah in vain! On top of it, whoever has still awaited the Messiah after Jesus has been deceived. They have not considered what Daniel said elsewhere: "In the days of those kings, the God of heaven will set up a kingdom that shall never be destroyed," namely, the heavenly kingdom of Christ.[363]

Jews, I beg you, state why those divine Magi set out for Jerusalem to see the Messiah as soon as Jesus was born, and why did Herod, when he asked experts in the law about the time and birthplace of the

---

358 Paul. *Scrut.* 1.3.4, 33v–34r; cf. Hier. Sanctaf. *Contr.* 1.2, 31.
359 Latin: Chahadias.
360 *The Book of Beliefs and Opinions* (Arabic: *Kitāb al-Amānāt wa l-Iʿtiqādāt*) is a book written by Saʿadiah Gaon in 933. It provides a systematic account for the philosophical foundations of Jewish belief.
361 I.e., *Mishneh Torah*.
362 Paul. *Scrut.* 1.3.4, 33r–34r; 2.6.10, 280v.
363 Dan 2:44; Paul. *Scrut.* 1.7.6, 83r; 2.6.11, 283r; Hier. Sanctaf. *Contr.* 1.6, 71–2.

Messiah, kill those babies and his own son – which Macrobius, both philosopher and pagan, attests – if not because the sages believed the times and places pertained to the Messiah?[364] Hence many experts in the law venerated Jesus like a god while He was alive.[365] Nathaniel and Nicodemus and others, whom John the Evangelist calls "leaders," who venerated him in secret for fear of the Jews.[366] Why did many around the time of Jesus boast about being the Messiah although, as Gamaliel says, they suddenly disappeared as if they were fakes?[367] Josephus tells that when Felix was the procurator of Judea, there had been many who were deceiving the people by their persuasion, among others a certain pseudo-prophet from Egypt who had a very large group gathered around him, and who was crushed by Felix's army during an attempted coup.[368] This agrees with the Acts of the Apostles, in which the following is said to Paul by a tribune: "Art thou not that Egyptian who before these days didst stir up and lead forth into the desert four thousand men?" The tribune, since he did not recognize Paul, was suspicious that perhaps he was that Egyptian.[369] A certain Galilean named Judas also rose up at the time of enrolling in the census, as Luke the Evangelist says and Josephus confirms, under the governor of Syria Quirinius, and he deceived the people. Not long after, however, he and all his followers were scattered. Such a thing also happened to a certain Theudas, about whom Luke and Josephus, on the whole, wrote similar things.[370] Such also was Simon Magus and Bar-Kozeba besides, about whom Moses the Egyptian, the most learned of the Jews, says in the book of *Judges*: "Achilayl, wise Bar-Kozeba beyond the other Jews, and all those who were experts in the law at his time, claimed that, a most warlike leader, was the Messiah, all the way up until he was killed by Hadrian for his crimes."[371] So says Moses. Eusebius also makes mention of this, following the history of Aristo of Pella, who says that from the time of Hadrian's decree, the entire Jewish nation was utterly banished from the sight of Judea and that the region of Jerusalem had its name changed: it was called Aelia after Aelius, the

---

364 Macrobius, *Saturnalia* 2.4.11, ed. Willis, 144.
365 John 1:45; 3:1.
366 Hier. Sanctaf. *Contr.* 1.6, 71–2.
367 Acts 5:36.
368 Eus. *Hist.* 2.21.1–3 (*PG* 20.191–4); cf. Josephus, *De bello Iudaico*, 2.261–3.
369 Acts 21:38.
370 Acts 5:37; Eus. *Hist.* 1.5.5–6 (*PG* 20.83–6).
371 Ficino renders Akiba's name here and below as "Achilayl," breaking from his source, Hier. Sanctaf. *Contr.* 1.2, 43, who provides "Achiba"; cf. Paul. *Scrut.* 2.6.2, 265r.

praenomen of Hadrian.[372] But one reads in the Talmud, a peculiar body of knowledge belonging to the Jews, in the book *Sanhedrin*, that Bar-Kozeba himself had reigned for thirty and a half years and that he had been accustomed to claiming himself to be the Messiah and that the sage Achilayl had agreed with Bar-Kozeba. So it reads.[373] Bar-Kozeba, moreover, had necessarily lived as close as possible to Jesus's time.[374]

Therefore, what else are you waiting for, most obstinate men, when all the sages of your race had once reckoned that the age of Jesus was striving towards Christ? Why, a little after Jesus, did you wretches rebel so many times against the Romans, unless because all of you then thought that the promises of the prophets would soon reach their end? Suetonius the pagan attests to this: "The old and enduring opinion," he says, "had become very widespread in oracles across the East such that at that time men setting out from Judea would seize the highest position in world affairs," and he said that on account of this the Jews had rebelled and perished. Of course, at that time you were awaiting some armed Christ to suddenly establish a perpetual monarchy over the world in Judea.[375] How much wiser than you was Virgil, who reckoned that the utterances of the Sibyl regarding the king of the world could coincide with and be fulfilled in the time of Jesus! But this we have discussed elsewhere.

Josephus writes that before the siege of Jerusalem, an oracle was discovered in holy writ which pointed out that, at the same time, a man would come forth from their region who would seize an empire over the entire world. Someone supposed that the prediction of this oracle meant Vespasian, but Vespasian was ruling over only those peoples who were subjects of the Roman Empire, and no one else; therefore, these oracles ought to be thought of as referring to Christ, to whom the Father had said: "Ask of me, and I will give thee the nations for thy inheritance, and the utmost parts of the earth for thy possession."[376]

---

372 Eus. *Hist*. 4.6.2–4 (*PG* 20.311–14).
373 Ficino reports the length of Bar Kokhba's reign as he receives it from his source Hier. Sanctaf. *Contr*. 1.2, 42–3; its true length, however, was considerably shorter, lasting closer to four and a half years at most, see Menahem, *The Second Jewish Revolt*, 143–5, 177.
374 Ficino is here fallaciously supporting his argument by repeating the same historical person, Simon bar Kokhba, under two different names.
375 Suetonius, *Divus Vespasianus*, 4.5. Ficino reiterates the reference to Suetonius in a sermon of unknown date that was published in translation in the Appendix to Marsilio Ficino, *The Letters of Marsilio Ficino. Volume 6, being a Translation of Liber VII*, transl. Language Department of the London School of Economic Science (London: Shepheard-Walwyn, 2009), 61.
376 Ps. 2:8; Eus. *Hist*. 3.5 (*PG* 20.221–4); cf. Josephus, *De bello Iudaico*, 6.311–15.

And the sound of this went forth at that time through His apostles into every country.

ISAIAH: "He is the Lord of Hosts – sanctify Him: He is your fear, and He is your dread. And He shall be a sanctification to you and a stumbling-stone, and a rock of scandal to the two houses of Israel, and a snare and a ruin to the inhabitants of Jerusalem, and very many of them shall stumble."[377] Similarly: "I shall lay in Zion a stumbling-stone and rock of scandal; whosoever believeth in Him shall not be confounded."[378] From this, it is obvious that the awaited Christ is God, the same who made holy the souls of the believers, and because of Him the two houses of Israel would fall, namely, the royal house and the priestly house, and that not everyone, but very many, would be obstinate, and those who would believe could not be confounded. It is not proper to explain this as two houses, as some twist it, that is, as two kings. For the convention of the Hebrew writers is to designate the entire line of priests as one priestly house, and to designate the entire line of kings as one royal house, that is, the house of David.[379]

JEREMIAH: "'And when they shall be multiplied and increase in the land in those days,' saith the Lord, 'they shall say no more: the ark of the covenant of the Lord: neither shall it come upon the heart, neither shall one remember it, neither shall it be visited, neither shall that be done any more,'"[380] That is to say, after the Messiah, as Mohammad also thinks is right, both the offices and the ceremonies of the Old Testament had ceased, nor was this at all wrong, for those were the images of the future sacraments. When the substance is present, however, what need is there of an image?

ISAIAH: "Before she was in labour, she brought forth. Before her time came to be delivered, she brought forth a boy child."[381] The most ancient commentaries of the Hebrews explain it so, that is, before the one was born who reduced the Jews to their final slavery, that is, Titus, their redeemer had already been born. Hence the Chaldean text has: "Still the difficulty will not come for her, and still the trembling will not come to her, with birth pangs the Messiah will be revealed." Regarding this Chaldean text the Hebrew Jonathan says: "Before the difficulty can come to her, she is saved, and before the pangs of birth

---

377 Isa. 8:13–15.
378 This is not directly from Isaiah but the above quote mediated through Rom. 9:33 and 10:11 with only the former verse being a reference to the Hebrew prophet.
379 Paul. *Scrut.* 1.1.3, 9r.
380 Jer. 3:16.
381 Isa. 66:7.

can come to her, the Messiah is revealed." The sage Samuel affirms something similar in the very same place. From all this, it is apparent that the Messiah had arisen before the destruction of Jerusalem. Very many of the Hebrews, however, grant that he was born on the day when the city was razed to the ground; then they take refuge in trifles, as is their custom, saying that he is hidden until such time as God commands him to show himself openly to all. Some place him on Mount Sinai with angels, others remove him beyond the Caspian mountains, yet others see him wandering and begging here and there, and so they confuse each other with their madness and discord.[382]

ISAIAH: "The Lord Himself shall give you a sign. Behold a virgin shall conceive in her womb, and bear a son and His name shall be called Emmanuel."[383] In Hebrew it is "hahalma," which means "a girl hidden away and kept."[384] But "Emmanuel" means "God with us," namely because He who would be born from that girl was to be not only a man, but also God. For a birth of this kind, I say, from an ever-virgin girl is promised as a kind of prodigious sign, about which David: "Truth is sprung out of the earth."[385] And Isaiah says elsewhere: "Let the heavens exult from above, and let the clouds rain down justice, let the earth be opened and spring forth a saviour. For I the Lord God have created Him."[386] We notice two extremes and two middle grounds in the human species: each one of us is born from a man and a woman, Adam from neither, Eve only from a man because of divine power, Jesus only from a woman because of the Divine Spirit. Mohammad, the king of the Arabs, greatly admires and venerates this mystery in his dialogue.[387] In the Qur'an, compelled by the truth, he also says: "Jesus, son of Mary, messenger of God, His Spirit, and His Word was sent from heaven to the virgin Mary."[388]

DANIEL: "I saw in my vision of the night, and lo in the clouds of heaven, one like the son of man came, and He came even to the Ancient of Days, and those who were in attendance presented Him. And a kingdom was given to Him, and glory, and an empire, and all people, tribes, and tongues shall serve Him, and His power is an everlasting one that shall never pass, and His kingdom that shall not be

---

382 Hier. Sanctaf. *Contr.* 1.2, 34–6.
383 Isa. 7:14; cf. Matt. 1:23.
384 Cf. Petrus Alfonsi, *Dialogus contra Iudaeos*, Titulus 7 (Resnick, 180).
385 Ps. 85:12 (Vulg. Ps. 84:12).
386 Isa. 45:8; cf. Paul. *Scrut.* 2.6.3, 267r.
387 Hier. Sanctaf. *Contr.* 1.4, 57.
388 *Alcor.* 4.171 (Petrus Pons, 71).

destroyed."[389] For all the Jewish interpreters explain this parable as being about the King Messiah. Although there is here a debate regarding the final coming of Christ, with these words Daniel means that God will come in the guise of a man, and that the kingdom of Christ will not be temporal but eternal and spiritual. On this, Isaiah is also consistent, for there God speaks thus about Christ: "I will give thee hidden and invisible treasures."[390]

HOSEA: "I will call that which was not my people, my people; and her that was not beloved, beloved; and her that had not obtained mercy, one that hath obtained mercy. And it shalt be in the place where it was said: you are not my people; there they shall be called the sons of the living God."[391] In these lines, the conversion of pagans and the obstinacy of the Jews are foretold, such as had occurred around the time of Jesus.[392]

ISAIAH: "I was found by them that did not seek me. I appeared openly to them that asked not after me. All the day long have I spread my hands to a people that believeth not, but contradicteth me."[393] In these verses, there is the same prediction as a little above.

DAVID: "The stone which the builders rejected; the same is become the head of the corner. This is the Lord's doing; it is wonderful in our eyes. This is the day which the Lord hath made: let us be glad and rejoice therein. O Lord, save me: O Lord, give good success. Blessed is he that cometh in the name of the Lord."[394] Jesus, being rejected by the crooked as useless, by divine power became "the head of the corner" to which two walls are connected, that is, the Gentiles and those among the Jews who converted.

MALACHI: "My will is not in you, saith the Lord, and I have not accepted a sacrifice from your hands, since from the rising of the Sun even to the going down, my name will be made known among the nations."[395] These lines show a rejection of the faithless Jews and of Jewish ceremonies and an approval of the faithful Gentiles at the coming of Christ. Moses: "I placed[396] thee to be the light of the nations, that thou mayst be in a state of salvation even to the farthest part of the earth."[397]

---

389 Dan. 7:2; 7:14.
390 Isa. 45:3; Paul. *Scrut.* 1.3.1, 21v–22r; 1.10.7, 166r-v.
391 Rom. 9:25–6; cf. Hosea 2:23–4.
392 Rom. 9:24; cf. Paul. *Scrut.* 1.2.1, 12r–13v; 1.2.4, 20r-v.
393 Rom. 10:20–1; cf. Isa. 65:1–2.
394 Ps. 118:22–6 (Vulg. Ps. 117:22–6).
395 Mal. 1:10–11.
396 Bartolucci has "*Posuit*" here, whereas the 1500 Latin edition of *De Christiana religione* (f. XLIr) has "*Posui te,*" and "*dedi*" appears in the Vulgate. Ficino's Italian is "io tho posto" and it is also noteworthy that he uses *dedi* below when he cites Isa. 49:6 again.
397 Isa. 49:6; Paul. *Scrut.* 1.1.1, 4v; 1.8.4, 100r; 2.3.10, 212r.

ISAIAH: "I come to gather all nations and tongues, and they shall come and shall see my brilliance. And I will send around a sign upon them, and I will send of them that are saved to the nations that are far away, that have not heard of my glory and they shall declare my brilliance to the nations. And I will take of them to be priests, and Levites, saith the Lord."[398] And elsewhere in *Isaiah* God addresses the Messiah so: "It is a small thing that thou shouldst be my servant to sustain the tribes of Jacob, and to convert the dregs of Israel. I have given thee to be the light of nations."[399] Likewise, he says: "The first shall say to Zion: 'Behold I am here, and to Jerusalem I will give an evangelist. I saw, and there was no man even among them to consult, and who, when he asked, could see the word. Behold they are all in the wrong, and their works are vain."[400] And in the following chapter he adds: "Behold my servant, I will uphold Him: my elect, my soul delighteth in Him: I have given my Spirit upon Him, and He shall bring forth judgment to the nations. He shall not cry, nor have respect to person, the bruised reed He shall not break, till He set judgment in the earth, and the islands shall look upon His law."[401] Similarly, elsewhere: "I will bring forth a seed out of Jacob, and out of Judah a possessor of my mountains: and my elect shall inherit it, and my servants shall dwell there. Behold my servants shall eat, and you shall be hungry, my servants shall rejoice, and you shall be ashamed and you shall leave your name for an execration to my elect: and the Lord shall slay thee, and call His servants by another name."[402] He also has God speaking thus elsewhere: "Israel hath not known me, and my people hath not understood me."[403] Likewise, he says: "By hearing you shall hear, and shall not understand, and seeing you shall see, and shall not perceive. For the heart of this people is grown gross, and with their own ears they have been dull of hearing, and their eyes they have shut: lest at any time they should see with their eyes, and hear with their ears, and understand with their heart, and be converted, and I should heal them."[404] "I will send of them that are saved to the nations," that is, I will send the Messiah's disciples who escaped the clutches of the Jews to convert the pagans, and "I will take (*assumam*)," that is, from among the Gentiles who were

---

398 Isa. 66:18–19.
399 Isa. 49:6.
400 Isa. 41:27–9; Paul. *Scrut.* 1.2.2, 14r–15r.
401 Isa. 42:1–4; Paul. *Scrut.* 1.5.5, 50r.
402 Isa. 65:9; 65:13–15; Paul. *Scrut.* 1.2.3, 15v–16r.
403 Isa. 1:3.
404 Matt. 13:14–15; cf. Isa. 6:9–10.

converted, I will establish lawful priests, from which it is obvious that even Gentiles were capable of being raised (*assumi*) to the dignity of Israel. Hence the Jew Rav Huna[405] in his commentaries on *Exodus* says: "At the time of the Messiah, converted pagans will be priests ministering to the Lord."[406] "It is a small thing that he should be," by this, it is clear that the Messiah, like Jesus, was to be sent for the salvation not only of the Hebrews but also of the Gentiles. Solomon, a Jewish interpreter, while explaining the passage "The first shall say to Zion," says that all this must be understood as being about the Messiah king and ultimate deliverance; Jonathan's Chaldean translation reveals the same thing. But in these words of Isaiah, it is apparent that Christ was to preach first and foremost among the Jews, and there He was to found the gospels and the evangelists, but because the Jews would be wicked and obstinate, he adds: "There was not a man, and thus He shall bring forth judgment to the Gentiles,"[407] namely, through His disciples, He will disseminate the gospel's teaching among the pagans; and, in order to show that the gospel's judgments must be spread in the utmost humility, not with pride, by force, in the commotion and the sounding of trumpets, as the law of Moses was, he added: "He shall not cry."[408] In the remaining words, Isaiah reveals that the Messiah is to be descended from Jacob and that His followers for the most part would be foreigners who would be chosen before God, and they would no longer be Israelites but would be named by another name: Christians.[409] He also reveals that the Jews would oppose the Messiah and would pay the penalty, just as it happened previously during the time of Jesus, and that the obstinacy of the Jews would also be everlasting, such as we still experience today.

JEREMIAH: "The turtle hath known its time, and the swallow and the sparrow have observed the times of their entry; but my people have not known the judgment of the Lord. How do you say 'We are wise, and the law of the Lord is with us?' The false measurement is done in vain. The scribes are confounded, the wise men are dismayed and taken, for they have rejected the word of the Lord."[410] Why do the

---

405 Ficino provides Ravanais for Rav Huna, thereby not only preserving, but compounding the error found in his copy of Paul of Burgos's *Scrutinium Scripturarum*, which has Ravanay (cf. Paul. *Scrut.* 1.2.1, 13v).
406 Paul. *Scrut.* 1.2.1, 13v.
407 Isa. 50:2; 42:1.
408 Paul. *Scrut.* 1.5.2, 45v–46r.
409 Paul. *Scrut.* 1.2.3, 15v.
410 Jer. 8:7–9.

prophets often relate what will happen as what has already passed? Because in the divine mind, for which all things are present, they see those things as present, and after they have seen them, as past (that is, they speak of matters that are manifest and that have already been fulfilled). But let us return to Jeremiah. He makes it clear in the words above that scribes would not have perfect knowledge of the time of Christ's coming, and the time of reaping. This is certainly not surprising, for the interpretation of the divine sense is most difficult for the unjust. What one reads in Deuteronomy agrees with this: "The Lord strike thee with madness and blindness and stupor of mind. And mayst thou grope at midday as the blind man is wont to grope."[411] "Midday" is the light of the works of Christ, in which a great many Jews have been blinded.[412] Elsewhere, Jeremiah says the same: "Lord my God, to thee the Gentiles shall come from the ends of the earth, and shall say how our parents have possessed false idols, and there was no use in them. If a man shall make gods unto himself, those will not be gods."[413] These words predict the tearing down of idols through the Messiah, which was done through Jesus; this squares up with what Isaiah says when, speaking of Christ, he says: "He will teach you His ways,"[414] and quite a bit further down: "In that day a man shall cast away his idols of silver, and his idols of gold, which he had made for himself, lest he adore them."[415] Daniel means the same thing when, speaking of Christ, he says that a stone hewn not with hands will destroy a statue made of iron, woven fabric, gold, and silver.[416] The "stone hewn" is Jesus, cut down by the power of the priests; He destroyed the statue (i.e., idolatry, which worshipped statues), "not with hands" (i.e., without human force). A statue, I say, consisting of four parts: for it was scattered into four particular kingdoms of the world (namely, the Chaldeans, the Medians, the Greeks, and the Romans).[417]

---

411 Deut. 28:28–9.
412 Paul. *Scrut.* 2.6.3, 268v; 284r; 2.6.13, 284r; Cf. Giovanni Pico della Mirandola, *Heptaplus*, 7.4 (Carmichael, 157); a decade after the publication of *DCR*, Pico would elaborate this theme of Christ as theological Sun in great detail: "Then came the fourth day [of Creation], on which the sun, the lord of the firmament, that is, Christ, the lord of the law ... began to shine for eternity, calling the world to eternal life. The sun did not destroy the firmament, but perfected it, and Christ came not to destroy the law, but to perfect it."
413 Jer. 16:19–20; Paul. *Scrut.* 1.7.2, 79r-v.
414 Isa. 2:3.
415 Isa. 2:20.
416 Cf. Dan. 2:36–45.
417 Paul. *Scrut.* 1.7.1, 78r–79r.

Elsewhere, Jeremiah says the same: "The Lord shall be terrible upon them, and shall destroy all the gods of the earth: and man shall adore Him from his own place, all the islands of the Gentiles."

ISAIAH: "For the Lord hath mingled for you the spirit of a deep sleep, He will shut up your eyes, He will cover your princes, that see visions. And the vision of all shall be unto you as the words of a book that is sealed which when they shall deliver to one that is learned, they shall say: 'Read this,' and he shall answer: 'I cannot, for it is sealed.' And the book shall be given to one that knoweth no letters, and it shall be said to him: 'Read,' and he shall answer: 'I know no letters.' And the Lord said: 'Forasmuch as this people draw near me with their mouth and glorify me with their lips, but their heart is far from me, and they have feared me with the commandment and doctrines of men.' Therefore behold I will proceed to cause an admiration in this people, by a great and wonderful miracle. For wisdom shall perish from their wise men, and the understanding of prudent men shall be hid."[418] Likewise, one reads elsewhere: "God hath given them the spirit of insensibility; eyes that they should not see and ears that they should not hear, until this present day."[419] All this predicts that as many Jews as possible, the learned as much as the ignorant, because of their crimes and impiety, will not recognize the prophecies of the awaited Christ, or Christ when He is present; because of this error they are in misery, today until the end of the world as, just as we have said elsewhere, Hosea sang: "The children of Israel shall sit many days without king, and without prince, and without sacrifice, and without altar, and without ephod, and without teraphim."[420] But since around the end of the world they will believe in our Christ, he adds: "And after this the children of Israel shall return and seek the Lord their God, and David, their king."[421] The Chaldean translation contains: "And they will obey the Messiah, son of David, their king, and they will be terrified at the Lord." In Hebrew it has: "And they will stream to the Lord and to His goodness in the last days."[422] Let no one understand this to be about the Babylonian captivity, in which they held kings and leaders as honoured for the time being. The fourth book of Kings in fact teaches us this where it recounts that the king of Judah, Jehoiakim, had been placed in the royal seat along with other kings by the king of Babylon, and

---

418 Isa. 29:10–14.
419 Rom. 11:8; Paul. *Scrut.* 2.6.5, 270r-v.
420 Hosea 3:4.
421 Hosea 3:5.
422 Paul. *Scrut.* 2.6.13, 285v–286r.

all other men of this race were honoured in like fashion.[423] They have been deprived of these honours today. They are also lacking sacrifice and an altar, since they lack a temple arranged according to Mosaic law; they lack an "ephod," that is, a priestly vestment, and a "teraphim," which is a kind of instrument built for foretelling the future in a sort of idolatrous ritual. With these words, it is meant that today the Jews neither worship the true God lawfully nor worship idols, but in all other times, they either duly worshipped God, or worshipped idols. But "after many days" and "in the last days," that is, after many centuries such as those after Jesus and near the end of the world, "shall return and seek their God," namely, the one of their fathers and "David their king," that is, the Messiah born from the line of David, as the Chaldean translation teaches.[424] But the liberation from Babylon was not after many centuries and in most recent times. Let no one understand that the Messiah will then come for the first time, for – if I may clear up this error – the prophet did not say "their king will come," but "they shall return and seek" Him, as if He already has come, but they abandoned and ignored Him, and at last they will seek Him. The Chaldean words make this clear when they say: "They will obey the Messiah to the extent that they had been obstinate beforehand." About this, Isaiah says: "Thus saith the Lord to the house of Jacob, Jacob shall not now be confounded, neither shall his countenance now be ashamed because when he shall see his children sanctifying my name, and they shall sanctify the Holy One of Jacob, and shall glorify the God of Israel, and they that erred in spirit, shall know understanding, and they that murmured, shall learn the law."[425] In these words, Jacob's confusion is lifted because the apostles were as sons from his progeny, who exalted Jesus, and by whose teaching all the Jews will finally place their faith in Christ. Paul demonstrates this most keenly in the *Epistle to the Romans*.[426] Because of this, while speaking about the first coming of Christ, Isaiah says: "In that day the bud of the Lord shall be in magnificence, and it shall come to pass that every one shall be left in Zion, and that shall remain in Jerusalem, shall be called holy."[427] "In that day," that is, in the time of light; "the bud of the Lord," that is, Christ the Son of God; "in magnificence," namely,

---

423 Cf. 2 Kings 25:27–30 (Vulg. 4 Rg. 25:27–30).
424 Ficino is providing exegesis from his source (Paul. *Scrut.* 2.6.13, 286r) for two Bible verses he omitted: Gen. 4:3 and Hosea 3:5.
425 Isa. 29:22–4.
426 Cf. Rom. 9:11.
427 Isa. 4:2–3.

On the Christian Religion   137

of His works and portents; "everyone shall be left" means that the few disciples of Christ, abandoned by nearly everyone, are the holy relics of Christ. Those relics will be exalted with Christ in the second coming of Christ.[428]

But what is to be said about the Jews in the meantime? Few will be chosen, and seldomly. For the following verse of Isaiah is understood to be about them: "And the fruit thereof that shall be left upon it shall be as one cluster of grapes, and the shaking of the olive tree, two or three berries in the top of a bough."[429] Afterward, because of their perfidy, they were shaken from the natural tree and separated from the root of the olive tree, as Paul the Apostle says,[430] and still, a good many seem either to have been left behind there, or rather to have been grafted to it again in the meantime, like Evaristus the Hebrew, a distinguished man, who was the seventh pope[431] of the Christians after Peter, and who lived more than ten years in that office and died a martyr. Thereafter, at the time of the Goths, Julian the Jew ruled the first bishopric in Spain in the holiest manner. Petrus Alfonsi, from the same nation, also wrote a dialogue against the perfidy of the Jews; Alfonso of Burgos,[432] a top metaphysicist, took up the faith of Christ in the sixtieth year of his life and wrote many exceptional things against the Jews.[433] What shall I say about Nicholas of Lyra, a great gentleman of learning and an exceptionally holy man? What about Jerome [of Santa Fe] the physician, who at the time of Pope Benedict argued subtly against the Jews? There were also others, a great number in fact, although few were exceptional over such a long period of time. I reckon that this verse of Jeremiah is about them: "I will take you, one of a city, and two of a kindred"[434] – or "of

---

428 Paul. *Scrut.* 1.3.2, 25r; 2.6.13, 285v–286r.
429 Isa. 17:6; Paul. *Scrut.* 2.6.14, 286v–287r.
430 Cf. Rom. 11:16–24; Paul. *Scrut.* 2.6.7, 275r.
431 By today's reckoning, Ficino is mistaken about the identity of the seventh pope. Evaristus (d.105) was actually the fifth pope, while the seventh was Sixtus I (d.125). This is an error that Ficino is passing on from Paul of Burgos, who places Evaristus's term as beginning in 112 AD and lasting ten years, seven months, and twelve days. Cf. Edelheit, *Ficino, Pico, and Savonarola*, 227; in Fic. *TP* 4.361, n. 48.
432 Before his conversion, this individual was known as Abner of Burgos, an Aristotelian philosopher, and afterward as Alfonso of Valladolid, a Christian Platonist and author of the *Mostrador de Justicia*. He lived c. 1260–1347.
433 Paul. *Scrut.* 2.6.14, 287r.
434 We have kept the wording from the Douay-Rheims Bible, Ficino's source Paul of Burgos (see *Scrut.* 2.6.10, 282v), and Ficino's own Italian version all maintain "cognatione" instead of the erroneous "cognitione" that appears in Ficino's Latin.

a congregation" – "and will bring you into Zion,"[435] namely, heaven. The bishop Paul of Burgos, a distinguished theologian, covered this material diligently.

DAVID: "He shall come down like rain on the fleece," that is, unknown to many, and adds: "In His days shall justice spring up, and abundance of peace."[436]

ISAIAH: "In His days shall justice spring up, and a multitude of peace." Jesus was born during Octavian's reign and introduced evangelical grace and justice against the original injustice contracted from the root of Adam.[437] The reign of Octavian was also the most just. There was even such peace at the time throughout the entire world that there has never been a wider or a longer-lasting one. Hence Virgil: "The doors of war shall be closed." The peace lasted for thirty-seven years after Jesus.[438]

ISAIAH: "Egypt, the merchandise of the Ethiopians, and Saba are exhausted. Men of stature shall cross over to thee and shall be thine servants. They shall walk after thee, they shall go bound with shackles, and they shall worship thee and shall make supplication to thee, since in thee is God, and there is no other God except thee. For you are God, God of Israel our saviour, and we knew not. All those who are hostile to you shall be confounded and fall into confusion, and they shall stand in awe."[439] These things show precisely how at some point pagan empires were to become subject to Christ; likewise, how Christ was not recognized as God our saviour for some time, how He was worshipped thereafter, and how it was fitting that His adversaries – obstinate Jerusalem and idolatry – fell, just as it has happened. That Christ would also be a man, Isaiah reveals thus: "God shall send them a man, and He shall save them, while judging, He shall heal them."[440] He rightly calls the Messiah the saviour, and He Who Will Save. For He is called Jesus, that is, the saviour. But he shows that He will not heal bodies by violence and arms, but souls by His judgment. David, similarly, reveals that Christ is God when he is speaking about God: "He sent His word, and healed them, and delivered them from their destructions."[441] For this reason, Abraham recognized God in the form

---

435 Jer. 3:14.
436 Ps. 72:6–7 (Vulg. Ps. 71:6–7).
437 Cf. Paul. *Scrut.* 1.3.3, 27v.
438 Virgil, *Aeneid*, 1.293.
439 Isa. 45:14–16.
440 Isa. 19:20.
441 Ps. 107:20 (Vulg. Ps. 106:20).

of a man, and worshipped Him as the king of all.[442] Similarly, God appeared to Jesus, the successor of Moses, likewise also to Jacob.

JEREMIAH: "This is our God, and there shall be no other counted, aside from Him who found every path to prudence, and gave it to Jacob His servant, and to Israel His beloved. Afterwards He was seen upon earth, and conversed with men."[443] This shows the Messiah to be God and man. Jeremiah, elsewhere: "And He is a man, and who knew Him?"[444] as if to say, because of His humility and man's pride, many did not recognize Him. It is no wonder that many Jews, not particularly pious, did not know the profound mystery of the Messiah and the divinity of Jesus. Nevertheless, many Jews – some pious, some even learned – knew from the beginning; for Christ converted many thousands of Jews to His law, His disciples many more. But even Mohammad claims in the Qur'an that those Jews who believed in Jesus were given far greater preference by God than the rest of the Jews.[445] As Jeremiah foretold elsewhere, these men, along with the Gentiles, "called [the Messiah] our Lord the Just," and they truly called Him that, for He would not have allowed Himself to be called God falsely.[446]

MOSES IN *NUMBERS*: "A star shall rise out of Jacob and a man shall rise up from Israel."[447] Through this and what precedes it, the Messiah is shown to be God and man. Therefore, in depicting God, Ezekiel places Him upon a throne of sapphire in the likeness of a man, precisely because God was to be a man.[448] Whence Rabbi Johanan, in his commentaries on the *Psalter*, says that although the Jews were previously freed from captivity by other leaders, their ultimate redemption must be completed by God in His own person. With that, he concedes that the Messiah is God and explains this verse about Him: "Blessed is he that cometh in the name of the Lord, the Lord God hath shone upon us."[449]

---

442 Cf. Gen. 18:1–5; Paul. *Scrut.* 1.10.7, 164v–165r.
443 Bar. 3:36–8; Ficino is maintaining the misattribution of this passage to Jeremiah from his source, see Lact. *Inst.* 4.13.8 (*PL* 6.483; Monat, 114–15).
444 Jer. 17:9; Lact. *Inst.* 4.13.10 (*PL* 6.484; Monat, 114–15).
445 *Alcor.* 9.30 (Petrus Pons, 119).
446 Jer. 23:6; Paul. *Scrut.* 1.3.3, 27v; note that Ficino intentionally changes the verb tense from what appears in the Vulgate, where we read *"vocabunt"* ("they will call") to *"vocaverunt"* ("they called"), which reading strengthens Paul's point that the day of prophecy has already come.
447 Num. 24:27.
448 Ezek. 1:26; Paul. *Scrut.* 1.10.7, 165v–166r.
449 Ps. 118:26–7 (Vulg. Ps. 117:26–7); Paul. *Scrut.* 1.10.9, 168r–v.

Speaking of Christ, who is more excellent among the others anointed by God (who themselves can be called Christs because of that anointing), David says: "God, thy God, has anointed thee with the oil of gladness beyond thy fellows."[450] Where he makes clear that Christ is a man, he even a little earlier pointed out that Christ is God, by saying: "Your seat, O God, is for ever and ever: the sceptre of thy kingdom is a sceptre of righteousness."[451] He clarifies what he says about the Messiah based on the fact that where it is said in the Hebrew, "Thou art beautiful above the sons of men," the Chaldean translation of Jonathan (which is of equal authority among the Jews to the Hebrew text) has: "Thy beauty, King Messiah, is greater than that of the sons of man." Everyone rightly cedes to the authority of this translation, for it was prepared by Jonathan, a great man, based on the agreement and the word of Eleazar and Joshua, most excellent men, a long time before the destruction of the temple, and all the ancient Talmudic Hebrews maintain that the translation had descended from the prophets Haggai, Zechariah, and Malachi.[452] Rabbi Alba, moved by David's words above and the like, asks in his commentaries on Genesis what Daniel means when he says of God: "He revealeth deep and hidden things, and knoweth what is in darkness, and light is with Him,"[453] and then answers: "Surely this is light, the light of the King Messiah, about whom it is written in the Psalm: 'In thy light we shall see light.'"[454] So he says. Here, he acknowledges that the divine light, which is always with God and is itself God, is the light of the Messiah, and is itself the Messiah.[455] The ancient and illustrious theologian Rabbi Nehunya, in a work entitled the *Book of Light*,[456] while explaining the following verse in Proverbs, "the just is an everlasting foundation,"[457] asks what Solomon means, and answers thus regarding the Messiah: "God has or will have in His age a just man who is beloved to Him, because He sustains the entire world and He is its foundation, He governs the world and He makes it to be governed; He is the foundation of all souls, and this is what is meant by 'the just is an everlasting foundation.'"[458] So he says, and with that he reveals that the Messiah is not only a man

---

450 Ps. 45:7 (Vulg. Ps. 44:8).
451 Ps. 45:6 (Vulg. Ps. 44:7); cf. Eus. *Hist.* 1.3.16–18 (*PG* 20.74).
452 Paul. *Scrut.* 1.5.7, 52r.
453 Dan. 2:22.
454 Ps. 36:9 (Vulg Ps. 35:10).
455 Paul. *Scrut.* 1.10.9, 169r.
456 I.e., *Sefer HaBahir*, *The Book of Brightness*.
457 Prov. 10:20.
458 Paul. *Scrut.* 1.10.9, 169r-v.

but also God. David himself also reveals the same elsewhere: "Mother Zion shall say: This man and that man is born in her, and the highest himself hath founded her,"[459] that is, God, who founded Zion, is born as a man in the same place and calls Zion mother.

ISAIAH: "There shall be in that day the root of Jesse and in him who shall rise up to rule over the nations, nations shall have hope, and their place of rest shall be held in honour."[460] And elsewhere: "There shall come forth a rod out of the root of Jesse, and a flower shall rise up out of his root. And the Spirit of God shall rest upon him; the spirit of wisdom, and of understanding, the spirit of counsel, and of fortitude, the spirit of godliness. And he shall be filled with the spirit of the fear of God."[461] Jesse was the father of David.[462] Consequently, by these verses, the prophet predicted that the Messiah would spring forth from the line of David to the benefit of the Gentiles more than the Jews, to hold dominion by spiritual rather than physical arms, as Jesus would. Isaiah says the same thing elsewhere in the person of Christ: "The Spirit of the Lord is upon me. Wherefore He hath anointed me to preach the gospel to the poor, to preach deliverance to the captives, and sight to the blind."[463] Here it is made clear that a Messiah would be born from the Holy Spirit, to be named Christ solely by divine anointment, likewise that he would preach the gospel to the poor, that he would deliver them from sin, that he would banish ignorance.[464]

DAVID: "The kings of Tarshish and the islands shall offer presents. The kings of the Arabians and of Saba shall bring gifts."[465]

ISAIAH: "All they from Saba shall come, [bringing] gold and frankincense: and shewing forth praise to the Lord."[466] Some of this happened immediately when Jesus was born, some after His ascension, especially during the reign of Constantine all the way to our present times. And elsewhere one reads: "I called my son out of Egypt."[467] Likewise, elsewhere it is said: "He will be called the Nazarene."[468] But our Jesus

---

459 Ps. 87:5 (Vulg. Ps. 86:5).
460 Isa. 11:10.
461 Isa. 11:1–3.
462 Lact. *Inst.* 4.13.18 (*PL* 6.485–6; Monat, 118–19).
463 Luke 4:18–19.
464 Eus. *Hist.* 1.3.13 (*PG* 20.74).
465 Ps. 72:10 (Vulg. Ps. 71:10).
466 Isa. 60:6; Ficino misquoted the Vulgate and omitted the word "*deferentes,*" which we have supplied in brackets.
467 Hosea 11:1.
468 Matt. 2:23; contrary to what Ficino is implying, this passage does not have any corresponding section in the Old Testament.

turned back out of Egypt, lived in Nazareth, and was dubbed the Nazarene.

ZECHARIAH: "The Lord God shewed me Jesus the high priest standing before the face of the angel of the Lord, and the Devil stood on His right hand to be His adversary. And the Lord said to the Devil: 'The Lord command thee, that chose Jerusalem.' And behold the firebrand thrown from the fire, and Jesus was clothed with filthy garments, and He stood before the face of the angel. He answered and said to those gathered around before his face: 'Take away the filthy garments from Him, and dress Him in a long tunic, and place a clean mitre upon His head.' And they covered Him with clothing, and they placed a clean mitre upon His head. And the angel of the Lord stood and appealed solemnly to Him, saying: "Thus saith the omnipotent Lord: 'If thou wilt walk in my ways, and preserve my commands, thou shalt judge my house, and I will give thee those who will convert in the midst of those who are gathered around.' Therefore, hear, O Jesus thou high priest.'"[469] The prophet's words correspond to God, Jesus the Nazarene, not to Jesus Nave or Jesus Josedech, who were both before Zechariah, and they neither underwent nor did such things.[470] For these words portend the future, and they designate a man in the form of an extinguished firebrand, at first despised and filthy, then adorned by God and judge of the divine house.[471]

SOLOMON IN THE *BOOK OF WISDOM*: "Let us lie in wait for the just, because he is not disagreeable to us and he upbraideth us with transgressions of the law. He boasteth that he hath the knowledge of God, and calleth himself the son of God. He is become a surrenderer of our thoughts. He is grievous unto us, even to live: for his life is like[472] other men's, and his ways are very different. We are esteemed by him as triflers, and he restraineth himself from our ways and from filthiness, and he preferreth the latter end of the just, and glorieth that he hath God for his father. Let us see then if his words be true, and let us prove what shall happen to him, and let us examine him by outrages and tortures, that we may know his meekness, and try his patience. Let us condemn him to a most shameful death. These things they thought, and were deceived, for their own foolishness blinded them,

---

[469] Zech. 3:1–8.
[470] I.e., Joshua, Son of Nun, and Joshua, son of Yehozadak, the first man chosen as high priest for the Second Temple.
[471] Cf. Lact. *Inst.* 4.14 (*PL* 6.489; Monat, 122–31).
[472] Ficino has "*similis*" ("like"), whereas the Vulgate has "*dissimilis*" ("unlike").

and they knew not the secrets of God."[473] So says Solomon and nothing is clearer. God rightly allowed such men, who had been blind and cruel heralds against the prophets of the Messiah, also to be against the Messiah.

ISAIAH: "Behold my boy shall understand, He shall be exalted, and glorified, and shall be exceedingly high. Just as many will be astonished at thee, thus men will rob your beauty of glory, and your glory of beauty. Thus, many nations shall wonder, kings shall shut their mouth at Him, for they to whom it was not announced of Him, shall see, and they that heard not, shall understand. Lord, who hath believed our report? And to whom is the arm of the Lord revealed? We have announced in His presence that he is like a sick man, like a root in thirsty ground; there is no beauty for Him, nor glory. And we have seen Him and there was no beauty nor grace, but His beauty is without honour, lacking beyond all men, a man in a state of affliction and knowing that He bears sickness, since His face is turned away, not honoured, nor reckoned of great worth.[474] This man carries our sins and grieves for us, and we ourselves have considered Him to be like a leper, stricken by God and humbled." (Or "to be in pain, in a state of affliction, and in torment"). "But He was wounded for our iniquities, and He was sickened for our sins. The teaching of our peace was in Him, by His bruises we are healed. All we, like sheep, have gone astray, man hath strayed from His path and the Lord hath offered Him up for our sins, and He, since He was in torment, opened not His mouth. Like a sheep He was led to the slaughter, and like a speechless lamb before his shearer, thus He did not open His mouth. In humility, the judgement upon Him was lifted, who shall declare His generation? Since His life shall be lifted away from the earth, He was led to His death by the iniquities of my people, and I shall give the wicked for His burial and the rich for His death, since He hath done no iniquity, nor was deceit found in His mouth. And the Lord is pleased to cleanse Him of affliction. If you were to give your life for sin, you will see a long-lived seed, and the Lord wishes to remove its soul from pain, to show it the light and to shape its understanding, to justify a just man serving the many well. And He bore their sins, therefore He shall inherit many and divide the spoils of the strong, because His soul was delivered unto death. And He was counted among the wicked, and He

---

473 Wisd. of Sol. 2:12–17, 19–22.
474 For "sick man," Bart. *DCR* 244, line 689 has "*infimus*" ("the smallest"), whereas the 1500 Latin edition (f.XLVIv) has "*infirmus*" ("sick man"), which suits the context much better; Augustine's text has "*infans*" ("small child") here.

shall bear the sins of many, and because of their sins He was offered up."[475] But what Isaiah uttered in the above words regarding ultimate redemption, which was to be received through the Messiah, is obvious from what he prefaces them with: "How beautiful upon the mountains are the feet of Him that bringeth good tidings, and that preacheth peace: of Him that sheweth forth good, that preacheth salvation, that saith: 'Zion, thy God shall reign!'"[476] And below that: "The Lord hath prepared His holy arm in the sight of all the nations: and all the ends of the earth shall see the salvation of our God."[477] And below that: "For the Lord will go before you, and the God of Israel will gather you together."[478] Everyone, Jews as much as Christians, agree that these and many other similar things there pertain to the Messiah.[479] He then adds below: "Behold my boy (or "servant")[480] shall understand." That this "servant" is the Messiah, the Chaldean translation also makes clear in this way: "Behold my servant shall understand the Messiah."[481] Likewise, the Jewish Talmudic interpreters explaining this passage of Isaiah show that this Messiah is God with the following: "He shall be exalted more than Abraham, he shall be elevated more than Moses, he shall be exceedingly higher than the angels."[482] But how precious a redemption of this kind is through the Messiah is obvious from the words of Isaiah: "Israel is saved in the Lord with an eternal salvation. You shall not be confounded, and you shall not be ashamed for ever and ever."[483] Therefore, salvation through the Messiah was not to be corporeal or temporal, like the Egyptian and the Babylonian and the like, but spiritual and everlasting.[484] But although that prophecy of Isaiah, "Behold [my boy] shall understand,"[485] manifestly pertains to our Jesus, only Rabbi Salomon – a man of wayward will – dared to

---

475 Isa. 52:13–53:12; Paul. *Scrut.* 1.5.7, 53r-v; cf. Augustine, *De civitate Dei*, 18.29.1 (*PL* 41.585–6; Dombart and Kalb, 619–20).
476 Isa. 52:7.
477 Isa. 52:10.
478 Isa. 52:12.
479 Paul. Scrut. 1.5.4, 48r.
480 The Vulgate has *servus* ("servant"), but Augustine's text, derived from the *Vetus Latina* translation has *puer* ("boy") for its translation of "παῖς" (*pais*, meaning "servant" or "boy"), which is to be found in the Greek Septuagint.
481 Isa. 52:13; Paul. *Scrut.* 1.5.4, 48r-v; cf. Augustine, *De civitate Dei* 18.29.1 (*PL* 41.585; Dombart and Kalb, 619).
482 Paul. *Scrut.* 1.5.4, 48v.
483 Isa. 45:17.
484 Paul. *Scrut.* 1.5.4, 48r-v.
485 Isa. 52:13.

pervert those words, twisting them to be about the Jewish people living in their present misery. As we have said, the Chaldean translation certainly contradicts him. Even all the ancient Jewish interpreters of the prophets who maintain that the servant is the Messiah and exceedingly higher than the angels, contradict him. Such excellence cannot agree with this vile and vice-ridden rabble of Jews. Accordingly, Rabbi Moses Gerondi followed the ancients in his contempt for this Salomon and so he says in his commentaries on Genesis that the King Messiah would offer his heart to beg for Israel, also that he would suffer many fasts and the basest degradations on their behalf, citing this verse of Isaiah: "But He was wounded for our iniquities, He was bruised for our sins."[486] So he says. And although the Jewish dregs today are greatly afflicted as if wounded and bruised, almost in the same way as Isaiah portrays the afflicted servant of God, nevertheless, in no way are the words of Isaiah able to correspond with this rabble, chiefly on account of the six signs they provide us.

The first [sign]: even if these people are heavily oppressed, they still do not suffer this because of the iniquities and sins of the nations so that the nations which torment them may obtain pardon and salvation from God due to the suffering and merits of the Jews; on the contrary, all Jews await vengeance from God against the nations. Therefore, when Isaiah asserts of the servant of God that others were healed by His bruises, and that God laid the iniquity of everyone else upon Him, he certainly is not speaking about the Jewish people, since on account of their punishment others are not saved but punished, as they themselves assert.

The second sign: Isaiah says that the servant of God did not cause iniquity, nor was deceit found in His mouth. But the Jews have been given over to avarice, usury, lies, and sins. And they themselves even grant that it is because of their sins that they live in this misery, and compelled by the authority of Deuteronomy, they admit that if, after giving up their depravity, they converted to God, they would be delivered forthwith.[487] Hence their teachers, admitting that this misery arises from their sins, ask what in the world those sins may be. Rabbi Salomon denounced the worship of a calf built in the desert. God had already punished and pardoned this crime prior to Jesus. Some hold that each individual commits various transgressions, others that there is a hidden sin for whose guilt they pay the price.

---

486 Isa. 53:5.
487 Cf. Deut. 30.

The third sign: Isaiah says at the end of the chapter that the servant of God pleaded for the transgressors. On the contrary, at least thrice daily in their execrable rituals, the Jews call down the most terrible things upon the Roman Empire, the Church of Christ, and all the nations other than the Jews, and in their Talmudic decrees, they are ordered to harm Christians to the extent that they can, either by force or by fraudulent deceit.

The fourth [sign]: how in the world is it that the teaching and the discipline of peace, which Isaiah says exists in the servant of God, is to be placed in this ignorant and twisted rabble of Jews?

The fifth [sign]: how in the world is that wretched people higher than the angel of God? All the ancient Jews agreed beyond any doubt that the servant of God was just that.

The sixth [sign]: When Isaiah says: "He was led to His death by the iniquities of my people," who, pray tell, cannot see that the one is the servant of God who is led to His death, and the other is the people of God for whose iniquities He is killed? Unless perhaps one were to posit that Isaiah, the most elegant writer of all, had been speaking so absurdly that he meant to be understood as saying: "my people was led to death by the iniquities of my people." Hence if the Jewish people has no sin, Isaiah is speaking falsely here about the Jewish people, and if it does, he is speaking falsely as soon as he adds: "He hath done no iniquity,"[488] if just at that moment he is speaking about the people. Therefore, in no way can the servant of God be the people.[489]

But it is worthwhile to render the very words of Isaiah into twelve conclusions, just as Paul of Burgos, the bishop and distinguished theologian, rendered them.

The first: the servant of God is described in Isaiah as more excellent than all creatures, for he says: "He shall be exalted and elevated,"[490] and so on.

The second: He himself was small from the start, and was of humble origin, for he says: "He grows up as a tender plant, and as a root out of a thirsty ground."[491]

The third: He was despised in his course and thought worthless, for Isaiah says: "We saw that he was despised, and the most abject of men; we esteemed him not."[492]

---

488 Isa. 53:7.
489 Paul. *Scrut.* 1.5.7, 52r–54r.
490 Isa. 53:13.
491 Isa. 53:2.
492 Isa. 53:3.

The fourth: He was wounded because of our iniquities, namely, those that must be cleansed, whence the following verse: "And by His bruises we are healed," and below that: "The just one Himself shall make just many of my servants, and He shall bear their iniquities."[493]

The fifth: all just men aside from Him wandered from the shared law, off the path of salvation, but He bore all their iniquities"; that is, He paid the price for everyone, hence this verse: "All we like sheep have gone astray, and the Lord hath laid on Him the iniquity of us all."[494]

The sixth: He endured these punishments and afterward He also willingly endured death, about which Isaiah says: "He was offered because it was His own will, and He shall be led as a sheep to the slaughter, and as a lamb before his shearer."[495] But the Jews do not bear their suffering willingly, but with a reluctant and bitter spirit.

The seventh: it happened for the sin of the people, although that man was innocent; about this Isaiah says: "For the wickedness of the people have I struck him,"[496] and below that: "He who hath done no sin, neither was deceit found in His mouth."[497]

The eighth: the servant of God was to divide the spoils of the strong, acquired in victory, because[498] He had delivered His own life unto death; the following verse addresses this: "Therefore will I appoint to Him very many, and He shall divide the spoils of the strong, because He hath delivered His soul unto death."[499]

The ninth: He would be thought unjust; therefore Isaiah says: "And He was reputed with the wicked."[500]

The tenth: A servant of this kind, although through what He bore well enough, He could shoulder and erase the sins of all, He still did not in effect wash away the evils of all, but of many, for which reason Isaiah added: "And He hath borne the sins of many."[501]

---

493 Isa. 53:11.
494 Isa. 53:6.
495 Isa. 53:7.
496 Isa. 53:8.
497 Isa. 53:9.
498 Bart. *DCR* 247, line 800 has "*eo quo*," which is an unusual and difficult to translate construction, whereas the 1500 Latin edition (f. XLVIIIv) has "*eo quod*" ("because"), which is not only the more idiomatic reading but is also the same construction frequently used by Paul of Burgos.
499 Isa. 53:12.
500 Isa. 53:12.
501 Isa. 53:12.

The eleventh: there was so great a love in Him that he even prayed to God for His enemies and murderers; to this Isaiah adds: "He prayed for the transgressors."[502]

The twelfth: the things related in this prophecy exceed the natural powers of the mind, concerning which Isaiah exclaimed: "Who hath believed our report?"[503] All these things apply solely to Jesus the Nazarene.[504]

JEREMIAH: "The breath of our mouth, Christ the Lord, is taken in our sins: to whom we said: 'Under His shadow we shall love among the nations.'"[505] Likewise, one reads: "In that day thou shalt not be ashamed for all thy doings, which thou hast impiously done against me for then I will take away from thee the depravities of thine injustice, and now thou shalt no more be honoured upon my holy mountain, and I will leave in thee a meek and humble people, and they who remained of Israel shall stand in reverence in the name of the Lord."[506] Likewise: "Lord, show me so that I may recognize. Then I saw their thoughts. I was like an unblemished lamb, led to be a victim. They made plans against me, saying: 'Come, let us put wood (*lignum*) on His bread, and strike His life from the earth, and there shall be no more memory of Him.'"[507] Likewise: "She who bears is frightened, she hath become weary of life, and her Sun is set while it was yet midday. She is confounded and cursed. The rest of them I will give up to the sword in the sight of their foes."[508] Likewise: "I have forsaken my house, I have left my inheritance into the hand of her foes. My inheritance is become to me just as a lion in the forest. It hath cried out against me, therefore have I hated it."[509] With this, Jeremiah teaches that the Messiah was to be seized and given to torment to cleanse our sins, and that He would leave the people of the Christians at first humble and subject to persecutions, for He wishes the remnants of Israel to be apostles and martyrs. After these verses, he also makes mention of the wood (*lignum*) of the cross, and an eclipse at midday during Christ's passion. He also adds the martyrdom of Christians and the vengeance against the obstinate Jewish people, then he adds that the people of God rose like a lion against Christ, like a lamb, and

---

502 Isa. 53:12.
503 Isa. 53:1.
504 Paul. *Scrut.* 1.5.7, 54r-v.
505 Lam. 4:20.
506 Zeph. 3:11–13.
507 Jer. 11:18–19.
508 Jer. 15:9; Lact. *Inst.* 4.19.4 (PL 6.511; Monat, 176–7).
509 Jer. 12:7–8; Lact. *Inst.* 4.20.7 (PL 6.515; Monat, 182–3).

therefore God will cast out that people. Solomon: "If you turn away from me, says the Lord, and will not keep my truth, I will cast Israel out from the land which I have given to them, and this house will be abandoned, and everyone who shall pass by it shall wonder and say: 'For what reason did the Lord do such wicked things to this land and to this house?' And he shall say: 'Because they abandoned the Lord their God, and persecuted their king, the most beloved God, and crucified Him in great humiliation. For this, God brought these evils upon them.'"[510] So he says. Therefore, who will deny that Jesus the Nazarene was the Messiah, and that He was equally man and God?

EZRA: "This passover is our saviour and our refuge. Consider it, since we have to humiliate Him upon wood (*lignum*), and after these things we will hope in Him, lest this place be deserted for all time. God Lord of virtues says: 'If you will not believe in Him, nor hear His annunciation, you shall be a laughing stock among the nations.'"[511] So he says, and nothing could be clearer. But the threat from Ezra corresponds with that from Moses: "I" – namely, God – "will provoke you to jealousy by that which is not a nation, by a foolish nation I will anger you."[512] Above all of Ezra's other words, we should especially consider those that state that the Jews would humiliate the saviour – that is, Jesus, which means "saviour" – upon wood (*lignum*) at the time of Passover. Similarly, it is important to remind ourselves that at the fourteenth Moon,[513] the law instructs the Jews to celebrate Passover and to sacrifice a lamb. Whence Anatolius, a philosopher from Alexandria, precisely demonstrates, at first by reasoning, then by law and also the authority of Philo, Josephus, Agathobulus, and Aristobulus, that the correct and customary Mosaic Jewish ritual to be celebrated at Passover was during the month of March, after the Sun and the Moon have crossed the vernal equinox, and the Moon is opposite to the Sun. Hence Polycrates, the disciple of the apostolic disciples, claimed that the apostles and also their successors were accustomed to celebrate Passover in the manner of the Jews at the fourteenth Moon, when the Jewish people were making unleavened bread. Where are we going with this? Simply confirming what we have said elsewhere, namely that the eclipse of the Sun, which happened during Christ's passion, was not natural.[514] But that it did happen Lucian of Antioch attested

---

510 1 Kings 9:6–9 (Vulg. 3 Rg. 9:6–9).
511 Lact. *Inst.* 4.18.22 (*PL* 6.507; Monat, 168–71).
512 Rom. 10:19.
513 I.e., the full Moon.
514 Eus. *Hist.* 7.32.13–19 (*PG* 20.726–30); cf. Josephus, *Antiquitates Iudaicae*, 20.10.1.

before the tribunal of his judge: "Seek in your annals, you will discover that in Pilate's time, during Christ's passion, after the Sun was driven off, the day was broken by darkness."[515] Tertullian also proclaimed to judges: "You have this account of the world passed down in your annals."[516]

ISAIAH: "I the Lord God have called thee to justice, and I shall hold thee by the hand and strengthen thee. And I have given thee for a testament of my race, for a light of the nations, to open the eyes of the blind, to lead forth the fettered from their chains, and them that sit in darkness out of the prison house."[517] So he says, and therein God addresses Christ, sends Him to introduce a New Testament, to convert the Gentiles no less than the Jews, to release those who are fettered in limbo, and to cleanse sins. Elsewhere in Isaiah Christ speaks thus: "I am not stubborn, nor do I resist. I set my back to whips and my cheeks to open palms, and I do not turn my face away from the filthiness of spit."[518] Likewise: "In that day the root of Jesse, who shall be as an ensign of the people, him the Gentiles shall beseech, and his sepulchre shall be glorious."[519] All of this corresponds to Jesus the Nazarene.

AMOS: "'And it shall come to pass in that day,' saith the Lord, 'that the Sun shall go down at midday and the day of light shall be made dark, and I shall turn your feast days into mourning, and your songs into lamentation.'"[520] "In [that] day," namely, the one on which the Messiah suffered; "the Sun shall go down," means an eclipse of the Sun at noon while Jesus was suffering; "the day of light," that is, Christ, who is the light of light. After these words, God established as perpetual vengeance that the Jews be vexed daily and repeat the lamentations of Jeremiah and similar protestations.

EZEKIEL: "I have exalted the low tree (*lignum*)."[521]

JOB: "Who shall give us of His flesh so that we may glut ourselves?"[522]

ZECHARIAH: "With these I was wounded."[523] Likewise, regarding God saving Jerusalem, he so speaks elsewhere: "I will pour out upon the house of David, and upon the inhabitants of Jerusalem, the spirit

---

515 Eus. *Hist.* 9.6.3 (*PG* 20.810).
516 Tert. *Apol.* 21.19 (*PL* 1.401).
517 Isa. 42:6–7.
518 Isa. 50:5–6.
519 Isa. 11:10.
520 Amos 8:9–10.
521 Ezek. 17:24.
522 Job 19:22.
523 Zech. 13:6.

of grace and power. And they shall look upon me, whom they have pierced, and they shall mourn for Him as though mourning an only child."[524] So he says. He who, as God, pours in the spirit of grace and power, is pierced as a man. And therefore, so that we would understand Christ as created from different natures, in one regard performed wonders, and in another regard suffered horrors. In the first person, Zechariah said, "I will pour out," in the third, "for Him"; "I will pour out," namely, "I" as God, "they shall look upon me, whom they have pierced," namely, as a man; "and they shall mourn for Him," namely, a man assumed by me, God – but it is permitted to no one to modify the text, which should say "they shall look upon Him," for every Bible, the Hebrew as much as the Chaldean, says "they shall look upon me" – "they shall mourn," that is, they will pay the price in this age and the next. But how does He pour in the spirit of grace, if they are mourning for Him?[525] Surely He pours in the grace of the Holy Spirit and the pardon of ancient sins, for He freed the willing from hell. He also poured the spirit of power to punish the unbelievers, for these are the ones who are mourning.

HABAKKUK: "In the midst of two animals thou shalt be recognized, thou hast issued forth for the salvation of thy people to make the saved thy Christs, thou hast sent death unto the heads of thy foes."[526] "Of two animals," that is, of the two testaments; likewise, of the two prophets on Mount Tabor, Moses and Elijah; furthermore, of the two criminals on the cross; and perhaps also of the two beasts when He was born in the stables. "For the salvation of thy people," to render the souls of the believers saved from hell. He calls the obstinate Hebrews "foes."

David speaks often under his own name regarding the Messiah, whom he knew would spring up from his line, and he says the following: "Scourges were gathered together upon me, and I knew not, they were separated, and repented not; they tempted me, they scoffed at me with scorn, and they gnashed upon me with their teeth";[527] "they gave me gall for my food, and in my thirst they gave me vinegar to drink";[528] "Many dogs have encompassed me, the council of the malignant hath besieged me. They have dug my hands and feet. They have numbered all my bones. And they have stared upon me and seen

---

524 Zech. 12:10.
525 Paul. *Scrut.* 1.10.8, 167v.
526 Hab. 3:2.
527 Ps. 35:15–16 (Vulg. Ps. 34:15–16).
528 Ps. 99:22 (Vulg. 68:22).

me, they parted my garments amongst them, and upon my vesture they cast lots";[529] "They shall strive after the soul of the righteous, and condemn the innocent blood, and the Lord is become my defence";[530] "Thou wilt rescue me from the contradictions of the people, thou wilt make me head of the nations. A people which I knew not, hath served me, at the hearing of the ear they have obeyed me";[531] "Let these things be written in another generation, and the people that shall be created shall praise the Lord";[532] "The Lord hath made known His salvation, He hath revealed His justice before the sight of the nations";[533] "I will give thee the nations for thy inheritance";[534] "The kings of the earth stood up,[535] and the princes met together, against the Lord, and against His Christ";[536] "Let their" – namely, the Jews' – "table become as a snare before them, and a recompense, and a stumbling block. Let their eyes be darkened that they see not; and their back bend thou down always";[537] "Pour out thy wrath upon them, and let the rage of thy wrathful anger take hold of them. Let their dwelling be made desolate, and let there be none to dwell in their dwelling place, because they have persecuted Him whom thou hast sent, and they have added to the grief of their wounds. Add thou iniquity upon their iniquity, and let them not come into thy justice. Let them be blotted out of the book of the living, and with the just let them not be written. I am poor and sorrowful, thy salvation, O God, hath raised me up."[538] King David was not poor, but the Messiah to be born from him was poor. Regarding the traitor Judas, David foretold the following: "He who eats bread with me, shall lift his heel against me";[539] likewise, the following regarding the Jews: "[They] have hated me without cause."[540] About this, Paul the Apostle prophesied the following: "They shall fill up their sins always, for the wrath of God is come upon them to the end"[541]

---

529 Ps. 22:17–19 (Vulg. 21:17–19).
530 Ps. 94:21–2 (Vulg. 93:21–2).
531 Ps. 18:44–5 (Vulg. Ps. 17:44–5).
532 Ps. 102:19 (Vulg. Ps. 101:19).
533 Ps. 98:2 (Vulg. Ps. 97:2).
534 Ps. 2:8.
535 Bart. *DCR* 251, line 923 has *"abstiterunt"* ("stood back"), whereas the 1500 Latin edition (f.Lv) has *"astiterunt"* and the Vulgate has *"adstiterunt."* We have rendered the latter.
536 Ps. 2:2.
537 Ps. 69:23–4 (Vulg. 68:23–4).
538 Ps. 69:25–30 (Vulg. Ps. 68:25–30).
539 Ps. 41:10 (Vulg. Ps. 40:10); cf. John 13:18.
540 Ps. 35:19 (Vulg. Ps. 34:19).
541 1 Thess. 2:16.

– and so he foretold both the Jews' everlasting obstinacy and suffering. But why have we omitted what Jeremiah plainly foretold regarding Judas's act of selling out Christ, both the price and the purchase of the field, as it is related in the gospel? For he says: "And they took the thirty pieces of silver, the price of Him that was prized, that they prized of the children of Israel, and they gave them unto the potter's field, as the Lord appointed to me."[542] Matthew adds that the field, bought at the price of Christ, was called the field of blood even in his times.[543] On the resurrection of Christ, David says the following: "My flesh shall rest in hope, because thou wilt not leave my soul in hell, nor wilt thou give thy holy one to see corruption,"[544] that is, because the body of Christ did not decay. Similarly: "Thou hast brought forth, O Lord, my soul from hell. I have slept and have taken my rest, and I have risen again, because the Lord hath raised me up. I rose up and am still with thee."[545] Hosea agrees with David.

HOSEA: "He will heal us after two days; on the third day, we will rise again," or better yet, the following: "Come, and let us return to God, for He hath taken us, and He will save us; He will strike and He will cure us, He will visit us after two days; on the third day, He will raise us up, and we will come into His sight."[546] Likewise, one reads: "Death is swallowed up in victory! O death, where is thy victory? O death, where is thy sting?"[547] meaning that the resurrection of our body is also marked by the resurrection of Christ, for just as all of us have trespassed and died in Adam alone, thus we are all cleansed and rise again in Christ alone. But regarding this Paul the Apostle speaks precisely and divinely.[548]

But why was the prophet Jonah taken out of the belly of the huge fish and on the third day returned to the light still living, if not to signify the resurrection of Christ?[549] Accordingly, the deeds no less than the words of the Old Testament are prefigurations of the New. The New is by all means the end point of the Old, no differently than a completely coloured and finished painting is the end point of some sketch, and so the New Testament is far superior to the Old.

---

542 Matt. 27:9–10.
543 Matt. 27:8.
544 Ps. 16:9–10 (Vulg. Ps. 15:9–10); cf. Acts 2:26–7.
545 Ps. 30:4 (Vulg. Ps. 29:4); Ps. 3:6–7; Ps. 139:18 (Vulg. Ps. 138:18).
546 Hosea 6:1–2.
547 1 Cor. 15:54–5; cf. Hosea 13:14; Augustine, *De civitate Dei*, 14.9.2 (*PL* 41.413; Dombart and Kalb, 426).
548 Rom. 5:12–21.
549 Cf. Jon. 2.

David thus sang of the ascension of the Lord: "God is ascended with jubilation, and the Lord with the sound of the trumpet: 'Sing ye to the Lord, who ascendeth above the heaven of heavens to the East. Thou hast ascended on high, thou hast led captivity captive, thou hast given gifts to men.'"[550] He also thus sang the mission of the Holy Spirit: "Thou shalt send forth thy Spirit, and they shall be created, and thou shalt renew the face of the earth."[551]

JOEL: "And it shall come to pass after this, that I will pour out my Spirit upon all flesh and your sons and your daughters shall prophesy. Your old men shall dream dreams, and your young men shall see visions, and onto my servants and my handmaids in those days I will pour out my Spirit."[552] After the ascension of Christ, not only the apostles but also a great many others, women as much as men, Gentiles as much as Jews, the learned, the untaught, the elderly, the young, accepted the gifts and the amazing grace of the Holy Spirit.

ISAIAH: "Let me speak in other tongues and in other lips to this people, but thus they will not hear me, sayeth the Lord."[553] And accordingly, although the apostles who had previously been uncultivated suddenly poured forth divine mysteries in various languages once they accepted the gift of the Holy Spirit, even still not all the Jews believed.

EZEKIEL: "I will give you my Spirit in your entrails."[554] And elsewhere regarding baptism he says the following: "I will pour upon you clean water and you shall be cleansed from all your filthiness, and I will cleanse you from all your idols."[555] The Jews' teachers, when they interpret their book about Jonah, and when they explain the Talmud (that is, their novel body of law made after Jesus), cite a prophecy of this kind to prove that at the time of the Messiah, not only the Jews, but even every nation will wash off the filth of sins with some sort of sprinkling of water.

ISAIAH IN SONG: "Thou shall draw water with joy out of the saviour's sources, and you shall say in that day: 'Praise ye the Lord, and call upon His name.'"[556] "Of the saviour," that is, of Jesus the Messiah, for "Jesus" means "saviour"; "Praise ye the Lord," namely because Christ leads to the worship of the one God, while idols fall into disuse. A little later, he adds the preaching of the apostles to the nations in this

---

550 Ps. 47:6 (Vulg. Ps. 46:6); Ps. 68:33–4 (Vulg. 67:33–4); Ps. 68:19 (Vulg. 67:19).
551 Ps. 104:30 (Vulg. Ps. 103:30).
552 Joel 2:28–9; cf. Acts 2:17–18.
553 Cf. Isa. 28:11.
554 Ezek. 36:26.
555 Ezek. 36:25.
556 Isa. 12:3–4.

manner: "Sing ye to the Lord, for He hath done great things; shew this forth in all the earth."[557] But since Christ is born in Judea, he further adds: "Rejoice, and praise, O thou habitation of Zion, for great is He that is in the midst of thee, the Holy One of Israel."[558]

David deals with many obvious things about Christ in the second, third, fifteenth, and twenty-first psalms, and in many others, but this verse reveals the mission of the apostles to far-off nations: "Their sound hath gone forth into all the earth, and their words unto the ends of the world."[559]

On the Messiah and on the mission of the apostles, Isaiah: "How beautiful are the feet of they that bring good tidings of peace, of they that bring good tidings of good?"[560] Also, he thus presaged and had a foretaste of the apostles' torments: "For thy sake, we are put to death all the day long. We are accounted as sheep for the slaughter."[561] Origen, in the third of his *Commentaries on Genesis*, says the following: "As it is handed down to us, Thomas was allotted the Parthians, Matthew was allotted Ethiopia, Bartholomew was allotted Nearer India, Andrew was allotted Scythia, John was allotted Asia, Peter was allotted Pontus, Galatia, Bithynia, Cappadocia, and the rest of the neighbouring provinces, preaching only to the Jews. He is understood to have gone around, and finally remained at Rome, where he too was crucified turned upside down, for he pleaded it so be done lest he seem to be made equal with God. But what can I say about Paul? He filled all the lands from Jerusalem to Illyricum with the gospel of Christ, and in the end was martyred under Nero."[562] So says Origen. Thaddeus as well, who was one of the seventy disciples of Christ, set out beyond the Euphrates and was preaching the gospel in the town of Edessa. He converted the entire kingdom of king Abgar to Christ and wondrously released Abgar himself from an incurable illness. For so, in a letter to Abgar, Christ had earlier promised that this would happen, after Abgar had asked Him by letter to set out to cure him. This, which had been written in Syriac in the public histories of the city of Edessa where Abgar had ruled, Eusebius read and translated into Greek.[563]

---

557 Isa. 12:5.
558 Isa. 12:6.
559 Ps. 19:5 (Vulg. 18:5).
560 Isa. 52:7; cf. Rom. 10:15.
561 Rom. 8:36.
562 Eus. *Hist*. 3.1 (*PG* 20, 214–15).
563 Eus. *Hist*. 1.13 (*PG* 20.119–30).

CHAPTER 28 – RESOLVING DOUBTS AROUND THE PROPHECIES

At the present time, we must explain some of the prophets' words that, if they are not properly understood, provide the stubborn and stupid Jews the opportunity not to admit that Jesus was the Messiah, that is, the true Christ.

ISAIAH: "There shall be in the last days ...,"[564] that is, at the end of the age of the prophets and at the end of the Jewish kingdom and priesthood. For he means not that Christ will first come in the last days of the world, as some dream up, otherwise His teaching would be entirely useless, or at least useful for only a short time, but in the last days of the prophets, the Jewish priesthood, and the Jewish kingdom: these three came to an end in the time of Jesus of Nazareth. And this follows: "the mountain of the house of the Lord prepared on the top of mountains."[565] Some Jews, raving mad on account of this verse, say that God will move Mount Tabor, Mount Sinai, Mount Carmel all the way to Jerusalem and place them atop the peak of Mount Zion. Stupid small-minded men always ascribe the incorporeal works of an incorporeal God to bodies. But Rabbi Salomon, a Jew, actually explains Isaiah here far more correctly, saying that Mount Zion would surpass all other mountains not by the height of the place but by the greatness of its miracles. Furthermore, on that mountain our Jesus gave sight to a man born blind, healed a paralytic, and there performed many other miracles; there He also finally poured out the Holy Spirit from heaven onto His disciples.[566]

Afterward, this follows: "and all nations shall flow unto it,"[567] that is, many from every nation.[568] Similarly, they say every animal had been on Noah's ark, that is, there had been some from every kind of animal. "Nation shall not lift up sword against nation, neither shall they be exercised any more to war."[569] The phrasing "any more" signifies not an everlasting world peace but a universal and long-lasting one. There had been, moreover, such a peace in Jesus's time that Virgil then sang of the doors of war being closed, just as we have said elsewhere.[570] The

---

564 Isa. 2:2.
565 Isa. 2:2.
566 Hier. Sanctaf. *Contr.* 1.9, 85.
567 Isa. 2:2.
568 Nic. *Quaest.* 5vb–6ra.
569 Isa. 2:4.
570 Virgil, *Aeneid*, 1.293–4; cf. Chapter 27 above (Bart. *DCR* 238, line 504).

Hebrews have in the fourth book of Kings: "robbers of Syria came no more into the land of Israel."[571] After that time, however, it is reported that Syrians had often invaded the land of Israel. "[No] more," therefore, signifies up to a set time. Eusebius, however, reports that from Jesus's times until his own (that is, Constantine's), there had not been as many destructions of kingdoms and massacres of peoples as there had been before.[572] Isaiah, likewise, says the same thing elsewhere concerning the time of the Messiah: "The wolf shall dwell with the lamb, and the leopard shall lie down with the kid."[573] The high priest Eleazar and Aristobulus, the wisest Jewish interpreters before Christ, and Philo, the wisest after Christ, all reckoned that the sacred scripture had to be explained through allegory, because of its mystical sense, and they even attempted it themselves.[574] Nevertheless, the childish minds of many Jews stand in expectation of such a Golden Age with the Messiah reigning absolutely, as is depicted in the words of poets, and in paintings. Moreover, while Jesus lived, the golden truth, peace of mind, and eternal reward shone enough in the souls of men who are not stubborn; and after Him, because of His works and teaching, anyone with the will can enjoy the Golden Age: Jesus secured for man eternal peace with God, although even for many years "the wolf" (meaning the stronger ruler or people) did not devour "the lamb" (meaning the weaker ruler or people). Before Jesus, the Gentiles and the Jews were wholly at odds in all matters; after Him, many of the Jews and most of the Gentiles lived, and still live, harmonious in custom and belief by His teaching. Every day, all over the world, the bites of venomous animals are rendered harmless by the miracles of the apostles. Each one of these things, it seems, applies to the Golden Age.[575] The Golden Age ought to be placed entirely in the rewards of the soul rather than in those of the body; the poets' trifles, however, are best left to children. Even Rabbi Moses judged this to be so, for in his book *On Judges*[576] he says: "Beware lest you believe that in the time of the Messiah the order of the world and the progression of natural things ought to behave differently than normal. That Isaiah says, 'the wolf shall dwell with the lamb' and so forth, is enigmatic, for it

---

571 2 Kings 6:23 (Vulg. 4 Rg. 6:23).
572 Cf. Eus. *Hist*. 10.9 (*PG* 20.902–6).
573 Isa. 11:6.
574 Eus. *Prae*. 8.9–11 (*PG* 21.626–44).
575 Nic. *Quaest*. 6ra.
576 Cf. Chapter 27 above (cf. Bart. *DCR* 232).

signifies that Israel will live untroubled amid the impious men of this world, who are depicted as wolves and leopards."[577] So he says.

MOSES IN *DEUTERONOMY*: "If thou be driven as far as the poles of heaven, the Lord thy God will fetch thee back from hence, and will take thee to Himself, and bring thee into the land which thy fathers possessed."[578] For this reason, the Jews that have gathered[579] together hoping for Christ's support do not admit that Jesus was the true Christ since they were scattered on His account. The response to be given to these Jews is that this prophecy was fulfilled when they were freed from servitude in Babylon. For at that time, as Ezra attests, King Cyrus not only allowed all the Jews to return to their fatherland, but he even offered gifts to those returning.[580] Should, however, anyone argue that a flock of this sort pertains to the Messiah, I would say that any souls scattered by Jesus for their sin that have the will gather together in the heavenly fatherland. For David called it "the land of the living": "I believe," he says, "to see the good things of the Lord in the land of the living."[581] Hence Rabbi Moses the Egyptian in Deuteronomy[582] says that the divine good, which is intelligible, is named by many names in holy scripture, for it is called: the mountain of God and His holy place, the place of sanctuary, the holy way, the halls of the Lord, the temple of the Lord, the house of the Lord, the gate of the Lord.[583] So he says. Rabbi Salomon and Rabbi Abba also reckon that the building of the temple described by Ezekiel pertains to the heavenly Jerusalem.[584] False, therefore, are those who hope to see a visible temple built by the Messiah; false, likewise, those who are waiting for Him to gather the people of Israel together in some set location; and false, thirdly, those who think that all Jews will be saved in the time of the Messiah.[585]

Let us hear Jeremiah speaking thus: "'Return, O ye revolting children,' saith the Lord, 'for I am your husband, and I will take you, one of a city, and two of a flock, and will bring you into Zion. And I will give you pastors according to my own heart, and they shall feed you

---

577 Paul. *Scrut.* 1.5.2, 46v.
578 Deut. 30:4–5.
579 In this chapter, Ficino uses two cognate words for "gather" (*"congregare"*) and "flock" (*"grex"*).
580 Cf. Ezra 1:1–4.
581 Ps. 27:13 (Vulg. Ps. 26:13).
582 I.e., *Mishneh Torah*.
583 Paul. *Scrut.* 1.4.3, 39r–41r; Nic. *Quaest.* 6rb; Hier. Sanctaf. *Contr.* 1.1, 16–17.
584 Cf. Ezra 40:5–49; 41:1–26.
585 Hier. Sanctaf. *Contr.* 1.4, 49–50.

with knowledge and teaching."[586] So he says. In fact, these words are to be understood as being about the final redemption, which was to be fulfilled by the Messiah, but not about the redemption from servitude in Babylon, as others believe. For in the same context one reads: "At that time Jerusalem shall be called the throne of the Lord, and all the nations shall be gathered to it, in the name of the Lord."[587] Concerning this, Rabbi Salomon explains in his *Sanhedrin* book that the words of Jeremiah above, namely, "I will take you, one of a city, and two of a flock,"[588] are about the final redemption, which they await. For there he says the following: "I shall elect the just and bring them into Zion," from which it is clear that in the final redemption through the Messiah not all Israelites are saved, but only the just; they, moreover, are far fewer than the unjust, who are not saved. Therefore the prophet said: "one of a city, and two of a flock," – or "of a kindred" – "as if to say very few will be chosen from the many."[589] So he says. Likewise, in that spot, another of the ancient Talmudists says that, just as only two – namely, Caleb and Joshua – of the 600,000 men who left Egypt are said to have entered the Promised Land, thus it will be in the time of the Messiah, for so it is written in Hosea: "and she shall sing there according to the days of her youth, and according to the days of her coming up out of the land of Egypt."[590] So he says.

ZECHARIAH, SPEAKING OF CHRIST, SAYS: "He shall build a temple to the Lord."[591] The Jews expect Christ to erect the largest construct on earth from dead stones. Jesus, however, by an all too divine skill erected a temple from the living stones of souls. But these people are even refuted by what has been said above.

JEREMIAH: "In His days," namely, the Messiah's, "Judah shall be saved, and Israel shall dwell confidently."[592] The Jews hold that the days that Jeremiah names pertain to the Christ by whose hands they hope to be returned to that ancient and earthly kingdom, and to be enriched by earthly wealth as they desire. We, however, say that by the grace and teaching of Christ, the souls of the willing, everyone else as much as the Jews, are cleansed of that original guilt, and through this cleansing they can inhabit the body with the confidence that after the dissolution of

---

586 Jer. 3:14–15.
587 Jer. 3:17.
588 Jer. 3:14.
589 Paul. *Scrut.* 2.10.6, 282v.
590 Hosea 2:15; Hier. Sanctaf. *Contr.* 1.4, 50.
591 Zech. 6:13.
592 Jer. 23:6.

the body, they will fly back to the heavens. "Judah," that is, the human race that wholly has its origin in that region (that is, in Judea). "Shall be saved," specifically, should it have the will. But from whatever shall it be saved? Specifically from the guilt conceived through Adam, and it will dwell in heaven.[593] We ought to remember that, in holy scripture, Israel occasionally signifies men of every race, so long as they follow the true worship of the God of Israel, even if they are not descended from Israel or Jacob by blood. For this reason, when Isaiah expounds on the propagation of the people of Israel through the calling of the nations under the Messiah's teaching, he says: "I will pour out my spirit upon thy seed," and so on, "And they shall spring up among the herbs, as willows beside the running waters." In the same context he makes clear that this propagation of the seed of Israel or Jacob is not to be understood as only according to the lineage of the body. Therefore, he adds: "One says: 'I am the Lord's,' and he shall be called by the name of Jacob, and another shall subscribe on his hand, 'To the Lord,' and he shall be made in name like unto Israel."[594] So he says. The one who says, "I am the Lord's," is thus of Israel according to the flesh, and about him this verse is added, "and he shall be called by the name of Jacob." What follows beyond this in the text pertains to those who are similar to Israel in belief and customs. Hence Rabbi Salomon, interpreting these words, "and he shall be made in name like unto Israel," thus says, "they are those who are converted from the Gentiles' mode of worship to the true worship of God, for they are worthy to be called by the name of Israel." So says Salomon.[595]

Therefore, when the prophets say that Israel will be saved under the Messiah, they do not understand it as this race of man or that, but all who both in their worship and way of life render themselves similar to Israel and Jacob. But if you maintain that a specific people is signified by the name Judah and Israel in the text of Jeremiah, so long as it signifies the people of God, so be it! Those who denied the son of God, however, degenerated and were punished by the Romans, but those of the Jews who followed Him – many great men indeed – were truly to be called by the name of Israel. The chief among these men, since they were given a sign from God before the siege of the city of Jerusalem, fled into the realm of king Agrippa, who was a friend of the Romans, and were kept safe.[596] It is worth no small consideration what Paul the

---

593 Nic. *Quaest.* 6rb.
594 Isa. 44:3–5.
595 For the last three paragraphs, see Paul. *Scrut.* 1.1.1–2, 5r-v and 6v–7r.
596 Eus. *Hist.* 3.5.3 (*PG* 20.222–3).

Apostle truly prophesied, that some Jews to be sure would remain stubborn until every gentile the world over converted completely to Christ and at last they would be converted at the end of the ages.[597] He also cited these prophetic verses: "There shall come out of Zion He that shall deliver, and shall turn away the ungodliness from Jacob and this is to them my covenant when I shall take away their sins."[598] Thus, at last, in the predetermined times, Judah will be saved and there will be then, as was divinely predicted, one shepherd and one fold. Then will be fulfilled this verse of Zechariah: "In that day there shall be one Lord, and His name one."[599] There is also this verse of Zephaniah: "Then I will restore to the people a chosen lip, that all may call upon the name of the Lord, and may serve with one shoulder."[600] Likewise, add this verse of Ezekiel: "Then I will turn back (*convertam*) the captivity of Jacob, and will have mercy on the house of Israel."[601] Similar to that is this verse: "And I will bring back your captivity from all regions."[602] But when will this be? Every day all the Jews who have the will are delivered from captivity by the Messiah – not only from the captivity of sin but also from that of men. This will become especially clear when they have the greatest will, that is, during the second coming of Christ near the end of the world's course. Then the Messiah, by force of arms of some sort, will bring battle against the impious; these battles Zechariah foretells will take place in a war to come over Jerusalem, and afterward adds: "in that day, the Lord shall be one."[603] Then the Messiah will forcefully pour out His wrath over the nations and kingdoms with all His might, just as the prophet Zephaniah threatens, adding this: "Then I will restore to the people."[604] Then the battle of Gog and Magog that Ezekiel described will be fulfilled, and Ezekiel foretells that when it comes to an end, the redemption of Israel will take place: "Then I will turn back the captivity."[605] Christ, therefore, in His first coming gently remitted the sins of the willing with His teaching, His example, and His works; in His second He will approach the matter more boldly, and He will purge more bitterly, and by force

---

597 Rom. 11:26–7.
598 Cf. Isa. 59:20–1.
599 Zech. 14:9.
600 Zeph. 3:9.
601 Ezra 39:25.
602 Ezra 29:14.
603 Zech. 14:9.
604 Zeph. 3:9.
605 Ezra 39:25.

He will overcome the stubborn with their leader the Antichrist: for so demands the order of God, of nature, of instruction.[606]

DANIEL SAYS: "I beheld in the vision of the night, and lo, one like the Son of Man came on the clouds of heaven."[607] On account of this and the like, Jews expect a Christ not humble in appearance and circumstances, as our tradition maintains of Jesus, but rather a majestic and powerful one, since they know not that His coming is twofold: "Long ago, He came humbly to be judged, in the end He shall come majestically to judge."[608] Furthermore, it becomes clear that Daniel is talking about the final judgment of the world there when he adds: "Thrones were placed, and the books were opened."[609] That the first coming would be humble we have demonstrated above with many of the prophets' utterances, and there is the following one of David about this: "But I am a worm, and no man: the reproach of men, and the outcast of the people. All they that saw me have laughed me to scorn, they have spoken with the lips and wagged the head: 'He hoped in the Lord, let Him deliver Him, let Him save Him, seeing He delighteth in Him.' For thou art He that hast drawn me out of the womb, my hope from the breasts of my mother, I was cast upon thee from infancy out of my mother's womb. Thou art my God, depart not from me."[610] He adds much in the same passage quite clearly pertaining to the same thing.[611] Many of the Jews, since they were reading different utterances about a different coming, put forward two messiahs: the one would be the son of Joseph, that is in a long line descended from Joseph, father of Ephraim, who would be subject to suffering and murder; the other would be descended from David, whom they are accustomed to call the son of David, who was to revive the other messiah that had been slain and forcefully restore the kingdom of Israel. But they are clearly mad; for holy scripture maintains that the salvation of the human race depends on one, by one, and for one, and when they speak of the Messiah, they almost always call Him the child of David or Judah, but never that of Joseph, father of Ephraim. Hence Rabbi Moses in his book of *Judges*, citing all the prevalent opinions concerning the Messiah, concludes that the Messiah would be from the line of David,

---

606 Paul. *Scrut.* 1.5.5, 49r–50v.
607 Dan. 7:13.
608 Bart. *DCR* 260 has *"indicaturus"* ("shall prosecute") where one should read *"iudicaturus"* ("shall judge").
609 Dan. 7:9–10.
610 Ps. 22:7–12 (Vulg. Ps. 21:7–12).
611 Nic. *Quaest.* 6va.

and he makes no mention of another Messiah. Therefore, those who groundlessly put forward the pair of Messiahs are raving mad since one is enough. How much more correctly do we sufficiently fulfil all the prophecies, however diverse, through Jesus alone, and we ourselves are sufficiently filled! If in fact Jesus was the son of one Joseph as though by adoption, reputation, and guardianship, He was also the son of King David from His mother who descended from David. At one point, in humility, He was judged by the inhabitants of the world; at another point, He also judged the world with the utmost force.[612]

ISAIAH: "And the light of the Moon shall be as the light of the Sun."[613] He is not speaking of the time of the first coming, when the usual order of the world was not to change, as we have said elsewhere, but about the age after the second coming of Christ. For neither the heavenly bodies nor the elements will cease to be after the final judgment, but only their motion, which was instituted for the sake of repose (*quies*), and then, by an overflow of light, the universe will be rendered more beautiful. He adds: "Then the wound of the people and the affliction of their wound shall be healed, because death, which was introduced to us on account of the sin of our first parents, shall die."[614] For all men shall rise again to an immortal life, as many prophets plainly foretell. Moreover, we have addressed the methods of the resurrection in that *Theology* of ours, which we composed in the countryside at Rignano with Giovanni Cavalcanti, our Achates. In our *Theology* we even added that Zoroaster, Mercurius, and Plato had predicted the resurrection of bodies. What is more, nobody doubts that the Hebrews' many prophets foretold it.

ISAIAH: "He shall see a long-lived seed."[615]

DAVID: "I will make His seed to endure forevermore."[616] These two predictions, Christ is promised a spiritual seed, not a bodily one. Likewise, a spiritual priesthood and kingdom are promised when David says: "Thou art a priest forever according to the order of Melchizedek,"[617] "and I will make His throne as the days of heaven."[618] Likewise: "Thy throne, O God, is forever and ever: the sceptre of thy kingdom is a sceptre of righteousness."[619] Shortly afterward, he also adds what pertains

---

612 Paul. *Scrut.* 1.10.8, 167v.
613 Isa. 30:26.
614 Isa. 30:26.
615 Isa. 53:10; last two paragraphs: Fic. *TP* 18.9 (Allen and Hankins 6.164–79).
616 Ps. 89:30 (Vulg. Ps. 88:30).
617 Ps. 110:4 (Vulg. Ps. 109:4).
618 Ps. 89:30 (Vulg. Ps. 88:30).
619 Ps. 45:6 (Vulg. Ps. 44:7).

to the name of the Messiah by saying: "God, thy God, has anointed thee with the oil of gladness beyond thy fellows."[620] For He has been anointed and ordained beyond all other kings, clearly because it was by God and for eternity. Furthermore, he had rightly said that he was a priest according to the order of Melchizedek, for this Melchizedek is reported to have been a priest of the highest God in the holy scrolls, but one who was not anointed with oil in the common way and who did not receive the priestly office following the succession of race, as was customarily done among the Hebrews.[621] And therefore it is foretold that, according to Melchizedek's order, Christ will be a priest who is to be consecrated not by liquid oil, but by virtue of the heavenly Spirit.[622]

Nathan, too, was ordered by God to foretell the following to King David about a Messiah to be born of his line: "When thy days shall be fulfilled, and thou shalt sleep with thy fathers, and I will raise up thy seed after thee, which shall be from thy bowels."[623] This man, therefore, who is born after the death of David, cannot be Solomon; on the contrary, the Messiah is an eternal king, not temporal like Solomon, and one who builds not a temporal temple to God, as Solomon did, but an eternal one. For God continues to say to Nathan: "And I shall restore His kingdom. He shall build a house to my name, and I will establish His throne forever. I will be to Him a father and He shall be to me a son,"[624] namely because the Messiah is more the son of God than of David. A little later he adds: "and His kingdom shall be before me forever,"[625] namely because it will be in the goods of the spirit, not of the body. Therefore, he adds: "and His throne shall be raised up forever."[626] Understanding this kingdom better than the obstinate Jews, Mohammad says in the Qur'an: "The Word of God, Jesus Christ, the son of Mary was sent by the Creator of the world to be the face of all nations in this age and the next."[627]

The kingdom of Jesus of Nazareth was just as the prophets promised Christ. Therefore, He says: "My kingdom is not of this world."[628] He accordingly left to His pontifical successors authority in spiritual

---

620 Ps. 45:7 (Vulg. Ps. 44:8).
621 Cf. Eus. *Hist.* 1.3.16–18 (*PG* 20.74).
622 Paul. *Scrut.* 2.1.4, 174r–v; 2.3.15, 220v–221r.
623 2 Sam. 7:12 (Vulg. 2 Rg. 7:12).
624 2 Sam. 7:12–14 (Vulg. 2 Rg. 7:12–14).
625 2 Sam. 7:16 (Vulg. 2 Rg. 7:16).
626 2 Sam. 7:13 (Vulg. 2 Rg. 7:13).
627 *Alcor.* 3.45 (Petrus Pons, 45).
628 John 18:36.

matters, and not until the end of the world does the substantial and chief jurisdiction of the pontiffs, insofar as the pontiffs are also the vicars of Christ, extend itself any further. The dominion and administration over earthly matter are supplementary roles for pontiffs – almost by accident – not insofar as they are God's vicars, but insofar as they are the heirs of Constantine the Caesar. Moreover, this is said not to detract from the pontiff's authority over temporal matters – for he really does hold it, although it happened by accident, since without it he had long been a true pontiff for three hundred years, and can still be – but to more easily deflect the barbs of the Jews with this truth.[629] For where Daniel signifies the four kingdoms under the figures of the four beasts, all the Jews maintain that the fourth beast is to be understood as the Roman Empire.[630] Since, however, Daniel says that the fourth beast would be destroyed by a kingdom to be raised up by the God of heaven, the Jews explain that the Roman Empire ought to be destroyed with the coming of the Messiah.[631] They add that the Church's rule is entirely the same as its ancient Roman counterpart, albeit smaller, for which reason they conclude that it is an impious rule, and it is later to be dissolved by their long-awaited Messiah. In fact, they corroborate this with the fact that Daniel says that from the fourth beast a small horn sprouts to speak out against God on high, and they maintain that such was Jesus and His vicar.[632] Truly a contrivance of this sort is false, not only because the basis for Roman rule lies in the material, whereas the basis for Christian rule lies entirely in the immaterial – therefore they are distinct sorts of rule, for which reason even today we see our emperor as distinct from the pontiff – but also because Daniel says that the horn made war against the saints and prevailed against them, which in no way can be said of Jesus and His vicar, who is similar to Him.[633] In addition to that, Daniel foretells in the same place that the fourth beast will perish when "one like the Son of Man on the clouds of heaven"[634] will come. All this will be fulfilled in the second coming of Christ, when He will approach in the greatest majesty and power to render judgment, but by no means in the first coming, when Daniel foretells that He will come not in power and magnificence, but as a stone that has been hewn and thrown. That "horn," in fact, will be the

---

629 Paul. *Scrut.* 1.7.7–10, 83r–87r.
630 Cf. Dan. 7:1–8; Paul. *Scrut.* 1.7.12, 90v.
631 Dan. 7:13.
632 Cf. Dan 2:34 and 2:45.
633 Cf. Dan. 7:8.
634 Dan. 7:13.

Antichrist; "small," clearly because the Antichrist will derive its origin from the vile dregs of the Jews. "Attached to the fourth beast," that is, to tyrannical power, for this beast signifies the whole tyranny of the world, from the beginning of Rome until the end of the world, which tyranny will fall together with the greatest tyrant, the Antichrist, with the second coming of Christ: for Daniel says concerning the judgment near the end of the world: "the judgment sat," he says again "suddenly an end."[635] There are those who maintain that by this horn not only is the Antichrist signified, but also the tyrannical heresy and heretical tyranny of Mohammad, the King of Arabia, for he is the image of the Antichrist, just as John the Baptist was the image of Christ.[636] Furthermore, that the fourth beast signifies a universal tyranny in any and every part of the world, which arose from the first Romans up until the Antichrist and the end of the world is clear from the fact that even all the Jews agree that the first beast signifies a universal tyranny of the world from the beginning of the world up until Nebuchadnezzar. For the ends of things ought to correspond to their beginnings[637] with a degree of symmetry.[638]

CHAPTER 29 – AGAINST THE JEWS: THAT THEY ARE WRETCHED IN CHRIST'S VENGEANCE[639]

Should anyone examine the histories of the Hebrews, he would find that they have never been oppressed by any serious misfortune, except for whenever they have committed some most despicable crime. Before their servitude in Babylon they fell into idolatry and filled the streets of the city of Jerusalem with the blood of the prophets, just as one reads in the book of Kings, and they perpetrated other outrages of a very similar nature. This is why they suffered seventy years of servitude in the land of Babylon. Thereafter, they lived justly enough up until the times of

---

635 Cf. Dan. 7:10 and 7:26; Paul. *Scrut.* 1.7.12, 91r.
636 Paul. *Scrut* 1.7.12, 90v.
637 Bart. *DCR* 263 has *"ex ordinis,"* an incomplete prepositional phrase where the 1500 Latin edition (f. LVIIv) has *"exordiis"* ("beginnings"), which fits the intent Ficino expressed in the corresponding passage of the Italian text.
638 Paul. *Scrut.* 1.7.12, 90r.
639 Bart. *DCR* 264 has *"quam"* ("how"), whereas both the list of chapter headings at the beginning of the book as well as the 1500 Latin edition (f. LVIIv) have *"quod"* ("that"), which we have kept. The Italian version also has "che" ("that").

our Jesus Christ, whom they treated no differently than the prophets before Him that had been sent for His sake. Since, however, after murdering Jesus, they have been punished longer and more harshly than ever before, one can draw no other conclusion than that they had committed a crime greater than idolatry and the murder of the prophets. Hence Jeremiah: "They have not hearkened to me, nor inclined their ear, but have hardened their neck, and have done worse than their fathers."[640] This, in fact, demonstrates that Jesus, the true Messiah, was both more than a prophet and more than a divine man; indeed, He truly was God.[641]

Tell me, Jews, I beg of you, why in the Talmud – that book of yours containing novel laws which you composed nearly four hundred years after Jesus – did you establish laws against the Christians more savage than Nero or Domitian could have devised, even though you were scattered not by Christians but by the idolatrous Romans?[642] Why do you call down the most serious evils on us with venomous curses, particularly at least three times on any given day during your rituals, when we ourselves pray to God for you, and we are even kinder to you than the Mohammadans are? You do not think the Christian law to be baser than the Mohammadan law, but rather superior. In fact, its very nature secretly goads your spirits, as I see it, towards hatred of Christians, because clearly on account of Jesus Christ divine justice scattered you. It is plain to see how you cleared the way for Christ's vengeance, although unwittingly. Surely many among you, out of an impious disregard and ignorance of the scriptures, did not believe that Jesus was the true Messiah, since He was unarmed. Because of this, and because you were either expecting to have another Messiah soon, as Suetonius says, or, as many among you thought, you already had another one who was mighty in arms, you audaciously rebelled against the Romans. Due to this rebellion, the city was utterly destroyed, the men slain and scattered. We know this from Suetonius.[643]

So you have been ruined because you did not believe in Jesus Christ. We can even confirm this with the words of your Josephus. For he mentions the many signs of divine anger against the Jews and the most undeniable dreadful miracles. He also maintains that the Romans besieged the city of Jerusalem, where nearly all of Judea had then come

---

640 Jer. 7:26.
641 Paul. *Scrut.* 2.6.3, 266v.
642 Hier. Sanctaf. *Contr.* 2.1, 123; cf. Ps. 59:12 (Vulg. Ps. 58:12).
643 Suetonius, *Divus Vespasianus*, 4.5.

together for the feast of the unleavened bread, and so your crowds were at their densest. Moreover, it is indisputable that during those very days you murdered Jesus years before.[644] Josephus adds that Titus, who had besieged the city, after receiving many portents, would often say that God was so angry at the Jews that he feared that God would also grow angry at him if he forgave the Jews. So although Titus was not cruel – and so too for Vespasian – nevertheless, with God pushing him on, the war was conducted with more cruelty – nay, with more justice – than the Romans were ever accustomed to at any other time. Despite the fact that over 1.1 million Jews perished in that city by famine and sword, more than 90,000 captives were still sold into slavery. Josephus, who was even present for it, and Eusebius say this.[645] Josephus adds the following: "When Titus, going around the city, saw the ramparts piled with the corpses of the dead and my fatherland drenched with the putrid gore of the human body, with a great sigh and raising his hands to the sky, he called on God as his witness that this was not his doing."[646] Then he adds: "I for my part judge that, even if Roman arms had let up for just a little against the impious, the city would have suffered the penalty of death, whether by being swallowed by the earth, or by a flood of water, or by the fires of Sodom and thunderbolts sent down from heaven. This city would have produced a far more unfortunate generation of men living today than those who had endured such horrors, and a viler generation at that, and because of them, so too would every nation equally deserve to be exterminated."

Philostratus confirms as much in his *Life of Apollonius of Tyana* with these words: "With the capture of Jerusalem, Titus had filled all the environs with corpses. What is more, the neighbouring peoples wanted to crown him because of his victory, but he responded that he was unworthy of such an honour, for he had not been the author of such deeds, but rather he had merely let God work through his hands to show His anger against the Jews." So says Philostratus.[647]

Present at the siege was Vespasian, who when he was holding his triumph over the Jews after the city was destroyed, just as Suetonius relates, suddenly performed two miracles before the people: by touch alone, he healed a blind man and a lame man.[648] He, however, never before or after is reported to have performed another deed of

---

644 Eus. *Hist.* 3.5.5–7 (*PG* 20.223); cf. Josephus, *De bello Iudaico*, 6.420–7.
645 Eus. *Hist.* 3.7.2 (*PG* 20.234).
646 Eus. *Hist.* 3.6.15–16 (*PG* 20.230); cf. Josephus, *De bello Iudaico*, 5.519.
647 Philostratus, *Vita Apollonii Tyanensis*, 6.29.
648 Suetonius, *Divus Vespasianus*, 7.2.

that sort, as though he performed those miracles with the aid of God immediately after he avenged Christian blood at God's incitement. For although he was sufficiently just, nevertheless, he was not of such holiness, or of such learning and skill that he could perform miracles, as it seems to me. Clement and Hegesippus, disciples of the apostles, write that James, the brother of our Lord, stood out in everyone's opinion as excellent in his righteousness to such a degree that even all the wisest of the Jews believed that the reason for the storming of Jerusalem under Vespasian that followed immediately on the heels of James's death was because they laid their wicked hands on him.[649] Josephus clearly indicates that he too thinks this is the case when he says the following: "All this happened to the Jews to avenge James, a righteous man, who was the brother of Jesus that is called Christ,[650] the most righteous and pious of all men by everyone's agreement whom the Jews murdered." So he says. Furthermore, that God ruined them to avenge Christian blood is clear from the fact that they perpetrated no other crime in those times for which God, it would seem, ought to grow so bitterly outraged. He was nevertheless wholly outraged, as Josephus himself, who was present, shows in the seventh book of *The Jewish War*: "Some of the worst men," he says,

> and deceivers uttering false prophecies persuaded the unfortunate people not to believe the obvious signs and evidence of divine anger and wrath, although the future destruction of both the city and the nation was clearly being presaged to them. But just as the insane and those who possess neither eyes nor a mind, they heaped scorn upon every sign from the heavens – and indeed a bright shining star just like a sword was seen looming over the city and, what is more, the comet was seen burning with fateful flames for the entire year. But even before the time of destruction and war, when the people gathered for the feast day of the unleavened bread, on the eighth day of Xanthicus – which is April – during nighttime, at the ninth hour, such a brilliant light surrounded the altar and the temple that everyone thought that it had become the clearest day, and the light lasted for half an hour. To the inexperienced and ignorant, this fateful omen in fact seemed favourable, but its true meaning did not escape those experienced in the laws, the learned, and each and every upright teacher. Also during the same feast, when the calf was brought forth during the sacrifices and was standing beside the altar, it birthed a lamb while in

---

649 Eus. *Hist.* 2.23.19–20 (*PG* 20.203).
650 Cf. Matt. 27:22.

the very hands of its attendants. But even the door of the inner temple, which looked to the East, suddenly appeared to have opened itself on its own during the sixth hour of the night, although it was decked in solid bronze and of so great a weight that it could only be closed with the utmost effort of twenty men pushing it, and although it was held in place by being equipped with iron locks and bars, and by being fastened with bolts extending along its length. But even some days after the feast day had passed, on the twenty-first day of the month of Artemisius (i.e., May) an ominous vision appeared that was almost beyond belief – certainly they would have thought it untrue, had not the calamity of ills that followed confirmed their trust in their own eyes – for around sunset, they saw four-horse chariots borne everywhere through the air, cohorts of armed men mingling with clouds, and the host surrounding cities with unforeseen columns of men. Furthermore, on another feast day, which is called Pentecost, when the priests entered the temple at night to perform the customary mysteries, first they felt some tremors and heard a loud din, and then heard unexpected voices saying: "Let us depart from here." In addition to this was something more frightful: before the fourth year of the war, when the city had been enduring in peace and abundance, a certain son of Ananias named John, a simple commoner, suddenly began shouting on the feast day of the tabernacles:[651] "Woe from the East, woe from the West, woe from the four winds, woe over Jerusalem and over the temple, woe over bridegrooms and brides, woe over the people," and he was shouting this incessantly, day and night, going around through all the streets, until some leading men from among the people, as if moved by anger at the dire portent, seized the man and flogged him with many lashings. But, saying nothing else on his own behalf and not even pleading with those who were present, he kept repeating the same utterances with equal determination and uproar. Then, understanding that there was a movement of the divine presence (*numen*) in this man – as was the case – the leaders brought him before a Roman judge, and there the man, now lacerated to the bone by scourges, poured out neither pleas nor tears, but kept producing the same utterance, letting it out wretchedly and with a wail after nearly every blow, even adding this: "Woe, woe to Jerusalem."[652]

Josephus has been speaking up to this point.

Even before him, Jesus had thus foretold these ills: "Woe to them that are with child and that give suck in those days. But pray that your flight be not in the winter or on the Sabbath. For there shall be then great

---

651 I.e., Sukkot.
652 Eus. *Hist.* 3.8.1–9 (*PG* 20.235–9); cf. Josephus, *De bello Iudaico*, 6.288–304.

tribulation, such as hath not been from the beginning of the world until now, neither shall be."[653] Therefore, upon seeing the city, Jesus wept over it saying: "If thou also hadst known, and that in this day, the things that are to thy peace, but now it is hidden[654] from thy eyes. For the days shall come upon thee, and thy enemies shall cast a trench about thee and compass thee round and hem thee in on every side, and cast thee to the ground, and thy children who are in thee."[655] "There shall be great necessity[656] in the land, it shall be upon this people, and they shall fall by the edge of the sword and shall be led away captives into all nations. And Jerusalem shall be trodden down by the nations till the times of the nations be fulfilled."[657] "And when you shall see Jerusalem compassed about with an army, then know that the desolation thereof is at hand."[658] He even foretold other things like this, and if anyone were to compare them with Josephus's history, he would not be able to hold any doubt concerning the divinity of Christ.[659]

Since you have not merely been struck down once or for a short time, just as is usual for those who pay the price for their human transgression, but, paying the price to God eternal for the crime of *lèse-majesté*, you wander miserably both everywhere and always, what more will you to say this, you wretches? Nor in fact is this an injustice, for you always sin, both in that you are obstinate and in that you detract from the mystery of Christ. Furthermore, although many nations opposed Christians, you nevertheless were and will be rightly punished more sternly than the others because you were too ungrateful after God once honoured you above all others, because you murdered the prophets and Christ. You were the first of everyone to set yourselves against the Christians, both in Judea with murder and rapine, and everywhere else in the world with your treachery. Everywhere you would rouse the strength of the nations against Christians, for which reason they were tormented far and wide because of the example and instigation

---

653 Matt. 24:19–21.
654 The Latin of the Vulgate has *abscondita sunt* ("are hidden"), but Ficino provides the singular, following the Greek *ekrybeē* ("is hidden"), which is itself due to the fact that in Greek neuter plural nouns do not take a plural verb, but rather a singular.
655 Luke 19:42–4.
656 The Greek of the New Testament is *anagkeē*, which can carry the sense of both necessity or inevitability and distress or anguish, which is rendered in the Latin Vulgate as *pressura* ("distress"), but Ficino provides "*necessitas*" ("necessity" or "inevitability") instead, a word laden with greater philosophical connotations.
657 Luke 21:23–4.
658 Luke 21:20.
659 Eus. *Hist*. 3.7.1–5 (*PG* 20.234–5).

of many Jews. Nevertheless, the heavenly leader, in a way that beggars belief, restored his host that had been cut down on all sides, and miraculously enlarged it. What is more, even Mohammad admits that you were scattered in Christ's vengeance. For he says in the Qur'an that God rescued Jesus's soul from the hands of the Jews, brought it back to Himself and exalted it, exposed the followers of Christ to persecutors even up to the judgment and end of the world, and on top of that resolved to afflict the disbelieving Jews, who are deprived of every avenger and guardian, with the greatest torments in this life and the next.[660]

But listen to your Moses of Egypt in his book of Ordinary Judges saying this: "Jesus of Nazareth was recognized as the Messiah and was killed by the verdict of the judges: it was the reason why Israel would be destroyed by the sword."[661] So he says. Indeed, although divine justice oppressed you with various severe calamities and massacres immediately after Jesus nearly every year until Titus (as Florus, Josephus, Philo, and Eusebius demonstrate), it nevertheless delayed the utter destruction of your city for forty years after Jesus so that even you would have time for penitence and so that the rise of Christian law would become more clearly known to all the ages while your city still stood and without the confusion of the events of those times. It also happened that while the city was standing, you could more violently torture Christians and put them through more exacting trials. Christ, however, punished you through the hands of idolaters, not of Christians, in order to show that His Christians both ought to live and are able to rule without any violence. And He punished you so miraculously that there has never been nor will there ever be anything more wretched. Christ foretold it just as Josephus confirmed it.[662] Read Josephus's fifth book on these matters, you will also see mothers eating their children out of famine. However, that I may wrap this all up in brief, one cannot devise a more lamentable tragedy, and even your own people once foretold this wretchedness in Christ's vengeance. For when Pilate said: "I am innocent of the blood of this just man: you handed Him over," they responded: "His blood be upon us and upon our children."[663]

---

660 *Alcor.* 4.157–8 (Petrus Pons, 70); cf. Irenaeus, *Adversus haereses*, 1.24.4 (PG 7,1.676–8).
661 Nic. *Quaest.* 5va.
662 Eus. *Hist.* 3.6.21–7 (PG 20.230–4); cf. Josephus, *De bello Iudaico*, 6.201–13.
663 Matt. 27:24–5.

Continuing the Proof of Christ's Vengeance in Three Chapters

Since, however, you diligently mull over the causes of this calamity of yours on a daily basis in order to escape the guilt of Christ's murder, let us recall everything from the beginning and collect it into three chapters. We judge that it is by necessity best of all for three chapters to correspond on the matter of that crime, for whose guilt you have been scattered.

First, in fact, that crime – one that we have touched upon from the beginning, which is obviously far more severe than the guilt for which you were once scattered in Babylonia – is at the very least commensurably more severe with how much worse your condition is after Jesus than it was in the previous diaspora. This calamity is reported to have begun with the unspeakable slaughter of your people and the cheapest sale of them into slavery – indeed, such happened often and severely at other times: before Titus and after Jesus, but especially in Jerusalem under Titus, in Mesopotamia under Trajan, in Betar under Hadrian, and everywhere under Gallus.[664] In fact, this did not happen in the calamity that preceded Christ. Add to this the fact that under Claudius, aside from the other calamities, as Luke says, God also overwhelmed you with extreme famine, which even Josephus asserts was great in Judea during the time of Claudius.[665] Likewise, in other diasporas you had everywhere honoured the leaders of your race and kept intact the lawful practice of your rituals, but not in this one. Moreover, God once would console you by sending prophets, who would either promise swift deliverance, such as Jeremiah and Ezekiel, or would show that it is now imminent, such as Daniel, Ezra, Haggai, and Zechariah. Accordingly, it is evident that God regarded you as children then, not as enemies, as He does today. For you have no prophet after Jesus, a warning that the Psalm made to you: "There is now no prophet, and He will know us no more."[666] Why did God long ago utterly deprive the great majority of you of your lives, and of your priesthood, kingdom, and prophets? To show that He had long ago rejected you as rebels, since you are without any divine hope and inheritance. How then can you expect a Messiah from whom you do not even receive heralds and likenesses of the Messiah? Finally, in other times you were banished for a brief time and to some region or another; after Jesus you have been banished for the longest time, nay for all time, and throughout all the world, as is to be expected for you,

---

664 Eus. *Hist.* 4.2.5 (*PG* 20.306); 4.6.3 (*PG* 20.311); 7.1 (*PG* 20.639).
665 Eus. *Hist.* 2.8 (*PG* 20.155); Acts 11:28–30.
666 Ps. 73:9 (Vulg. Ps. 72:9).

who, by killing Jesus, above all transgressed against God Himself, who is always and everywhere. When you murdered the prophets, you sinned against the messengers of God; when you worshipped idols, you deprived God of as much of the kingdom as was in you; what was still left for you except to rage against the person of God itself? Therefore, if by murdering Jesus, you committed a greater crime than the slaying of the prophets and idolatry, then certainly you raged against God; and put differently: if you ever laid your impious hands upon God, then it was only possible when you laid them upon Jesus, who alone in the world showed Himself by His powers and portents to be the true son of the highest God and to be God. So far we have spoken about the first matter.

In the second place, however, we concern ourselves with this guilt of yours for which you live wretchedly in exile, how it is shared among all of you everywhere and always: for each and every one of you continuously leads a wretched life the world over. In fact, no other crime can be imagined for which every one of you could be forever tainted, except that you rejected the lives of Jesus and His followers; what is more, you approved of their murder. For this reason, you are participants in the murder of Christ, as even Jeremiah touched on thus: "Why will you contend with me in judgment? For you have all transgressed against me."[667] But if you were to find fault in the calf made on Horeb, or the murders of the prophets, or whatever other of your ancestors' monstrous crimes, and if you were to lack any inclination either towards killing prophets or making idols, it would follow that you are in no way, properly speaking, participants in those crimes. Raving mad, therefore, are those who think you to be oppressed by this calamity because of the worship of idols or the murder of the prophets.

The third matter, however, as it seems to me, is what concerns the guilt that is the reason for such misery, how it is hidden and unknown to you, since in the book of the Talmud, which is entitled *Magnila*,[668] the question is posed why was an end of torment to those living abroad in Babylonia foretold, as Jeremiah thus attests: "When the seventy years shall be fulfilled in Babylon, I will visit you."[669] After Titus, however, no end has ever of the miseries been foretold for those living abroad. To this question, an answer is thus given there: "Then an end of their

---

667 Jer. 2:29.
668 We and others have failed to determine with any certainty what Talmudic text Ficino (and Paul of Burgos) are referring to here. See A. Lukyn Williams, *Adversus Judaeos: A Bird's-Eye View of Christian Apologiae until the Renaissance* (Cambridge: Cambridge University Press, 1935; repr. 2012), 274.
669 Jer. 29:10.

ills is shown to them, just as the guilt for which they suffered ills is revealed, but to them, for whom the guilt is unknown, so too is the end unknown."[670] So it is said there. But no other shared crime of yours is completely unknown to all of you, except that which your people committed against Jesus, and you support. For not only do you not know that it is evil, but, although it is the worst, you think it to be the best.

CHAPTER 30 – CONFIRMATION OF OUR MATERIAL FROM JEWISH SOURCES AGAINST THE JEWS REGARDING THE HOLY BOOKS

By the will of God, everywhere and always, you Jews circulate the Hebrew books of the prophets, from which everyone may understand that Christians did not make up the prophets' predictions, as David touched on: "My God let me see over my enemies: slay them not, lest they forget thy law. Scatter them by thy power."[671] So you are therefore unwilling witnesses to our truth. And where we too have the holy scripture of prophets, translated by many after Christ into Greek and Latin, we also have that translation, which was done by seventy-two Jews, chosen as the most outstanding of all from the entire people by the high priest Eleazar at the behest of king Ptolemy more than three hundred years before Christ, as Aristaeus the Greek (who was a close friend of the king) and Josephus write. They add that the king, for the sake of this translation, redeemed from slavery with his own money 100,000 Jews who were serving in Egypt, donated unbelievable gifts to the temple and the high priest, and bestowed unprecedented honours on the translators. I make use of this translation quite freely to defeat (*convicere*) this treacherous Jewish rabble with the excellent arsenal provided to me by those illustrious Jews.[672] Nor should it be thought that the earliest Christians had corrupted those books which had long ago been disseminated around the world, especially since they revered them as a thing sent from heaven and defended their mysteries with their own blood.

---

670 Paul. *Scrut.* 2.6.2, 265r-v.
671 Ps. 59:12 (Vulg. Ps. 58:12).
672 Eus. *Prae.* 8.2–3 (*PG* 21.587–91).

On Miracles

I come now to the miracles that you certainly do not deny; indeed, you confirm in your numerous histories that the apostles as much as Jesus performed miracles. But some among you say that Jesus, a beggar among the Egyptians in His childhood, had learned magic to the highest degree in a few short years – no mean feat. So many of the greatest philosophers, journeying to Egypt from everywhere, could not after many years learn this even in the slightest, even at a ripe old age. For what magus at any other time, when he was publicly captured and slain in the highest ignominy, was immediately able to accomplish being regarded everywhere as the highest God? What magic did those uneducated fishermen use once Jesus was dead? For it follows that they performed miracles, otherwise Jesus, after being killed, would have completely lost all authority in a short time. If they were magi, why did they not – as ambitious men are wont to do – preach themselves rather than the beggar Jesus, who was publicly executed suffering a shameful death? But by what stratagem either did those simple fishermen draw up in their net Paul and Apollo, Jews most learned of all men, and many other highly educated and brilliant men in order to suffer death, or did Paul likewise ensnare Hierotheus and Dionysus the Areopagite, the most outstanding philosophers among all the Platonists, and all other men like him? What was the joy, what was the use of magic put forward to those risking their lives daily not for the love of themselves, but for the love of Christ? Hence Justin, an outstanding philosopher, in the book that he wrote to the emperor Antoninus in defence of our religion, says: "I myself, having been trained in the ways of the Platonists, when I heard the Christians slandered and saw them unafraid to undergo death and to suffer every torture, began to consider that it was impossible that they abide in wickedness and in lust."[673] So says Justin.

But let us listen to Tertullian, a nigh contemporary of Justin, crying out to the Roman judges: "Nature soaks all evil in either fear or shame. In short, the wicked greatly desire to remain hidden, they shun being seen, when caught they tremble, when accused they deny, nor even do they easily or always confess to a foe. For sure, they grieve when they are condemned, they render accounts to themselves, they ascribe the impulses of their wicked mind either to fate or to the stars. For they do not wish it to be theirs because they recognize the evil. But what here is similar to Christians? No one is ashamed, no one is sorry, except simply

---

673 Eus. *Hist.* 4.8.5 (*PG* 20.323–6).

for not having been Christian earlier. If the Christian is reproached, he boasts; if he is accused, he makes no defence. When interrogated, he confesses of his own accord; when condemned, he gives thanks. What sort of evil is this which does not have any of the natural characteristics of evil: fear, shame, subterfuge, regret, lamenting? What evil is this whose culprit rejoices, and the accusation thereof is wished for, and its punishment is a blessing?"[674] Tertullian, furthermore, finds fault in the rashness of the pagan judges because they cruelly condemned Christians in the name of their religion alone, without ever having discovered a crime. What, however, this religion thought, they neither asked nor wished to hear from Christians. Finally, as I have said elsewhere, the holiest goal of this teaching makes very clear that Christ and His disciples performed miracles not with magic but with divinity. There remains among you a book on the life of Jesus of Nazareth, where one reads that Jesus, among the other miracles that are there recounted in great number, even revived the dead, clearly because only He knew how to correctly pronounce the proper name of God, which among you is revered more than anything else, and since it consists only of four letters – and those in fact are all vowels *(vocales)* it is pronounced with the utmost difficulty.[675] It sounds almost like this: "*hiehouahi,*" that is, "was, is, shall be," and the majority of Hebrews hold this opinion.[676] If this is so, since nothing among you is regarded as holier than this name and therefore you cannot confirm anything profane, undoubtedly our Christ's teaching is divine, because it, just as you say, is rooted in the power of that most divine name and, just as we assert, in the power of God.

The Testimony of John the Baptist and Josephus

Stop with your raving already, you Jews, who are as mad as you are wretched! Do you believe that man of God, John the Baptist, whom everybody without exception honours, and who, as Josephus says, was truly and publicly regarded as an exemplar of all virtues?[677] The greatest throngs of Jews and of all others flocked to him from everywhere, as if to an oracle. So says your Josephus. John the Baptist, moreover,

---

674 Tert. *Apol.* 1.10–13 (*PL* 1.266–9).
675 Nic. *Quaest.* 5va.
676 On Ficino's potential use of Kabbalistic sources for this pronunciation of the Tetragrammaton, see Bartolucci, "Per una fonte cabalistica del *De Christiana religione*: Marsilio Ficino e il nome di Dio," 35–46 and "Marsilio Ficino e le origini della Cabala Cristiana," in *Pico e la Cabalà*, 47–67.
677 Eus. *Hist.* 1.11.3–6 (*PG* 20.115); cf. Josephus, *Antiquitates Iudaicae*, 18.3.3.

openly without a shred of doubt affirmed that Jesus of Nazareth was the Messiah and ordered everyone to follow Him; otherwise everyone, who then spoke of Jesus, would not have set their beginning from the testimony of John and his affirmation, and they would not have lavished him with astonishing praise. It is clear to everyone that the evangelists recounted the life of Jesus and of John at the same time. Since Mohammad also knew of their friendship, he recited the origins, the lives, and the praises of each, namely, John the Baptist and Jesus, in the same chapter of the Qur'an.[678] He called Jesus the spirit and word of God and said in the same place that John was a great prophet, a guarantor of the divine word. And certainly, John made sure that Jesus gained His first disciples from him. Finally, listen to what your Josephus says about Christ in his books on *The Jewish Antiquities*, which he wrote in Greek, just as one can read today and could read then in ancient Greek as well as Latin copies, even before Constantine's time, as Jerome and Eusebius attest. Neither could those books be corrupted at all, since they were dispersed so widely and held in the highest authority by everyone, especially at the time when Christians everywhere were most of all subject to slanderers, nor do I yet find the books marked by any of our foes to indicate that they corrupted the books of Josephus or of the prophets. But let us come now to Josephus: "There was," he said, "during those same times, Jesus, a wise man, if in fact it is right to call Him a man, for He was a performer of miracles and a teacher to those men who freely hear what is the truth, and He even brought over to Himself many of the Jews and also many from the nations: this man was Christ" (or, "He was believed to be"). "When Pilate sentenced Him to be crucified because of an accusation made by the leaders of our people, those who loved Him from the beginning did not abandon Him. For on the third day, He appeared alive to them again, just as the prophets inspired by God had foretold both this and His countless other future miracles. Rather, the name and race of Christians, who are named after Him, persevere up to the present day."[679] He also says the following elsewhere: "Ananias the younger, a man shameless and arrogant in his manners, handed over a man named James – the brother of Jesus that is called Christ – and several others besides to be stoned on the accusation that they were acting against the law. Those, however, who were seen to be the most moderate men of the city and to be concerned with the integrity of the law, bore this with difficulty and secretly sent messages

---

678 *Alcor.* 3.39 and 3.45 (Petrus Pons, 45); cf. *Alcor.* 6.85 (Petrus Pons, 90).
679 Eus. *Hist.* 1.11.7–8 (*PG* 20.115–18); cf. Jerome, *De viris illustribus*, 13 (*PL* 33, 629–31).

to the king, asking him to write to Ananias not to perpetrate such a crime, since the latter had acted improperly on previous occasions." So says Josephus in the twentieth book of the *Antiquities*.[680]

On the Resurrection of Christ

At any rate, none of you dares to deny the rest of Jesus's miracles since they were many and performed often, and performed openly before the people, and since many still sing of them. Yet you completely deny the resurrection, although many have written of it, because it was not known to everyone. Still, you see that it was confirmed by Josephus. Or is it that you are unaware that, because the body of Jesus had been made wholly immortal and divine, it was not fitting to be seen by the eyes of just any mortals, but only by those who had been chosen by God as witnesses for others? Over the course of forty days, Jesus was often seen revived from the dead and He was seen by many people, not only by the apostles and the disciples but also by more than five hundred of their brethren gathered together at once, as Paul the Apostle attests when he says that many of them were still alive when he was writing of it.[681] Indeed, they attest that not only was Jesus resurrected, but so too was a myriad of men, Jews as much as Gentiles, who, like them, most gladly underwent a certain and bitter death for the sole glory of Jesus who had been publicly and ignominiously executed. So we ought to mock that history you invented that Jesus's disciples took His body from its tomb and hid it among the plants in a garden, but a little later spies sent for it by the high priest found it. O ye all too ignorant and silly men! Why did you not hang that corpse in the marketplace if you were so deeply devoted to erasing the glory of Jesus? For in this way all would have immediately abandoned the sect of the Nazarene.

CHAPTER 31 – CONFIRMATION OF GOD'S TRINITY AND OF CHRIST'S DIVINITY FROM THE JEWS

Why do you disparage the divine Trinity while utterly ignorant of your own mysteries? Read the commentaries of your own interpreters on the Psalm: "God, the Lord God hath spoken, and He hath

---

680 Eus. *Hist.* 2.23.21–3 (*PG* 20. 203–6); cf. Josephus, *Antiquitates Iudaicae*, 20.9.1.
681 Cf. 1 Cor. 15:6.

called the earth."[682] For in those commentaries, the question is posed why the Psalm invokes God three times, and the answer given is to show specifically that God had created an age (*seculum*) with these three names according to the three properties by which the world was created; these are wisdom, knowledge, and prudence, as one reads in Solomon's Proverbs: "The Lord in wisdom hath founded the earth, hath arranged the heavens in prudence, and in His knowledge the depths break out."[683] God is also named three times in Exodus: "I am the Lord, your God, a jealous God."[684] Behold the three divine names according to the three properties of God, by which all things are made. Likewise, one reads in the book of Joshua: "God, the Lord God, He knoweth."[685] Such is what one finds there. You will find a similar explanation in your commentaries on Genesis, especially on this part: "In the beginning, God created heaven and earth,"[686] where Rabbi Eleazar says: "The world was not created except through or with the word of God, as one sees in the Psalm: 'The heavens were established by the word of the Lord.'" And so it follows in the same passage: Rabbi Shimon[687] says: "God breathed, or blew the Holy Spirit and the world was created, just as one reads in the Psalm: 'All the power of them' – (or 'host') – 'by the breath of His mouth.'"[688] Such is what one finds there.[689]

You deny that God has a natural son, that is, of the same nature. Yet God says in the *Psalms*: "Thou art my son, this day have I begotten thee."[690] This cannot be said of angels and souls, which are not begotten but created, for they proceeded not from the substance of God, but from nothing. Therefore, even if at times in holy scripture "the sons of God" are mentioned, nevertheless God never mentions sons as being begotten.[691] But he said "this day," that is, in the eternal today, specifically in the present state of eternity, which has neither beginning nor end – for whatever is of the substance of God is also eternal within God. Therefore, there is in the Psalm: "Give to the king thy judgment,

---

682 Ps. 50:1 (Vulg. 49:1).
683 Prov. 3:19–20.
684 Exod. 20:5.
685 Josh. 22:22.
686 Gen. 1:1.
687 Latin: *Simeon*.
688 Ps. 33:6 (Vulg. Ps. 32:6); Hier. Sanctaf. *Contr.* 2.3, 153–4. Latin: *"spiritus"* for "breath."
689 Paul. *Scrut.* 1.9.5, 130r.
690 Ps. 2:7.
691 Paul. *Scrut.* 1.9.9, 133r.

O God,"[692] where it is clearly discussing the Son of God. Regarding the Son Himself it is said: "His name shall be forevermore, and His name continueth before the Sun."[693] The fact, however, that where our translation says "continueth," the Hebrew text has "*ynnon*"[694] – which actually is a word derived from "*nyn*"[695] and "*nyn*" means 'son' – makes clear that the language is about the eternal Son of God. Therefore, what else does "*ynnon*" signify but a son, begotten, born, and absolute? That God has a son, Solomon attests in Proverbs: "Who hath ascended up into heaven, and descended? Who hath held the wind in his hands? Who hath bound up the waters together as in a garment? Who hath raised up all the borders of the earth? What is His name and the name of His son, if thou knowest?"[696] Listen further to Isaiah as he cries out to God: "Holy, Holy, Holy Lord God Sabaoth."[697] The thrice repeated "Holy" signifies the Trinity of divine persons, "Lord" in the singular signifies the one substance of God. "All the earth is full of His glory,"[698] by this Isaiah signifies that the assumption of man was done from the word of God, for in the same passage, he places God on His throne in the shape of a man.[699]

To show that you will not sufficiently understand these kinds of mysteries, he adds much about your blindness, your deafness, your stubbornness, which we recounted at another time.[700] He even records God speaking thus elsewhere: "Come ye near unto me, and hear this: from the beginning, I have spoken not in secret. From the time when it was done, I was there, and now the Lord God hath sent me, and His spirit."[701] Therefore, the one who "from the beginning" (namely of the law) did not speak "in secret" (namely because he spoke openly to all those listening on Mount Sinai) and who was there "at that time" (namely God Himself, founder of the law) now is sent by God, that is, God the Son, begotten of God the Father, assumed a human nature. "The spirit of God" also sends Him, since the joining of God and man happened through the Holy Spirit.[702] Any one of those who "send" is

---

692 Ps. 72:1 (Vulg. Ps. 71:2).
693 Paul. *Scrut.* 1.9.10, 134v; Ps. 72:17 (Vulg. Ps. 71:17).
694 I.e., ינון (yin-nō-wn); Paul. *Scrut.* 1.9.10, 136v.
695 I.e., נין (nuwn) verb derived from "a primitive root," meaning "to resprout, i.e., propagate by shoots; figuratively, to be perpetual, be continued," see Strong's H5125.
696 Paul. *Scrut.* 1.9.11, 138r–139r; Prov. 30:4.
697 Isa. 6:3.
698 Paul. *Scrut.* 2.6.3, 267r; Isa. 6:3.
699 Cf. Isa. 6:1.
700 See above, Chapter 27, Bart. *DCR* 237, lines 465–7.
701 Isa. 48:16.
702 Paul. *Scrut.* 1.9.13, 143v.

necessarily God since the one who is sent is God, and although there is only one God, there is nevertheless some distinction, albeit inconceivable, between those who send and the one who is sent. But given the preceding verses, it is clear that the one who is recorded as speaking here is God Himself; for He says: "I am the first, and I am the last, my hand hath founded the earth";[703] for that is also clear given the following verse, since after everything we have brought up, this is added: "So saith the Lord, thy Redeemer, Holy One of Israel."[704] But let us hear David crying out: "Whither shall I go from thy spirit? And whither shall I flee from thy face? If I ascend into heaven, thou art there."[705] In these words, he means that the Spirit of God is everywhere, but the Jews and the Christians posit that only God is everywhere. Therefore, we are in agreement that the Spirit is not some breath outside of God, but the Holy Spirit and God, of which Job says: "The spirit of God made me, and the breath of the Almighty gave me life."[706] It is the office of God alone to make man, that is, the soul, and to give it life. What is more, in your commentaries on Genesis, the question is asked what is "the spirit of God that moved over the waters,"[707] and there too the answer is provided: "This is the spirit of the Messiah about which one reads in Isaiah: 'And the spirit of the Lord shall rest upon him, the spirit of wisdom, and of understanding.'"[708] So it says there. From this it is also clear that God is both the Spirit and the Messiah. Likewise, Rabbi Shimon says in the same commentaries: "What does one make of what one reads in the Psalm: 'All the power of them by the spirit of His mouth?'[709] And the answer is given: 'it is the following: 'God breathed the breath of His mouth, and the world was created.'" In addition to this, when Rabbi Moses Gerondi was explaining "In the beginning God created heaven and earth,"[710] he said: "'In the beginning (*in principio*),' that is, 'in wisdom,' which is the principle of principles (*principium principiorum*)." And therefore, the Jerusalem translation has "in wisdom" in the place of "in the beginning." But that some kind of wisdom is in God, conceived by God from eternity as progeny, the prophet Solomon thus reveals, by representing wisdom speaking in this way: "Hear, for I will

---

703 Isa. 48:12–13.
704 Isa. 41:14.
705 Ps. 139:7–8 (Vulg. Ps. 138:7–8).
706 Job 33:4.
707 Gen. 1:2.
708 Isa. 11:2; Paul. *Scrut.* 1.9.15, 149v.
709 Ps. 33:6 (Vulg. Ps. 32:6).
710 Gen. 1:1.

speak of great things.[711] God possessed me in the beginning of His ways, before He made any thing from the beginning. I was set up from eternity, and of old, before the earth was made. The depths were not as yet, and I was already conceived, neither had the fountains of waters as yet sprung out. The mountains, with their huge bulk, had not as yet been established. Before all the hills, I was brought forth. He had not yet made the earth, nor the rivers, nor the poles of the world. When He prepared the heavens, I was present. When with a certain lay, and compass, He enclosed the depths,"[712] all the way to this part: "I was with Him forming all things, and rejoiced before Him at all times."[713] In these words, it is clear that a wisdom of this sort was not only "conceived from eternity," but also was "brought forth" from it. Indeed, as wisdom, being absolute, already "was present" and "rejoiced," and as it was distinct from its progenitor in its own way, it was "with Him" and "forming all things," just as if wisdom itself were God. Although it is begotten of the Father, it nevertheless always existed with the Father simultaneously. For what is made without motion is produced in a single moment; such things, while they are being made, in fact already exist, just as the air has already been illuminated while it is being illuminated, and the truth and reason of things while they are being understood, have already been understood. Therefore, the word and very reason of God, because it is begotten both without motion and in an intelligible way, is already being born as it is being conceived, and as it is being born, it is simultaneously present and forming everything.

This opinion had the greatest antiquity among your forefathers since Moses says: "In the beginning Heloym created"[714] and so on. "Heloym" is plural, and its singular is "Heluel,"[715] "created" is in the singular. Of course, since there is a certain number of persons in the one simple essence of God, Moses and many other Hebrews on that account employed this construction for God alone: making use of a plural noun and a singular verb and vice versa. A similar number in God is also signalled in the last book of Joshua: "You will not be able to serve the Lord, because He is a holy God";[716] the actual Hebrew (*Hebraica veritas*) has: "because He (*ipse*, sg.) is the holy (*sancti*, pl.) Heloym." Likewise, Jeremiah: "You have perverted the words of the

---

711 Prov. 8:6.
712 Prov. 8:22–7.
713 Prov. 8:30; Paul. *Scrut.* 1.9.16, 152r-v.
714 I.e., Elohim, rendered in Italian editions as "*Eloyn*"; Gen. 1:1.
715 I.e., El, rendered variously in Italian editions as "*Euel*" and "*Eluel.*"
716 Josh. 24:19.

living God, of the Lord of Hosts, your God";[717] the actual Hebrew has "Heloym haym," that is, "of the living gods." However, it has what follows in the singular, just as we also have it. The plural noun for God is joined to a plural verb in the second book of Kings: "What nation is there, as the people of Israel, whom God went to redeem for a people to Himself."[718] The actual Hebrew says: "The Heloym went," that is, "the Gods." Similarly, one reads in Ecclesiastes: "Who is man, that he can follow the king his maker?";[719] the Hebrew text says: "Who is man, that he enters after the king who have already made him?" When David speaks with God Himself: "God, thy God, has anointed thee with the oil of gladness,"[720] does he not make some distinction in God between him who is anointed, and Him who anoints, or more precisely, them who anoint? For David mentioned the Son, who is anointed, and the Father and the Spirit when he said of those anointing: "God God." But what he says to God Himself is clear from the following; for he foretold: "Thy seat, O God."[721] But also when he says of his Lord God: "The Lord said to my Lord: sit thou at my right hand,"[722] does he not indicate that there is a distinction in persons between the one who sits to the right and the one near whom He is sitting? The Chaldean translation, however, demonstrates that those two are consistent in nature, for it says: "The Lord spoke with His word."[723] Also, through what follows in the same Psalm: "From the womb before the day star I begot thee," that is, before anything created, out of my innermost substance and from within myself, it is clear that what befits God alone befits the Son of God. Still, two persons are also indicated when "I begot thee" is said, for the one that begets and the begotten differ in their person. What more can we say? Moses settles the matter, for he says: "God said let us make man to our image and likeness,"[724] and he adds: "God made man."[725] In this speech, he attributes a singular number to God twice, and twice a plural number too, so as to more effectively demonstrate that there is a number of persons within a unity of essence. Hence, when God is speaking to Moses, he says: "I am the God of thy

---

717 Jer. 23:36.
718 2 Sam. 7:23 (Vulg. 2 Rg. 7:23).
719 Eccles. 2:12.
720 Ps. 45:7 (Vulg. Ps. 44:8).
721 Cf. Ps. 45:6 (Vulg. Ps. 44:7).
722 Ps. 110:1 (Vulg. Ps. 109:1).
723 Ps. 110:3 (Vulg. Ps. 109:3).
724 Gen. 1:26.
725 Gen. 1:27.

fathers, the God of Abraham, the God of Isaac, the God of Jacob."[726] He first denotes that there is one substance of God, then by a triple repetition, he makes clear a number of three persons. One, however, ought to remember that, although power, wisdom, and will (or, goodness) differ in some way in the human craftsman, still no one says because of this difference "that craftsman have made," or "those craftsmen has made," because those three do not constitute different persons; only in the case of God, however, and almost every time, the holy scripture joins the plural with the singular because specifically in Him alone is there a single nature and three persons, and also in Him not only are there three powers, just like in a craftsman, but also three persons distinct from each other and united in an amazing way.[727]

CHAPTER 32 – CONFIRMATION OF THE MESSIAH'S SUFFERING AGAINST THE JEWS FROM JEWISH SOURCES

Do you buffoons mock us because we believe that the Messiah would suffer for the guilt of the original sin? But we have repeatedly shown previously that He would suffer many hardships, first by using reasoned arguments, then by using the authority of the prophets as much as those of your own interpreters. But I know what you wanted, specifically for God to forgive man's trespasses by some generosity or clemency of His without the suffering of the Messiah. Have you forgotten the ancient maxim that always prevailed above all else among your teachers: God governs all human affairs by a twofold measure, namely, mercy and justice? "All the ways of the Lord," David says, "are mercy and truth,"[728] the latter being justice. Likewise, he states: "Holy and terrible is His name."[729] Your interpreters think that a measure of mercy is signified in holy scripture where "Adonay," meaning "Lord," is said, and a measure of justice where "Eloym," meaning "God," is said. Therefore Rabbi Joshua, considering the power of both names joined together, when Moses says: "The Lord God sent Adam out of the pleasure garden to till the earth," he says, "with a certain measure of justice and mercy God created Adam, with the same measure He gave him

---

726 Exod. 3:15.
727 Nic. *Quaest.* 1va-b; Paul. *Scrut.* 1.9.2, 122r–124r; 2.1.4, 174r-v.
728 Ps. 25:10 (Vulg. Ps. 24:10).
729 Ps. 111:9 (Vulg. Ps. 110:9).

an order, with the same measure He expelled him."[730] So says Joshua, precisely because Moses similarly pairs together "Lord God" not only in the expulsion, but also in the creation and the order. God employed justice in creating Adam because He formed him in no other way than to correspond equally to His idea (which is always in God and through which He forms) and to divine goodness, for whose sake He forms. Similarly, He employed mercy because He did not confer life and the other good things to Adam without any prior merits.

He was merciful in giving orders since He abundantly granted the enjoyment of nigh-innumerable fruits. What is more, He was just since, with threats of some sort, He forbade the eating of the tree of knowledge of good and evil. For it was only right that man should acknowledge and declare that he was subject to God by some law. Lastly, He was just when, after the transgression, He punished Adam with expulsion; He was, however, also very merciful when He only afflicted a finite penalty upon him who had offended and had somehow sinned infinitely against an infinite God. Therefore, do you actually wish for Adam and the human race, his progeny, to be reconciled to God the creator under the Messiah without the constraint of His mercy and justice, that is, by His mercy alone? God forbid.

Remember what you reflect on in Deuteronomy every day: "The works of God are perfect, and all His ways are judgments."[731] God is faithful without any iniquity, righteous, and just. Therefore, it befitted God's mercy that at some point He would reconcile the human race with Himself. It befitted His justice that some satisfaction would intercede and at least the Messiah would make satisfaction for the everyone else, about which Isaiah said: "All we like sheep have gone astray, and man hath gone astray from his own way,"[732] that is, all men have gone astray, because the father of them all, Adam, went astray from his own way. Isaiah adds about the Messiah: "And God hath laid on him the iniquity of us all."[733]

I know that you are nevertheless accustomed to object here: it is absurd to think that by the greatest crime, which many committed when they killed the Messiah, the crimes of man are washed away, nor does the suffering of one man make satisfaction for the sins of all, nor is it just that the innocent Messiah make satisfaction for others who are

---

730 Gen. 3:23–4.
731 Deut. 32:4.
732 Isa. 53:6.
733 Isa. 53:6; Paul. *Scrut.* 1.5.9, 56r–57v.

guilty. But we shall respond briefly in this way: evils were erased not by the wickedness of the murderers but by the virtue of the Messiah in suffering evils. For this reason, the love and power in Christ's suffering was greater than the hatred and vice in everyone's wrongdoings, and the life of the one Christ was more worthy than everyone else's lives. Therefore, when He gave up His life for everyone, He made a satisfaction that was far more than satisfactory: one can make satisfaction for another. We see this done every day in civil matters: for satisfaction rests in outside acts; for these, both bonds and friends can be employed. But since penance consists of an internal act of the mind and will, it depends on the very person who sinned. Therefore, as it is necessary that every sinner give penance for their crimes, only in this way was it that the Messiah made satisfaction for everyone. Thus these verses of Isaiah are fulfilled: "Surely he hath borne our infirmities, and carried our sorrows. He was bruised for our sins, by His bruises we are healed."[734] Yet we do not get let off without punishment, as from the beginning of the world to its end we undergo many hardships on account of that original sin; in Christ, however, there was a brief suffering, a wondrous power and perfection, and happiness (*felicitas*) everlasting. God had established from eternity that the Messiah would be the redeemer of the human race, a redeemer, I say, who would redeem from the servitude of the guilt that brings death, about which Isaiah said: "There shall come a redeemer to Zion."[735] And there is in the Messiah this excellent dignity, which He certainly would have lacked had He not washed away the stains of the people by the sacrifice of His own flesh. We have found in the sacred histories that holy men always appease God by offering sacrifices, especially by spilling blood; that they obtain gifts from Him; that they deliver the people from imminent dangers; that they are accustomed to ratify divine laws and purge the sins of the people once every year – this the pagans also imitated, albeit not in keeping with the law.[736]

But let us come now to the Hebrews. First, we read in Genesis about where Noah, after the Great Flood, "built an altar unto the Lord on which he offered holocausts,"[737] and for this reason God, now appeased, decided that a flood of this kind would not befall the earth again. For this follows in the same passage: "And the Lord smelled a sweet savour, and the Lord said to him: 'I will no more curse the earth for the sake of man.'"[738] Second,

---

734 Isa. 53:4–5.
735 Isa. 59:20.
736 Paul. *Scrut.* 1.5.7, 53v–54v.
737 Gen. 8:20.
738 Gen. 8:21.

also in Genesis, where Abraham was first ready to sacrifice his own son at God's command, then he was forbidden from doing so by God through an angel, finally he offered a ram and sacrificed it to God. Because of Abraham's willingness (*voluntas*) and offering, God promised him a unique gift after swearing an oath. His gift was that all the nations from Abraham's seed that had the will (*voluerint*) would be saved.[739] The third is found in Exodus. For there, the people of God is delivered from its misfortune in Egypt by the sprinkling of the blood of the Passover lamb across the doorposts and thresholds of its houses. "I shall see," He says, "the blood, and shall pass over it; and the plague shall not be upon you to destroy you."[740] The fourth is also in Exodus. There, as Moses wished (*volens*) to ratify the law he had received from God, he sprinkled the blood of the victims upon the people, in order to confirm thereby the covenant between God and man. For so one reads there: "Moses took the blood and sprinkled it upon the people, and said: 'This is the blood of the covenant, which the Lord hath made with you concerning all these words.'"[741] Fifth, in Leviticus, the day of atonement is dealt with, about which one reads there: "Upon this day shall be the atonement and the cleansing. You shall be cleansed from all your sins before the Lord."[742] The high priest, of course, would enter the Holy of Holies once per year and pour forth the blood of the sacrifices before the place of atonement and upon the place of atonement. And by this blood, according to the custom established by God, the uncleanliness of the people was washed away. The reason for an arrangement of this kind is described in Leviticus: "Because the life of the flesh is in the blood, and I have given the blood to you, that you may make atonement upon my altar for your souls, because the blood may be for an expiation of the soul."[743]

The cleansing and the deliverance of the people under the Messiah ought to have encompassed these five things that we have related, and things greater than even them. Therefore, He rightly offered a sacrifice of His own blood to God on behalf of all; the sprinkling of His blood, as the most perfect sacrifice, was prefigured in all the above sacrifices, like signs, especially in the offering of Isaac made by his father, at Passover, and, in addition to the above, in the circumcision of all boys. Divine mercy did not wish (*noluit*) that all men should shed their lives with blood for their sins, but that on behalf

---

739 Cf. Gen. 22:1–18.
740 Exod. 12:13.
741 Exod. 24:8.
742 Lev. 16:30.
743 Lev. 17:11; Paul. *Scrut.* 1.5.10, 60v–61r.

of everyone, one man should spill His blood, and for this reason divine mercy exalted Him above all others. This spilling of blood is still reckoned to have been a divine sacrifice by intent of the ready will of Christ offering Himself most freely, although it was an impious murder by the intent of the murderers. Indeed what you once enacted every year with the sacrifice of a Passover lamb as a sign of your atonement and salvation, and what was at last fulfilled on Passover by the sacrifice of Jesus the meek saviour, that is also in a way repeated every day in the Eucharist. Christ, therefore, is thus "the priest in eternity," sacrificing Himself once for God, who alone was able to cleanse others perfectly, since neither was He unclean nor did He need holocausts to cleanse Himself, unlike the rest of the priests before Him, since He perfectly purified the uncleanliness of man and that of His own house not with the blood of beasts, not with impure blood, not with the blood of someone else, but with His own pure human blood. Paul the Apostle speaks about these things in the Epistle to the Hebrews.[744] For this reason, the absolution of sins was more seemly through the suffering of Christ than if God had forgiven through His absolute power.[745] For aside from the fact that this mode of absolution suited God's justice and mercy, and likewise suited demonstrating Christ's most excellent virtue, it also greatly, in fact more than anything else, contributed a mystery of this kind to human teaching by its example – specifically one of obedience, meekness, love, high-mindedness, courage, contempt for the mortal, and longing for the eternal. Thus, these verses of Isaiah are fulfilled: "The learning of our peace (*disciplina pacis*) was upon Him."[746] He did this so we might have peace with God, and He taught so we might have peace with each other; "by His bruises we are healed,"[747] that is, not only because He made satisfaction on our behalf but also because He instructed us by teaching and example.

---

744 Cf. Heb. 1–2.
745 "*Potentia absoluta*" and "*potentia ordinata*" were concepts widely in use by late medieval scholastic theologians in discussions of God's justice vs. his mercy, especially among the nominalists; see, for example, Heiko Oberman, *The Harvest of Medieval Theology* (Cambridge, MA: Harvard University Press, 1963), 30ff.
746 Isa. 53:5.
747 Isa. 53:5.

CHAPTER 33 – CONFIRMATION AGAINST THE JEWS OF ORIGINAL SIN, AND THEREBY OF THE MESSIAH'S SUFFERING, FROM JEWISH SOURCES

You often reproach our notion of hereditary (*originalis*) guilt, you of all people who are ignorant of how to interpret your own prophets; for we ourselves have learned this from them. Isaiah cries out to the people: "Thy first father sinned, and thy interpreters have transgressed against me, and I have polluted" – or "profaned" – "the holy princes, and I have given Jacob to death, and Israel to blasphemy."[748] The "first father," specifically Adam, sinned when he ignored a commandment from God, on account of which "the holy princes," that is, the patriarch and the rest of the just men descended from him are cut off from divine vision as "polluted," that is, as profane, just as the polluted used to be cut off from the temple. Punishment for the first sin passed to all those descended from Adam since, after the transgression, God threatened Adam so: "Cursed is the earth in thy work, in labour shalt thou eat"; so too He threatened the woman: "In pain shalt thou bring forth children."[749] Therefore, since the punishment passed to everyone, the guilt also passed to everyone: for it is unlikely that such a long-lasting punishment, common to all men, has been without guilt. Furthermore, hear what God says to the people in Isaiah: "Thou hast made me to serve with thy sins"[750] because the Lord God took the form of a servant to atone for the crimes of the servant people. God could not serve as God, so He served as a man. The Messiah was, therefore, both God and man, which is evident also through the following: "Thou hast wearied me with thy iniquities," that is, the punishments for your iniquity. "Fear not, O my servant Jacob, I am, He that will blot out thy sins,"[751] that is, although your transgression was dire to the extent that the human species could not atone for it alone, nevertheless, I, God and man, shall wholly atone for it.

Regarding baptism too, and the Holy Spirit, he adds: "I will pour out water upon the thirsty, I will pour out my spirit upon thy seed, and my blessing upon thy stock."[752] Perhaps also in this is signified the water that the pierced side of Christ spilled forth, and the spirit of life that He gave up on the cross for us.[753] Read the commentaries on Genesis of your ancients, especially in the section where Moses says: "These are

---

748 Isa. 43:27–8.
749 Gen. 3:16–17.
750 Isa. 43:24.
751 Isa. 43:24–5; 44:2.
752 Isa. 44:3.
753 Paul. *Scrut.* 1.6.2, 66v–69r.

the generations of the heaven and the earth, when they were created."[754] There you will find that all things had been created perfect by God from the start, but immediately after the sin of the first parent, all things, especially all things human, degenerated from their perfection, nor will they revert to their original state before the son of Perez is come, that is, the Messiah who is descended from Perez. From this, you can conclude that the sins of the first parents had been passed down onto their descendants and had to be remedied by the Messiah.

But He remedied them one way in His first coming, He will remedy them another way in His second. Also, many of your teachers are of the opinion that the prophets and holy fathers of the Old Testament descended to hell before the coming of the Messiah. For instance, they prove this using what God tells Abraham in Genesis: "Thou shalt go to thy fathers."[755] From this, Rabbi Rhahamon makes the argument that, because the fathers of Abraham worshipped idols, as one reads in Joshua, when Abraham went to them, he descended to hell.[756] The same is related about Isaac in Genesis: "Isaac has died, is dead, and has been added to his people";[757] there the same is said of Jacob; in the third book of Kings, the same is said of David: "David slept with his fathers."[758] Rabbi Rhahamon makes a similar argument about all these men, since they are sent to the place of those who were unjust and worshipped idols.[759] But Christ, by His death, delivered the holy fathers from death, that is, from the darkness of their souls.[760] Zechariah touched upon this: "And thou by the blood of thy testament hast sent forth thy prisoners out of the lake wherein there is no water,"[761] that is, the saints were sent forth from limbo, an arid place (namely, void of light and joy). Christians, therefore, did not discover that the great Messiah, by His labour and suffering, would redeem the souls of the fathers and their descendants from hell, but many Jews of old thought so too. Chief among them was Rahamon, whom I mentioned, and in addition to him were Joshua,[762] Hana, Abba, and Judah, who in their Talmudic

---

754 Gen. 2:4.
755 Gen. 15:15.
756 Hier. Sanctaf. *Contr.* 1.7, 76; cf. Josh. 42:2.
757 Gen. 35:29.
758 1 Kings 2:10 (Vulg. 3 Rg. 2:10).
759 Paul. *Scrut.* 1.6.4, 71v–72r.
760 Paul. *Scrut.* 1.5.10, 63v; cf. Ramon Martí, *Pugio fidei*, 3.2.8–10 (Frankfurt and Leipzig: Friedrich Lanckisus, 1687), 598–601.
761 Zech. 9:11.
762 Latin: Osuas; Ficino spells Rabbi Joshua above "Iosue," similar to his source, Jerome of Sante Fe, who provides Osua (*Contr.* 1.11, 108.) and Iosue (*Contr.* 1.7, 76).

disputations, after much pertinent discussion, also cite the following verse of Hosea for this purpose: "I will deliver them out of the hand of death; I will restore them from death."[763] Likewise, this verse of Isaiah: "The redeemed of the Lord shall return, and shall come into Zion with everlasting praise and joy upon their heads."[764] They explain that "Zion" is the heavenly fatherland, and rightly so: for there is no everlasting praise and joy on earth. Rabbi Moses Gerondi agrees with this; in fact all Jews actually admit that the patriarchs and the saints prior to the coming of the Messiah do not enter paradise but remain at its outer fringes until the son of Perez, namely, Christ, son of David, comes, and all this on account of Adam's sin.[765]

And although this is so, nevertheless a good many among you who are not sufficiently learned deny that hereditary guilt had been transferred onto succeeding generations and had to be atoned for through Christ, as if it were fitting that there be so long-lasting a punishment on all the guiltless. So why does Moses write in Genesis that after Adam's transgression, God placed the Cherubim and the spinning flaming sword to block the path of the tree of life, unless to signify that because of a likeness with the first parents and the guilt contracted therefrom, the entry to paradise is closed to all?[766] We ought to keep in mind that the entry to the kingdom of heaven is so difficult and so precious that it can and should be blocked not only on account of every individuals' own day-to-day sins but also on account of the common fault belonging to all human nature and contracted by birth through descent from the first parents. And although the saints before Christ delivered and cleansed themselves from their own sins by the strength of human virtue – for which reason they ought not to have been tormented in hell – nevertheless, not one of them had enough virtue to be able to remove the obstacle that comprised the shared guilt of all human nature and throw open the entrance to paradise. But such a guilt and such a debt was dissolved for all by the suffering of Christ. "For God," as Isaiah says, "hath laid on Him the sin of us all";[767] therefore through Him God opened the gates of the heavenly fatherland. Jeremiah conveyed this mystery so: "We have sinned against thee, O expectation of Israel, the saviour in time of trouble. Why wilt thou be like a stranger in the land, and as a wayfaring man turning in to lodge? Why wilt thou be as a wandering man, and as a man

---

763 Hosea 13:14.
764 Isa. 35:10.
765 Hier. Sanctaf. *Contr.* 1.7, 77–8; Paul. *Scrut.* 2.6.9, 278v–279v.
766 Cf. Gen. 3:24.
767 Isa. 53:6.

that cannot save? But thou, O Lord, art among us, and thy holy name is called upon by us, forsake us not, O Lord our God."[768]

There are no few among you who ask why Christ, in removing the guilt, did not remove the punishment: "In the sweat of your brow"[769] and "in pain shalt thou bring forth children"[770] and the like. Clearly in order for us to acknowledge daily by these prods that spurning God's commandments was the absolute worst thing and remains so; and in order that we may accomplish more by exercising moral virtues to achieve blessedness. In addition to this, the redemption, the victory, the freedom, the abundance, and the peace that was promised to us at the time of the Messiah pertained to the spiritual, which leads to blessedness, not to the corporeal, which either does not lead to blessedness or impedes it. So, by Christ's suffering and true faith, original sin was removed, that is, insofar as it concerns the guilt that impedes ultimate blessedness; but the toilsome things remain that not only do not impede, but in fact contribute to this blessedness. But you retort with that verse from Ezekiel: "The son shall not bear the iniquity of the father."[771] We, however, explain it in this way: clearly the son, if he is utterly without guilt, is not punished for the sin of the father. Everyone, however, used to be born partaking of that first guilt, for just as everyday sins pass from father to son by imitation, thus the first sin passes by descent. Nor is it any wonder that the fault of the first parent passed to succeeding generations; for every day in children we observe the gestures, passions, and mannerisms of their grandparents as much as those of their parents. Thus it is ordained by nature that the body and the soul meet in some harmonious proportion and come together in one being in such a way that the movements of the body somehow penetrate[772] easily and with utmost potency into the soul and so too the movements of the soul into the body. The soul of the son is derived from neither the body nor the soul of the father, but such a body with such an inclination is derived from such a body as that of its progenitors, thus fathers have eaten sour grapes and the teeth of their sons were set on edge. The soul, because of a certain affinity and affection towards its own body is in some way rendered a participant of that inclination, especially according to the soul's inferior force, which approaches the body and acquiesces much to it. Finally, the superior force of the soul often, out of a

---

768 Jer. 14:7–9; Paul. *Scrut*. 1.6.4, 73r-v; 1.6.5, 74r-v.
769 Gen. 2:16.
770 Gen. 2:19.
771 Ezek. 18:20.
772 Italian here has *"siriflectino,"* "reflect in."

sort of natural love, for the most part yields to the inferior force, just as the inferior does to the body; it yields, I say, almost in a similar way, but not to the same degree. But movement, which is an action in the soul, becomes suffering (*passio*) in the body; what becomes suffering in the body becomes sense and empathy (*compassio*) in the soul; the disposition, which in the body is a punishment for guilt, is guilt in the soul.

Moreover, you retort with this: the stain contracted from one's progenitor through descent is not a sin since it is not willingly contracted by the offspring. On the contrary, it is indeed a sin, since it is a sort of crookedness diverging from rectitude and thus unsuited to achieving its end, just as with a defect in a cripple. It is a sin, I say, not of one's particular nature so much as of our universal nature, but it somehow happens willingly in offspring, inasmuch as offspring freely follow this kind of inclination. Furthermore, it is voluntary not by the offspring's particular will so much as by the will of Adam himself, who by the movement of generation somehow sets in motion all who spring from his stock, no differently than the will of a single soul moves to action the many limbs of the body. Therefore, in this way the movement of the foot is said to be done willingly, not by the particular will of the foot but by the universal will of the soul, which primarily sets the limbs in motion, and so too for the movement of the head, and of the hands, and of everything else. In this way, the natural crookedness of man is judged to be wilful because of the will of Adam, who somehow sets everyone in motion, rather than because of one's particular will.

There are those among you who argue against us for this reason: if the sin from the first parents were poured into us, since we were in them and we have received our human nature from them, for the same reason it would necessarily follow that each and every sin of each and every progenitor, from the beginning of the world until our time, would be planted[773] in us at birth. To this our theologians respond that no fault either of the first parent, or of anyone else is necessarily transferred to us at birth aside from the first, for indeed man produces with himself a being that is the same not in number and in person, but in species. And therefore, what pertains to the particular person of every particular individual is not passed down to children by descent, but what concerns the species is. For musicians and philosophers do not produce musicians or philosophers respectively; nevertheless, the man who sees, hears, and has two legs – unless something were to prevent

---

773 Bart. *DCR* 287 has "*inferentur*" ("will be inflicted"), whereas the 1500 edition (f.LXXIr) has "*insererentur*" ("would be planted"), which makes more sense in this context.

him – produces a biped also capable of seeing and hearing. But the first fault becomes a natural inheritance of the human species; the rest are uninherited and are particular to each individual.

I know that here you tend to retort that the sin of Adam pertained to his particular person rather than to the species since it proceeded from his particular act of free will. To this I respond according to the minds of our theologians: something pertains to everyone's person in two ways, either according to the person itself, or by a gift of grace. Similarly, something can concern nature in two ways, either according to nature itself, namely, what is entailed by the principles and elements of its nature, or by the gift of a supernatural grace. From the beginning, human nature had an original justice not from its inner principles, but by the gift of God's grace, which is said to have been bestowed to all human nature by descent through the first parent. He lost this gift because of the guilt of the first transgression; accordingly, just as that original justice would have been preserved in his descendants along with the propagation of nature had he not transgressed, thus an opposite perversity and crookedness is passed down with nature to subsequent generations. Therefore, such a fault became a defect more of nature than of a person. All other faults, Adam's or anyone else's, pervert nature not to a degree that belongs to one's nature, but to a degree that belongs to one's person; therefore, it is not necessarily passed down to children and grandchildren. What therefore did the suffering of Christ confer on us? By removing the obstacle of hereditary guilt, He opened the entrance to paradise, which, before Him, the holy men were unable to enter. We shall discuss this better at another time.[774]

I omit minor details, such as that the Devil, once prince of this world (that is, of worldly men), was cast out by Christ. The Devil no longer deludes us through idolatry, nor vexes the souls and bodies of so many nations as bitterly as he once did, except when it is occasionally permitted by God for a specific purpose. Through faith in the Messiah, who is now come, we resist the Devil; through faith in the Messiah who would come, the saints before Christ resisted the Devil. Still, at that time, none could flee his hand in such a way as to avoid hell's threshold (that is, limbo), about which David sang: "Who is the man that shall live, and not see death, and shall liberate his soul from the hand of hell?"[775] Against this poison and the like, virtue, suffering, mysteries, teaching, exempla, and faith in Christ offer us more than enough

---

[774] For this paragraph and the previous three, see Paul. *Scrut.* 1.6.6, 74v–76v.
[775] Ps. 89:49 (Vulg. Ps. 88:49).

remedies. Above all others, baptism in the virtue of the Holy Spirit and faith in Christ dissolves the guilt and debt in the soul of the one who is washed in baptism, but it does not uproot the innate inclination of the body's nature. For the Spirit and the spiritual mystery have no concern for the body, but rather an exclusive concern for the spirit and the will. Hence it happens that all who are begotten from the body of a baptized man are compelled daily to acknowledge the gift of purification from the mystery of Christ, since they are born unclean, as they too are in need of baptism. So too, a grain of wheat, even if it is cleaned with skill, still produces uncleaned grains, such that they are likewise in need of skill. For skill had cleaned the property of a particular grain rather than the nature of the species and the generative force.

CHAPTER 34 – PROOF AGAINST THE JEWS, FROM JEWISH SOURCES, THAT THE CEREMONIES OF THE OLD TESTAMENT HAVE BEEN COMPLETED AND FULFILLED BY THE ARRIVAL OF THE NEW TESTAMENT

If the Old Testament's kingdom, prophecy, priesthood, and sacrifice ought to have been set aside according to God's plan with the introduction of a New Testament at the time of the Messiah, king and priest eternal, and end of the prophets, as we have demonstrated previously, the far more insignificant ceremonies, in which there was little of import, rightly disappeared. I have made this clear previously from no small number of the prophets' oracles. Since, after all, those prophecies used to foretell nothing but Christian things and ceremonies, now that the predictions of the prophets have at last been fulfilled, the former ceremonies have for good reason been completed. Nevertheless, you Jews, more obstinate than anyone else, still hold fast to those things, citing what Moses said in Deuteronomy against us: "And now, O Israel, hear the commandments and judgments which I teach thee: that doing them, thou mayst live, and entering in thou mayst possess the land which the Lord God of our fathers will give us. You shall not add to the word that I speak to you, neither shall you take away from it."[776] These words must be pored over diligently. Moses speaks to the flock under his authority, for he says, "O Israel, hear"; he did not say, "let none add to or take away from it," but "*you* shall not add" and "neither shall *you* take

---

776 Deut. 4:1–2.

away." Therefore, he took the power of making changes away from the flock (*gregi*) under his authority, but not from God, who is above Moses, or from his exceptional messenger (*egregio nuntio*), who received from God the power to make changes.[777]

Jeremiah protested against your obstinacy in this way:

> "Behold the days shall come," saith the Lord, "and I will strike" (or "I will bring about") "a new covenant" (or "testament") "with the house of Israel, and with the house of Judah, not according to the testament" (or "agreement") "which I made" (or "agreed to") "with their fathers in the day that I took them by the hand to bring them out of the land of Egypt, the agreement which they made void" (or "since they did not abide by my testament") "and I disregarded them" (or "I loathed") "saith the Lord. But this shall be the testament" (or "agreement") "that I will set up with the house of Israel. After those days, saith the Lord, I will give my law to their minds" (or "in their bowels"), "and I will write it in their heart, and I will see them, and I will be their God, and they shall be my people. And each man shall not teach his neighbour, and each man his brother saying: "Know the Lord, since all shall understand me,"

namely, that God is one (*unicus*). It continues: "From the greater even to the lesser, for I will be forgiving of their iniquities, and I will remember their sins no longer."[778] In these words God promises that someday He will set up a new agreement and testament and that He will hand down a new law, different from the one which He had given to Moses after He had delivered the Jews from Egypt, and that He will no longer write it on tablets, but in the minds of men, as if to say that first one could be destroyed, not the second, and the old ceremonies ought to be maintained according to the spiritual understanding (*intelligentia spiritalis*) once the New Testament is introduced. Certainly, as Paul the Apostle says, when the prophet speaks of a "new agreement and testament," he means that the other can grow old and falter.[779] But when did this occur? When was this verse fulfilled: "I will see them and I will be their God"?[780] God always sees men with the intellect, but when He assumed the form of a man, He saw with eyes as well. The form of a man, I say, that was in fact regarded as God by men. About this David: "The God

---

777 Paul. *Scrut.* 1.8.1, 93r-v.
778 Jer. 31:31–4; Augustine, *De civitate Dei*, 17.3.2 (*PL* 41.525–6; Dombart and Kalb, 553); cf. Heb. 8:8–10.
779 Cf. Heb. 8:8–12.
780 Cf. Heb. 8:13.

of gods shall be seen in Zion,"[781] and Zechariah: "Thou art God, and in thee is God, nor is there any God besides thee,"[782] which points to the divinity of the Messiah, the founder of the New Testament and agreement, and also signifies the distinction between divine persons.

But lest someone be confused because there are different words in different translations, in some place "agreement," elsewhere "testament," it should be known that this word, namely, "*Berith*,"[783] which equally means "law" (*lex*), "agreement" (*pactum*), "covenant" (*fedus*), and "testament" (*testamentum*), was introduced by Jeremiah. But your interpreters admit that the new law is understood as the law of the Messiah, for which reason the teachers of the Talmud say that the law of the Messiah will surpass the law of Moses.[784] Read the brief commentaries on this in Solomon's Ecclesiastes, there you will find this: "Every law of the current age is a kind of vanity according to the law of the future age," that is, according to the law of the Messiah. For in the following the matter is made clear: "All law, which one learns in this age is a vain thing when compared to the law of the Messiah." So one reads there. Therefore, you see that the law of the Messiah differs from the law of Moses, and that Moses's ceremonies completely fade away in the sight of the Messiah. But the law of Moses is called vain not in absolute terms, but relative to the law of Christ, for it is more outstanding than all the rest. But why is it called vain? Because it can only guide the human race through civic virtues to the path of heavenly blessedness, but not to that end. Christian law leads perfectly towards exemplary virtues and perfect heavenly happiness through purgative virtues and those of a purified soul. For perfect happiness (*felicitas*) is not given, except to perfectly purified souls; the law of Moses does not effect this, but the law of Christ does. The law of Moses, therefore, is a kind of preparation for the law of Christ, almost a perfect form and habit, since he who has the habit does not need preparation. As we have said above, you admit that the saints do not enter paradise under the law of Moses, but rather await the law and grace of the Messiah. For this reason, as I see it, Moses promises only temporal rewards for those who keep his law, as that teaching cannot aspire to anything greater. Moses in *Deuteronomy* reveals the whole matter thus: "I will raise them up a prophet out of the midst of their brethren, like to thee, and I will put my words in his

---

781 Ps. 84:8 (Vulg. Ps. 83:8).
782 Isa. 45:14.
783 I.e., בְּרִית.
784 Paul. *Scrut.* 1.8.2, 94r-v.

mouth, and he shall speak to them all that I shall command him. And if anyone will not hear His words, which he shall speak in my name, I will be the avenger."[785] Do you not see that God would create some prophet aside from Moses among your people and give him the authority to make the laws anew? To this prophet it is granted to change everything as he deems fit – to change, I say, image into substance, in order to perfect the imperfect. By the command of God you ought to believe Him in all matters no less than you believe Moses, and since neither have all of you believed, nor have you believed everything, you have been driven into exile, as God threatened.[786]

Do not let the Arabs pretend that Mohammad was so great a king, but actually a tyrant; for his law did not keep the law of Moses in check, which had grown unchecked, but rather expanded it too far, since no time, or place, or utterances of the prophets are in agreement with it. In what way could Mohammad be that supreme prophet supposed to be raised up from the Jewish people, when he himself admits in the Qur'an that Jesus of Nazareth had been the last and greatest prophet of the Hebrews? At one time, the Jews, especially those of Africa, were admonished by these words of Moses and so were awaiting the Messiah as a maker of new laws. But Rabbi Moses[787] wrote to them that God did not promise a prophet as lawmaker, but merely a prophet as messenger of things to come: "God," he says, "wanted to drive out auguries, which the Canaanites were using, from among the Jews." Hence he would say to them: "Those nations, whose land you will possess, heed augurs and diviners, but you have been instructed otherwise by the Lord your God," that is, to foretell the future not through auguries, but through the prophets sent by God. Therefore, he adds: "The Lord your God will raise up for you a prophet from your nation and your brethren just as He has raised me up; you will heed him." So said Rabbi Moses to the Jews of Africa. We also maintain that these words of Moses are not to be explained in any other way than how Rabbi Moses explained them to the Jews of Africa.[788]

---

785 Deut. 18:18–19.
786 Paul. *Scrut.* 1.8.3, 94v–95r; Macrobius, *Commentarius in somnium Scipionis*, 1.8.5–11, ed. J. Willis (Stuttgart and Leipzig: Teubner, 1970; repr. 1994), 37–9; cf. above, Chapter 21.
787 I.e., Moshe ben Maimon (Moses Maimonides).
788 Paul. *Scrut.* 1.8.4, 96r-v.

But let us consider the great Moses in the same chapter of Deuteronomy, speaking so in the following verses: "As thou desirest of the Lord thy God in Horeb, when the assembly was gathered together, and saidst: 'Let me not hear any more the voice of the Lord my God, neither let me see any more this exceeding great fire, lest I die.' And the Lord said: 'To me they have spoken all things well. I will raise them up a prophet out of the midst of their brethren like to thee, and I will put my words in his mouth, and he shall speak to them all that I shall command him. And if anyone will not hear the words which he shall speak, I will be the avenger.'"[789] Do you see that the people, when the law was handed over on Mount Horeb, had been terrified by fire and all the other horrible signs? that God was then asked not to speak to the people in that way again? For this reason, God promised previously that, without causing any terror, He would pass down the law to the people through a prophet who would be a true man like Moses. Therefore, in the earlier words of the chapter, Moses is speaking about a prophet as herald of things to come, of which there were many, but in the subsequent words, he is speaking about a prophet as lawmaker, which we maintain was Jesus the Nazarene.

But it troubles you too much, I know, because Moses ordered His commandments to be kept forever. Remember that your grammarians treat the wording pertaining to the everlasting as twofold: sometimes it referred to the everlasting in absolute terms, at other times it referred to the everlasting conditionally. In the first category is "cela,"[790] and where among us the Psalm says: "They shall praise thee unto the ages of ages,"[791] according to the Hebrew, it is "cela"; there is also in this category "necali," and when the Greek and Latin Psalm says: "He will live forever," in Hebrew one hears "necali." In the second category the Hebrew has "halam,"[792] the Latin has "age" (*seculum*). In this manner, in Deuteronomy it is said regarding the servant that was bought: "He will be a servant to you 'holam,'"[793] that is, "for the age" – for the age, I say, of your life or of that of the servant, no longer. Thus "age" in this verse does not mean the lifespan of everything, but the lifespan of this or that man. But when Moses orders that the ceremonies surrounding the Sabbath, Passover,

---

789 Deut. 18:16–19
790 I.e., *selah*, סֶלָה.
791 Ps. 84:5 (Vulg. Ps. 83:5).
792 I.e., *olam*, עוֹלָם.
793 Deut. 15:17.

Pentecost, and the Feast of the Tabernacles, the Day of Atonement, and the like be maintained, he never uses the wording that means an absolute eternity, but simply "holam," which means a specific age, that is, the entire age of the Old Testament until the Messiah establishes the New Testament, and until the old ceremonies, while they seem to wither, grow green again and are fulfilled in new ceremonies rather than being completed.[794] Thus our Jesus fulfilled the law when He perfected what had been imperfect. And this very perfection of Christian law makes it clear that there is a goal to the vast body of Mosaic law and an ultimate end of its lifespan which, as we have said, God had foretold through Jeremiah, promising a new law different from that of Moses.[795]

Moreover, should anyone inquire in what respect the new is more perfect than the old, let him consider that, inasmuch as it regards the current matter, there are five principal excellencies of the new – that is, Christian – law.

The first is the Mosaic Law: it was handed down on tablets, corruptible and made of stone; the new law was, as Jeremiah says, to be burned into hearts and minds, which in fact signifies that this new teaching is more spiritual – and also eternal – since the form of natural law is eternally impressed onto eternal minds; the old, however, was given to a temporal subject for a time.

The second: The old body of law, aside from what pertains to natural law, bound only the nation of Israel, to whom it was given. Hence the Psalm says of God: "Declaring His word to Jacob, His justices and His judgments to Israel. He hath not done so to every nation, and His judgments He hath not made manifest to them."[796] The new law, however, which is purely natural and nothing else, binds all, and for this reason Isaiah says of the Messiah and His teaching: "Till I set judgment in the earth, and the islands shall look to His law."[797]

The third: The oldest decrees, aside from those which pertain to natural justice, are said to have bound the subject people not everywhere, but only in the region of the Promised Land, as the words of Deuteronomy make clear: "You know that I have taught you statutes

---

794 Cf. Deut. 16:1–17; note that in each other instance where Ficino has used the verbs *"consumere"* (to fulfil) and *"consummare"* (to complete), he joined them with a conjunction, whereas here, curiously, he places them in opposition.
795 Paul. *Scrut.* 1.8.5, 97r-v.
796 Ps. 147:8–9 (Vulg. Ps. 147:19–20).
797 Isa. 42:4.

and justices, as the Lord my God hath commanded me, that you might do them in the land which you shall possess";[798] likewise: "And He commanded me at the same time that I should teach you ceremonies and judgments, which you ought to do in the land that you shall possess";[799] similarly: "But stand thou here with me, and I will speak to thee all my commandments, and ceremonies and judgments, which thou shalt teach them, that they may do them in the land, which I will give them for a possession."[800] The statutes of the Messiah, however, since they are no less than natural, must be observed everywhere. Therefore we read in Malachi, when God rejects the old sacrifices: "My will is not in you, saith the Lord of Hosts, and I will not receive a gift of your hand";[801] he then adds: "From the rising of the sun even to the going down, my name is great among the nations, and in every place there is sacrifice, and there is offered to my name a clean oblation."[802] Therefore, the sacred rites, which, under the old law, it was lawful to celebrate solely in the temples and tabernacles of the Promised Land, would at some point – that is, under the Messiah – be pleasing to God everywhere.

The fourth: The old law promises only material and temporal rewards and threatens similar punishments, as is often clear in Leviticus and elsewhere; the new law promises spiritual and eternal rewards and punishments.[803]

The fifth: The old law leads only to civic and common virtues, by which it staves off unrest; the new leads to purgative virtues and those of the purified soul, by which it uproots the passions and consigns the kindling of vice into oblivion, as though into a fire.[804] But why is that? Because God was instructing a still uncultivated people with more digestible teachings[805] – as was fair – and He decided to move them with rewards as much as punishments that were clearer to them. Even Rabbi Moses the Egyptian admits this in the commentaries of the book of Sanhedrin: "But by the time of Christ, the people had now become more cultivated. Then, as Isaiah says: 'The earth is filled with the knowledge

---

798 Deut. 4:5.
799 Deut. 4:14.
800 Deut. 5:31.
801 Mal. 1:10.
802 Mal. 1:11.
803 Deut. 20:1–21.
804 Cf. Macrobius, *Commentarius in somnium Scipionis*, 1.8.5–11, ed. Willis, 37–9.
805 Cf. 1 Cor. 3:1–3; cf. Paul. *Scrut.* 2.1.2, 171v; 2.4.3, 228r-v: Paul of Burgos uses the metaphor of digestion to explain that humanity needed to be weaned off Mosaic Law and introduced to Christian Law in the manner that infants must first take their mother's milk before being ready for solid food.

of the Lord, as the water of the overflowing sea.'"[806] So then God called forth and formed the human race with truer rewards and more complete statutes. Rightly, therefore, with the new law coming as a form, the old law, just as a preparation, either goes away or passes into the new one, and is fulfilled in the new one. Rabbi Moses was not at all able to keep quiet about this in Deuteronomy,[807] where he divides the whole duration of the world into two ages, specifically the present age and the age of the Messiah. The interpreters of the Talmud, as we have said previously, maintain that the present age and future age are the ages of the law and of the Messiah, and he admits that the law of this age is vain in respect to the law of the Messiah, as though in the age and law of Christ, the old age and the old law are brought to an end and fulfilled.[808]

The Distinction between the Commandments of Moses

The chief commandments of Moses are those that are contained in the decalogue. They were given directly by God to all people upon tablets of stone, then, as everlasting, they were sealed in the Ark of the Covenant in the Holy of Holies. All the other commandments, however, are less significant, were given through Moses, written on paper by him, and placed outside the Holy of Holies. But among these, some are simply moral instructions and, since they imitate the law of nature, are nigh-everlasting, like the chief commandments; others pertain to judgments, which varied, since they were entrusted to the principle of fairness just as the custom for legal matters demanded; others, likewise, pertain to ceremonies, which are of little importance, for they are used to indicate and signify something else, being figures similar to Pythagorean symbols.[809] One who is ordered to abstain from pork is ordered to avoid living like a pig, and one who is ordered to rest his body on the Sabbath is ordered to rest his mind in contemplation.

These and the like have been refined through Christ to their original sense and purpose. Therefore, sacrificing to God, the rule that a thief should make restitution for what was stolen, and the like all pertain to natural and moral law, for which reason they are commanded to be forever maintained. But to make a corresponding sacrifice in this manner on this day or in that manner on that day, to make restitution four times or twice as much, and the like are either ritual or judicial matters, and they

---

806 Isa. 11:9.
807 I.e., *Mishneh Torah*.
808 Paul. *Scrut.* 1.8.6, 99r–101r.
809 Cf. Thom. Aq. *S. Theol.* I–II, 99.1–6.

could and ought to have been changed according to how it suited the place, the times, and the people. In these kinds of matters, change occurs not only under Christ – and it occurs rightly – but also among the ancients. For in the first age, according to God's plan, it was not lawful for man to eat anything but plants, just as Genesis teaches us. Yet in the second age, after the Great Flood, with God's leave, it was lawful to eat animals, as is also made clear in Genesis. Hence in the book *Bereshith Rabbah*,[810] namely, in the commentaries on Genesis, while explaining this verse of a Psalm, "the Lord looseth them that are fettered,"[811] it is said: "Every beast that is considered unclean in this age," namely, in the age of the law, "will be made clean by God in a future age," namely, in the age of the Messiah, "just as beasts, which had been unclean for earlier people, were clean for the sons of Noah. Just as God allowed only plants as clean to more ancient people, and thereafter every animal as clean to the sons of Noah, so in the future age, God will allow whatever He previously prohibited."[812] So it is said there. Thus it is clear that in the age of the Messiah, the less significant customs of the old age, now being empty and void, must be dissolved. Do you Jews still demand more witnesses for this? Although they are unnecessary, I shall nevertheless cite some of the many that remain.[813]

MALACHAI: "My testament will be with Him of life and peace, and I gave to Him that He fear me with fear, and He was afraid before my name. The law of truth will be in His mouth, and He will walk with me guiding the way in peace. And He will convert many from iniquity, for the lips of the priest shall keep knowledge, and seek the law from His mouth, because He is the angel of the Lord almighty."[814] In these words, God promises His testament anew to the Messiah, the testament, I say, to restore peace between man and God, from whom the life of man comes forth. Likewise, He promises the Messiah a mild and almost fearful life, and also a priesthood. He promises that not by force and arms, but with peace and knowledge will He convert men – not all but many. Similarly, He promises that man will receive a new law from Him. But to whom does all this correspond, if not Jesus of Nazareth?

NAHUM: "I will cast out the graven and molten things, I will make thy grave, for behold the swift feet upon the mountains of Him that bringeth good tidings, and that preacheth peace. O Judah, keep thy feast

---

810 Latin: *Veresiht Rabba*.
811 Ps. 146:7 (Vulg. Ps. 145:7).
812 Cf. Gen. 9:1–3.
813 Paul. *Scrut.* 1.8.12, 107v–108v.
814 Cf. Mal. 2:5–7.

days, and pay thy vows, for they shall no longer pass into old age; it is fulfilled, it is completed, it is lost. He is come up that shall breathe into your face, rescuing thee from tribulation."[815] This clearly predicts at the coming of the Messiah the fall of idols, the fulfilment of the prophecies and of the Old Testament, the completion of the ancient ceremonies, the loss of the Jews' kingdom, the preaching of the gospel of peace, the ascension of Christ, the exhalation of the Holy Spirit, and finally the deliverance from tribulation, to wit, of hell.

MICAH: "The law shall go forth out of Zion, and the word of the Lord out of Jerusalem. And He shall judge among a great many people, and He will conquer and guide strong nations afar off."[816] By this it was meant that the Messiah would bring a new teaching and a new law beyond the Mosaic one; it would come not from Sinai, as the old one did, but from Zion; nor would it instruct only the Jews, as the old one did, but it would be spread everywhere by the word of the apostles' preaching, and undo the institutions of strong nations.

ISAIAH: "Thus saith the Lord to the men of Judah, who live in Jerusalem: 'Renew reform amongst yourselves, and sow not upon thorns. Circumcise yourselves to the Lord your God, and circumcise the foreskin of your heart, lest my wrath come forth as fire, and there be none that can quench it."[817] Moses: "In the last days, the Lord will circumcise your hearts that thou mayst love the Lord thy God."[818] Jesus Nave, who prefigured Jesus Christ, said: "The Lord said to Jesus: 'Make thee very sharp knives of rock, and sit, and circumcise the second time the children of Israel,'" namely, by a circumcision of the heart.[819] By these three oracles it was shown that circumcision of the body would be changed under Christ to circumcision of the spirit. The Jews concerned themselves with the tip of the foreskin; Christ purifies and washes the whole. So why is it fitting, after Jesus, to shed the blood of boys on their eighth day? Spare your infant sons, you Jews, as cruel as you are superstitious! Spare your newborn sons! By being fully circumcised, Jesus shed His blood once and for everyone. But if circumcision, the first of the ceremonies, would not be enduring – for it was not established in the beginning, but under Abraham, and without it, anyone could be a just man whenever – much less enduring would all the others be.[820] Why, therefore, do you still observe

---

815 Nah. 1:14–2:2.
816 Mic. 4:2–3.
817 Jer. 4:3–4.
818 Deut. 30:6.
819 Josh. 5:2.
820 Cf. Paul. *Scrut.*, 1.8.15, 117v–118v.

the Sabbath? Surely at one time the Lord's Day was prefigured to you by the Sabbath.[821] Why do you still sacrifice temporal offerings to this day? It is evident that they all had their end in the eternal offering, Jesus. Why in vain do you daily attempt to restore the ancient priests, who foreshadowed Jesus the eternal priest?[822] He is the true priest in eternity according to the succession of Melchizedek. Tell me then, why do you still expect a king? Your temporal kingdom was long ago transferred to Christ, king in eternity. And when you wretches said or read, "Jesus the Nazarene, King of the Jews," at that time you received the one, final, perpetual king, the dying man and living God. Even your Moses had signified this to us when, relating the rite for appointing a priest through the sacrament of some kind of mystical ointment, he named it Christ;[823] likewise, when appointing a king to succeed him, he named him Jesus, who had been named Auses beforehand.[824] And so, through the evidence of these two names – the trappings of the high priesthood are conveyed by the one, and those of the kingship by the other – Jesus Christ is named, being the one who was both king and high priest.[825]

CHAPTER 35 – ON THE AUTHORITY OF CHRISTIAN DOCTRINE

There are many things that confirm the doctrine of Christ: first, the predictions of the sibyls and the prophets, then the holiness and the miracles of Christ and of the Christians. In addition, there is the incomparably astonishing depth and majesty that was captured with the sober pen of those who had previously been uncultivated men and fishermen, especially Peter, Jacob, and John; and that is to say nothing of Paul, who, even though he was a most learned man prior to his conversion, still far transcends what is human in his epistles afterward. What is more honourable than Peter's epistles? What is more venerable than the epistles of James and Jude? What shall we say about John's Revelation, the book

---

821 Paul. *Scrut.* 1.8.14, 113r–117r.
822 Here we have used the 1474 Italian edition, fol. o iiii v ("equali come ombre prenuntiavano Giesu sacerdote eterno") rather than the Latin ("qui tanquam minimi Ihesum sacerdotem preferebant eternum"), since the latter poses unsolvable syntactical problems.
823 Lev. 8:12.
824 Cf. Num. 27:18–23. This "Auses" is Iosue in the Vulgate, i.e., Joshua. This name appears as "Ause" in Ficino's source Eusebius.
825 Eus. *Hist.* 1.3.2–7 (*PG* 20.70–1).

that reveals the face of heaven and contains as many sacraments as it has words? What shall we say about this man's epistles, in which there is the sweetness of nectar and a sense of the divine, without the adornment of words? It seems that his gospel was written by the hands of God, not by man. For when Amelius the Platonist read it, he swore "by Jove!" in astonishment that the barbarian (that is, a Jew) had quickly comprehended what Plato and Heraclitus contended regarding divine reason, the principle and order of things.[826] Simplicianus says that he had heard some Platonist saying that the opening of the *Gospel of John* ought to be written with golden letters on the pediments of temples everywhere. Finally, everyone was in their speech just as they were in life, for just as they were the mildest in their conduct, yet the bravest and most steadfast in perils and hardships, thus they were equally the humblest and loftiest in speaking. Philosophers believe these kinds of conjunctions are beyond nature (*supra naturam*). Therefore, those simple folks and fishermen were rendered fishers of men by their teacher Christ, as He had promised. What is amazing is that after His ascent into heaven, with a breath from heaven He suddenly and miraculously taught so much to men, who were still uncultivated, that in the presence of all people they forthwith prevailed in all tongues and teachings. A sign of this fact is that they taught the greatest number of learned men, and many of the wisest men submitted their own necks most freely to their yoke. The Platonists Hierotheus, Dionysius the Areopagite, and Justin, whose writings are full of all wisdom, took up the cross of Christ along with the apostles. So too did Panthenus the Stoic, the philosophers Quadratus, Agrippa, Aristides, Luke and Mark, Tenas and Apollo, both outstanding experts in Jewish law. What shall I say about the wise Ignatius, disciple of Christ, bishop of Antioch, who wrote many letters about martyrdom and Christian doctrine to the Ephesians, Magnesians, Thracians, Smyrnians, Philadelphians, Polycarp, and the Romans while he was being led to Rome in fetters to be devoured by beasts. In the letter to the Romans he says:

> From Syria all the way to Rome, I struggle, as I am to be devoured by beasts. Meanwhile, bound day and night, I struggle with ten leopards, that is, the soldiers who keep watch over me, and the better I am to them, the worse they are to me. Their iniquity becomes more apparent by my doctrine, but I am not justified by it. If only I could enjoy the beasts that are prepared for me. I pray both that they are ready to kill me and enticed

---

826 I.e., the Logos; Eus. *Prae.* 11.18–19 (*PG* 21.891–902).

to eat, lest they dare not touch my body, as has happened with other martyrs. But if one will not come, I shall provoke it to devour me. Forgive me, my sons, I know what benefits me; now I begin to be a disciple. Will I not forsake this world I see in order to find Jesus Christ? Let the fire, the cross, the beasts, the crushing of bones, the severing of limbs, the grinding of the entire body, all the torments obtained by the devil's cunning come upon me, only so that I may rejoice in Jesus Christ."[827]

So he says, and when he was at last condemned to the beasts and he heard the roaring lions, he said with an ardour for suffering: "Let me be ground by the lions' teeth that I may become pure bread."[828]

Polycarp as well, the bishop of the Smyrnaeans, companion of John the Evangelist, the great teacher of Asia, often being asked by judges to deny Jesus, answered that he could not deny the one whom he had already been happily serving for eighty-six years. Therefore, since he burned entirely with the love of Christ, he endured the flames of the fire and death with the greatest ease.[829] The Smyrnaeans wrote this about him to the churches of Pontus. The pupil of the apostles, Justin the Platonist, in the book he offered to the judges in defence of our religion, listed many famous martyrs and then prophesied that he too would be consumed in the fires of martyrdom because of the treachery of one Crescens the Cynic, saying: "And, for my part, I expect that I shall suffer treachery from one among them whom I oppose on behalf of the truth; I expect that I shall be beaten with staff and club perhaps by this Crescens who is no lover of wisdom (*philosophus*), but a lover of boasting (*philopompus*)." So it happened, and the bravery with which Justin bore it was equal to the clarity with which he had foreseen it.[830]

John the Evangelist also had foreseen, and at the end of his gospel had predicted that, although he would suffer the harshest torture, he could not be killed. He had even foretold most clearly in Revelation, among the other calamities to befall Christians, the one which happened under Emperor Valerian, about which Dionysius, bishop of Alexandria and martyr of that time, says: "It was revealed to John to say: 'And a mouth speaking proud words and blasphemies, and power was given to him for two and forty months.'[831] Both are fulfilled in Valerian."

---

827 Jerome, *De viris illustribus*, 16.8–9 (PL 23.666–7).
828 Cf. Eus. *Hist.* 3.36 (PG 20.287–91).
829 Cf. Eus. *Hist.* 4.15.20–1 (PG 20.362–4).
830 Eus. *Hist.* 4.16.1–6 (PG 20.363–6).
831 Rev. 13:5; note that we have here chosen to translate the text as it appears in the Vulgate and in the 1500 Latin edition (f.LXXVIIIr), which both read *"magna"* (great things, i.e., arrogant things) rather than Bart. DCR 299 which has *"magni."*

So says Dionysius.[832] But before discussing other martyrs, it was fitting to mention Christ's cousin Simeon, who, at the age of 120 years and after prolonged torture, also freely took up the cross.[833] One finds Timothy, Titus, Clement the Roman, Barnabas, the elder John, Aristion, Sosthenes, Silvanus, Sosipater, Demophilus, Dorotheus, Philemon, Andronicus, Urbanus, Lucius, Jason, Tertius, Crescens, Linus, Cletus, Paul, Sergius the proconsul of Cyprus, Silas, Hegesippus the Jew, Crispus, Epaphras, Demas, Mark, Aristarchus, Epaphroditus, Tychicus, Onesimus, Evodius, Papias, Hermas, Justus, Gaius, and Melito of Asia,[834] the philosopher who wrote a book for Marcus Antoninus Verus that defended Christ, and very many other exceedingly wise men, disciples of the apostles. From among them, one would look on another's cross without fear, soon await his own cross undaunted, and bear it unconquered.[835]

Other wise men imitated them: Theophilus; Dionysius; Pinytus of Crete; Tatian; Philip; Musanus; Modestus the philosopher; the Syrian logician and mathematician Bardaisan, and the philosopher Apollinaris – these last two gave books in defence of our religion to Marcus Antoninus Verus; Victor; Irenaeus; Rhodo; Clement of Alexandria; the most learned Miltiades, who bequeathed a book in defence of the Christian religion to Marcus Antoninus Commodus;[836] the philosopher, Roman senator, and martyr of Christ Apollonius, who wrote an outstanding volume to Commodus Severus to render an account of his faith;[837] the other Apollonius; Serapion; Bacchyllus; Polycrates; Heraclitus; Maximus; Candidus; Apion; Sextus; Arabianus; Narcissus; Judas; Tertullian, the source of doctrine, who flourished under Emperor Severus and cried out against his judges: "We say openly, and we say to you as you torture us, we cry out tormented and bleeding: 'We worship God through Christ!' Realize that God is man; He wishes to be recognized and worshipped through Christ and in Christ.[838] We are grateful for your verdicts: when you condemn us, God absolves us."[839]

Add to these men Ammonius of Alexandria, a noble Platonist; the sage Leonides, father of Origen; Origen, a most admirable man both in his doctrine and his lifestyle, whom Porphyry ranked ahead of all men

---

832 Eus. *Hist.* 7.10.1–3 (*PG* 20.658).
833 Eus. *Hist.* 3.32.6 (*PG* 20.282–3).
834 Latin: Melitus; see page 40 above.
835 Cf. Eus. *Hist.* 4.26 (*PG* 20.391–8).
836 Eus. *Hist.* 4.20–1 (*PG* 20.378); cf. 4.27–30 (*PG* 20.398–403).
837 Eus. *Hist.* 5.17.5 (*PG* 20.475); 5.21 (*PG* 20.486–90).
838 Tert. *Apol.* 21.28 (*PL* 1.462).
839 Tert. *Apol.* 50.16 (*PL* 1.604).

of his age in doctrine, and who refuted Celsus the Epicurean's disputations against the Christians in eight volumes, and composed as many on Christian doctrine that one could hardly hope to read them all over the course of a very long life.[840] As Eusebius says, Origen also endured frequent torments for the glory of Christ, unheard of in any other time; his illustrious disciples, Plutarch, Heraclides, Hero,[841] and the two Sereni bore the martyr's crown for Christ.[842] There follow Tryphon and Ambrose, students of Origen; Minutius; Gaius; Beryllus; Hippolytus; Alexander; Julius Africanus; Geminus; Theodorus; Cornelius; Cyprian the African, a martyr and man of the most outstanding wisdom and eloquence; Cyprian's student Pontius; Dionysius; Novatian; Marcion; Archelaus; the famous philosopher Anatolius of Alexandria; Victorinus; the martyr Pamphilus, a very wealthy man, and his student Eusebius of Caesarea (who took after his teacher); Pierius; Lucian; Peleus; Arnobius; Lactantius; Rheticius;[843] the distinguished philosopher Methodius, who refuted Porphyry's arguments against us in an outstanding volume; Juvencus; Eustathius;[844] Marcellus; Athanasius the Great; Antoninus; Basilias; Theodorus; Eusebius the Sardinian; Emisenus; Triphylus; Lucifer; Eusebius; Acacius; Serapion; Hilary the Great; Victorinus; Titus; Damasus; Apollinaris; Gregory Baeticus; Pacian; Phoebadius; the holy man Didymus of Alexandria and his pupil Ambrose of Alexandria; Optatus the African; Achillius; Cyril; Euzoius;[845] Epiphanius; the great Ephrem the Syrian; Basil and his brother Gregory; Gregory of Nazianzus, dubbed "the theologian," who responded in detail and at length to the invectives of the emperor Julian against the Christians; Diodorus; Ambrose; the greatest philosopher Evagrius; Maximus; John Chrysostom; Gelasius; Theotimus; Dexter; Amphilochius; Sophronius, and other nigh-innumerable men outstanding in their doctrine, who defended the glory of Christ amid fire and sword – some before Emperor Julian, some during his reign – with their pens, their tongues, their lives, and their deaths, for which reason they are called "martyrs," being witnesses of Christ's glory.

---

840 Eus. *Hist.* 6.1 (*PG* 20.522).
841 Latin: Heros; see page 40 above.
842 Eus. *Hist.* 6.4.1–3 (*PG* 20.531).
843 Latin: Rethnicus; see page 40 above.
844 Latin: Eustachius; see page 40 above.
845 Latin: Cuzonius; Rheticius, Eustathius, and Euzoius can be identified with a degree of confidence in large part due to the fact that Ficino mostly observed the order of Jerome's *De viris illustribus*, 57–134 (*PL* 23.669–716) in compiling this list.

Jerome counts Josephus, Seneca, and Philo among the first Christians.[846] Also, just after the rise of this religion, seventy-two heresies of clever men, some arising from man's pride, some from the subtlety of demons, came swarming in, and certainly they honoured Christ, but not in the right way as others did. But now, if I wanted to count the Jeromes, the Ambroses, the Augustines, the Gregories, and countless other men most outstanding in their knowledge – Greeks, barbarians, and Latins alike – who laboured for the longest time after Julian the Apostate for the glory of Christ by writing with cleverness and distinction, and by acting piously, their sheer number would beggar all attempts at an exhaustive tally. At any rate, Christian law excels the others to the extent that it had more learned men, and these were always more learned and more eloquent than other learned men, and those who followed this law were always holier than those who took up other laws.

Had logicians or orators or poets thrown down the first foundation of this religion, we would suspect that the common people had been deceived by man's subtlety; had all learned men consistently rejected it, we would conclude that perhaps it should be despised. Had rulers fully favoured this law either from its beginning or shortly thereafter, we would think, as we suppose of *certain* religions, that the weaker had been coerced by the stronger, then that following generations, as it happens, had been nursed on that law along with their mother's milk. Therefore, divine providence wanted the simple truth of its religion to derive its first origin first from uncultivated and simple men, and the shrewd and learned to be happily caught in the nets of the simple and uncultivated.[847] What is more, God allowed His religion to be cruelly assailed for more than three hundred years by the powerful among all the nations in order that the number of learned and faithful witnesses would be that much greater and their authority on this matter be that much truer, more certain, and more steadfast; for it is easy to offer faith in prosperity, but difficult in adversity. Cornelius Tacitus – to say nothing of our own histories – attests that Christians were afflicted with the most elaborate torments; but he blamed the Christians, I believe, in order to placate his contemporaries.[848] Tertullian even shows that Tacitus lied in his history because he said that the Jews worship the head of an ass and wrote in the same history that Pompey inspected the

---
846 Cf. Jerome, *De viris illustribus*, 11–13 (*PL* 23.657–63).
847 Cf. Thom. Aq. *C. Gent.* 1.6.3.
848 Tacitus, *Annales*, 15.44.3.

Jews' sanctuary (*arcana*) and found no statue in it.[849] So, from this one falsehood you can gather the quality of the rest. There is also the fact that, as Irenaeus attests, suspicion then arose about our people being impious and impure for no other reason than the entirely incestuous and obscene way some Gnostic heretics lived.[850] But the disrepute did not last long once the truth began to make itself known. When Lucian the pagan was deriding some travelling sophist and, as he himself describes, not even a real Christian, but a boaster and braggart, he said: "Besides, this man has learned the Christians' wondrous wisdom from their priests and teachers who scorn all other religions, although they adore that great man who had been nailed to a cross in Palestine. Following the law of their master, they bind themselves to each other in fraternal love and hope that they will live forever; led by this hope those poor little wretches hold this life and its benefits in contempt, and voluntarily subject themselves to slaughter every day."[851] So Lucian says. Aulus Gellius, a close friend of the traveller, is witness to the fact that Lucian lied about the traveller because of his hatred, for he shows that this traveller was a serious and steadfast man and a true philosopher.[852]

Pliny the Younger, in a letter to Trajan, lamented that cities of Christians were being massacred, although they were doing nothing against the Romans' law except singing hymns before dawn to their god, a certain Christ; indeed, just to compare their teaching, they forbade murder, theft, adultery, robbery, and the like.[853] Trajan even wrote back that, in any event, the Christians were not to be sought out, but once brought forth, it was fitting for them to be punished. Tertullian thus reproaches Trajan's decree: "O inevitably confused decree! It says that they should not be sought out, as if innocent, and it commands them to be punished, as if guilty. It shows mercy and cracks down; it looks the other way and focuses its attention. Why, judgment, do you beset yourself? If you condemn, why do you not also seek out? If you do not seek out, why do you not also acquit?"[854] He also refutes in the greatest detail an empty rumour against Christian customs that had arisen, and he shows that the Christians had been persecuted not for any crime, but in the name of their religion; and, as we have said previously,

---

849 Tert. *Apol.* 16.1 (*PL* 1.420); cf. Tac. *Hist.* 5.9.
850 Cf. Irenaeus, *Adversus haereses* (*PG* 7).
854 Lucian, *De morte Peregrini*, 11–13.
855 Aulus Gellius, *Noctes Atticae*, 12.11.
856 Eus. *Hist.* 3.33.1 (*PG* 20.286).
854 Tert. *Apol.* 2.8–9 (*PL* 1.322).

Serenus Granius[855] similarly lodged a complaint in a letter to Hadrian, for which reason Hadrian wrote to Minucius Fundanus, proconsul of Asia, that he should not allow innocent Christian men to be harassed, nor should he allow an opportunity to rob them to be granted to their persecutors. Our Eusebius attaches Hadrian's entire letter. Melito, the bishop of Sardis, wrote a book in defence of our religion to Emperor Verus, and in it he makes mention of edict to the people of Asia from Antoninus, who reproached them for disrupting the worship of the immortal God that the Christians worship and for persecuting the Christians even to the death.[856] In the same edict, Antoninus adds that a large number of judges from the provinces had at one time written to his father about this and just recently an even greater number still had written to him; lastly, he adds that he came to the same conclusion as his father also had, which is that no one should pursue the Christians, at least for being Christian, unless perhaps it is proven that they are striving to undermine Roman rule.[857] It is my belief that Antoninus had also feared Christ because his brother Marcus Aurelius wrote that, when his army ran the risk of succumbing to thirst in German territory, through the prayers of some Christian soldiers they suddenly received from God, against all hope, the heaviest rains. With these rains their thirst was allayed, and the enemy was routed by the onset of the thunderbolts, and because of the miraculous nature of this notable deed, the legion changed its name and called itself Fulminea ("The Thunderous"). This is what Apollinaris and Tertullian write. Tertullian adds that the letters of Emperor Marcus still exist, whereby this may be proved more clearly.[858] Eusebius adds that the pagan historians had also reported this miracle but left out what the Christians accomplished through prayer.[859] Therefore, calamity chiefly befell the Christians due to either the ignorance of the mob or the irreverence of its leaders, of which Nero was the first, as Tertullian shows. Suetonius relates that Nero had persecuted the Christians simply because they had introduced a new religion and, as he says, a malefic one – that is, a magical one – for many of those who saw God's miracles attributed them to demons.[860] But infinite truth and goodness made its own truth known from the lies of its enemies and converted the evils of men to

---

855 I.e., Granius Serenus.
856 For Melito, see page 40 above.
857 Eus. *Hist*. 4.8.6 (*PG* 20.326); 4.26.3 (*PG* 20.391–8).
858 Eus. *Hist*. 5.5.1–5 (*PG* 20.442).
859 Eus. *Hist*. 2.25 (*PG* 20.207–10).
860 Suetonius, *Vita Neronis*, 16.2.

good. It also allows the society of its saints to be vexed, whether by heretics or enemies, until the end of the world. God does not compel men, whom He created as children from the beginning, to salvation; He entices each one with unremitting inspiration. For if one approaches Him, He hardens him with labours, He disciplines him with adversities, and, as gold with fire, thus He tests the soul with hardship.[861] If one perseveres until the end, just as gold in fire, so at last, in happiness, he will beam with divine light.

CHAPTER 36 – THAT THE HOLY SCRIPTURE OF THE CHRISTIANS IS NOT CORRUPTED

Mohammad strongly approves of the first Christians and admits that the Christian doctrine, that is, the books of the gospels and of the apostles, had received their wondrous authority from God Himself. He also ranks it above the Old Testament, but he says that, after the apostles, these books had been corrupted by Christians. A man as cunning as he was warlike made up this entire story since he asserts that his coming had been prophesied in the clearest words by Christ, who, allegedly, said in His gospel: "I foretell to you that after me shall come a messenger of God, named Mohammad," meaning the spirit of truth, "who will teach you all things."[862] Even if a fabrication of this kind chiefly had a place as much by force as by deceit among a people that was irrational and too soft for war – for such are the Mohammadans – nevertheless, it is just too laughable in the eyes of great and discerning men.[863] For before the coming of Mohammad, there was no reason why the name of Mohammad, rather than those of Pilate, Judas, the Antichrist, or the Devil ought to have been removed from the gospel.[864] Furthermore, after the coming of Mohammad, Mohammad himself would have been worshipped by those who revered the gospel, instead of his name being removed. He, however, wished to falsely add his name in John where Christ prophesies the Holy Spirit, whose outpouring was prophesied to His apostles not long after the resurrection of Jesus, but it was not

---

861 Cf. Fic. *TP* 12.2.3 (Allen and Hankins 4.29); Plotinus, *Enneads*, 4.7.10.
862 Cf. John 14:26 "But the Paraclete, the Holy Ghost, whom the Father will send in my name, He will teach you all things …"
863 Ricc. *Contr.* 2.61 and 3.1–7; cf. *Alcor.* 61.6 (Petrus Pons, 335).
864 Ricc. *Contr.* 3.93–8.

prophesied to the Arabs six hundred years later. On the fiftieth day after the resurrection, however, it was not a man but the incorporeal spirit and truth that happily blew over them and shone upon them, and all the leaders of the Christians agree on this, especially those who were witnesses of the prophecy in their words and letters. So how is it likely that all Christians had dared to alter the volumes that, at the time, they revered above all as gifts from heaven? But if some impious men had dared, being few in number and imprudent, they would have been overcome forthwith by the more numerous and prudent, and so would not have prevailed. Likewise, if the holy volumes scattered among all the nations had been distorted, many would have noticed immediately; if but one had been distorted somewhere, all other copies would have cried out in protest. Nevertheless, it is completely impossible to falsify with any precision books that had been published in different languages, places, and times, spread so far so suddenly, and used so often. Why do you think different sects of heretics kept offering different interpretations rather than different texts? We have heard from numerous Ethiopians, even the lettered among them, that our holy volumes, written in a barbarian script among them, are just as they are among the Greeks and the Latins. The theologian Riccoldo Ebron[865] writes that in Asia he had read the exact same texts among the Jacobites and the Nestorians – Christian heretics – as among us.[866]

From this it is clear that the Old Testament is correctly preserved by Christians. For, granted, we have many translations published both before and after Christ: some are rather loose, namely, those that were done by the Jews themselves; others are maintained word for word, especially the one by Jerome. Nevertheless, the foremost – nay, all – the mysteries of Jesus Christ are everywhere found to be nearly similar. All the Jews accept Jerome's word-for-word translation as accurate, and it is, in any case, more than enough to confirm Jesus.[867] As yet the most accurate translation was published before Christ by seventy-two Jews, and it remains similar among the Greek, the Latin, and the barbarian Christians. Tertullian also claims that the first copies of it – both Hebrew and Greek – were, in his time, present at the Serapeum in the libraries

---

[865] I.e., Riccoldus de Monte Crucis (1243–1320) was a Florentine Dominican who travelled extensively and wrote many polemical works and guidebooks for missionaries. His most famous text, the *Contra legem Saracenorum* was written in Baghdad and served to guide Latin Christians in their understanding of Islam for centuries.
[866] Ricc. *Contr.* 3.86–92.
[867] Ricc. *Contr.* 3.54–60.

of Ptolemy.[868] Nor was a translation of this kind at one time corrupted by the apostles or their successors, not only because it was difficult to corrupt manuscripts that are broadly disseminated, and thereby preserved, but also because it is utterly foolish to believe that so many great men had falsified the testimonies of the Jews in order to revive a slain Jesus only to bring ruin on themselves.[869] Finally, the frequent objections, false accusations, traps set against Christians on all sides, and the very oft-repeated disputes have served as an admonition for Christians to hold the right course of the scriptures. But if anyone ever heard from the Mohammadans that anything pertaining to Mohammad had been excised from the Old Testament, he would respond that the Jews were in no way ever able to come to agreement with the Christians in order to accomplish this. No Old Testament, however, whether it be Christian or Jewish, supports the Mohammadans' argument in any way.[870]

But, to return to the New Testament, it is established that it is free of errors according to the disciples of the apostles and the successors of the disciples, who bear witness regarding the integrity of the text both in their works and writings. The above is also established according to the most ancient councils that were frequently called, where around 10,000 of the most learned men who ever assembled examined the manuscripts with the utmost precision, for which reason nothing was ever accepted by the Church without the most rigorous examination. What is more, Mohammad babbles something about the apostles' successors adding to the gospels that the man Jesus was the highest God and had truly died. In response to this, I first contend that, in the writings of the apostles and the evangelists, the New Testament is so often connected in order and uniformity that in no way could such an interpolation have been made; then, that nothing either is more difficult to persuade someone of than that a man is the highest God, or seems more paradoxical to discover than that He is the true God and that He had truly died. So can it really be that they added this interpolation so they could all the more easily persuade others of what they preached? These Christians said almost nothing but this, which either upset the Jews, who did not grasp the union of God and man, or offended the Romans, masters of the earth, who had prohibited anyone from being called god without the authority of the Senate, and who posited many gods that were by no means the highest. But the Christians, without the Senate's approval,

---

868 Tert. *Apol.* 18.8 (*PL* 1.437).
869 Ricc. *Contr.* 3.49–53.
870 Ricc. *Contr.* 3.80–5.

called Jesus both the highest and the only God, and they knew that precisely on this account they were undertaking an altogether arduous task and were in the greatest danger among the Jews and the Gentiles. Therefore, what Mohammad says was inserted seems least of all to have been an interpolation, but was, in plain truth, simply placed there from the beginning.[871]

But he himself seems never to have understood the Christians' wholly profound mysteries, though he read them, for where he reads that Jesus is God and the son of God, he thinks that the Christians are introducing two gods, namely, the Father and the Son; and he renounces this pair of gods in the Qur'an. Christians are also hostile to this understanding of God since they believe God the Father, the Son, and the Spirit to be one.[872] Mohammad himself, although he knows not in what way, was still moved by Christ's miracles and admits that He is God and the son of God, when he calls Him the breath and spirit of God, God's own soul, the power of God, the word of God, born from a perpetual virgin by God's inspiration.[873] Besides, however often he happens upon the name of the Trinity, being a man entirely ignorant of such a thing, he all too falsely and incompetently accuses Christians of worshipping three gods, since he did not know how to distinguish the properties of the divine persons while preserving the unity of the divine substance. Nevertheless, compelled by truth, he introduces God everywhere speaking about Himself in the plural number, as Moses had also observed when in *Genesis* he attributed to God sometimes a singular noun, sometimes a plural verb, definitely preserving the unity of substance in God and, at the same time, the number of persons: "God said: Let us make man to our image and likeness,"[874] and a good many other unambiguous examples.[875] But listen to how Mohammad makes God speak to Mary, best of all women, and never touched by any man: "We blew our soul [into her], and we made her and her son a manifest miracle."[876] Likewise: "Once we sent many messengers, we finally sent Christ, Mary's son, whose faithful followers were of a meek and steadfast heart. We gave him the gospel, that through him men would pursue the love and grace of God."[877] Similarly: "We have conferred much goodness

---

871 Ricc. *Contr.* 3.61–70.
872 Ricc. *Contr.* 1.4–12.
873 Ricc. *Contr.* 1.41–6.
874 Gen. 1:26.
875 Ricc. *Contr.* 15.41–50.
876 *Alcor.* 21.91 (Petrus Pons, 198).
877 *Alcor.* 2.253 (Petrus Pons, 36).

upon Christ, and appointed him teacher to the sons of Israel."[878] Likewise: "We sent Christ to fulfill the divine law, made Christ and Mary a miracle, and gave them the best place to dwell in paradise."[879] And he often says the like.

For this reason, even if it is undeniable that he was arrogant, it seems that he should be faulted no less for his ignorance than his arrogance. For he greatly tempered his arrogance when he said in the Qur'an that he had not performed miracles, nor would he perform any, that he was unaware of a great many things, that he was merely a man, albeit a messenger inspired by God, and that he could not pardon sins.[880] He forbade that he be invoked and worshipped; moreover, he admitted that there are some things of dubious veracity in his books. From this fact it appears that he was not "the spirit of truth." Mohammad also detracted greatly from the authority of the Qur'an when he said: "Whoever has lived honestly by adoring the one God – whether Jew or Christian or Saracen – will obtain mercy and salvation from God."[881] But he admits the authority of the gospel most clearly when he calls it light, guidance, and perfection. For this reason even the adherents of Mohammad admit, with his acquiescence, that the rituals of the Old Testament had in large part come to a deserved end with the approach of the New Testament. They understand and observe the Old and New Testament in the way that was explained and mandated by Mohammad since he claimed himself to be the truest interpreter of both. They affirm the creation of the world, the line of Adam, all of Hebrew history, and Christ's teachings. They expect that the Antichrist will be the wickedest man, whom they believe will be killed by Christ; likewise they await the resurrection of bodies, the final judgment, everlasting rewards and punishments; they seat Christ next to God, and Mohammad next to Christ.[882] They, as we do, pray daily to God: "Our Father" and so forth, but where we say "and lead us not," they say: "God has been and God will be, and Mohammad was sent by God."[883]

---

878 *Alcor.* 5.110 (Petrus Pons, 82).
879 *Alcor.* 5.75 (Petrus Pons, 79).
880 Ricc. *Contr.* 8.85–97.
884 *Alcor.* 2.62 (Petrus Pons, 18); Ricc. *Contr.* 3.29–36; 9.20–8.
882 Ricc. *Contr.* 15.19–32.
883 Guillaume of Tripoli, *De statu Sarracenorum*, 286.

CHAPTER 37 – THE CAUSE OF THE ERROR OF THE JEWS, MOHAMMADANS, AND PAGANS

One often demands the cause for why so many Jews remain faithless to this day. The answer is the divine depth of the prophetic and Christian mysteries: because it is divine, it is therefore impenetrable to human understanding. Conversely, the character of the venal and wretched Jews is entirely uncultivated and obstinate: an insatiable greed not only to preserve what is theirs but also to earn interest; a natural love of their own people and an innate hatred for Christians. Furthermore, what was it that drew a great many barbarians into heresy after the time of blessed Gregory? The extraordinarily difficult interpretation of divine scripture; a race of barbarians all too unversed in these matters; the violent hand of Mohammad, King of the Arabs, and the laws of the seven kings, who, being of his family, followed in the order of succession. To this was added wanton abandon.

So what was it that in times past wrenched the pagans away from the true religion of the Hebrews? The commands of ambitious leaders, an age of scant cultivation, wanton abandon, and the lies of malign demons. Then, the blandishments and flatteries of the poets fuelled the error. Furthermore, ancestral custom and time-honoured tradition easily trap everyone in any error whatsoever. Tradition cannot trap lawful Christians in error since, from the beginning, they have taken up the religion that is free of error. But there is no need for me to confirm with a long argument what Christ and His disciples set forth for us to believe in, hope for, and carry out. For they have enough truth and authority, which we have already demonstrated proceeds from divine truth. Therefore, we ascribe the greatest reason (*ratio*) behind Christian institutions and prophecies, whenever we say in the Pythagorean fashion: "*He* said it."[884] We shall, however, remember that it is not right to be bothered if we do not quite have the capacity for it, for I judge this to be the greatest sign of their divinity. Certainly, if our mind deeply comprehends these things, they are lesser things than the mind; if they are such, they cannot be divine; for if they are divine, they exceed every capacity of the human mind.[885] Faith, as Aristotle posits, is the foundation of knowledge, and by faith alone (*fide sola*), as the Platonists prove, we draw nearer to God. "I have believed," says

---

884 Cicero, *De natura deorum*, 1.5.10–11.
885 Cf. Thom. Aq. *C. Gent.* 1.5.5–6.

David, "and therefore I have spoken."[886] Therefore, if we believe, and if we approach the source of truth and goodness, we shall draw a wise and blessed life.

The end. Thanks to God. Amen.

---

[886] Ps. 116:10 (Vulg. Ps. 115:10).

Appendix: Table of References to *On the Christian Religion* in Ficino's Correspondence

Ficino's letters	*LSE* vol. & page	Recipient	Cross-ref. for duplicate text	Date	Relevant quotes & comments
1.21	1.59	Angelo Poliziano			In response to a request from Poliziano for a list of Ficino's writings, *On the Christian Religion* appears in the supplied list.
1.48	1.92	Filippo Controni of Lucca			"I am sending you my book on love as I promised and also my book *On Religion*, so that you may appreciate that my love is religious and my religion full of love."
1.80	1.125–7	Francesco Marescalchi		11 Sept. 1474	"I have not yet finished the book about the Christian religion, because during August, while I was correcting it, I caught a fever and diarrhoea."
1.88	1.138–9	Lorenzo de' Medici			"Hitherto, most religious Lorenzo, I have only spoken to you on religious matters in your Church of *the Christian Religion*. Having thus spoken through God, I considered a letter unnecessary."
1.126	1.193–4	Andrea Cambini			"You ask me to give you my book on religion to Francesco, son of Berlinghieri, ... so that he can send it to you. ... But why are you asking for our Religion, dearest companion?"

(Continued)

Appendix

Ficino's letters	*LSE* vol. & page	Recipient	Cross-ref. for duplicate text	Date	Relevant quotes & comments
3.9	2.15	Pietro Placentino			"The Pope has sent you, as a vigorous general, to take up arms against the enemies of divine wisdom. ... I am therefore sending you these arms with which I fight unceasingly with all my strength against the enemies of truth."
3.27	2.36	Antonio da Forli	Bart. *DCR* App. II.6	~1476	"This book ... will reveal the true nature of [my religion]. ... it may not seem beautiful, but I hope that at least it is not ill-informed."
3.28	2.36–7	Filippo Sacromoro		~1476	"I am sending you our *Religion* as a pledge of religious love. If, perhaps, it should seem very poor, remember that the Christian religion was founded in poverty. ... Bear in mind we have no printers here, only misprinters."
3.39	2.47	Alberto Parisi	Bart. *DCR* App. II.5		"In the book I send, my mind [is] reasoning with all its power on divine faith and hope."
3.41	2.50	Francesco Marescalchi			"Why are you in doubt whether I have given you my book treating of divine grace *gratis*?"
3.57	2.72	Naldo Naldi		13 Feb. 1476 [= 1477]	"I now give you a small gift that is new: a book recently composed by me about holy faith. ... I give it lest, while discoursing on faith and devotion, I myself seem to be lacking in faith and devotion."
3.63	2.81	D. Francesco Guasconi	Bart. *DCR* App. II.3 and II.4	20 May 1477	"Our *Religion*, a pledge of religious love, [by which] I shall fulfil my due to Piety itself. If it should ... seem very poor to you, remember that the Christian religion was founded in poverty. Remember that we have no printers here, only misprinters."
4.5	3.8	Giorgio Antonio Vespucci	Bart. *DCR* App. II.1		"Our book on true piety, given not to instruct, but to satisfy piety itself." Sent by Ficino and Giovanni Cavalcanti.

Appendix 223

Ficino's letters	LSE vol. & page	Recipient	Cross-ref. for duplicate text	Date	Relevant quotes & comments
5.1	4.3–4	Ad familiares	Bart. DCR App. III	before 15 Sept. 1477	Abstract summary of On the Christian Religion; translated into Italian by Ficino for inclusion in his Sermoni morali della stultitia et miseria degli uomini.
5.2	4.4	Naldo Naldi			Refers to 5.1 as a "very brief summary of our book On Religion"; this letter accompanies the summary which Ficino was sending to Naldi.
5.3	4.5	Antonio Ivani		15 Sept. 1477	Letter that accompanies 5.1 sent to Ivani: "a summary of our book On Religion," which Ficino says Ivani has read.
5.28	4.43	Raffaele Riario		after 10 Dec. 1477	"I am sending you this Religion as the handmaiden of Truth, similarly naked and defenseless [as Truth is]."
5.42	4.57	Antonio Vinciguerra	Bart. DCR App. II.4		"May both you and [Bernardo] Bembo enjoy reading our book on religion."
5.44	4.59	Girolamo Rossi	Bart. DCR App. II.2	29 Oct. 1478	"Read well our book on the holy faith ... do not measure the stature of what is divine from the base level of humanity."
6.17	5.33	Bernardo Bembo		15 July 1479	"In the same year [1474], ... I wrote the book On the Christian Religion. So enjoy reading this book."
6.46	5.70	Antonio Lanfredini (+ his father Jacopo)		~1480	"If faith is in need of any witness, then my letter will bring with it this most potent testimony of my faith in you, a book written by us on true faith."
7.17	6.29	Federico da Montefeltro		6 Jan. 1482	"We speak more fully of the divine oracles of the sibyls and prophets in our book on religion."
7.18	6.33–4	Antonio Zilioli			"Marsilio, a follower of the ancients, always joins the religious with the philosophical to the best of his ability, not only in this one book On Religion that you are asking for, but in all his writings."

(Continued)

224 Appendix

Ficino's letters	*LSE* vol. & page	Recipient	Cross-ref. for duplicate text	Date	Relevant quotes & comments
9.12	8.19–20	Martin Uranius Prenninger		12 June 1489	In response to a request from Prenninger for information about Ficino's writings, *On the Christian Religion* appears in the list that Ficino supplies.
12.36	11.44	Gian Stefano Castiglioni		4 Nov. 1494	"Let not the poor and humble appearance of this book offend you, I pray, since the Christian religion has taught humility from the beginning and gladly endures poverty. In fact, a book written on Christian piety is wholly fitting for you … [T]his book *On Religion* … will be the proof and pledge of how constant my love for you will be."
Bart. *DCR* App. II.1		Giorgio Antonio Vespucci	4.5		"Our book on true piety, given not to instruct, but to satisfy piety itself." (short excerpt from 4.5); sent by Ficino and Giovanni Cavalcanti.
Bart. *DCR* App. II.2		Girolamo Rossi	5.44	29 Oct. 1478	"Read well our book on the holy faith … do not measure the stature of what is divine from the base level of my feeble intellect."
Bart. *DCR* App. II.3		Donato Ugolino	3.63	25 July 1477	"Our *Religion*, a pledge of religious love, [by which] I shall fulfil my due to Piety itself. If it should … seem very poor to you, remember that the Christian religion was founded in poverty. Remember that we have no printers here, only misprinters."
Bart. *DCR* App. II.4		Antonio Vinciguerra	3.63; 5.42	10 Nov. 1479	"Our *Religion*, a pledge of religious love, [by which] I shall fulfil my due to Piety itself. If it should … seem very poor to you, remember that the Christian religion was founded in poverty. Remember that we have no printers here, only misprinters."
Bart. *DCR* App. II.5		Rainaldo Ursini [sic; = Orsini]	3.39		"In the book I send, my mind [is] reasoning with all its power on divine faith and hope."

Ficino's letters	*LSE* vol. & page	Recipient	Cross-ref. for duplicate text	Date	Relevant quotes & comments
Bart. DCR App. II.6		Daniel Placentino	3.27		"This book ... will reveal the true nature of [my religion]. ... it may not seem beautiful, but I hope that at least it is not ill-informed."
Bart. DCR App. III		*Ad familiares*	5.1		Abstract summary of *On the Christian Religion*; translated into Italian by Ficino for inclusion in his *Sermoni morali della stultitia et miseria degli uomini*.

Bibliography

Allen, Michael J.B. *Icastes: Marsilio Ficino's Interpretation of Plato's Sophist: Five Studies and a Critical Edition with Translation*. Berkeley: University of California Press, 1989.
– *Marsilio Ficino: Commentaries on Plato: Volume I, Phaedrus and Ion*. The I Tatti Renaissance Library 34, Cambridge, MA: Harvard University Press, 2008.
– Marsilio Ficino: *On Dionysius the Areopagite: Vol. 1: On Mystical Theology & The Divine Names* and *Vol. 2: On the Divine Names*. The I Tatti Renaissance Library 66 and 67, Cambridge, MA: Harvard University Press, 2015.
– "Marsilio Ficino on Plato, the Neoplatonists and the Christian Doctrine of the Trinity." In *Third Eye: Studies in Marsilio Ficino's Metaphysics and its Sources*, edited by Michael J.B. Allen, 555–84. Aldershot: Variorum, 1995.
– "Marsilio Ficino on Saturn, the Plotinian Mind, and the Monster of Averroes." In *Studies in the Platonism of Marsilio Ficino and Giovanni Pico*, edited by Michael J.B. Allen, 253–72. London and New York: Routledge, 2017.
– *Marsilio Ficino: The Philebus Commentary*. Berkeley: University of California Press, 1975.
– *Plato's Third Eye: Studies in Marsilio Ficino's Metaphysics and its Sources*. Aldershot: Ashgate Variorum, 1995.
Allen, Michael J.B., trans., and James Hankins, ed. *Marsilio Ficino: Platonic Theology*. 6 vols. London: I Tatti Renaissance Library, 2001–6.
Ashdowne, Richard K., David R. Howlett, and Ronald E. Latham, eds. *Dictionary of Medieval Latin from British Sources*. 3 vols. Oxford: The British Academy, 2018.
Attrell, Dan. "Honoring the Outermost: Saturn in *Picatrix*, Marsilio Ficino, and Renaissance Cosmology." *Preternature* 9, no. 2 (2020): 169–208.
Attrell, Dan, and David Porreca. *Picatrix: A Medieval Treatise on Astral Magic*. University Park: The Pennsylvania State University Press, 2019.

Bibliography

Bacon, Roger. *Secretum secretorum cum glossis et notulis, tractatus brevis et utilis ad declarandum quedam obscure dicta fratris Rogeri*. Edited by Robert Steele and translated by A.S. Fulton. Oxford: Clarendon, 1920.

Bartolucci, Guido. "Marsilio Ficino e le origini della Cabala Cristiana." In *Pico e la Cabalà*, edited by F. Lelli, 47–67. Florence: Olschki, 2014.

– "Per una fonte cabalistica del *De christiana religione*: Marsilio Ficino e il nome di Dio." *Revue de la Société Marsile Ficin* 6 (2004): 35–46.

– *Vera religio: Marsilio Ficino e la tradizione ebraica*. Turin: Paideia, 2017.

Bibliander, Theodor, ed. *Machumetis Saracenorum principis Alcoran*. Basel: Iohannes Oporin, 1543.

Botley, Paul. *Learning Greek in Western Europe, 1396–1529*. Philadelphia: American Philosophical Society, 2010.

Brucker, Johann Jakob. *Historia critica philosophiae a mundi incunabulis ad nostram usque aetatem deducta*. 5 vols. Leipzig: Bernhard Christoph Breitkopf, 1742–4.

Bühler, Curt F. "The First Edition of Ficino's *De Christiana religione*: A Problem in Bibliographical Description." *Studies in Bibliography* 18 (1965): 248–52.

Carmichael, Douglas. "Heptaplus." In *Pico Della Mirandola: On the Dignity of Man*, translated by Charles Glenn Wallis, Paul J.W. Miller, and Douglas Carmichael. Indianapolis and Cambridge: Hackett Publishing Company, 1965/1998.

Cecco d'Ascoli. *Sphaera cum commentis*. Venetiis: impensa heredum quondam domini Octaviani Scoti Modoetiensis ac sociorum, 1518.

Chazan, Robert. *Daggers of Faith: Thirteenth-Century Christian Missionizing and Jewish Response*. Berkeley: University of California Press, 1989.

Clausen, Wendell. *A Commentary on Virgil, Eclogues*. Oxford: Clarendon Press, 1994.

Copenhaver, Brian P. "Scholastic Philosophy and Renaissance Magic in *De vita* of Marsilio Ficino." *Renaissance Quarterly* 37, no. 4 (1984): 523–54.

Copenhaver, Brian P., and Charles B. Schmitt. *Renaissance Philosophy*. Oxford and New York: Oxford University Press, 1992.

Cosenza, Mario Emilio. *Biographical and Bibliographical Dictionary of the Italian Humanists and of the World of Classical Scholarship in Italy, 1300–1800*. 6 vols. Boston: G.K. Hall & Co., 1962.

Courcelle, Pierre. "Les exégèses chrétiennes de la quatrième Églogue." *Revue des Études Anciennes* 59, nos. 3–4 (1957): 294–319.

Deferrari, Roy J., and M. Inviolata Barry, eds. *A Lexicon of St. Thomas Aquinas*. 2 vols. Washington, DC: Catholic University of America Press, 1948–9.

Dombart, Bernard, and Alphonse Kalb. *Sancti Aurelii Augustini De civitate Dei*. Turnhout: Brepols, 1955.

Drum, Walter. "Paul of Burgos." In *Catholic Encyclopedia*, vol. 11, edited by Charles Herbermann. New York: Robert Appleton Company, 1913.

Du Cange, Charles du Fresne, et al. *Glossarium mediae et infimae latinitatis*. 10 vols. Niort: L. Favre, 1883–7.
Edelheit, Amos. *Ficino, Pico and Savonarola: The Evolution of Humanist Theology*. Leiden: Brill, 2008.
Egbi, Raphael. *Voluptas: la filosofia del piacere nel giovane Marsilio Ficino (1457–1469)*. Pisa: Edizioni della Normale, 2019.
Eusebius. *Die Preaeparatio Evangelica, Teil 1: Einleitung, die Bücher I bis X*. Edited by Karl Mras. Berlin: Akademie, 1982.
– *Die Preaeparatio Evangelica, Teil 2: Die Bücher XI bis XV, Register*. Edited by Karl Mras. Berlin: Akademie, 1983.
– *The Ecclesiastical History*, vol. 1. Edited by E. Capps, T.E. Page, and W.H.D. Rouse and translated by Kirsopp Lake. London: William Heinemann, 1926.
Evelyn-White, Hugh G., trans. *The Homeric Hymns and Homerica with an English Translation*. Cambridge, MA: Harvard University Press, 1914.
Farndell, Arthur, ed. *Gardens of Philosophy: Ficino on Plato*. London: Shepheard-Walwyn, 2006.
Ficino, Marsilio. *De Christiana religione*. Edited by Guido Bartolucci. Pisa: Edizioni della Normale, 2019.
– *Della cristiana religione*. Florence: Nicolò di Lorenzo, 1474.
– *Della cristiana religione*. Pisa: Lorenzo & Angelo Florentino, 1484.
– *The Letters of Marsilio Ficino*. Volume I. Preface by Paul Oskar Kristeller. Translated by members of the Language Department of the London School of Economic Science. London: Shepheard-Walwyn, 1975.
– *The Letters of Marsilio Ficino*. Volume 2: *Being a Translation of Liber III*. Translated by members of the Language Department of the London School of Economic Science. London: Shepheard-Walwyn, 1978.
– *The Letters of Marsilio Ficino*. Volume 3: *Being a Translation of Liber IV*. Translated by members of the Language Department of the London School of Economic Science. London: Shepheard-Walwyn, 1981.
– *The Letters of Marsilio Ficino*. Volume 4: *Being a Translation of Liber V*. Translated by members of the Language Department of the London School of Economic Science. London: Shepheard-Walwyn, 1988.
– *The Letters of Marsilio Ficino*. Volume 5: *Being a Translation of Liber VI*. Translated by members of the Language Department of the London School of Economic Science. London: Shepheard-Walwyn, 1994.
– *The Letters of Marsilio Ficino*. Volume 6: *Being a Translation of Liber VII*. Translated by members of the Language Department of the London School of Economic Science. London: Shepheard-Walwyn, 1999.
– *The Letters of Marsilio Ficino*. Volume 7: *Being a Translation of Liber VIII*. Translated by members of the Language Department of the London School of Economic Science. London: Shepheard-Walwyn, 2003.

- *The Letters of Marsilio Ficino.* Volume 8: *Being a Translation of Liber IX.* Translated by members of the Language Department of the London School of Economic Science. London: Shepheard-Walwyn, 2009.
- *The Letters of Marsilio Ficino.* Volume 10: *Being a Translation of Liber XI.* Translated by members of the Language Department of the London School of Economic Science. London: Shepheard-Walwyn, 2015.
- *The Letters of Marsilio Ficino.* Volume 11: *Being a Translation of Liber XII.* Translated by members of the Language Department of the London School of Economic Science. London: Shepheard-Walwyn, 2020.
- *Liber de Christiana Religione. Marsilii Ficini Florentini Liber de Christiana Religione ad Laurentium Medicem.* Venetiis: Ottinus Papiensis, 1500.
- *Opera, et quae hactenus extitere, et quae in lucem nunc primum prodiere omnia.* 2 vols. Basel: Henricpetrina, 1576.
- *Three Books on Life.* Edited by Carol V. Kaske and John R. Clark. New York: Medieval and Renaissance Texts and Studies, 1989.

Florio, John. *Queen Anna's New World of Words, or Dictionarie of the Italian and English Tongues.* London: Melchisidec Bradwood, 1611.

Gentile, Sebastiano, ed. *Lettere, I: Epistolarum familiarum liber I.* Florence: Olschki, 1990.

Gill, Joseph. *The Council of Florence.* Cambridge: Cambridge University Press, 1959; repr. 2011.

Gottheil, Richard, and Meyer Kayserling. "Ibn Vives Al-Lorqui (Of Lorca), Joshua Ben Joseph (Hieronymus [Geronimo] de Santa Fé)," in *The Jewish Encyclopedia*, vol. 6. New York: Funk & Wagnalls, 1906.

Grafton, Anthony. *Worlds Made by Words.* Cambridge, MA and London: Harvard University Press, 2011.

Guillaume of Tripoli. *Notitia de Machometo, De statu Sarracenorum.* Edited and translated by P. Engels. Würzburg: Echter and Altenberge: Oros, 1992.

Hames, Harvey J. "Elia Del Medigo: An Archetype of the Halachic Man?" *Traditio* 56 (2001): 213–27.

Hanegraaff, Wouter. "Beyond the Yates Paradigm: The Study of Western Esotericism between Counterculture and New Complexity." *Aries* 1, no. 1 (2001): 5–37.
- *Esotericism and the Academy: Rejected Knowledge in Western Culture.* Cambridge: Cambridge University Press, 2012.
- "How Hermetic Was Renaissance Hermetism?" *Aries* 15, no. 2 (2015): 179–209.
- "How Magic Survived the Disenchantment of the World." *Religion* 33, no. 4 (2003): 357–80.

Hankins, James. "Cosimo de'Medici and the 'Platonic Academy.'" *Journal of the Warburg and Courtauld Institutes* 53 (1990): 144–62.

- *Humanism and Platonism in the Italian Renaissance*. 2 vols. Rome: Edizioni di Storia e Letteratura, 2003/4.
- *Plato in the Italian Renaissance*. 2 vols. Leiden, New York, Copenhagen, Cologne: Brill, 1990.

Howlett, Sophia. *Marsilio Ficino and His World*. London: Palgrave Macmillan, 2016.

Idel, Moshe. *Kabbalah in Italy 1280–1510*. New Haven, CT: Yale University Press, 2011.

Inowlocki, Sabrina. *Eusebius and the Jewish Authors*. Leiden and Boston: Brill, 2006.

Jerome. *Sancti Eusebii Hieronymi Epistulae*. Edited by Isidorus Hilberg in *Corpus Scriptorum Ecclesiasticorum Latinorum* 54. Vienna: F. Tempsky and Leipzig: G. Freytag, 1910.

Johnson, Aaron P. *Ethnicity and Argument in Eusebius' Praeparatio Evangelica*. Oxford and New York: Oxford University Press, 2006.

Kern, Otto, ed. *Orphicorum fragmenta*. Berlin: Weidmann, 1922.

Klibansky, Raymond, Erwin Panofsky, and Fritz Saxl. *Saturn and Melancholy*. Montreal: McGill–Queen's University Press, 1964/2019.

Kristeller, Paul Oskar. "The Alleged Ritual Murder of Simon of Trent (1475) and Its Literary Repercussions: A Bibliographical Study." *Proceedings of the American Academy for Jewish Research* 59 (1993): 103–35.
- *Eight Philosophers of the Italian Renaissance*. Stanford, CA: Stanford University Press, 1964.
- "Marsilio Ficino as a Man of Letters and the Glosses Attributed to Him in the Caetani Codex of Dante." *Renaissance Quarterly* 36 (1983): 1–47.
- *Philosophy of Marsilio Ficino*. Translated by Virginia Conant. New York: Columbia University Press, 1964.
- *Renaissance Thought and Its Sources*. New York: Columbia University Press, 1975.
- *Supplementum Ficinanum*. 2 vols. Florence: Olschki, 1937.

Lewis, Charlton T., and Charles Short, eds. *A Latin Dictionary*. Oxford: Clarendon, 1879; repr. 1993.

Liddell, Henry George, and Robert Scott, eds. *A Greek-English Lexicon*. Oxford: Clarendon, 1996.

Macrobius, Ambrosius Theodosius. *Commentarii in Somnium Scipionis*. Edited by Jacob Willis. Stuttgart and Leipzig: Teubner, 1970; repr. 1994.
- *Saturnalia*. Edited by Jacob Willis. Stuttgart and Leipzig: Teubner, 1994.

Magee, John, ed. and trans. *On Plato's Timaeus. Calcidius*. Cambridge, MA: Harvard University Press, 2016.

Martí, Ramon. *Pugio fidei*. Leipzig: Friedrich Lanckisus, 1687.

McGinn, Bernard. "Cabalists and Christians: Reflections on Cabala in Medieval and Renaissance Thought." In *Jewish Christians and Christian*

Jews, edited by R.H. Popkin and G.M. Weiner, 11–34. New York: Kluwer Academic Publishers, 1994.
– *Thomas Aquinas's* Summa Theologiae: *A Biography*. Princeton, NJ: Princeton University Press, 2004.
McMichael, Steven J. "Alfonso de Espina on the Mosaic Law." In *Friars and Jews in the Middle Ages and Renaissance*, edited by Steven J. McMichael and Susan E. Myers, 199–224. Leiden: Brill, 2004.
McMichael, Steven J., and Susan E. Myers, eds. *Friars and Jews in the Middle Ages and Renaissance*. Leiden: Brill, 2004.
Menahem, Mor. *The Second Jewish Revolt: The Bar Kokhba War, 132–136*. Leiden and Boston: Brill, 2016.
Monat, Pierre, ed. *Lactance*. Institutions divines. Livre IV. Paris: Les Éditions du Cerf, 1992.
Nakamura, Byron J. "When Did Diocletian Die? New Evidence for an Old Problem." *Classical Philology* 98, no. 3 (2003): 283–9.
Nauert, Charles. *Historical Dictionary of the Renaissance*. Lanham, MD: Scarecrow Press, 2004.
Netanyahu, Benzion. *The Origins of the Inquisition in Fifteenth-Century Spain*. New York: Random House, 1995.
Nicholas of Lyra. *Quaestiones disputatae contra Hebraeos*. In *Biblia: Cum postillis Nicolai de Lyra et expositionibus Guillelmi Britonis in omnes prologos S. Hieronymi et additionibus Pauli Burgensis replicisque Matthiae Doering*. 4 vols. Nürnberg: Anton Koberger, 1485.
Nicoli, Elena. "Ficino, Lucretius and Atomism." *Early Science and Medicine* 23 (2018): 330–61.
Oberman, Heiko. *The Harvest of Medieval Theology*. Cambridge, MA: Harvard University Press, 1963.
Passannante, Gerard. "Burning Lucretius: On Ficino's Lost Commentary." *Studies in Philology* 115, no. 2 (2018): 267–85.
Paul of Burgos (a.k.a. Pablo de Santa Maria). *Dialogus Pauli et Sauli contra Judaeos, Scrutinium Scripturarum*. Rome: Ulrich Han, 1471.
– *De nomine divino quæstiones duodecim*. Edited by Iohannes Drusius. Franeker, 1604; Amsterdam, 1634; London, 1660; Utrecht, 1707.
Petrus Pons, Nàdia, ed. *Alchoranus Latinus quem transtulit Marcus canonicus Toletanus*. Madrid: Consejo superior de investigaciones científicas, 2016.
Poliakov, Leon. *The History of Anti-Semitism*, vol. 2. Philadelphia: University of Pennsylvania Press, 2003.
Resnick, Irven. *Petrus Alfonsi: Dialogue against the Jews*. Washington, DC: The Catholic University of America Press, 2006.
Robichaud, Denis. "Ficino on Force, Magic, and Prayers: Neoplatonic and Hermetic Influences in Ficino's *Three Books on Life*." *Renaissance Quarterly* 70, no. 1 (2017): 44–87.

Saffrey, Henri D. "Florence 1492: The Reappearance of Plotinus." *Renaissance Quarterly* 49, no. 3 (1996): 488–508.
Saif, Liana. *The Arabic Influences on Early Modern Occult Philosophy*. London: Palgrave Macmillan, 2015.
Schoene, Alfred, ed. *Eusebi Chronicorum libri duo*. 2 vols. Berlin: Widemann, 1866–76.
Serracino-Inglott, Peter. "Ficino the Priest." In *Marsilio Ficino: His Theology, His Philosophy, His Legacy*, edited by Michael J.B. Allen, Valery Rees, and Martin Davies. 1–14. Leiden, Boston, Cologne: Brill, 2002.
Soykut, Mustafa. *Image of the "Turk" in Italy: A History of the "Other" in Early Modern Europe, 1453–1683*. Berlin: Klaus Schwarz Verlag, 2001.
Strong, James. *Strong's Exhaustive Concordance of the Bible*. New York: Hunt & Eaton, 1890.
Tanturli, Giuliano. "Marsilio Ficino e il volgare." In *Marsilio Ficino. Fonti, testi, fortuna. Atti del convegno internazionale (Firenze, 1–3 ottobre 1999)*, edited by Sebastiano Gentile and Stéphane Toussaint, 183–213. Rome: Edizione di Storia e Letteratura, 2006.
– "Osservazioni lessicali su opere volgari e bilingui di Marsilio Ficino." In *Il volgare come lingua di cultura dal Trecento al Cinquecento: atti del convegno internazionale, Mantova, 18–20 ottobre 2001*, edited by Arturo Calzona, F.P. Fiore, A. Tenenti, and C. Vasoli, 155–85. (Florence: Olschki, 2003).
Vasoli, Cesare. "Da Giorgio Gemisto a Ficino: nascita e metamorfosi della 'Prisca theologia.'" In *Miscellanea di studi in onore di Claudio Varese*, edited by Giorgio Cerboni Baiardi, 787–800. Rome: Vecchiarelli, 2001.
– "Il mito dei 'prisci theologi' come 'ideologia' della 'renovatio.'" In *Quasi sit deus. Studi su Marsilio Ficino*, edited by Cesare Vasoli, 11–50. Lecce: Conte, 1999.
– "Note sul volgarizzamento ficiniano della Monarchia." In *Miscellanea di studi in onore di Vittore Branca*. 5 vols. III, 451–74. Florence: Olschki, 1983.
– "Per le fonti del *De christiana religione* di Marsilio Ficino." *Rinascimento* 28 (1988): 135–233.
– "'Prisca theologia' e scienze occulte nell'umanesimo fiorentino." In *Storia d'Italia. Annali 25: Esoterismo*, edited by Gian Mario Cazzaniga, 175–205. Turin: Einaudi, 2010.
– "La tradizione cabbalistica e l'esperienza religiosa cristiana del rinascimento." *Italia* 9 (1994): 11–35.
Walker, D.P. *The Ancient Theology: Studies in Christian Platonism from the Fifteenth to the Eighteenth Century*. London: Duckworth, 1972.
– *Spiritual and Demonic Magic: from Ficino to Campanella*. University Park: The Pennsylvania State University Press, 2000.
Weill-Parot, Nicolas. *Les "images astrologiques" au Moyen Âge et à la Renaissance. Spéculations intellectuelles et pratiques magiques (XIIe-XVe siècle)*. Paris: Honoré Champion, 2002.

Williams, A. Lukyn. *Adversus Judaeos: A Bird's-Eye View of Christian Apologiae until the Renaissance*. Cambridge: Cambridge University Press, 1935; repr. 2012.

Wirszubski, Chaim. *Pico della Mirandola's Encounter with Jewish Mysticism*. Cambridge, MA: Harvard University Press, 1989.

Yates, Frances. *Giordano Bruno and the Hermetic Tradition*. Chicago: University of Chicago Press, 1964.

Index of Citations

Note that this portion of the index covers only Ficino's text of *On the Christian Religion*, and not the Introduction.

1. Scripture

Gen. 1:1, 180, 182–3
Gen. 1:2, 182
Gen. 1:26, 184, 217
Gen. 1:27, 184
Gen. 2:4, 191
Gen. 2:16, 193
Gen. 2:19, 193
Gen. 3:16-17, 190
Gen. 3:23-4, 186
Gen. 3:24, 192
Gen. 4:3, 136
Gen. 8:20, 187
Gen. 8:21, 187
Gen. 9:1-3, 204
Gen. 15:15, 191
Gen. 18:1-5, 139
Gen. 22:1-18, 188
Gen. 35:29, 191
Gen. 49:10, 119
Exod. 3:15, 185
Exod. 12:13, 188
Exod. 20:5, 180
Exod. 24:8, 188
Lev. 8:12, 206

Lev. 16:30, 188
Lev. 17:11, 188
Num. 24:17, 76
Num. 24:27, 139
Num. 27:18-23, 206
Deut. 4:1-2, 196
Deut. 4:5, 202
Deut. 4:14, 202
Deut. 5:31, 202
Deut. 15:17, 200
Deut. 16:1-17, 201
Deut. 18:16-19, 200
Deut. 18:18-19, 199
Deut. 20:1-21, 202
Deut. 28:28-9, 134
Deut. 30, 145
Deut. 30:4-5, 158
Deut. 30:6, 205
Deut. 32:4, 186
Josh. 5:2, 205
Josh. 22:22, 180
Josh. 24:19, 183
Josh. 42:2, 191
2 Sam. 7:12 (Vulg. 2 Rg. 7:12), 164
2 Sam. 7:12-14 (Vulg. 2 Rg. 7:12-14), 164
2 Sam. 7:13 (Vulg. 2 Rg. 7:13), 164

236 Index of Citations

2 Sam. 7:16 (Vulg. 2 Rg. 7:16), 164
2 Sam. 7:23 (Vulg. 2 Rg. 7:23), 184
1 Kings 2:10 (Vulg. 3 Rg. 2:10), 191
1 Kings 9:6-9 (Vulg. 3 Rg. 9:6-9), 149
1 Kings 17 (Vulg. 3 Rg. 17), 125
2 Kings 6:23 (Vulg. 4 Rg. 6:23), 157
2 Kings 25:27-30 (Vulg. 4 Rg. 25:27-30), 136
Ezra 1:1-4, 158
Ezra 29:14, 161
Ezra 39:25, 161
Ezra 40:5-49, 158
Ezra 41:1-26, 158
Job 19:22, 150
Job 33:4, 182
Ps. 2:2, 152
Ps. 2:7, 110, 180
Ps. 2:8, 128, 152
Ps. 12:9 (Vulg. Ps. 11:9), 71
Ps. 16:9-10 (Vulg. Ps. 15:9-10), 153
Ps. 18:44-5 (Vulg. Ps. 17:44-5), 152
Ps. 19:5 (Vulg. Ps. 18:5), 155
Ps. 22:7-12 (Vulg. Ps. 21:7-12), 162
Ps. 22:17-19 (Vulg. Ps. 21:17-19), 152
Ps. 25:10 (Vulg. Ps. 24:10), 185
Ps. 27:13 (Vulg. Ps. 26:13), 158
Ps. 33:6 (Vulg. Ps. 32:6), 180, 182
Ps. 35:15-16 (Vulg. Ps. 34:15-16), 151
Ps. 35:19 (Vulg. Ps. 34:19), 152
Ps. 36:9 (Vulg. Ps. 35:10), 140
Ps. 41:10 (Vulg. Ps. 40:10), 152
Ps. 44:22 (Vulg. Ps. 43:22), 56
Ps. 45:6 (Vulg. Ps. 44:7), 140, 163, 184
Ps. 45:7 (Vulg. Ps. 44:8), 140, 164, 184
Ps. 47:6 (Vulg. Ps. 46:6), 154
Ps. 50:1 (Vulg. Ps. 49:1), 180
Ps. 59:12 (Vulg. Ps. 58:12), 167, 175
Ps. 68:10 (Vulg. Ps. 67:19), 154
Ps. 68:33-4 (Vulg. Ps. 67:33-4), 154
Ps. 69:23-4 (Vulg. Ps. 68:23-4), 152
Ps. 69:25-30 (Vulg. Ps. 68:25-30), 152
Ps. 72:6-7 (Vulg. Ps. 71:6-7), 138

Ps. 72:1 (Vulg. Ps. 71:2), 181
Ps. 72:7 (Vulg. Ps. 71:7), 123
Ps. 72:10 (Vulg. Ps. 71:10), 141
Ps. 72:17 (Vulg. Ps. 71:17), 181
Ps. 73:9 (Vulg. Ps. 72:9), 173
Ps. 78:2 (Vulg. Ps. 77:2), 116
Ps. 84:5 (Vulg. Ps. 83:5), 200
Ps. 84:8 (Vulg. Ps. 83:8), 198
Ps. 85:12 (Vulg. Ps. 84:12), 130
Ps. 87:5 (Vulg. Ps. 86:5), 141
Ps. 89:30 (Vulg. Ps. 88:30), 163
Ps. 89:49 (Vulg. Ps. 88:49), 195
Ps. 94:21-2 (Vulg. Ps. 92:21-2), 152
Ps. 98:2 (Vulg. Ps. 97:2), 122, 152
Ps. 99:22 (Vulg. Ps. 68:22), 151
Ps. 102:19 (Vulg. Ps. 101:19), 152
Ps. 104:30 (Vulg. Ps. 103:30), 154
Ps. 107:20 (Vulg. Ps. 106:20), 138
Ps. 110:1 (Vulg. Ps. 109:1), 109, 184
Ps. 110:3 (Vulg. Ps. 109:3), 109, 184
Ps. 110:4 (Vulg. Ps. 109:4), 163
Ps. 111:9 (Vulg. Ps. 110:9), 185
Ps. 116:10 (Vulg. Ps. 115:10), 220
Ps. 118:22-6 (Vulg. Ps. 117:22-6), 131
Ps. 118:26-7 (Vulg. Ps. 117:26-7), 139
Ps. 139:7-8 (Vulg. Ps. 138:7-8), 182
Ps. 146:7 (Vulg. Ps. 145:7), 204
Ps. 147:8-9 (Vulg. Ps. 147:19-20), 201
Prov. 3:19-20, 180
Prov. 8:6, 183
Prov. 8:22, 110
Prov. 8:22-7, 183
Prov. 8:28, 110
Prov. 8:30, 183
Prov. 10:20, 140
Prov. 30:4, 181
Eccles. 2:12, 184
Wisd. of Sol. 2:12-17, 143
Wisd. of Sol. 2:19-22, 143
Isa. 1:3, 132
Isa. 2:2, 156
Isa. 2:3, 134

Index of Citations 237

Isa. 2:4, 156
Isa. 2:20, 134
Isa. 4:2-3, 136
Isa. 6:1, 181
Isa. 6:3, 181
Isa. 6:9-10, 132
Isa. 7:14, 130
Isa. 8:13-15, 129
Isa. 9:6, 117
Isa. 9:7, 118
Isa. 11:1-3, 141
Isa. 11:2, 182
Isa. 11:6, 157
Isa. 11:9, 203
Isa. 11:10, 141, 150
Isa. 12:3-4, 154
Isa. 12:5, 155
Isa. 12:6, 155
Isa. 17:6, 137
Isa. 19:20, 138
Isa. 28:11, 154
Isa. 29:10-14, 135
Isa. 29:14, 84
Isa. 29:22-4, 136
Isa. 30:26, 163
Isa. 35:3-6, 110
Isa. 35:10, 192
Isa. 40:35, 122
Isa. 41:14, 182
Isa. 41:27-9, 132
Isa. 42:1, 133
Isa. 42:1-4, 132
Isa. 42:4, 201
Isa. 42:6-7, 150
Isa. 43:24, 190
Isa. 43:24-5, 190
Isa. 43:27-8, 190
Isa. 44:2, 190
Isa. 44:3, 190
Isa. 44:3-5, 160
Isa. 45:3, 131
Isa. 45:8, 130

Isa. 45:14, 198
Isa. 45:14-16, 138
Isa. 45:17, 144
Isa. 48:6, 181
Isa. 48:12-13, 182
Isa. 49:6, 131–2
Isa. 50:2, 133
Isa. 50:5-6, 150
Isa. 52:7, 144, 155
Isa. 52:10, 144
Isa. 52:12, 144
Isa. 52:13-53:12, 144
Isa. 53:1, 148
Isa. 53:2, 146
Isa. 53:3, 146
Isa. 53:4-5, 187
Isa. 53:5, 145, 189
Isa. 53:6, 147, 186, 192
Isa. 53:7, 146–7
Isa. 53:8, 147
Isa. 53:9, 147
Isa. 53:10, 163
Isa. 53:11, 147
Isa. 53:12, 147–8
Isa. 53:13, 146
Isa. 56:1, 123
Isa. 59:20, 187
Isa. 59:20-1, 161
Isa. 60:6, 141
Isa. 64:4, 88
Isa. 65:1-2, 131
Isa. 65:9, 132
Isa. 65:13-15, 132
Isa. 66:7, 129
Isa. 66:18-19, 132
Jer. 2:29, 174
Jer. 3:14, 138, 159
Jer. 3:14-15, 159
Jer. 3:16, 129
Jer. 3:17, 159
Jer. 4:3-4, 205
Jer. 7:26, 167

238 Index of Citations

Jer. 8:7-9, 133
Jer. 11:18-19, 148
Jer. 12:7-8, 148
Jer. 14:7-9, 193
Jer. 15:9, 148
Jer. 16:19-20, 134
Jer. 17:9, 139
Jer. 23:5, 117
Jer. 23:6, 117, 123, 139, 159
Jer. 23:36, 184
Jer. 29:10, 174
Jer. 31:31-4, 197
Lam. 4:20, 148
Bar. 3:36-8, 139
Ezek. 1:26, 139
Ezek. 17:24, 150
Ezek. 18:20, 193
Ezek. 36:25, 154
Ezek. 36:26, 154
Dan. 2:22, 140
Dan. 2:34, 165
Dan. 2:36-45, 134
Dan. 2:44, 126
Dan. 2:45, 165
Dan. 7:1-8, 165
Dan. 7:2, 131
Dan. 7:8, 165
Dan. 7:9-10, 162
Dan. 7:10, 166
Dan. 7:13, 162, 165
Dan. 7:14, 131
Dan. 7:26, 166
Dan. 9:24, 123
Dan. 9:26, 124
Hosea 2:15, 159
Hosea 2:23-4, 131
Hosea 3:4, 120, 135
Hosea 3:5, 135–6
Hosea 3:14, 153
Hosea 11:1, 141
Hosea 13:14, 192
Joel 2:28-9, 154

Amos 8:9-10, 150
Jon. 2, 153
Mic. 4:2-3, 205
Mic. 5:2, 118
Nah. 1:14-2.2, 205
Hab. 3:2, 93, 151
Hag. 2:7-8, 121
Hag. 2:10, 121
Zeph. 3:9, 161
Zeph. 3:11-13, 148
Zech. 3:1-8, 142
Zech. 6:13, 159
Zech. 9:9-10, 119
Zech. 9:11, 191
Zech. 12:10, 151
Zech. 13:6, 150
Zech. 14:9, 161
Mal. 1:10, 202
Mal. 1:10-11, 131
Mal. 1:11, 202
Mal. 2:5-7, 204
Mal. 3:1-2, 122
Matt. 1:23, 130
Matt. 2:1-16, 75
Matt. 2:23, 141
Matt. 4:19, 66
Matt. 5:21-39, 116
Matt. 5:44, 66
Matt. 6:19-20, 66
Matt. 6:22, 51
Matt. 7:6, 48
Matt. 7:12, 95
Matt. 7:29, 66
Matt. 10:5-42, 66
Matt. 10:33-5, 66
Matt. 13:14-15, 132
Matt. 13:35, 116
Matt. 16:24-6, 66
Matt. 19:21, 66
Matt. 22:37, 97
Matt. 24:19-21, 171
Matt. 27:8, 153

Index of Citations

Matt. 27:9-19, 153
Matt. 27:22, 169
Matt. 27:24-5, 172
Luke 1:32, 118
Luke 2:1-5, 121
Luke 2:29-30, 109
Luke 3:1, 76
Luke 4:18-19, 141
Luke 6:31, 95
Luke 10:27, 95
Luke 12:33, 66
Luke 14:25-7, 66
Luke 18:22, 66
Luke 19:42-4, 171
Luke 21:20, 171
Luke 21:23-4, 171
John 1:1-5, 68, 96
John 1:45, 127
John 3:1, 127
John 5:39, 116
John 10:37-8, 81
John 13:18, 152
John 13:31-2, 68
John 14:26, 214
John 18:36, 117, 164
John 19:35, 68
John 21:24, 68
John 21:25, 78
Acts 2:17-18, 154
Acts 2:26-7, 153
Acts 5:36, 127
Acts 5:37, 127
Acts 5:40-1, 62
Acts 9:15-16, 63
Acts 10:24-7, 62
Acts 11:28-30, 173
Acts 12:3-17, 83
Acts 14:11-14, 62
Acts 21:38, 127
Acts 25:23-4, 63
Acts 26:24, 63
Acts 26:26, 55

Acts 28:20, 72
Acts 28:22, 72
Rom. 1:8, 65
Rom. 5:3-5, 58
Rom. 5:12-21, 153
Rom. 8:15-19, 59
Rom. 8:35, 56
Rom. 8:36, 56, 155
Rom. 8:38-9, 57
Rom. 9:11, 136
Rom. 9:24, 131
Rom. 9:25-6, 131
Rom. 9:33, 129
Rom. 10:11, 129
Rom. 10:15, 155
Rom. 10:19, 149
Rom. 10:20-1, 131
Rom. 11:8, 135
Rom. 11:16-24, 137
Rom. 11:26-7, 161
Rom. 15:17-19, 79
1 Cor. 1:22-5, 63
1 Cor. 1:25, 84
1 Cor. 1:26-8, 55
1 Cor. 2:1-6, 78
1 Cor. 2:9, 88
1 Cor. 3:1-3, 202
1 Cor. 3:4-8, 61
1 Cor. 3:19, 84
1 Cor. 3:21-3, 61
1 Cor. 4:9, 58
1 Cor. 4:9-21, 57
1 Cor. 4:11-12, 58
1 Cor. 4:12-13, 58
1 Cor. 6:19, 51
1 Cor. 9:24-7, 56
1 Cor. 12, 71
1 Cor. 13:4-5, 61
1 Cor. 13:7-8, 61
1 Cor. 15:6, 179
1 Cor. 15:19, 55
1 Cor. 15:29-32, 59

240   Index of Citations

2 Cor. 1:6-8, 59
2 Cor. 3:17-18, 69
2 Cor. 4:1-9, 70
2 Cor. 4:10-11, 58
2 Cor. 4:16-18, 70
2 Cor. 5:1, 70
2 Cor. 7:4-5, 59
2 Cor. 10:4-6, 84
2 Cor. 11:20, 61
2 Cor. 11:23-33, 61
2 Cor. 12:12, 79
Gal. 2 :19-20, 59
Gal. 5:14, 95
Gal. 6:14, 59
Gal. 6:17, 58
Eph. 1, 71
Eph. 3:1, 59
Eph. 3:13, 59
Phil. 1:12-13, 55
Phil. 1:25-6, 57
Phil. 1:29-30, 57
Phil. 2:7-8, 78
Phil. 2:9-11, 78
Phil. 3:7-14, 71
Phil. 3:8, 59
Phil. 3:10, 59
Phil. 3:20, 60
Phil. 4:1, 60
Phil. 10:20-4, 57
Col. 1:5-6, 65
Col. 1:15-20, 71
Col. 1:23, 55
Col. 1:23-4, 57
1 Thess. 1:4-5, 79
1 Thess. 1:6, 60
1 Thess. 2:1-2, 60
1 Thess. 2:16, 152
1 Thess. 3:7-8, 60
1 Thess. 3:3-4, 57
1 Tim. 1:15-17, 62
1 Tim. 3:15-16, 79
1 Tim. 4:10, 62
2 Tim. 1:7-8, 57

2 Tim. 1:12, 58
2 Tim. 2:9-13, 58
2 Tim. 3:11-12, 58
2 Tim. 4:5-8, 70
Heb. 1-2, 189
Heb. 1:1-4, 70
Heb. 4:12-13, 71
Heb. 4:14, 60
Heb. 8:8-10, 197
Heb. 8:8-12, 197
Heb. 8:13, 197
Heb. 10:32-5, 60
Heb. 12:1-2, 60
James 1:2-6, 68
James 1:17-18, 68
James 2:8, 95
1 Pet. 2:9, 69
1 Pet. 3:15, 55
1 Pet. 4:12-14, 69
1 Pet. 5:1-2, 69
1 Pet. 5:10-11, 69
2 Pet. 1:16, 69
1 John 1:1-5, 67
1 John 3:13-14, 67
1 John 4:13-14, 68
1 John 4:16, 68
1 John 4:18, 61
1 John 5:4, 65
1 John 5:7-9, 67
1 John 5:10-15, 67
1 John 5:18-20, 67
Rev. 13:5, 208
Rev. 19:10, 62
Rev. 20:4-5, 62
Rev. 22:8-9, 62

2. Non-Scriptural Premodern Sources

Alcoranus 2.253, 85, 217
Alcoranus 2.62, 218
Alcoranus 3.39, 178
Alcoranus 3.45, 164, 178

Index of Citations 241

Alcoranus 4.157-8, 172
Alcoranus 4.171, 130
Alcoranus 5.46, 85
Alcoranus 5.75, 218
Alcoranus 5.82-5, 85
Alcoranus 5.110, 218
Alcoranus 6.85, 178
Alcoranus 9.30, 139
Alcoranus 21.91, 217
Alcoranus 22.17, 85
Alcoranus 61.6, 214
Alcoranus 61.14, 85
Alfonsi, Petrus, *Dialogus contra Iudaeos* Tit. 7, 130
Ambrose, *Epistulae* 6 [28].6, 114
Ammianus Marcellinus, *Res gestae* 23.1.2-3, 122
Anonymous, *Epistola de Casaribus* 39.7, 83
Anonymous, *Orphicorum fragmenta*, 113
Augustine, *Confessiones* 7.6.8-10, 73
Augustine, *Confessiones* 7.9.13, 103
Augustine, *De civitate Dei* 10.27, 107
Augustine, *De civitate Dei* 14.9.2, 153
Augustine, *De civitate Dei* 17.3.2, 197
Augustine, *De civitate Dei* 18.23, 111
Augustine, *De civitate Dei* 18.23.1, 106, 111
Augustine, *De civitate Dei* 18.23.2, 106
Augustine, *De civitate Dei* 18.29.1, 144
Augustine, *De civitate Dei* 18.53-4, 74
Augustine, *De civitate Dei* 19.23.2, 81
Augustine, *De natura et grati* 64.77, 51n15
Aulus Gellius, *Noctes Atticae* 1.19, 106
Aulus Gellius, *Noctes Atticae* 12.11, 212

Basil of Caesarea, *Homilia* 16, 103

Calcidius, *Commentarius* 126, 76
Cecco d'Ascoli, *Sphera cum commentis*, 77

Cicero, *De natura deorum* 1.5.10-11, 219
Ps.-Clement, *Recognitiones* 4.27.1-4, 113

Diogenes Laertius 1.1, 48
Ps.-Dionysius, *Caelestis hierarchia* 6-7, 89
Ps.-Dionysius, *Caelestis hierarchia* 8.1, 90
Ps.-Dionysius, *Caelestis hierarchia* 9.1-2, 90
Ps.-Dionysius, *Epistulae* 7, 112
Ps.-Dionysius, *Epistulae* 7.2, 77

Eusebius Caesariensis, *Chronicon* 2, 77, 82
Eusebius Caesariensis, *Historia ecclesiastica* 1.3.2-7, 206
Eusebius Caesariensis, *Historia ecclesiastica* 1.3.13, 141
Eusebius Caesariensis, *Historia ecclesiastica* 1.3.16-18, 140, 164
Eusebius Caesariensis, *Historia ecclesiastica* 1.5, 121
Eusebius Caesariensis, *Historia ecclesiastica* 1.5.2, 77
Eusebius Caesariensis, *Historia ecclesiastica* 1.5.5-6, 127
Eusebius Caesariensis, *Historia ecclesiastica* 1.6.2, 120
Eusebius Caesariensis, *Historia ecclesiastica* 1.6.9-10, 124
Eusebius Caesariensis, *Historia ecclesiastica* 1.8.1, 121
Eusebius Caesariensis, *Historia ecclesiastica* 1.8.1-9, 170
Eusebius Caesariensis, *Historia ecclesiastica* 1.9.1-2, 124
Eusebius Caesariensis, *Historia ecclesiastica* 1.11.3-6, 177
Eusebius Caesariensis, *Historia ecclesiastica* 1.11.7-8, 178
Eusebius Caesariensis, *Historia ecclesiastica* 1.13, 155

Eusebius Caesariensis, *Historia ecclesiastica* 2.2.1-6, 82
Eusebius Caesariensis, *Historia ecclesiastica* 2.21.1-3, 127
Eusebius Caesariensis, *Historia ecclesiastica* 2.23.19-20, 169
Eusebius Caesariensis, *Historia ecclesiastica* 2.25, 213
Eusebius Caesariensis, *Historia ecclesiastica* 2.7.1, 83
Eusebius Caesariensis, *Historia ecclesiastica* 2.8, 173
Eusebius Caesariensis, *Historia ecclesiastica* 2.9.4, 83
Eusebius Caesariensis, *Historia ecclesiastica* 2.23.21-3, 179
Eusebius Caesariensis, *Historia ecclesiastica* 3.1, 155
Eusebius Caesariensis, *Historia ecclesiastica* 3.5, 128
Eusebius Caesariensis, *Historia ecclesiastica* 3.5.3, 160
Eusebius Caesariensis, *Historia ecclesiastica* 3.5.5-7, 168
Eusebius Caesariensis, *Historia ecclesiastica* 3.6.15-16, 168
Eusebius Caesariensis, *Historia ecclesiastica* 3.6.21-7, 172
Eusebius Caesariensis, *Historia ecclesiastica* 3.7, 65
Eusebius Caesariensis, *Historia ecclesiastica* 3.7.1-5, 171
Eusebius Caesariensis, *Historia ecclesiastica* 3.7.2, 168
Eusebius Caesariensis, *Historia ecclesiastica* 3.7.2, 115
Eusebius Caesariensis, *Historia ecclesiastica* 3.8.1-9, 169
Eusebius Caesariensis, *Historia ecclesiastica* 3.8.6, 77
Eusebius Caesariensis, *Historia ecclesiastica* 3.17, 121

Eusebius Caesariensis, *Historia ecclesiastica* 3.20.1-7, 121
Eusebius Caesariensis, *Historia ecclesiastica* 3.32.6, 209
Eusebius Caesariensis, *Historia ecclesiastica* 3.33.1, 212
Eusebius Caesariensis, *Historia ecclesiastica* 3.36, 208
Eusebius Caesariensis, *Historia ecclesiastica* 4.2.5, 173
Eusebius Caesariensis, *Historia ecclesiastica* 4.3.1-3, 82
Eusebius Caesariensis, *Historia ecclesiastica* 4.6.2-4, 128
Eusebius Caesariensis, *Historia ecclesiastica* 4.6.3, 173
Eusebius Caesariensis, *Historia ecclesiastica* 4.8.5, 176
Eusebius Caesariensis, *Historia ecclesiastica* 4.8.6, 82, 213
Eusebius Caesariensis, *Historia ecclesiastica* 4.15.20-1, 208
Eusebius Caesariensis, *Historia ecclesiastica* 4.16.1-6, 208
Eusebius Caesariensis, *Historia ecclesiastica* 4.18, 82
Eusebius Caesariensis, *Historia ecclesiastica* 4.20-1, 209
Eusebius Caesariensis, *Historia ecclesiastica* 4.26, 209
Eusebius Caesariensis, *Historia ecclesiastica* 4.26.3, 213
Eusebius Caesariensis, *Historia ecclesiastica* 4.27-30, 209
Eusebius Caesariensis, *Historia ecclesiastica* 5.5.1-5, 213
Eusebius Caesariensis, *Historia ecclesiastica* 5.10.3, 105
Eusebius Caesariensis, *Historia ecclesiastica* 5.17.5, 209
Eusebius Caesariensis, *Historia ecclesiastica* 5.21, 209

Eusebius Caesariensis, *Historia ecclesiastica* 5.23, 78
Eusebius Caesariensis, *Historia ecclesiastica* 6.1, 210
Eusebius Caesariensis, *Historia ecclesiastica* 6.4.1-3, 210
Eusebius Caesariensis, *Historia ecclesiastica* 7.1, 173
Eusebius Caesariensis, *Historia ecclesiastica* 7.10.1-3, 209
Eusebius Caesariensis, *Historia ecclesiastica* 7.32.13-19, 149
Eusebius Caesariensis, *Historia ecclesiastica* 8.13, 83
Eusebius Caesariensis, *Historia ecclesiastica* 8.15, 83
Eusebius Caesariensis, *Historia ecclesiastica* 10.9, 83, 157
Eusebius Caesariensis, *Praeparatio evangelica* 1.4.7, 103
Eusebius Caesariensis, *Praeparatio evangelica* 4.16.8, 103
Eusebius Caesariensis, *Praeparatio evangelica* 5.1.9-11, 101
Eusebius Caesariensis, *Praeparatio evangelica* 5.17.6-9, 101
Eusebius Caesariensis, *Praeparatio evangelica* 5.26.4, 101
Eusebius Caesariensis, *Praeparatio evangelica* 5.29, 101
Eusebius Caesariensis, *Praeparatio evangelica* 5.32, 101
Eusebius Caesariensis, *Praeparatio evangelica* 6.6.70-1, 74
Eusebius Caesariensis, *Praeparatio evangelica* 8.1.6, 115
Eusebius Caesariensis, *Praeparatio evangelica* 8.2-3, 115, 175
Eusebius Caesariensis, *Praeparatio evangelica* 8.9-11, 157
Eusebius Caesariensis, *Praeparatio evangelica* 8.11.3, 47
Eusebius Caesariensis, *Praeparatio evangelica* 9.2, 114
Eusebius Caesariensis, *Praeparatio evangelica* 9.3, 114
Eusebius Caesariensis, *Praeparatio evangelica* 9.4, 115
Eusebius Caesariensis, *Praeparatio evangelica* 9.5.6, 114
Eusebius Caesariensis, *Praeparatio evangelica* 9.6.3, 150
Eusebius Caesariensis, *Praeparatio evangelica* 9.6.5, 114
Eusebius Caesariensis, *Praeparatio evangelica* 9.6.6-9. 113
Eusebius Caesariensis, *Praeparatio evangelica* 9.10.1-2, 114
Eusebius Caesariensis, *Praeparatio evangelica* 9.10.3, 113
Eusebius Caesariensis, *Praeparatio evangelica* 9.11, 112
Eusebius Caesariensis, *Praeparatio evangelica* 9.13, 112
Eusebius Caesariensis, *Praeparatio evangelica* 9.27.3, 113
Eusebius Caesariensis, *Praeparatio evangelica* 10.1-2, 112
Eusebius Caesariensis, *Praeparatio evangelica* 10.4.20-1, 113
Eusebius Caesariensis, *Praeparatio evangelica* 10.5, 113
Eusebius Caesariensis, *Praeparatio evangelica* 10.8.2, 47
Eusebius Caesariensis, *Praeparatio evangelica* 10.11.27-30, 47
Eusebius Caesariensis, *Praeparatio evangelica* 11.18-19, 207
Eusebius Caesariensis, *Praeparatio evangelica* 13.12.5, 113

Ficino, Marsilio, *Epistolae*, 128
Ficino, Marsilio, *Epistolae*, 4.19, 111
Ficino, Marsilio, *Epistolae*, 8.7, 111

244 Index of Citations

Ficino, Marsilio, *In Charmidem*, 98
Ficino, Marsilio, *In Philebum*, 103
Ficino, Marsilio, *Theologia Platonica* 1.2, 92
Ficino, Marsilio, *Theologia Platonica* 4.305, 52
Ficino, Marsilio, *Theologia Platonica* 4.361, 51, 137
Ficino, Marsilio, *Theologia Platonica* 11.4, 86-88
Ficino, Marsilio, *Theologia Platonica* 12.2.3, 214
Ficino, Marsilio, *Theologia Platonica* 13.1.4, 98
Ficino, Marsilio, *Theologia Platonica* 14.8, 51
Ficino, Marsilio, *Theologia Platonica* 14.9, 50
Ficino, Marsilio, *Theologia Platonica* 14.10, 47, 72
Ficino, Marsilio, *Theologia Platonica* 16.1, 90
Ficino, Marsilio, *Theologia Platonica* 16.7.12, 98
Ficino, Marsilio, *Theologia Platonica* 18.8, 90
Ficino, Marsilio, *Theologia Platonica* 18.9, 162-3
Firmicus Maternus, Iulius, *Mathesis* 4.17.2, 113

Guillaume de Tripoli, *De statu Sarracenorum*, 218

Herman of Carinthia, *De generatione Machumet*, 100
Herman of Carinthia, *Doctrina Machumet*, 100
Hermes Trismegistus, *Corpus Hermeticum* 1.9, 87
Hieronymus de Sanctafide (Jerome of Santa Fe), *Contra Iudeos ... libri duo* 1.1, 158

Hieronymus de Sanctafide, *Contra Iudeos* 1.2, 118-19, 123-4, 126-8, 130
Hieronymus de Sanctafide, *Contra Iudeos* 1.4, 130, 158-9
Hieronymus de Sanctafide, *Contra Iudeos* 1.6, 126-7
Hieronymus de Sanctafide, *Contra Iudeos* 1.7, 119, 191-2
Hieronymus de Sanctafide, *Contra Iudeos* 1.9, 156
Hieronymus de Sanctafide, *Contra Iudeos* 1.11, 191
Hieronymus de Sanctafide, *Contra Iudeos* 1.12, 122
Hieronymus de Sanctafide, *Contra Iudeos*, 2.1, 167
Hieronymus de Sanctafide, *Contra Iudeos*, 2.3, 180
Horace, *De arte poetica* 1.78, 79

Iamblichus, *De vita Pythagorica* 28.145-7, 100
Irenaeus, *Contra haereses*, 212
Irenaeus, *Contra haereses* 1.24.4, 172

Jerome, *De viris illustribus* 2.11, 105
Jerome, *De viris illustribus* 3.2, 104
Jerome, *De viris illustribus* 11-13, 211
Jerome, *De viris illustribus* 13, 178
Jerome, *De viris illustribus* 16.8-9, 208
Jerome, *De viris illustribus* 57-134, 210
Jerome, *De viris illustribus* 79, 84
Jerome, *Prologus Regum*, 117
Jerome of Santa Fe. *See* Hieronymus de Sanctafide
Josephus, *Antiquitates Iudaicae* 18.3.3, 177
Josephus, *Antiquitates Iudaicae* 19.8.2, 83
Josephus, *Antiquitates Iudaicae* 20.1.3, 124

Index of Citations   245

Josephus, *Antiquitates Iudaicae*
  20.9.1, 179
Josephus, *Antiquitates Iudaicae*
  20.10.1, 124, 149
Josephus, *De bello Iudaico*
  2.261-3, 127
Josephus, *De bello Iudaico* 4.420, 65
Josephus, *De bello Iudaico* 5.519, 168
Josephus, *De bello Iudaico* 6.201-13, 172
Josephus, *De bello Iudaico* 6.288-304,
  77, 170
Josephus, *De bello Iudaico* 6.311-15, 128
Josephus, *De bello Iudaico* 6.420, 115
Josephus, *De bello Iudaico* 6.420-7, 168
Justin, *Epitome* 36.2, 114

Lactantius, *Institutiones divinae* 1.6, 106
Lactantius, *Institutiones divinae*
  4.3.4-9, 48
Lactantius, *Institutiones divinae*
  4.4.1-6, 48
Lactantius, *Institutiones divinae*
  4.6.5, 109
Lactantius, *Institutiones divinae*
  4.6.6, 110
Lactantius, *Institutiones divinae*
  4.10.18, 77
Lactantius, *Institutiones divinae*
  4.12.20, 99
Lactantius, *Institutiones divinae*
  4.13.8, 139, 141
Lactantius, *Institutiones divinae*
  4.13.10, 139
Lactantius, *Institutiones divinae*
  4.13.11, 81
Lactantius, *Institutiones divinae*
  4.14, 142
Lactantius, *Institutiones divinae*
  4.15.15, 110
Lactantius, *Institutiones divinae*
  4.15.18, 110
Lactantius, *Institutiones divinae*
  4.15.24, 110

Lactantius, *Institutiones divinae*
  4.15.25, 110
Lactantius, *Institutiones divinae*
  4.15.29, 111
Lactantius, *Institutiones divinae*
  4.16.17, 110
Lactantius, *Institutiones divinae*
  4.17.4, 111
Lactantius, *Institutiones divinae*
  4.18.15, 110
Lactantius, *Institutiones divinae*
  4.18.17, 111
Lactantius, *Institutiones divinae*
  4.18.18, 111
Lactantius, *Institutiones divinae*
  4.18.20, 111
Lactantius, *Institutiones divinae*
  4.18.22, 149
Lactantius, *Institutiones divinae*
  4.19.4, 148
Lactantius, *Institutiones divinae*
  4.19.5, 111
Lactantius, *Institutiones divinae*
  4.20.7, 148
Lactantius, *Institutiones divinae*
  4.20.11, 111
Lactantius, *Institutiones divinae*
  4.23.10, 99
Lactantius, *Institutiones divinae*
  4.24, 99
Lactantius, *Institutiones divinae*
  4.25.3-5, 88
Lactantius, *Institutiones divinae*
  4.27.1-3, 102
Lactantius, *Institutiones divinae*
  4.27.20, 87
Lucian, *De morte Peregrini* 11-13, 212

Macrobius, *Commentarius in somnium
  Scipionis* 1.8.5-11, 199, 202
Macrobius, *Saturnalia* 2.4.11,
  75, 127
Mishneh Torah, 126, 158, 203

Moses Maimonides, *Guide for the Perplexed*, 117

Nehunya, Rabbi, *Sefer HaBahir* (*The Book of Brightness*), 140
Nicholas of Lyra. *See* Nicolaus Lyrensis
Nicolaus Lyrensis (Nicholas of Lyra), *Quaestiones disputatae contra Hebraeos*, 116, 121, 123, 125, 156-8, 160, 162, 172, 177, 185

Origen, *Contra Celsum* 1.59-60, 76
Origen, *Contra Celsum* 2.47-8, 75
Origen, *De principiis* 2.6.3, 91
Origen, *De principiis* 4.1, 64

Pablo de Santa Maria (Paulus Burgensis / Paul of Burgos), *Dialogus Pauli et Sauli contra Judaeos, Scrutinium Scripturarum* 1.1.1, 116, 131
Pablo de Santa Maria, *Scrutinium Scripturarum* 1.1.1-2, 158-60
Pablo de Santa Maria, *Scrutinium Scripturarum* 1.1.3, 129
Pablo de Santa Maria, *Scrutinium Scripturarum* 1.2.1, 131, 133
Pablo de Santa Maria, *Scrutinium Scripturarum* 1.2.2, 132
Pablo de Santa Maria, *Scrutinium Scripturarum* 1.2.3, 132-3
Pablo de Santa Maria, *Scrutinium Scripturarum* 1.2.4, 131
Pablo de Santa Maria, *Scrutinium Scripturarum* 1.3.1, 119, 131
Pablo de Santa Maria, *Scrutinium Scripturarum* 1.3.2, 121, 137
Pablo de Santa Maria, *Scrutinium Scripturarum* 1.3.3, 123-4, 138-9
Pablo de Santa Maria, *Scrutinium Scripturarum* 1.3.4, 124-6
Pablo de Santa Maria, *Scrutinium Scripturarum* 1.4.3, 158
Pablo de Santa Maria, *Scrutinium Scripturarum* 1.5.2, 119, 133, 158
Pablo de Santa Maria, *Scrutinium Scripturarum* 1.5.4, 144
Pablo de Santa Maria, *Scrutinium Scripturarum* 1.5.5, 132, 162
Pablo de Santa Maria, *Scrutinium Scripturarum* 1.5.7, 140, 144, 146, 148, 187
Pablo de Santa Maria, *Scrutinium Scripturarum* 1.5.9, 186
Pablo de Santa Maria, *Scrutinium Scripturarum* 1.5.10, 119, 188, 191
Pablo de Santa Maria, *Scrutinium Scripturarum* 1.6.2, 190
Pablo de Santa Maria, *Scrutinium Scripturarum* 1.6.4, 191, 193
Pablo de Santa Maria, *Scrutinium Scripturarum* 1.6.5, 193
Pablo de Santa Maria, *Scrutinium Scripturarum* 1.6.6, 193-5
Pablo de Santa Maria, *Scrutinium Scripturarum* 1.7.1, 134
Pablo de Santa Maria, *Scrutinium Scripturarum* 1.7.2, 134
Pablo de Santa Maria, *Scrutinium Scripturarum* 1.7.6, 126
Pablo de Santa Maria, *Scrutinium Scripturarum* 1.7.7-10, 165
Pablo de Santa Maria, *Scrutinium Scripturarum* 1.7.12, 165-6
Pablo de Santa Maria, *Scrutinium Scripturarum* 1.8.1, 197
Pablo de Santa Maria, *Scrutinium Scripturarum* 1.8.2, 198
Pablo de Santa Maria, *Scrutinium Scripturarum* 1.8.3, 199
Pablo de Santa Maria, *Scrutinium Scripturarum* 1.8.4, 131, 199
Pablo de Santa Maria, *Scrutinium Scripturarum* 1.8.5, 201
Pablo de Santa Maria, *Scrutinium Scripturarum* 1.8.6, 203

Index of Citations 247

Pablo de Santa Maria, *Scrutinium Scripturarum* 1.8.12, 204
Pablo de Santa Maria, *Scrutinium Scripturarum* 1.8.14, 206
Pablo de Santa Maria, *Scrutinium Scripturarum* 1.8.15, 205
Pablo de Santa Maria, *Scrutinium Scripturarum* 1.8.16, 122
Pablo de Santa Maria, *Scrutinium Scripturarum* 1.9.2, 185
Pablo de Santa Maria, *Scrutinium Scripturarum* 1.9.5, 180
Pablo de Santa Maria, *Scrutinium Scripturarum* 1.9.9, 180
Pablo de Santa Maria, *Scrutinium Scripturarum* 1.9.10, 181
Pablo de Santa Maria, *Scrutinium Scripturarum* 1.9.11, 181
Pablo de Santa Maria, *Scrutinium Scripturarum* 1.9.13, 181
Pablo de Santa Maria, *Scrutinium Scripturarum* 1.9.15, 182
Pablo de Santa Maria, *Scrutinium Scripturarum* 1.10.5, 118
Pablo de Santa Maria, *Scrutinium Scripturarum* 1.10.6, 117
Pablo de Santa Maria, *Scrutinium Scripturarum* 1.10.7, 118, 131, 139
Pablo de Santa Maria, *Scrutinium Scripturarum* 1.10.8, 151, 163
Pablo de Santa Maria, *Scrutinium Scripturarum* 1.10.9, 139–40
Pablo de Santa Maria, *Scrutinium Scripturarum* 2.1.2, 202
Pablo de Santa Maria, *Scrutinium Scripturarum* 2.1.4, 164, 185
Pablo de Santa Maria, *Scrutinium Scripturarum* 2.3.10, 131
Pablo de Santa Maria, *Scrutinium Scripturarum* 2.3.15, 164
Pablo de Santa Maria, *Scrutinium Scripturarum* 2.4.3, 202
Pablo de Santa Maria, *Scrutinium Scripturarum* 2.6.2, 127, 175
Pablo de Santa Maria, *Scrutinium Scripturarum* 2.6.3, 130, 134, 167, 181
Pablo de Santa Maria, *Scrutinium Scripturarum* 2.6.5, 135
Pablo de Santa Maria, *Scrutinium Scripturarum* 2.6.7, 137
Pablo de Santa Maria, *Scrutinium Scripturarum* 2.6.9, 192
Pablo de Santa Maria, *Scrutinium Scripturarum* 2.6.10, 126, 137
Pablo de Santa Maria, *Scrutinium Scripturarum* 2.6.11, 126
Pablo de Santa Maria, *Scrutinium Scripturarum* 2.6.13, 134–7
Pablo de Santa Maria, *Scrutinium Scripturarum* 2.6.14, 116, 137
Pablo de Santa Maria, *Scrutinium Scripturarum* 2.10.6, 159
Paul of Burgos. *See* Pablo de Santa Maria
Paulus Burgensis. *See* Pable d Santa Maria
Philostratus, *Vita Apollonii Tyrensis* 6.29, 168
Pico della Mirandola, Giovanni, *Heptaplus* 7.4, 125, 134
Pindar, *Pythian Odes* 8.95, 100
Plato, *Charmides* 157b-e, 98
Plato, *Epinomis* 986a-7c, 113
Plato, *Epinomis* 986c, 87
Plato, *Epistolae* 314a, 103
Plato, *Epistolae* 323d, 87
Plato, *Leges* 888a-d, 53
Plato, *Phaedrus* 241a-b, 53
Plato, *Phaedrus* 246a-d, 47
Plato, *Protagoras* 322a, 51
Plato, *Republica* 328d-9d, 53
Plato, *Republica* 515c-d, 52
Plato, *Timaeus* 41d-42b, 90
Plato, *Timaeus* 42a, 98
Plato, *Timaeus* 43e, 98

248 Index of Citations

Pliny, *Naturalis historia* 2.200.3-5, 76
Pliny, *Naturalis historia* 5.15.70, 115
Pliny, *Naturalis historia* 7.192, 113
Plotinus, *Enneads* 4.7.10, 214
Plutarch, *De defectu oraculorum*, 101
Plutarch, *De superstitione* 1.1, 48
Porphyry, *De abstinentia*, 51n15

Qur'an. *See Alcoranus*

Ramon Martí, *Pugio fidei* 2.4.23, 125
Ramon Martí, *Pugio fidei* 3.2.8-10, 191
Ramon Martí, *Pugio fidei* 3.21.9, 125
Riccoldus de Monte Crucis, *Contra legem Saracenorum* 1.4-12, 217
Riccoldus de Monte Crucis, *Contra legem Saracenorum* 1.12-25, 86
Riccoldus de Monte Crucis, *Contra legem Saracenorum* 1.35-40, 86
Riccoldus de Monte Crucis, *Contra legem Saracenorum* 1.41-6, 217
Riccoldus de Monte Crucis, *Contra legem Saracenorum* 1.41-60, 85
Riccoldus de Monte Crucis, *Contra legem Saracenorum* 1.50-1, 86
Riccoldus de Monte Crucis, *Contra legem Saracenorum* 2.61, 214
Riccoldus de Monte Crucis, *Contra legem Saracenorum* 3.1-7, 214
Riccoldus de Monte Crucis, *Contra legem Saracenorum* 3.29-36, 218
Riccoldus de Monte Crucis, *Contra legem Saracenorum* 3.49-53, 216
Riccoldus de Monte Crucis, *Contra legem Saracenorum* 3.54-60, 215
Riccoldus de Monte Crucis, *Contra legem Saracenorum* 3.61-70, 217
Riccoldus de Monte Crucis, *Contra legem Saracenorum* 3.80-5, 216
Riccoldus de Monte Crucis, *Contra legem Saracenorum* 3.86-92, 215
Riccoldus de Monte Crucis, *Contra legem Saracenorum* 3.93-8, 214
Riccoldus de Monte Crucis, *Contra legem Saracenorum* 8.85-97, 218
Riccoldus de Monte Crucis, *Contra legem Saracenorum* 9.20-8, 218
Riccoldus de Monte Crucis, *Contra legem Saracenorum* 15.19-32, 218
Riccoldus de Monte Crucis, *Contra legem Saracenorum* 15.41-50, 217

Sa'adiah Gaon, *The Book of Beliefs and Opinions*, 126
Sallust, *Bellum Iugurthinum* 1, 49
Strabo, *Geographica* 13.4.8, 76
Strabo, *Geographica* 16.2.34-8, 114
Suetonius, *Tiberius* 48.2, 76
Suetonius, *Vita Neronis* 16.2, 213
Suetonius, *Divus Vespasianus* 4.5, 128, 167
Suetonius, *Divus Vespasianus* 7.2, 168

Tacitus, *Annales* 2.47, 76
Tacitus, *Annales* 4.13.1-5, 76
Tacitus, *Annales* 15.44.3, 124, 211
Tacitus, *Historiae*, 5.9, 212
Tacitus, *Historiae*, 5.110, 114
Talmud, *Avodah Zarah* 9a, 125
Tertullian, *Apologeticum* 1.2, 73
Tertullian, *Apologeticum* 1.4, 73
Tertullian, *Apologeticum* 1.5, 73
Tertullian, *Apologeticum* 1.10-13, 177
Tertullian, *Apologeticum* 2.8-9, 212
Tertullian, *Apologeticum* 5.1, 82
Tertullian, *Apologeticum* 5.3-4, 83
Tertullian, *Apologeticum* 7.3-4, 73
Tertullian, *Apologeticum* 16.1, 212
Tertullian, *Apologeticum* 18.4, 63
Tertullian, *Apologeticum* 18.8, 216

Tertullian, *Apologeticum* 19.6, 112
Tertullian, *Apologeticum* 21.19, 150
Tertullian, *Apologeticum* 21.28, 209
Tertullian, *Apologeticum* 21.29, 47
Tertullian, *Apologeticum* 23.4-7, 101
Tertullian, *Apologeticum* 23.15-17, 102
Tertullian, *Apologeticum* 23.19, 102
Tertullian, *Apologeticum* 24.1, 102
Tertullian, *Apologeticum* 37.4-7, 64
Tertullian, *Apologeticum* 50.12-14, 64
Tertullian, *Apologeticum* 50.16, 209
Thomas Aquinas, *Summa contra gentiles* 1.3.5, 87
Thomas Aquinas, *Summa contra gentiles* 1.5.10-11, 219
Thomas Aquinas, *Summa contra gentiles* 1.6.3, 71, 211
Thomas Aquinas, *Summa contra gentiles* 4.11.1-7, 87
Thomas Aquinas, *Summa contra gentiles* 4.27.1, 92
Thomas Aquinas, *Summa contra gentiles* 4.39.2-3, 94
Thomas Aquinas, *Summa contra gentiles* 4.40.13, 94
Thomas Aquinas, *Summa contra gentiles* 4.41.8, 94
Thomas Aquinas, *Summa contra gentiles* 4.54, 94
Thomas Aquinas, *Summa theologica* I-II, 99.1-6, 203

Velleius Paterculus, *Historia Romana* 2.126.4, 76
Virgil, *Aeneid* 1.293, 138
Virgil, *Aeneid* 1.293-4, 156
Virgil, *Aeneid* 6.439, 90
Virgil, *Eclogae* 4.7, 107
Virgil, *Eclogae* 4.15-17, 107
Virgil, *Eclogae* 4.31, 108
Virgil, *Eclogae* 4.48-9, 108
Virgil, *Eclogae* 4.50-2, 108
Virgil, *Eclogae* 4.53, 109
Virgil, *Georgica* 1.242, 90
Virgil, *Georgica* 3.491, 102
Virgil, *Georgica* 4.480, 90

Index

Aaron, 114
Abba the Jew, 117, 158, 191
Abdalla, 100
Abdal Muttalib, 100
Abdera, 115
Abgar, 155
Abner of Burgos, 23, 137n431
Abraham, 113–14, 123, 125, 138, 144, 185, 188, 191, 205
absolution, 189
Abulafia, Abraham, 26
Abydenus, 112
Acacius, 210
Achates, 163
Achilayl, 127
Achillius, 210
Acusilaus, 112
Adam, 21, 98, 125, 130, 138, 153, 160, 185–6, 190, 192, 194–5, 218
Adonay, 117, 185
Adriatic Sea, 10
adultery, 116, 212
Aelia, 127
Aelius, 127
Africa, 84, 199
African(s), 118, 126, 210
Africanus, 112
afterlife, 16
Agathobulus, 149

age (era), 62, 78, 80, 82, 91, 93, 107, 110–11, 115, 117, 123, 140, 151, 164, 172, 180, 200–1, 204; dark/iron, 13–14, 48, 107; end of, 161; first/old, 156, 198, 201, 203–4; future, 109, 151, 164, 198, 203–4; golden, 13–14, 107, 157; second, 128, 163, 203–4
Aglaophemus, 9, 18, 47, 103
Agrippa (king), 63, 160
Agrippa (philosopher), 207
Akiba, 125
Alba, Rabbi, 140
Alcinous, 12
Alemanno, Yohanan, 27n53
Alexander, 112–13
Alexander (martyr), 210
Alexander of Aphrodisias, 14
Alexander of Macedon, 54, 115
Alexander Severus, 82
Alexandria, 12–13, 15n29, 112, 149, 208–10
Alfonsi, Petrus, 9, 18, 23–6, 32, 41, 137
Alfonso de Espina, 26
Alfonso of Burgos, 137
Alfonso of Valladolid. *See* Alfonso of Burgos
allegory, 157
Allen, Michael J.B., 4, 15–16, 37
alphabet, 113

Index

Alphaeus, 112
Alypius of Antioch, 122
ambition, 72–3
Ambrose, 210
Ambrose of Alexandria, 210
Ambrose of Milan, 114, 210–11
Amelius, 84, 207
Ammianus Marcellinus, 122
Ammonius of Alesxandria, 209
Amos, 150
Amphilochius, 210
Ananias, 170, 179
Anatolia, 10
Anatolius, 149, 210
Ancona, 80
Andrew, 155
Andronicus, 209
angel(s), 5, 56, 58, 70, 79, 83, 87–90, 92–3, 103, 108, 118, 122–3, 130, 142, 144–6, 180, 188, 204
animal(s), 19–20, 49–50, 79, 86, 91–2, 94, 151, 156–7, 165–6, 189, 204, 207–8
annunciation, 149
Antichrist, 162, 166, 214, 218
Antioch, 58, 122, 149, 207
anti-Semitism, 31
Antoninus, 210
Antoninus Pius, 82, 176, 213
Antonio of Forli, 34, 222
Apion, 112, 209
Apollinaris, 210
Apollinaris (philosopher), 209, 213
Apollo, 56, 61, 114, 176, 207
Apollo (Milesian), 81
Apollonius (antimontanist), 209
Apollonius (martyr), 209
Apollonius of Tyana, 100, 168
Apollophanes, 77
apologetics, 6, 8
apostle(s), 5, 12, 28, 30, 40, 54, 58, 62, 66, 78, 82, 84, 103, 105, 129, 136–7, 148–9, 152–5, 157, 161, 169, 176, 179, 189, 197, 205, 207–9, 214, 216
Arab(ians), 120, 130, 141, 199, 214, 219
Arabia, 100, 166
Arabianus, 209
Arabic (langauge), 126n360
Aragon, 119n322
Aramaic, 9, 26. *See also* Chaldean(s)
Arbonius, 84
Archangels, 89
Archelaus, 210
Aretas, 61
Argyropoulos, John, 11
Arian(s), 85–6
Aries, 77
Aristaeus, 112, 115, 175
Aristarchus, 209
Aristides the Athenian, 82, 207
Aristion. *See* Aristo of Pella
Aristippus, 52, 102
Aristo of Pella, 127, 209
Aristobulus, 112, 115, 149, 157
aristocrats, 82
Aristophanes, 112
Aristotelian(s), 14, 31n61, 137n432
Aristotle, 10–11, 14, 114, 219
ark, Noah's, 156
Ark of the Covenant, 129, 203
Arnobius, 210
arrogance, 29n57, 35, 53, 84, 178, 218
Artapanus, 112–13
ascension, 141, 154, 205, 207
asceticism, 21, 28–30, 66
Ashdowne, Richard, 37
Asia, 59, 76, 155, 208–9, 213, 215
assumption, 95, 181
astrologer(s), 74, 77
astrology, 5, 72, 77, 113
Athanasius, 210
Athena. *See* Pallas (Athena)
Athens, 77
Atlas, 113

atonement, 188–90, 192; Day of, 201
Attic (language), 113
Atticus the Platonist, 112
Attrell, Dan, 5n6
augur(ies), 199
Augustine, Aurelius, 16, 25n49, 32, 51n15, 80, 103, 111, 143n474, 144n480, 211
Augustus, 75, 77, 106, 121. *See also* Octavian
Aulus Gellius, 212
Aurelian, 83
Auses, 206
avarice, 145. *See also* greed
Averroes, 7, 12, 14–15, 15n29, 31n61
Avicenna, 15n29

Baal, 76
Babylon, 120, 135–6, 158, 166, 173–4
Babylonian(s), 112, 120, 135, 144
Bacchyllus, 209
Bactrians, 102
Baghdad, 215n865
Bahir, Sefer, 27n53, 140n456
Balkans, 10
baptism, 24, 77, 110, 154, 190, 196
Barachiah, 123
barbarian(s), 65, 101, 113, 207, 211, 215, 219
Barcelona, 119n322
Bardasian, 209
Bar Kokhba, 40, 125, 127–8
Bar-Koziba. *See* Bar Kokhba
Barnabas, 62, 209
Barry, Mary Inviolata, 37
Bartholomew, 105, 155
Bartolucci, Guido, 27, 32, 34–6, 131n396
Basil the Great, 103, 210
Basilias, 210
beast(s). *See* animal(s)
Bembo, Bernardo, 34, 223

Benedict (pope), 137
Benedict XIII (antipope), 25
Ben-Kozeba. *See* Bar Kokhba
Berlinghieri, 221
Berossus the Chaldean, 112
Bersabe, 104
Beryllus, 210
Betar, 125, 173
Bethlehem, 118
Bible, 27, 37–8, 112, 114–15, 136n424, 151; Douay-Rheims, 37–9, 137n434; Vetus Latina, 41n81, 144n480. *See also* Septuagint; Vulgate (Bible)
Bindello, 80
bishop(s), 24, 34, 48, 84, 137–8, 146, 207–8, 213
Bithynia, 76, 155
Black Sea, 10
blasphemy, 58, 190, 208
blessedness, 73, 79, 93, 95–8, 101, 111, 114, 131, 139, 193, 198, 220
body(-ies), 49, 53, 55, 57–8, 60, 71, 80, 86, 91–2, 94–8, 102, 111, 119, 138, 153, 156–7, 159–60, 163–4, 168, 193–6, 203, 205, 208, 218; heavenly, 112, 163; of Jesus, 81, 85, 153, 179
boldness, 53
Bologna, 34
books (prophetic), 23, 56, 66. *See also* prophecy(-ies); prophet(s)
Brahmins, 47, 114
Brucker, Johann Jakob, 5n4
Bruni, Leonardo, 11n18
Bruno, Giordano, 3
Burgos, 25, 137–8, 146, 147n498
Byzantine Empire, 11

Cabala (Christian), 23n45, 26. *See also* Kabbalah (Jewish)
Caesarea, 210
Calami, 114

254   Index

Calcidius the Platonist, 76
Caleb, 159
Cambini, Andrea, 221
Canaanites, 199
Candidus, 209
cannibalism, 102, 172
Cappadocia, 155
Careggi, 11
caritas, 20–21, 28, 38. *See also* love
Carmel, Mount, 156
Cartagena, 24
Carthage, 64
Carthaginians, 102
Caspian(s): - mountains, 120, 130; - people, 103
Castiglioni, Gian Stefano, 33–4, 224
Cavalcanti, Giovanni, 163, 222, 224
Cecco d'Ascoli, 77–8
Celsus, 75, 83, 210
Cephas, 61
ceremonies, 56, 74, 129, 131, 196–8, 200–3, 205
Chaeremon the Stoic, 75
Chaldean(s), 26, 75–6, 81, 112–13, 134
Chaldean (language), 116–19, 121, 129, 133, 135–6, 140, 144–5, 151, 184. *See also* Aramaic
Chanaham, 113
Charles VIII, 14n27
chastity, 24, 64
Cherubim, 89, 93, 192
childhood, 52
Choerilus, 112
Christ, 8, 12, 14, 18–19, 21–2, 23n44, 25n49, 27, 30–1, 40, 54, 56–65, 67, 69, 72, 74–5, 78, 81–6, 91, 94–109, 111, 115–16, 118, 121–4, 126, 128–9, 131, 133–41, 146, 148, 150–9, 161–7, 169, 171–9, 189–90, 192–3, 195–6, 198, 202–9, 211–15, 217–19; baptism of, 77; birth of, 77; death of, 28, 75, 77, 110, 191; disciples of, 14, 28, 30–1, 54–6, 62–6, 75, 83, 103, 105, 133, 137, 139, 156, 177, 207, 219; glory of, 56, 61–2, 69, 210–11; imitation of, 18, 28; Incarnation of, 5, 9, 13; life of, 36, 82, 105; name of, 69, 73; passion of, 76, 148–50; power of, 82; second coming of, 137, 161, 163, 165–6, 191; soul of, 81; suffering of, 28, 57, 69, 76–7, 187, 193, 195; works of, 82
Christendom, 26, 32; enemies of, 18, 33, 35
Christianity, 7, 19, 21, 28–32, 38–9, 48, 63–5, 72, 74–5, 77, 81–6, 88, 101–3, 105–6, 115, 119n322, 120, 124, 126, 133, 137, 144, 146, 148, 165, 167, 169, 171–2, 175–8, 182, 191, 196, 206, 208–19
Christology, 22
Chrysoloras, Manuel, 11n18
Church, 27, 31, 36, 47, 57, 71, 79, 146, 165, 208, 216; Fathers, 19, 40–1; Greek, 10; history, 17, 41; Latin, 10; primitive, 12, 17, 28, 30, 39
Cicero, 6, 28, 66
circumcision, 188, 205
Clark, John R., 37
Claudius, 173
Clearchus, 114
Clement of Alexandria, 112, 169, 209
Clement the Roman, 209
Cletus, 209
Colossians, 57, 65, 71
comet(s), 75, 109, 169
commandment(s), 81, 95, 135, 190, 193, 196, 199–200, 202–3
Commodus, Marcus Antoninus, 209
Comon, 112
Constantine, 82–8, 106, 109, 141, 157, 165, 178
Constantinople, 10–11
contemplation, 29, 66, 88–9, 97, 103–4

Controni, Filippo, 33–4, 221
conversion, 24–5, 30–2, 65, 131, 133, 137n432, 139, 142, 145, 150, 155, 160–1
conversos, 9, 23–4, 27, 31
Copenhaver, Brian, 12–14
Corinthians, 55, 57–61, 63, 70–1, 78–9
Cornelius, 62, 210
Corpus Hermeticum. *See* Hermes Trismegistus
Council of Ferrara-Florence, 10
courage, 189
covenant, 129, 161, 188, 197–8
creation, 19, 22, 59, 68, 71, 92–3, 95, 182, 186, 191, 218
Crescens the Cynic, 208–9
Crete, 209
Crispus, 209
cross, 59–60, 66, 71, 78, 102, 148, 151, 190, 207, 209, 212
crucifixion, 63–4, 77–8, 86, 109, 149, 155, 178
Cynic(s), 208
Cyprian, 210
Cyprus, 209
Cyril, 210
Cyrus, 158

Damascenes, 61
Damascus, 61, 112
Damasus, 210
Daniel, 123–6, 130–1, 134, 140, 162, 165–6, 173
darkness, 17, 67–9, 91, 111, 140, 150, 191
David, 71, 109, 117–18, 121, 123, 129–31, 135–6, 138, 140–1, 150–5, 158, 162–4, 175, 182, 184–5, 191–2, 195, 197, 220
death, 15–16, 21, 28–9, 55–61, 64–5, 67, 71, 73–4, 78, 81–3, 90, 99, 101, 103–4, 108, 110–11, 115, 119, 121, 124, 142–3, 146–7, 151, 153, 155, 163–4, 167–9, 172, 174, 176–7, 179, 186–7, 190–2, 195, 200, 206–8, 210, 212–13, 216, 218
deceit. *See* deception
deception, 50, 54, 107–8, 143, 145–7
Decerbices, 102
Deferrari, Roy J., 37
delights (earthly), 28
Demas, 209
Demetrius of Phalerum, 112, 115
demon(s), 75, 81, 100–3, 108, 211, 213, 219
Demophilus, 209
Demosthenes, 28, 66
Deucalion, 112
Devil, 107, 142, 195, 214
Dexter, 210
Didymus of Alexandria, 113, 210
dignity, 25n49, 66, 73
Diocletian, 83
Diodorus, 210
Dionysius (bishop of Alexandria), 208–10
Dionysius (bishop of Corinth), 209
Dionysius the Aeropagite, 13–14, 35–6, 77, 89, 103, 112, 176, 207
disciples, 75, 125, 132, 208, 210; of apostles, 82, 103, 149, 169, 208–9, 216; of Jesus, 156, 178–9; of Paul, 56. *See also* Christ, disciples of
disobedience, 84
Disputation of Tortosa, 25
divination, 50
divine law. *See* law(s), divine
divine mind. *See* mind, divine
divine names. *See* names (divine)
Divine Spirit. *See* Holy Spirit
diviner(s), 199
Dominicans, 9, 24–5, 40, 119n322, 215n865
Dominions, 71, 89
Domitian, 83, 121, 167

Dorotheus, 209
dream(s), 84, 100, 114, 154
druids, 48
Du Cange, Charles du Fresne, 37

Earth, 52, 71–4, 78, 80, 103, 107, 109–10, 117, 119, 121, 128, 130–2, 134–5, 139, 143–4, 148, 152, 154–5, 168, 180–3, 185, 187, 191–2, 201–2, 216
earthquake, 75–6, 121
East, 75–7, 88, 115, 128, 154, 170
eclipse, 75–8, 109, 121, 148–50
Edessa, 155
Effraim, 118
Egypt, 114, 127, 138, 141–2, 159, 172, 175–6, 188, 197
Egyptian(s), 17, 20, 22, 47, 112–14, 116–18, 120, 126–7, 144, 158, 176, 202
Eleazar (high priest), 140, 157, 175
Eleazar, Rabbi, 180
elements (four), 88, 109, 163
Elia del Medigo, 31n61
Elijah, 85, 125, 151
Eloym, 185. *See also* Heloym
Elysian Fields, 90
Emisenus, 210
Emmanuel, 130
empathy, 194
Empedocles, 100
emperor(s), 54, 64, 74, 81–3, 100, 106, 109, 122, 125, 165, 176, 208–10, 213
empire, 115, 118, 128, 130, 138
Empyrean (heaven), 89
enemy(-ies), 18, 28, 33, 35, 54, 63, 66, 72, 74, 148, 151, 171, 173, 175–6, 178, 213–14
Enlightenment, 5
Enoch, 113
Epaphras, 209
Epaphroditus, 209
Ephesians, 59, 71, 207
Ephesus, 59, 112

Ephorus, 112
Ephraim, 162
Ephraim the Syrian, 210
Epicureans, 83, 210
Epicurus, 102
Epiphanius, 210
equinox (vernal), 149
error(s), 85–6, 100, 104, 124, 135–6, 137n431, 216, 219
essence, 92–3, 183–4
Essenes, 17, 47, 114
eternity, 86–8, 90, 93–5, 107, 118, 134n412, 164, 180–3, 187, 189, 196, 200–1, 206
Ethiopia, 155
Ethiopians, 17, 20, 47, 138, 215
Eucharist, 189
Eugenius IV (Pope), 10
Euhemerus, 112
Eumolpus, 47
Euphrates, 155
Eupolemon, 112–13
Eusebius (bishop of Rome), 210
Eusebius of Caesarea, 32, 40, 73–4, 76–7, 82–3, 105, 112–13, 115, 121, 127, 155, 157, 168, 172, 178, 206n824, 210, 213
Eusebius of Sardinia, 210
Eustathius, 210
Euzoius, 210
Evagrius, 210
evangelist(s), 62, 66, 70, 78, 105–6, 132–3, 178, 208, 216
Evaristus the Hebrew, 137
Eve, 130
evil, 13n27, 28, 58, 66, 95, 98–101, 108, 116, 147, 149, 167, 175–7, 186–7, 213
Evodius, 209
Ezekiel, 112, 139, 150, 154, 158, 161, 173, 193
Ezra, 149, 158, 173

faith, 13, 19, 21, 25n49, 29, 31, 33–5, 48, 55, 57–8, 60, 63, 65, 68, 70, 72–4, 78, 97, 109–10, 136–7, 186, 193, 195–6, 209, 211, 219
falsehood(s), 105, 212
famine, 56, 58, 61, 65, 83, 99, 168, 172–3
fasting, 61, 114, 176
fate, 72–74, 111
fear, 57, 59, 61, 69, 78, 82, 84, 102, 104, 110, 127, 129, 135, 141, 148, 168, 176–7, 204, 209, 213; of God, 50, 83, 85; of hell, 50
Feast of the Tabernacles, 170, 201
Federico da Montefeltro, 34, 223
Felix, 127
Ferrara, 10
Ficino, Marsilio, 3, 5–24, 26–41, 47, 49, 51n15, 63n77, 70n119, 80, 90n198, 102n227, 106n235, 112n274, 122n332, 123n338, 125n354, 127n371, 128n373–4, 133n405, 136n424, 137n431, 137n434, 139n443, 139n446, 141n466, 141n468, 142n472, 158n579, 166n637, 171n654, 171n656, 174n668, 177n676, 191n762, 201n794, 206n824, 221–5; *Apologia*, 4; *Commentary on Cratylus*, 32, 36; *Commentary on Divine Names*, 36; *Commentary on Epinomis*, 4; *Commentary on Laws*, 4; *Commentary on Mystical Theology*, 36; *Commentary on Parmenides*, 4; *Commentary on Phaedo*, 32, 36; *Commentary on Phaedrus*, 4; *Commentary on Symposium*, 4; *Commentary on Timaeus*, 4; *De coelitus comparanda*, 3; humanist, 5–6, 18; *Introduction to Plotinus' Enneads*, 13n26, 15n29; Italian translation(s), 7–8, 33, 36–7, 85n180, 89n194, 131n396, 137n434, 166n637, 166n639, 183n714–15, 193n772, 206n822; letters, 14n27, 32–35, 221–5; magus, 3–5; mid–life crisis, 6; *On Love*, 33; *On the Christian Religion*, 7, 16–17, 19, 22, 26–8, 32–6, 39, 49, 221–5; philosopher, 4–6, 31, 34, 80; physician, 3–5; *Platonic Theology*, 3–4, 6–7, 15–17, 32, 35–7, 53, 72, 92, 163; Platonist, 4–5, 7, 35; priest(hood), 4–5, 31, 34, 36, 49; sermons, 35; theologian, 17, 20–1, 30–1; *Three Books on Life*, 3–4, 37; translator, 3, 6–7, 11–12, 32, 36
Firmicus, Julius, 113
Flaccianus, 111
Flood, Great, 187, 204
Florence, 6, 10–11, 14n27, 16, 31, 32n63, 34–5, 47, 80, 215n865
Florus, 172
foe(s). *See* enemy(-ies)
forgiveness, 96, 185
form(s), 89, 93–4
Franciscans, 25, 34
Fulminea (legion), 213

Gaius, 209
Gaius (martyr), 210
Galatia, 155
Galatians, 58
Galilee, 113, 121, 127
Gallus, 173
Gamaliel, 84, 127
Gaul(s), 17, 47
Gelasius, 210
gematria, 26
Geminus, 210
generation, 67, 70, 86, 88, 90
Genoa, 10
Gentiles, 18, 38, 59, 63–4, 79, 131–5, 139, 141, 150, 154, 157, 160–1, 179, 217
Germany, 213

258 Index

Gerónimo of Santa Fe. *See* Jerome of Santa Fe
Ghāyat al-Ḥal-a. See Picatrix
glory, 54, 58–60, 62, 64, 68–70, 79, 83, 90, 107, 121, 130, 132, 135, 143, 179. *See also* Christ, glory of
Gnostic(s), 212
God, 9, 16–22, 26, 28–9, 48–51, 53–4, 58–67, 69–74, 76, 78–100, 102, 104, 107–14, 116–19, 122, 126, 129–36, 138–60, 162–5, 167–9, 171–93, 195–207, 209, 211–14, 216–20; essence of, 88–9, 93; Father, 21–2, 47, 51, 59, 61, 67–8, 71, 78, 87, 89, 94, 97, 99, 107, 117–18, 128, 142, 181, 183–4, 214n862, 217–18; friendship of, 96–7; glory of, 78, 181; house of, 79; infinity of, 22; mind of, 20, 85; power of, 48, 57, 63, 65, 69–70, 78, 85, 90–3, 95, 177, 217; Son of, 20–2, 67–8, 70–1, 75, 86–90, 107, 109, 111, 136, 142, 164, 181, 184, 217; soul of, 85, 217; unity of, 22, 88, 92–3; wisdom of, 47, 63, 85, 92, 95; wrath of, 152, 167–9, 205. *See also* Lord of Hosts
gods (pagan), 13n27, 56, 62, 81–3, 100–2, 107–9, 118, 127, 134–5, 184, 198, 216–17
Gog, 161
good(ness), 50–1, 87–9, 91–3, 95–6, 100, 102n227, 116, 135, 144, 155, 158, 164, 185–6, 213–14, 217, 220; highest, 19–20, 54
gospel(s), 16, 30, 55, 57–8, 60, 65, 69, 73, 76–7, 85, 105, 115, 123, 133, 141, 153, 155, 205, 207–8, 214, 216–18
Goth(s), 137
grace (divine), 49, 73, 123, 138, 143, 151, 154, 159, 195, 198, 217
Great Conjunction of 1484, 7
Greece, 10, 47, 106

greed, 81, 219. *See also* avarice
Greek (language), 11, 16, 37–8, 40n81, 105, 111, 115, 117, 155, 171n654, 171n656, 175, 178, 200, 215. *See also* Attic (language)
Greek(s), 10, 17, 20, 22, 63, 65, 83, 102, 114, 134, 175, 211, 215
Gregory Baeticus, 210
Gregory the Great (pope), 80, 211, 219
Gregory of Nazianzus, 210
Gregory of Nyssa, 210
Guarini, Francesco, 34
Guasconi, D. Francesco, 222
Guido, prior of Santa Maria degli Angeli, 35
guilt, 96, 98–9, 107, 145, 159–60, 173–5, 185, 187, 190, 192–6, 212
gymnosophists, 47

Habakkuk, 93, 151
Hadrian, 82, 125, 127–8, 173, 213
Haggai, 121, 140, 173
halakha, 31n61
Ham, 113
Hana, 191
Hankins, James, 16, 37
happiness (*felicitas*), 21, 28, 97, 187, 214
hatred, 64, 67, 72–3, 148, 152, 167, 187, 212, 219
healing, 75, 78, 80
heat, 51
heaven(s), 13n27, 49, 55, 57, 59–60, 70–1, 73–4, 78, 81, 85–6, 88–9, 91–2, 95, 104, 107, 109–11, 121, 126, 130, 138, 154, 156, 158, 160, 162–5, 168–9, 172, 175, 180–3, 191–2, 198, 207, 215. *See also* Empyrean
Hebrew (langauge), 9, 26, 37, 104–5, 115–19, 123n338, 135, 140, 151, 181, 183–4, 200, 215
Hebrew (literature), 23, 26, 175, 218

Hebrews (people), 9, 17–18, 22, 29, 38, 47–8, 60, 70, 84–5, 98, 100, 105, 112–14, 120, 125–6, 129–30, 133, 137, 140, 151, 157, 163–4, 166, 177, 183, 187, 189, 199, 219
Hecataeus of Abdera, 112, 115, 212
Hecate, 81
Hegesippus, 121, 169, 209
Heliopolis, 77
hell, 50, 151, 153, 191–2, 195, 205
Hellanicus, 112
Hellenism, 29
Heloym, 183–4. *See also* Eloym
Heluel, 183
Heraclides, 210
Heraclitus, 207, 209
Hercules, 101
heresy(–ies), 86, 166, 211, 219
heretics, 74, 85, 212, 214–15
Hermas, 209
Hermes Trismegistus, 3, 6, 9, 12, 17–19, 22, 87, 103, 111, 113, 163
Hermogenes, 112
Hero, 40n80, 210
Herod Antipas, 83
Herod the Great, 75, 83, 120–1, 124, 126
Hesiod, 13–14, 112
Hestiaeus, 112
Hezekiah, 118
hierarchy(–ies) (of angels), 89
hierarchy (of being), 19
Hieronymus de Sancta Fide. *See* Jerome of Santa Fe
Hierotheus, 103, 176, 207
Hilary the Great, 210
Hippolytus, 210
Hiram the Phoenician, 112
Hircanians, 103
historian(s), 83, 122, 213
history, 5, 8–9, 12–14, 17, 21–2, 75–6, 105, 112, 114, 120, 127, 155, 166, 171, 176, 179, 187; Church, 17, 41; end of, 31; Jewish, 39; of religion(s), 6, 19, 39
holiness, 64, 103, 113–14, 119, 169, 206, 211
Holy Ghost. *See* Holy Spirit
Holy of Holies, 123, 188, 203. *See also* sanctum, inner
Holy Spirit, 22, 26, 58–60, 67, 69, 71, 78–9, 87–9, 91, 94–5, 109, 130, 132, 141, 151, 154, 156, 180–2, 184, 190, 196, 205, 214, 217
hope, 21, 33, 35, 55, 58–9, 62, 65, 69, 73–4, 96, 110, 141, 149, 153, 158–9, 173, 212–13, 219
Horeb, 174, 200
Hosea, 120, 131, 135, 153, 159, 192
humans, 16, 19–22, 34, 49–50, 54, 72, 91–2, 94–9, 101–4, 109, 119, 130, 160, 162, 181, 184, 186, 188, 190–2, 195, 198, 203–4, 213, 217
humility, 77–8, 133, 139, 143, 163
Huna, Rabbi, 40
hunger. *See* famine
hymns, 17, 212

Iamblichus the Chalcidian, 84, 100, 103
Iberia, 25
Iconium, 58
Idel, Moshe, 27
idol(s), 83, 134, 136, 154, 174, 191, 205
idolater(s), 84, 172
idolatry, 122, 134, 136, 138, 166–7, 174, 191, 195
Idumean(s), 120
Ignatius, 105, 207
ignorance, 48, 51, 53, 59, 95, 141, 167, 169, 179, 213, 217
illness, 72, 110, 155
Illyricum, 155
imagination, 86–7

impiety, 15n29, 48, 54, 74, 83, 96, 102, 135, 148, 158, 161, 165, 167–8, 174, 189, 212, 215
Incarnation, 20, 22–3. *See also* Christ, Incarnation
incest, 102
India, 104, 114, 155
Indians, 17, 20, 47
ingratitude, 51, 53–4, 97
iniquity(-ies). *See* injustice
injustice, 62, 73, 82–3, 110, 123, 138, 143, 145, 146–8, 152, 171, 186, 190–1, 193, 197, 204, 207
innocence, 64, 96, 147, 152, 172, 186, 212–3
inspiration (divine), 47, 79, 85, 178
intellect, 34, 47, 94, 197; angelic, 92; human, 15n29, 17–18, 20–1, 91
Irenaeus, 209, 212
Isaac, 185, 188, 191
Isaacides, Salomon. *See* Shlomo Yitzhaqi of Troyes
Isaiah, 84, 88, 110, 117–18, 122–3, 129–38, 141, 143–8, 150, 154–8, 160, 163, 181–2, 186–7, 189–90, 192, 201–2, 205
Islam, 7–8, 9, 14, 18, 22, 28–30, 35, 71, 75, 85–6, 100, 115, 167, 214, 215n865, 216, 219
Israel, 25n49, 63, 72, 76, 114, 118, 120, 129, 132–3, 135–6, 138–9, 144–5, 148–9, 153, 155, 157–61, 172, 182, 184, 190, 192, 196–7, 201, 205, 218
Israelite(s), 133, 159
Italy, 106
Ivani, Antonio, 34, 223

Jacob, 76, 119–20, 132–3, 136, 139, 160–1, 185, 190–1, 201, 206
Jacobites, 215
James, 68, 83, 105, 169, 178, 206
James I of Aragon, 119n322

Jason, 209
Jehoiakim, 135
Jeremiah, 117, 123, 129, 133–5, 137, 139, 148, 150, 153, 158–60, 167, 173–4, 183–4, 192, 197–8, 201
Jerome of Santa Fe, 9, 18, 23–6, 32, 41, 123n338, 137, 191n762
Jerome (St.), 6, 51n15, 84, 104–105, 117, 178, 211, 215
Jerusalem, 105, 115, 118–19, 122, 124–30, 132, 136, 138, 142, 150, 155–6, 158–61, 166–71, 173, 182, 205
Jesse, 141, 150
Jesus, 6, 8–9, 21–2, 57–62, 65–7, 69–70, 77–8, 81–2, 84–6, 94, 100–2, 106–7, 109, 111, 116, 119–21, 123–8, 130–1, 133–4, 136, 138–9, 141–2, 144–5, 148–50, 154, 156–9, 162–5, 167–79, 189, 199–201, 204–6, 208, 214–17
Jesus Josedech, 142
Jesus Nave, 142, 205
Jews, 8, 14, 18, 23–7, 29, 31–2, 35, 38, 40–1, 56, 60–5, 71–2, 75–6, 78, 85–6, 103, 111–29, 131–7, 139–41, 144–50, 152–62, 164–82, 185–6, 190–7, 199, 204–7, 209, 211–12, 215–19; "crypto–," 25; expulsions of, 25, 74; Sephardic, 25
Job, 150, 182
Joel, 154
Johanan, Rabbi, 139
John, 170
John the Baptist, 85, 122, 166, 177–8
John Chrysostom, 210
John the Elder, 209
John the Evangelist, 56, 61–2, 65, 67–8, 76, 78, 91, 96, 103–5, 116, 127, 155, 178, 206, 208, 214
Johnson, Aaron P., 38
Jonah, 153–4
Jonathan, 129, 133, 140

Jose (ben Halafta), 123–4
Joseph, 114, 162–3
Josephus, 65, 76, 83, 112, 115, 120–1, 124, 127–8, 149, 167–73, 175, 177–9, 211
Joshua, 140, 159, 180, 183, 191, 206n824
Joshua ha–Lorki. *See* Jerome of Santa Fe
Joshua, Rabbi, 185–186, 191
Joshua, Son of Nun, 142n470
Joshua, son of Yehozadak, 142n470
Jove. *See* Jupiter
joy, 16, 57, 59–60, 67–9, 131–2, 154, 176–7, 183, 186, 191–2
Juba, 112
Judah, 118–21, 132, 135, 159–62, 197, 204–5
Judah, Rabbi, 191
Judaism, 7, 9, 18, 22–4, 28, 30–1, 39
Judas, 83, 121, 127, 152–3, 214
Judas (philosopher), 209
Jude, 105, 206
Judea, 60, 63, 75, 105, 113, 120–1, 124, 127–8, 155, 160, 167, 171, 173
judge(s), 63–4, 79, 101, 142, 150, 170, 172, 176–7, 208–9, 213
judgment(s), 50, 52–3, 70, 75, 81–2, 108, 110–11, 117, 120, 124, 132–3, 138, 162–3, 165–6, 172, 174, 180, 186, 196, 201–3, 205, 212, 218
Julian (emperor), 64–5, 83, 122, 210–11
Julian the Jew, 137
Julius Africanus, 210
Julius Capitolinus, 82
Jupiter, 7, 87, 108, 207
justice, 35, 70, 83, 96, 104, 114, 117, 123, 130, 138, 150, 152, 168–9, 195, 201–2; God's, 22, 30, 167, 172, 185–6, 189
Justin, 82, 114, 176, 207–8
Justus, 209
Juvencus, 210

Kabbalah (Jewish), 26–7, 31n61, 177n676. *See also* Cabala (Christian)
Kaske, Carol V., 37
Kimhi, David, 119
king(s), 30, 47, 49, 51, 53–4, 61–3, 75, 85, 95, 100, 102, 112, 114–15, 117–21, 126, 128–31, 133, 135–6, 139–41, 143, 145, 149, 152, 155–6, 158–60, 163–4, 166, 173–5, 179–80, 184, 196, 199, 205–6, 219
kingdom. *See* king(s)
knowledge, 48, 69, 84, 97, 128, 134, 142, 159, 180, 186, 202, 204, 211, 219
Kristeller, Paul Oskar, 3

labour(s), 56–8, 60–2, 64, 70, 72, 94, 99–100, 108, 110, 132, 134, 137, 191, 211, 214
Lactantius, 77, 102, 106, 109–10, 113, 210
Lanfredini, Antonio, 34, 223
Lanfredini, Jacopo, 223
Lateran Council, Fifth, 15n30
Latin (language), 105, 111, 117, 171n654, 171n656, 175, 178, 180n688, 191n762, 200, 204n810, 206n822, 209n834, 210n841, 210n843–5
Latins, 4, 5n6, 10, 20, 23, 65, 211, 215
law(s), 53, 71–3, 102, 111, 115, 125–7, 132, 134n412, 136, 139, 142, 147, 149, 154, 167, 169, 175, 178, 181, 186–7, 197–205, 211–12, 219; Christian, 71–3, 86, 167, 172, 198, 201–3, 211; divine, 8, 17, 22, 53, 114, 187, 218; human, 50, 64, 114; Jewish, 115, 120, 207; Mohammadan, 167; Mosaic, 18, 26, 103, 124, 133, 136, 188, 198–9, 201–2, 205; Roman, 212
Leonides, 209
Levi, 120

Levi ben Gershom, 126
Levites, 132
Lewis, Charlton T., 37
Libra, 77
Liddell, Henry George, 37
life, 50, 57, 61, 66–8, 86–7, 90, 95, 98–100, 102, 104, 107, 114, 142, 148, 172–4, 178, 182, 186–8, 190, 196, 200, 204, 207, 210, 212, 220; active, 29; apostolic, 18, 28, 30; contemplative, 29; everlasting, 20, 62, 67, 116, 134n412, 163, 212; of Jesus, 58, 177–8
light, 51–2, 54, 67–70, 79, 85, 88–9, 91, 93, 96, 102–3, 111, 131–2, 134, 136, 140, 143, 150, 153, 163, 179, 191, 218; divine, 51–2, 69, 91, 93, 103, 140, 214
Limbo, 101, 119, 150, 191, 195
Linus, 47, 209
Livy, 106
logician(s), 209, 211
Logos (Word), 8–9, 17–18, 20–2, 27, 29, 58, 67–9, 71, 85, 87, 90–1, 94–6, 130, 164, 178, 180–1, 183, 217
Lord of Hosts, 121–2, 129, 184, 202
love, 29, 33, 35, 38, 57, 61, 66, 68, 70, 87–8, 95–7, 104, 148, 176, 187, 189, 194, 212, 219; of Christ, 56, 63, 176, 178, 208; divine, 20–1, 51; of God, 50, 54, 57–8, 93, 217. *See also caritas*
Lucca, 221
Lucian of Antioch, 149
Lucian of Samosata, 210, 212
Lucifer, 210
Lucius, 209
Lucretius, 7
Luke (evangelist), 25n49, 62–3, 72, 77, 83, 105, 127, 173
Luke (philosopher), 207
lust, 116, 176
Lycaonians, 62
Lynceus, 103
Lystra, 58

Maccabean(s), 120
Macedonia, 59
Macrobius, 75, 127
magic, 3, 101, 176–7, 213
Magnesians, 207
Magog, 161
magus(-i), 3–4, 47, 76, 81, 98, 121, 126, 176
Maimonides. *See* Moses Maimonides
Malachai, 122, 131, 140, 202, 204
malice, 53
Manetho the Egyptian, 40n80, 112
Manichaeans, 85–6
man(kind). *See* humans
Marcellus, 210
Marcion, 210
Marcus Aurelius, 213
Marescalchi, Francesco, 34, 221–2
Mark (evangelist), 105, 209
Mark (philosopher), 207
Maro. *See* Virgil
Martí, Ramon, 9, 18, 23, 25–6, 32, 41, 125n354
martyr(s), 102, 104, 137, 148, 208–10
martyrdom, 28–9, 70, 148, 155, 207–8
Mary (Virgin), 80, 85, 91, 100, 107, 130, 164, 217–18; tomb of, 85
massacre(s), 24, 121, 157, 172, 212
Massageteans, 102
materialism, 15
mathematicians, 47, 209
mathematics, 52
matter, 86–7, 93–4, 101, 165
Matthew, 104–5, 153, 155
Maximianus (emperor), 83
Maximus, 210
Maximus (martyr), 209
McMichael, Stephen J., 26
Medians, 134
Medici, 49
Medici, Cosimo de', 6, 10–11, 48

Medici, Lorenzo de', 6, 8, 34, 47–8, 74, 80, 221
Medici, Piero de', 48
Mediterranean Sea, 10
meekness, 52, 104, 142, 148, 189, 217
Megasthenes, 112, 114
Mehmed II, 10–11
Melampus, 47
melancholy, 6
Melchizedek, 163–4, 206
Melito, 40n80, 209, 213
Menander, 112
Mendesian(s), 112
mendicants, 9, 19, 27, 31
Mercurius Trismegistus. *See* Hermes Trismegistus
mercy, 22, 30, 62, 69, 93, 131, 161, 185–6, 188–9, 212, 218
Mesopotamia, 173
messenger(s) (of God), 100, 122, 130, 174, 197, 199, 214, 217–18
Messiah, 9, 22, 24, 26, 31, 40, 76, 117–19, 121–7, 129–36, 138–41, 143–5, 148–52, 154–65, 167, 172–3, 178, 182, 185–8, 190–3, 195–6, 198–9, 201–5
metaphysicians, 47, 137
metaphysics, 52, 80
Methodius, 210
Micah, 118, 205
Midrash, 25
Milan, 34
Miltiades, 209
mind, 103, 111, 169, 187, 197, 201, 203; angelic, 87; divine, 20, 52, 63, 94–5, 103, 134; human, 20–1, 49, 51–2, 54, 71, 91, 94, 96, 197, 219; power of, 33
Minucius Fundanus, 82, 213
Minutius, 210
miracle(s), 5, 15n29, 62–3, 66, 72, 74–5, 78–81, 83, 85, 89, 97–101, 104–5, 112, 135, 156–7, 167–9, 172, 176–9, 206, 213, 217–18
Mithridates, Flavius, 27, 31n61
Mnaseas, 112
moderation, 35, 104
Modestus (philosopher), 209
modesty, 35, 52
Mohammad, 85–6, 100, 129–30, 139, 164, 166, 172, 178, 199, 214, 216–19; tomb of, 85
Mohammadans. *See* Islam
Molon, 112
Molus. *See* Nicolaus Molus
money, 80
money-lenders, 81
Moon, 52, 77–8, 90, 149, 163
morality, 52
Moses, 18–19, 113–15, 120, 124, 131, 139, 144, 149, 151, 158, 183–6, 188, 190, 192, 196–201, 203, 205–6, 217
Moses ben Nahman of Girona, 24, 119, 123–4, 126, 145, 182, 192
Moses Maimonides, 9, 24, 116–18, 120, 126–7, 157–8, 162, 172, 199, 202–3
Moshe ben Maimon. *See* Moses Maimonides
Mount Sinai. *See* Sinai, Mount
murder, 75, 83, 116, 148, 162, 167–9, 171, 173–4, 187, 189, 212
Musaeus, 47, 113
Musanus, 209
muses, 53
mystery(-ies), 17, 47, 53, 56, 70–1, 80, 91, 103, 107, 112, 130, 139, 154, 170–1, 175, 179, 181, 189, 192, 195–6, 215, 217, 219

Nachmanides. *See* Moses ben Nahman of Girona
Nahum, 204
Naldi, Naldo, 32n63, 222–3

names (divine), 5, 36, 117, 158, 177, 180–1, 183, 185, 193, 204
Narcissus, 209
Nathan, 164
Nathaniel, 127
nature, 19–21, 29, 47, 52, 77, 80, 88, 98, 176, 180, 193–6, 203, 207; divine, 88, 94, 185; human, 16, 54, 66, 91–4, 98, 181, 194–5
Nazarene(s), 104, 121, 125, 141–2, 148–50, 179, 200, 206
Nazareth, 142, 156, 164, 172, 177–8, 199, 204
Nebuchadnezzar, 165
Nehunya, Rabbi, 27n53, 140
Neoplatonists, 14, 15n29
Nero, 83, 155, 167, 213
Nestorians, 215
New Testament. *See* Testament, New
Nicaea, 76
Nicholas of Lyra, 9, 24n46, 25, 32, 123, 137
Nicodemus, 127
Nicolaus Molus, 112
Nicolaus of Damascus, 112n274
Noah, 113, 156, 187, 204
notarikon, 26
Novatian, 210
Numa Pompilius, 48
Numenius, 84, 103, 112

obedience, 24, 78, 84, 98, 136, 189
obstinacy, 29n57, 30, 35, 65, 99, 122, 128–9, 131, 133, 136, 138, 148, 151, 153, 156, 161–2, 164, 171, 181, 196–7, 219
Ockhamism, 12
Octavian, 74–5, 117, 138. *See also* Augustus
Oenomaus, 100
ointment, 206
old age, 52–3, 102–3, 109

Old Testament. *See* Testament, Old
Olympiad(s), 76
omen(s), 169
Onesimus, 209
Optatus, 210
oracle(s), 71, 74, 82, 91, 101, 106, 115–16, 128, 177, 196, 205
orator(s), 211
Origen, 64, 75–6, 105, 155, 209–10
Orpheus, 9, 12n22, 18, 47, 52, 87, 103, 113
Orsini, Rainaldo, 34, 224
Ottomans, 10–11
Ovid, 13

Pablo Christiani, 119n322
Pablo de Santa Maria, 8n11, 9, 18, 23–5, 32, 39–41, 116n303, 125n354, 137n434, 138, 139n446, 146, 147n498, 174n668, 202n805
Pacian, 210
pagans, 6, 9–10, 13, 15, 17–19, 22, 28–30, 38, 56, 65, 71, 74–5, 81, 86, 100, 102–3, 112–13, 115, 118–19, 121–2, 124, 127–8, 131–3, 138, 177, 187, 212–13, 219
pain, 21
Palestine, 212
Pallas (Athena), 14n27, 17, 22, 48, 87
Pamphilus, 104, 210
Pan, 101
Panthenus the Stoic, 104, 207
Papias, 209
Paraclete, 214n862
paradise, 28, 192, 195, 198, 218
Parisi, Alberto, 34, 222
Parthian(s), 155
passion(s), 21, 66, 121, 148–50, 193, 202
Passover, 78, 149, 188–9, 200
patience, 58, 60, 62, 68, 72, 79, 142

patriarch(s), 190, 192
Paul of Burgos. *See* Pablo de Santa Maria
Paul of Middleburg, 14n27
Paul (St.), 13–14, 21, 25n49, 55–9, 61–3, 65, 69–70, 72, 78–9, 84, 91, 103, 105, 127, 136–7, 152–3, 155, 160, 176, 179, 189, 197, 206, 209
Paulus Burgensis. *See* Pablo de Santa Maria
peace, 13n27, 71, 107, 109–10, 117–19, 138, 143–4, 146, 155–7, 170–1, 189, 193, 204–5
Peleius, 210
Pella, 127
penitence, 126, 172
Pentateuch, 126
Pentecost, 76, 170, 201
Perez, 191–2
perfection, 49, 187
peripatetic, 14n29, 31n61, 114. *See also* Aristotle
persecution, 58, 65, 70, 74, 83–4, 102, 148–9, 152, 212–13
persecutor(s), 74, 83, 116n302, 172, 213
Persians, 17, 20, 22, 47, 83, 102, 112, 115
Peter (apostle), 55–6, 62, 68–9, 83, 105, 137, 155, 206
Petrus Alfonsi. *See* Alfonsi, Petrus
Phaethon, 112
Phalerum, 112, 115
Pharisees, 66
Philadelphians, 207
Philemon, 209
Philip (bishop), 209
Philip (emperor), 82
Philippi, 60
Philippians, 55, 57, 59, 71
Philo the Jew, 103, 149, 157, 172, 211
Philo the Pagan, 112

philology, 9, 27, 41n81
philosopher(s), 47–8, 65, 77, 80, 82, 84, 88, 100, 114–15, 127, 137n432, 149, 176, 194, 207–10
philosophy, 6–8, 12–14, 15n29, 17, 19–20, 31n61, 39, 47–8, 64, 74, 80, 104
Philostratus, 100, 168
Phlegon, 76
Phoebadius, 210
Phoenicia, 113
Phoenician(s), 112–13
Picatrix, 3
Pico della Mirandola, Giovanni, 3, 8n12, 14n27, 15n29, 26–7, 31n61, 134n412
Pierius, 210
piety, 8, 14, 16, 33, 48–9, 66, 73, 79, 81, 84, 139, 169, 211
Pilate. *See* Pontius Pilate
Pinytus of Crete, 209
Pisces, 77
Placentino, Daniel, 34, 225
Placentino, Pietro, 33, 222
planets, 88
plants, 21, 86, 92, 108, 146, 179, 204
Plato, 4, 6, 9, 11–12, 15n29, 16–19, 21–2, 29, 36, 47, 51–3, 84, 87, 90, 98, 102–3, 111–13, 163, 207
Platonic Academy (Florence), 12
Platonism(-ists), 7, 9–11, 13, 14–15n29, 16, 20–2, 28–30, 35–6, 39, 49, 76, 84, 101, 103, 112–13, 137n432, 176, 207–9, 219l Christian, 19, 31n61, 35
pleasure(s), 7n8, 28, 52, 64–6, 72–4
Plethon, George Gemistos, 10–11, 15n29
Pliny the Elder, 76, 113, 115
Pliny the Younger, 212
Plotinus, 3, 13n26, 15n29, 84, 103
Plutarch, 101, 210

266 Index

poet(s), 13, 32, 108–9, 157, 211, 219
polemic(s), 6, 8–10, 15, 19, 22–32, 39–41, 116n302, 125n354
Poliziano, Angelo, 14n27, 34, 221
Pollio, 106, 108
Polycarp, 77, 112, 207–208
Polycrates, 149, 209
Polyhistor, 112
Pompeius Trogus, 114
Pompey, 211
Pontius, 210
Pontius Pilate, 81, 83, 124, 150, 172, 178, 214
Pontus, 155, 208
pope, 137
Porcius Festus, 63
Porphyry, 15n29, 51n15, 81, 83, 100–1, 108, 113–14, 209–10
portent(s), 66, 75, 80, 112, 114, 137, 168, 174
poverty, 24, 29, 33
power, 51, 57, 65–6, 69, 73, 78, 84–5, 87, 90, 92–3, 99–102, 108, 115, 119–20, 130–1, 134, 148, 150, 165–6, 174–5, 177, 180, 182, 185, 187, 189, 197, 208, 217
Powers, 56, 71, 89
praise, 31, 61, 103, 113–14, 141, 152, 154–5, 178, 192
prayer, 82, 114, 148, 167, 170, 207, 213, 218
preaching, 18, 24, 29, 32, 55–8, 60, 63, 65, 69, 73, 77–9, 104–5, 122, 133, 141, 144, 154, 176, 204–5, 216
prediction(s), 30, 57, 65, 75–6, 84, 106, 116, 121, 128, 131, 134–5, 141, 161, 163, 175, 196, 205–6, 208
Prenninger, Martin Uranius, 224
pride, 52, 54, 104, 133, 139, 211
priest(s), 30, 47–9, 53, 56, 60, 76, 86, 100, 106, 113, 115, 120, 124, 129, 132–4, 142, 156–7, 163–5, 170, 173, 175, 179, 188–9, 196, 204, 206, 212
Principalities, 56, 71, 89
prisca theologia, 5, 8, 10, 12, 17–18, 29, 32, 103
prisci theologi. *See prisca theologia*
procession (divine), 21
Proclus, 12n22, 15–16, 84, 101, 103, 113
Promised Land, 120, 159, 201–2
prophecy(-ies), 5, 8–9, 17, 22–3, 28, 30, 40n81, 70, 103, 123, 135, 139n446, 144, 148, 152, 154, 156, 158, 161–2, 169, 196, 205, 208, 214–15, 219
prophet(s), 5, 9, 13, 17–19, 22, 28–31, 38, 40, 47, 56, 65–6, 70, 72, 74–6, 85, 91, 100, 103, 106, 109, 111–12, 114–17, 120, 128, 129n378, 134, 136, 140–3, 145, 151, 153, 156, 159–60, 162–4, 166–7, 171, 173–5, 178, 182, 185, 190–1, 196–200, 206; pseudo-, 127
providence, 9, 18, 53, 89, 99, 211
prudence, 79, 84, 98, 108, 135, 139, 180
Ptolemy the Mendesian, 112
Ptolemy Philadelphus, 115, 118, 175, 216
punishment(s), 56, 64, 90, 99, 111, 145, 147, 151, 160, 167, 171–2, 177, 186–7, 190, 192–4, 202, 212, 218
pupil(s). *See* disciples
purgatory, 115
purification, 47, 52, 85, 99–100, 107, 189, 196, 198
purity, 71
Pythagoras, 9, 12, 18, 47, 51n15, 100, 103, 113–14
Pythagorean(s), 51–52, 90, 112, 203, 219

Quadratus, 82, 207
quality, 71, 88
Quirinus, 127
Qur'an, 8n12, 71–2, 85, 100, 130, 139, 164, 172, 178, 199, 217–18

Rab, 126
Radak. *See* Kimhi, David
radiance, 88–9
Rahamon. *See* Rhahamon, Rabbi
Rambam. *See* Moses Maimonides
Ramban. *See* Moses ben Nahman of Girona
Ramon Martí. *See* Martí, Ramon
Rashi. *See* Shlomo Yitzhaqi of Troyes
Rav Huna, 133
reason, 20, 52, 55, 72, 80, 86–7, 91–3, 98, 149, 183, 185, 207, 219
redemption, 48, 79, 96, 104, 126, 139, 144, 159, 161, 187, 193
reform, 17–18
Reformation, 4
relic(s), 137
religion, 19–22, 31, 47–50, 52–3, 65, 71–2, 74, 81–4, 86, 108, 114, 176–7, 208–9, 211–13, 219; divine, 17; natural, 9, 17, 20, 29
République des Lettres, 4, 5n4
resurrection, 59, 101, 110–11, 125, 153, 163, 177, 179, 214–15, 218
Reuchlin, Johannes, 26, 36
revelation, 9, 13, 17, 29, 59, 208
reward(s), 60, 100, 111, 157, 203, 218; earthly, 71, 198, 202; heavenly, 72, 90, 202
Rhahamon, Rabbi, 191
Rheticius, 210
rhetorician(s), 84
Rhodo, 209
Riario, Pietro, 34
Riario, Raffaele, 34, 223
Riccoldo of Monte Cruce, 9, 215

Rignano, 163
rites (sacred), 47–9, 53, 81, 85, 90, 112, 167, 173, 202, 206
ritual(s). *See* rites (sacred)
robber(s), 61, 157
robbery, 143, 212–13
Roman Empire, 128, 146, 165
Romans, 17, 48, 58–9, 63–5, 79, 82–3, 101–2, 106, 109, 115, 120–1, 124–5, 128, 134, 136, 160, 165–8, 170, 176, 207, 209, 213, 216
Rome, 57, 72, 83, 106, 155, 166, 207
Rossi, Girolamo, 34, 223–4
Rufinus, 51n15

Sa'adiah Gaon, 39, 119, 123, 126
Saba, 138, 141
Sabbath, 170, 200, 203, 206
Sachoniato, 112, 114
sacrament(s), 79, 85, 129, 206–7
sacrifice(s), 20, 29, 47, 101–2, 120, 124, 131, 135–6, 149, 169, 187–9, 196, 202–3, 206; God's, 22; self-, 20, 70
Sacromoro, Filippo, 34, 222
sages (ancient), 9, 13, 18, 20, 33, 73, 127–8, 133, 190
saint(s), 114, 123–4, 165, 191–2, 195, 198, 214
Salomon, Rabbi, 116, 118–19, 124, 144–5, 156, 158–60
Saloninus, 106
salvation, 58–9, 95, 109, 119, 122–3, 131–3, 144–5, 147, 151–3, 159–62, 188–9, 193, 214, 218
Salvini, Sebastiano, 29n57, 34–5
Samuel, 130
sanctum, inner, 76, 124. *See also* Holy of Holies
Sanhedrin, 120, 126, 159, 202
Saracen, 218
Sardinian(s), 210

Sardis, 213
Sarepta, 125
Saturn, 7, 13, 107
saviour, 60, 68, 76, 111, 118–19, 130, 138, 149, 154, 189, 192
Savonarola, Girolamo, 14n27
schism, 10
Scientific Revolution, 4
Scotism, 12
Scott, Robert, 37
scribes, 66
Scripture(s), 7, 27, 30, 40, 41n81, 116, 157, 160, 162, 167, 175, 180, 185, 214, 216, 219
Scythia, 155
Scythians, 102–3
Second Temple. *See* temple(s), Second
secrecy, 55, 143, 181
Senate, 11, 81–2, 109, 120, 216
senator(s), 81–2, 209
Seneca, 211
senses, 21, 52, 92, 94, 97–8
sephiroth, 26
Septuagint, 38, 115, 117–18, 144n480, 175, 215. *See also* Bible; Vulgate (Bible)
Serapeum, 215
Seraphim, 89, 93
Serapion (bishop of Antioch), 209
Serapion (martyr), 210
Serenus, 210
Serenus, Granius, 82, 213
Sergius (proconsul), 209
servitude. *See* slavery
Severus, Commodus (emperor), 209
Sextus, 209
shame, 57–8, 60, 83, 102, 132, 136, 142, 144, 148, 176–7
Shimon, Rabbi, 180, 182
Shlomo Yitzhaqi of Troyes, 9, 24
Short, Charles, 37

sibyl(s), 23, 65, 72, 106–12, 128, 206; Cumaean, 106–8; Erythraean, 106, 109, 111
Sibylline Books, 17, 106, 108–9, 114
Silas, 209
Silvanus, 209
Simeon, 109, 209
Simon bar Kokhba. *See* Bar Kokhba
Simon ben Cosiba, 40, 125n354. *See also* Bar Kokhba
Simon Magus, 127
Simplicianus, 207
Simplicius, 15n29
sin(s), 60, 67, 70, 96, 98–9, 123, 141, 143–8, 150–2, 154, 158, 161, 163, 171, 174, 185–95, 197, 218. *See also* vice(s)
Sinai, Mount, 130, 156, 181, 205
sinner(s), 62, 187
Sixtus I (pope), 137n431
Sixtus II (pope), 51n15
slavery, 115, 129, 158, 166, 168, 173, 175, 187
Smyrnians, 207–8
Socrates, 102
Sodom, 168
soldier(s), 72, 84
Solomon, 110, 133, 140, 142–3, 149, 164, 180–2, 198
Solomon ha-Levi. *See* Pablo de Santa Maria
sophist(s), 77, 212
Sophronius, 210
Sosipater, 209
Sosthenes, 209
soul(s), 20, 28, 47, 51, 53, 71, 73, 80–1, 86–8, 90, 94, 97–9, 104, 108, 118–19, 126, 129, 132, 138, 140, 143, 147, 151–3, 157–9, 172, 180, 188, 191, 193–6, 198, 214, 217; divinity of, 53; human, 22, 79, 91–2, 94, 101, 182; immortality of, 14, 15n30, 16; intellectual, 14; nature of, 15;

purification of, 47, 100–1, 107, 202; rational, 29, 92, 94; unicity of, 14
Spain, 9, 25, 137
Speusippus, 12
sphere(s), celestial, 72–3, 88–9
Spirit (Holy). *See* Holy Spirit
spirit(s), 13, 57, 59, 67, 71, 73, 79, 85, 89–91, 101, 104, 135–6, 141, 147, 150–1, 160, 164, 167, 178, 181–2, 190, 196, 205, 215, 217–18
splendour, 70, 88, 90
star(s), 72–6, 90, 109, 121, 139, 169, 176, 184
Stoic(s), 75, 104, 207
Strabo, 114
Strong, James, 37
stubbornness. *See* obstinacy
Styx, 90
substance, 60, 70, 75, 86, 88, 90, 129, 180–1, 184–5, 199, 217
Suetonius, 128, 167–8, 213
suffering, 21, 28–9, 57–61, 64, 69, 91, 96, 98–9, 123, 153, 162, 176, 185–7, 189, 191, 193–5, 208
suicide, 83, 103
Sukkot, 170n651
Sun, 51–2, 75, 77, 91, 93–4, 112, 131, 134n412, 148–50, 163, 181, 202
superstition(s), 18, 48, 71, 102, 205
Syria, 104, 113–14, 127, 157, 207
Syriac (language), 155
Syrian(s), 113, 157, 209–10

tabernacles, 202; Feast of. *See* Feast of the Tabernacles
Tabor, Mount, 151, 156
Tacitus, Cornelius, 114, 124, 211
Talmud, 9, 24, 26–7, 71–2, 124, 125n354, 128, 140, 144, 146, 154, 159, 167, 174, 191, 198, 203
Tarquin, 106
Tarshish, 141

Tatian, 209
teacher(s), 47, 84, 99, 120, 145, 154, 169, 178, 185, 191, 198, 207–8, 210, 212, 218
teaching(s), 5, 19, 54–6, 63–4, 73, 79, 84, 99, 103–4, 107, 111–13, 115, 133–6, 143, 146, 148, 154, 156–7, 159, 161, 177, 189, 195–6, 198, 201–2, 204–5, 207, 212, 218
temple(s), 21, 51, 75–6, 82–3, 111, 122, 124, 136, 140, 158–9, 169–70, 175, 190, 202, 207; First, 121, 123; Second, 31, 121, 123–5, 142n470; third, 121
temptation, 68, 108
temurah, 26
Tenas, 207
Tertius, 209
Tertullian, 63–4, 72, 81, 83, 101–2, 112, 150, 176–7, 209, 211–13, 215
Testament, 119, 122, 150–1, 191, 197–8, 204; New, 22, 25, 66, 85, 112, 116, 122, 150, 153, 171n656, 196–8, 201, 216, 218; Old, 9, 18, 22, 25–6, 28, 30–1, 66, 85, 112, 116, 129, 141n468, 153, 191, 196, 201, 205, 214–16, 218
Tetragrammaton, 27, 36, 117, 177; *hiehouahi*, 177
Thaddeus, 155
Thallus, 112
theft, 212
Themis, 17, 48
Themistius, 15n29
Theodorus, 112
Theodorus (martyr), 210
theologian(s), 88–9, 103, 138, 140, 146, 189n745, 194–5, 210, 215
theology, 17, 19, 28, 30, 39, 71, 84, 103, 113, 134n412; negative, 21
theology, ancient. *See prisca theologia*
Theophilus, 112, 209

Theophrastus, 15n29, 114
Theotimus, 210
Thessalonians, 57, 60, 79
Theudas, 127
Thomas (apostle), 155
Thomas Aquinas, 9, 16, 24–5, 32
Thracians, 207
Thrones, 71, 89
Tibarenians, 103
Tiberius Caesar, 76–7, 81–2, 101, 109, 124
time, 13n27, 18, 21–2, 74, 90–1, 93, 110, 126, 134, 137, 157, 163, 172–3, 176, 181, 194, 199
Timocharis, 112
Timothy, 57, 61, 70, 79, 209
Titus, 210
Titus (bishop of Crete), 209
Titus (emperor), 82, 122, 129, 168, 172–4
torment(s), 54, 57, 64, 143, 145, 148, 155, 171–2, 192, 209–11
Tortosa, 25
torture(s), 64, 83, 172, 176, 208–9
Trajan, 173, 212
tranquility, 72
transgression, 30, 53, 123, 142, 145–6, 148, 171, 174, 186, 190, 192, 195
translation, 3–5, 7, 8n12, 12, 26–7, 32, 36–41, 51n15, 105, 111, 115–18, 122n332, 133, 135–6, 140, 144–5, 147n498, 155, 175, 181–4, 198, 208n831, 215–16
transvaluation (moral), 28, 30
Traversari, Ambrogio, 11n18
treachery, 108, 171, 175, 208
tree(s), 21, 86, 137, 150; of knowledge, 186; of life, 192
tribulation, 57–60, 70, 171, 205
Trinity, 9, 17, 21–22, 88–9, 94, 179–85, 217
Triphylus, 210

Trismegistus, Hermes Mercurius. *See* Hermes Trismegistus
Trophimus, 47
trust, 53, 80, 84, 97, 99, 125–6, 170
truth, 13–14, 20, 28, 30, 33, 48, 50, 53–6, 66, 68–9, 72–3, 75, 77, 79, 81, 100–2, 105, 111, 126, 130, 149, 157, 165, 175, 178, 183, 185, 204, 208, 211–13, 215, 217–20
Tryphon, 210
Turks, 8n12, 10–11
Tyana, 100, 168
Tychicus, 209
Tyre, 112

Ugolino, Donato, 34, 224
understanding, 67, 84, 87, 95, 135–6, 141, 143–4, 182, 197, 219; spiritual, 30, 197
unity, 22, 88, 92–3, 184, 217
University of Rome, 34
Urbanus, 209
Urbino, 34
Ursini, Rainaldo. *See* Orsini, Rainaldo
usury, 145

Valerian (emperor), 208
Valerius Soranus, 48
Varro, Marcus, 48, 102, 106
vengeance, 50, 116, 145, 148, 150, 166–7, 169, 172–3
Venice, 10, 34
Ventozara. *See* Bar Kokhba
Veronese, Guarino, 11n18
Verus, Marcus Antoninus, 209, 213
Vespasian, 82, 121–2, 128, 168–9
Vespucci, Giorgio Antonio, 34, 222, 224
vice(s), 72, 81, 99, 115, 145, 187, 202. *See also* sin(s)
Victor, 209

Victorinus, 210
Victorinus, Marius, 210
victory, 65, 83, 147, 153, 168, 193
Vinciguerra, Antonio, 223–4
Virgil, 13, 23, 106–9, 128, 138, 156
virgin, 91, 107, 130. *See also* Mary (Virgin)
Virgo, 77
virtue(s), 20, 36, 68, 71–3, 79–80, 96, 99, 104, 107, 114, 149, 177, 187, 189, 192–3, 195–6, 198, 202
Virtues (order of angels), 56, 89
vita activa. See life, active
vita apostolica. See life, apostolic
vita contemplativa. See life, contemplative
Viterbo, 34
Volterra, 34
Vulgate (Bible), 26, 40n81, 70n119, 131n396, 139n446, 141n466, 142n472, 144n480, 152n535, 171n654, 171n656, 206n824, 208n831. *See also* Bible; Septuagint

Walker, D.P., 3
war, 118, 125, 127, 138, 156, 161, 165, 168–70, 214; against Jews, 25
wealth, 48, 64, 114, 159
West, 77, 88, 170
wickedness, 67, 147, 176, 187
will, 47, 71, 73, 80, 151, 157–61, 185, 187–8, 194, 196; divine, 91, 95, 131, 189, 202; free, 20, 54, 195
wisdom, 13–14, 17–18, 33, 47–9, 51, 53, 63, 65, 68, 78, 81, 84, 100, 104, 113–14, 117, 135, 141, 180, 182–3, 185, 207–10, 212, 220. *See also* God, wisdom of

Word (of God). *See Logos* (Word)
works. *See* labour(s)
world (material), 13–14, 19–21, 29–30, 58–9, 61, 65, 67–8, 70, 72, 75, 79, 84, 87, 93, 96, 99–100, 108–9, 116–17, 128, 138, 140, 150, 157–8, 162–4, 166, 171, 173–5, 180, 182–3, 195, 203, 208, 218; beginning of, 72, 74, 90, 125–6, 166, 171, 187, 194; end of, 30, 65, 135–6, 156, 161, 165–6, 172, 187, 214. *See also* creation
worship, 47–50, 53–4, 56, 62, 73, 81–3, 90, 101, 114, 119, 134, 136, 138–9, 145, 154, 160, 174, 191, 209, 211, 213–14, 217–18
writing(s), 9, 13, 32–3, 63, 66, 103, 105, 107, 111–12, 115–16

Xenocrates, 12
Xistus the Pythagorean, 51

Yates, Frances Amelia, 3
yeshiva, 25
youth, 52–3

Zechariah, 118–19, 140, 142, 150–1, 159, 161, 173, 191, 198
Zephaniah, 161
Zeus, 22
Zilioli, Antonio, 223
Zion, 118, 129, 132–3, 136, 138, 141, 144, 155–6, 158–9, 161, 187, 192, 198, 205
Zohar, 26
Zopyrion, 40n80, 112
Zoroaster, 9, 18, 22, 87, 98, 100, 103, 113, 163

Lightning Source UK Ltd.
Milton Keynes UK
UKHW041903221122
412642UK00012B/45/J